MORE PRAISE FOR *The Ficti*

"HANDY, SNAPPY AND INSIGHTFU
— Fred Kl   )ks

"WHETHER YOU ARE READING A BOOK OR WRITING ONE, YOU could want no better companion." — Barnaby Conrad, author of The *Second Life of John Wilkes Booth, 101 Best Scenes Ever Written,* and *Last Boat to Cadiz*

"SHELLY LOWENKOPF distills a lifetime of fiction writing, teaching, and editing into a tool that is a writer's and storyteller's delight. This is a book to browse, consult, dip into, and above all to enjoy. There are vignettes of wisdom and delicious insights on every page that will inspire reader and writer alike. These pages have something for you, whether you write fiction or non-fiction, for we all tell stories. Lowenkopf's *Handbook* is a wonderful mentor for all of us and will surely become a classic." — Brian Fagan, author of *The Great Warming* and *Elixir*

"THIS IS THE MOST ACCESSIBLE AND COMPREHENSIVE BOOK about the art of writing and the pleasures of reading available anywhere. It will be an indispensable text for all writing workshops, seminars, classes, and general knowledge for all writers. The *Handbook* brings E.M. Forster's *Aspects of the Novel* into the twenty-first century. Its take on Wile E. Coyote is worth the price of the book." — J. R Freedman, author of *In My Dark Dreams* and *Against the Wind*

"I CAN NOW HONESTLY SAY THAT SHELLY LOWENKOPF WROTE the book on fiction. I can't imagine any serious writer (or for that matter, any serious reader) who would not benefit from its pages." — Catherine Ryan Hyde, author of *Pay It Forward* and *Jumpstart the World*

"DELIGHTFUL, FUNNY, AND REFRESHINGLY UNPRETENTIOUS, Shelly Lowenkopf's *The Fiction Writer's Handbook* is that rare book that is as instructive as it is entertaining. Reading it will give the budding writer the confidence to launch his career, and help the professional writer gain clarity and consciousness. It will enhance the casual reader's enjoyment and the serious reader's insight. And it will do all this with as much ease and amusement as any great page-turner." — Gina B. Nahai, author of *Caspian Rain* and *Sunday's Silence*

"WITH THE FICTION WRITER'S HANDBOOK, Shelly Lowenkopf has cooked up a literary gumbo for all writers, chock full of bite-sized tips and insights on the craft of writing. Once you've sampled it you won't be able to stop coming back for more." — Ehrich Van Lowe, producer of *The Cosby Show* and author of *Boyfriend from Hell* and *Earth Angel*

Books by Shelly Lowenkopf

FICTION

The City of Hoke

Love of the Lion

NONFICTION

Borderline Oddities, editor

Yesterday's California

Secrets of Successful Fiction Writing

THE
Fiction
Writer's
HANDBOOK

Shelly Lowenkopf

Foreword by Christopher Moore,
Author of A Dirty Job

White Whisker Books
Los Angeles

*For the two Annies
in my life:
The one who bore me,
and the one who
bore up with me.*

The Fiction Writer's Handbook
White Whisker Books paperback edition published November 2012
Published by White Whisker Books, Los Angeles, CA

LIBRARY OF CONGRESS CONTROL NUMBER 2012938842

Portions of this work have appeared in slightly different formats in *Ink Byte Magazine for Writers, The Montecito Journal, The Writer Magazine, Santa Barbara Review*, the *Fort Worth Star-Telegram, The Portable Writers' Conference, Writing Fiction*, and the University of Southern California's Politics and Society online resource.

*Editor: Christopher Meeks
Cover and book design: Deborah Daly*

Visit our website at www.WhiteWhiskerBooks.com

LIST OF ENTRIES

~A~

Act
Action is Character
Actioning
Adversary
Aftertaste
Agenda
Agreement
Alternate Universe (Also "AU")
Ambiguity
Antagonist
Anticipation
Anticlimax
Antigone
Anti-Hero
Apocalyptic Fiction
Arc
Arena
Attitude
Attribution
AU
Audience for Story, The
Authorial Intervention

~B~

Backpack
Backstory
Beat
Beating a Dead Horse
Beginnings
Being Right
Bigger Than Life
Bildungsroman
Block
Buyer's Remorse

~C~

Canary in the Mineshaft, The
Captain Ahab
Catalyst
Causality
Chaos
Chapter
Character-Driven Story
Characters
Character Arc
Chekhovian
Chemistry
Chick Lit
Choice
Choking Doberman, The
Chronology
Circumstances
Cliché
Cliffhanger
Cock-And-Bull Story, A
Coincidence
Collision
Combustion
Comedy
Comes to Realize
Coming-Of-Age Novel
Commercial Story, The
Complacency
Concept
Concept-Driven Story, The
Conflict
Conscience
Consequences
Content Editing
Contingency

5

Convention
Conversation
Copyediting
Counterpoint
Critical Reading
Crucible
Cutting

~D~
Deadline
Deadpan
Decisions
Defensiveness
Defining Moment
Degree of Intimacy
Denouement
Description
Design
Desire/Secret Desire
Details
Determinism
Deus Ex Machina
Device
Dialect
Dialogue
Digression
Disclaimer
Discovery
Distraction
Domino Theory, The
Don't Go There
Don't Tell the Reader What the Reader
Already Knows
Drama
Drunk in the Parking Lot, The
Dystopia, the Novel Of

~E~
Edge
Effect
Ego
Elephant in the Living Room, The

Elliptical Orbit
Emotion
Ending
Epiphany
Episode
Epistolary Novel, The
Euphemism
Event
Evoke
Exaggeration
Exit Strategy
Expectations

~F~
Family
Family History
Fantasy
Farce
Fatal Flaw
Fear
First-Person Narrative
First-Draft Strategy
Fish in a Barrel
Flash Fiction
Flashback
Foreshadowing
Formula
Fourth Wall, The
Frame
Frame-Tale Format
Frustration
Fun

~G~
Genre
Genre Promise
Ghost of Hamlet's Father, The
Goal
Goes Without Saying
Golem, The
Growth
Guilt

~H~
HIBK
Habit Words
Happy Ending, The
Hard-Luck Story
Hidden Agenda
Historical Novel, The
Horror Novel, The
Hubris
Humiliation
Humor

~I~
Iconic Characters
Imitation
Implications
In Medias Res
"In the Story"
Inevitability
Inference
Information Dump
Injustice
Inner Critic, The
Intensity in Language
Intent
Interior Monologue
Internal Conflict
Intrusive Author
Irony
"It's Eleven O'clock"

~J~
Jargon
Jealousy
Jeopardy
Journey, the Novel Of
Justice

~K~
Kafkaesque
Kicking a Character While He or She is Down

~L~
Landscape
Laundry List
Layer
Lewis (meriwether) and Clark (william)
Likely Story, A
Linkage
Lionel Essrog
Lit Fic
Literary Agent
Literary Story, The
Literature
Loss

~M~
Macguffin, The, (also Mcguffin)
Magic
Magical Realism
Manipulation
Manuscript
Marginal
Mars Probe, The
Matchmaker
Mcguffin, The
Messenger
Metaphor
Mickey Mouse Ending
Middle
Mise-En-Scene
Moment
ms
MTIWK
Multiple Point of View
Mystery

~N~
Naive Narrator
Narrative
Narrative Hook
Narrative Voice
Needs

Novel
Novelette
Novella
Nuance

~O~
Objective Correlative, The
Obligation
Obstacle
Occam's Razor
Occupation
Old Wives' Tales
Omar Little
Omniscient Point of View
On the Nose
One Character on Stage Alone
Opening Pages
Opening Velocity
Orbit
Order of Awareness, The
Organization
Other Shoe Dropping, The
Outline
Over the Top

~P~
Pace
Paper or Screen
Parody
Partner
Passivity
Pathetic Fallacy, The
Payoff
Picaresque
Plausibility
Plot
Plot-Driven Story
Point in Time
Point of View
Political Novel, The
Politics
PONR (Point of No Return)

Portal
POV
Power
Predictable
Premise
Problem Words
Process
Products
Protagonist
Publishers' Conventional Wisdom
Purple Prose

~Q~
Quest
Quiting
qy

~R~
Raisins in the Matzo
Rate of Discovery
Reaction
Reader, The
Reader Feeder, The
Reader's First Expectation, The
Reader's Second Expectation, The
Reality
Red Herring
Rejection
Relationships
Reliable Narrator
Response
Retrospect
Revelation
Revenge
Reversal
Revision
Ridicule
Risk
Roman A Clef
Romance
Romanticism

~S~
Sarcasm
Satire
Scene, The
Schadenfreude
Schrodinger's Cat
Science Fiction Novel, The
Second-Person Narrative
Secrets
Sensory Genome, The
Set-Up
Sexual Tension
Shaggy-Dog Story, The
Sherlock Holmes
Shift of Power
Short Story
Show, Don't Tell
Slice of Life
Slight
Sorcerer's Apprentice, The
Speculative Fiction
Speed Bumps
Stasis
stet
Story
Structure
Style
Submission
Subplot
Subtext
Surprise
Suspense
Synecdoche
Synopsis

~T~
TFS
Talking Heads
Tension
Theme
Third-Person Narration
Throughline

Time Frame
Time Sequence
Tipping Point, The
Tool Kit
Tradition
Tragedy
Transportation
Trigger
Turn
Two-Line Space Break

~U~
Unities
Unreliable Narrator, The
Unthinkable Come to Pass, The

~V~
Vector
Venture
Verb Tenses
Verisimilitude
Vernacular
Victim
Vision
Vital Lie
Voice
Volition
Voyage, The
Vulnerability

~W~
Weather Report
Western Novel, The
Whale, the Great White
What is the Story About?
Where Would They Rather Be?
Wile E. Coyote
Willing Suspension of Disbelief, The
Wisdom
Withholding Dramatic Information
Wizard of Oz, The
Worthy Opponent

Writer
Writer's Block
Writers Conferences
Writers Workshops

~Y~
YA novel
You

~Z~
Zeitgeist

FOREWORD:

Here Are Your Stones

To name something is to own it, to hold power over it. Pursue research in any academic discipline and eventually you will reach a level where you'll need to learn a completely new and specialized vocabulary. This is not simply a necessary consequence of specialization, but a mechanism of exclusion by which one group of people, be they academics or clergy, separate themselves, elevate themselves above a larger group. It's why the Catholic Mass was performed exclusively in Latin for nearly two millennia; it's why a Jewish boy must read from the Torah, in Hebrew, to enter the community as a man; and why Martin Luther's translation of the Bible into German, the English King James Bible, and even Dante's Inferno, written in Italian vulgate instead of Latin, were revolutionary. They were linguistic levelers; they gave God and poetry to the people, without the need for an interpreter.

Because of the mercurial nature of literature, a vocabulary specialized to the point of being arcane has developed around it. But these terms are largely used for interpretation and deconstruction; they are the tools that critics, as well as teachers and students of literature, lay out on a tray before (to paraphrase the poet, Billy Collins) tying a story to a chair and beating the meaning out of it. While identifying themes and motifs, metaphors and archetypes may help in dissecting a story, breaking its infinitely complex structure down to elements a critic or student can recognize, as is the case when dissecting a frog, you may understand the parts, but it ceases to be a fully functioning frog.

What this book does is supply the terms for construction of stories, not deconstruction. This is a lexicon of causes, not effects. These are the stones from which stories are built, not those by which they are dashed apart. When a writer starts out, all he really has going for him (or her) is the love of story and the blissful ignorance of just how much he does not know. Often a young writer pursues studies in literature, under the impression that by understanding great works of literature, he will be able to bring greatness to his own work. What happens, in my experience anyway, is that he is often crushed under the weight of literature. He's no longer protected by his ignorance, no longer buoyed by his passion and energy. The wall of literature is simply too high to climb, and while he has learned to pull stones out of it, he has no idea how to build it.

As Twain's Huck Finn puts it at the end of his narrative, having evidently learned what it takes to create a great story: "There ain't nothing more to write about, and I am rotten glad of it, because if I'd a knowed what a trouble it was to make a book I wouldn't a tackled it, and ain't a-going to no more."

This could be the lament of the sophomore writing student, trying to crawl out from under the rubble of deconstructed literature. I have been a writer for more than forty years, the last twenty of which I've made my living as a novelist. Writing fiction is the hardest and most rewarding thing I have ever done, and remains a challenge every day of my life as I try to learn more and get better at my craft. And there is always, always more to learn. Over the course of this very long quest, Shelly Lowenkopf is the best teacher I have ever had, and if not for the precepts he taught me, most of which are cataloged in this book, I would not have been able to do the work I so love to do, or have enjoyed any success at it.

Twenty-eight years ago I stumbled into Shelly Lowenkopf's pirate writing workshop in Santa Barbara with a handful of short horror stories and a sense of gratitude that there was anyone else in the world who thought that writing stories might be as important as, say, turning a profit or lowering taxes. (It was Santa Barbara, after all, and Ronald Reagan was in the process of molesting the country from his ranch outside that very city.) I read my stories, the students critiqued them, and finally Shelly would say something like, "The dialogue works, but perhaps if the characters each had an AGENDA it would add another layer to the TENSION." Then he would use that opportunity to explain to all of us what he meant, how considering AGENDA as you were writing would make your scenes better, more compelling to the reader. He had given us all a rock with which to build our stories. "The man's a lunatic," I lamented to my friends as I left the workshop, but a year later I would be back there, sitting next to Shelly, reading a story in which I had considered the AGENDA of each character, and Shelly might use that as an example of the concept, but might suggest strengthening the narrative VOICE. Another rock with which to build my stories.

And leaving the workshop I might say, "Well, he's right about AGENDA, but when it comes to this VOICE thing, he's clearly a lunatic."

"But last year you said he was a lunatic about AGENDA." "Yes, well, he got better." And so it went.

"Shelly, here is my brilliant sea monster story, full of CHARACTER, AGENDA and authorial VOICE."

"Thank you, Chris, here is your rock; it's called, COUNTERPOINT."

"He's a crazy person," I would say, only to realize a few months later how quickly Shelly recovered from his various mental health "episodes." And how often they resulted in my having become a better writer. Often I found that the truth in what Shelly was teaching me wouldn't seem relevant until I reached a point in my skill where I could recognize it. "Oh, that's what he was talking about?" There were never too many rocks in my basket to carry, because their use, their weight, their relevancy to storytelling and understanding story didn't manifest until I was ready to carry them. He gave them to me nonetheless, knowing at some point I might be able to use them. And so it has always gone, even unto this day, with this book, collecting new rocks I will use in building my next story.

(Twenty-five years after that first workshop, I would teach a master class in fiction writing at that same conference, and I prepared my class each day by attending Shelly's pirate workshop the night before and more or less just parroting what he had said. After all, I'd written and sold a lot of books, but everything I knew about teaching the craft had come from poor mad Shelly Lowenkopf, who gently delivered the stones of storytelling into the wee hours of the morning, then waited patiently, until his students became strong enough to pick them up. I'm sure my students thought I, too, was quite insane.)

So here they are, for you, in this book of terms by which a writer or a reader, a lover of fiction, can, when he or she is ready, come to understand how stories are made. Here, gentle reader, is your box of rocks.

Christopher Moore
San Francisco, California

PREFACE

The Fiction Writer's Handbook is a tool for writers of fiction and for readers who love story.

The moment a writer begins a story or a reader picks one up, a natural synergy begins. The writer sets forth with the reader somewhere in mind and heart, striving to make the reading experience more vivid, nuanced, and memorable. The reader, in addition to trying to second-guess and out-guess the writer, works at trying to figure how the writer does it. This book investigates the process of synergy from both sides—what techniques and strategies do writers use and how do they shape the richness of the reading experience—arriving at a strategy of its own to make the writing and reading experiences even more gratifying.

After thirty-plus years in the editorial trenches at book publishing and magazine venues as well as teaching writing and publishing-related courses at the Master of Professional Writing Program at the University of Southern California, I see a clear connection between writer and reader. The techniques and strategies in these pages have been forged from my observations in my own writing sessions, editorial meetings, actual editing of manuscripts, and teaching. They have come out of those focused hours where stories are experienced as intimate reality rather than mere words on a printed page. This is where I've been palpably aware of the trust implicit on both sides of the reader/writer equation.

Where does this trust come from? The reader invests faith in the writer to supply a satisfying experience. The writer harbors confidence that her words will be understood and appreciated. This connection is a mystery all students of writing, be they creators or consumers of it, try to unlock. I know this because in all the venues of my life—including, every year since 1980, for one hectic week at the tail of June, when I lead the late-night fiction workshop at the Santa Barbara Writers Conference—I've been barraged with questions that reflect confusion in the terms writers, editors, and writing instructors use, and even more questions about who the readers are and what they hope to find in the stories they read. I've come to understand these questions as ways of trying to access the key to the mystery.

Alas, I have no key—there isn't one. And, in some ways, trying to explain the reason for the heady rush that accompanies Philip Roth's literary pyrotechnics or why the creepy calm in a story such as Margaret Atwood's

The Handmaid's Tale is so unsettling is like trying to explain why a joke is funny.You may end up understanding the mechanics but you forget to laugh.

I'm convinced that a more intimate understanding of literary technique and strategy can sweeten the experience of literature, and even *deepen* the delicious mystery, for both sides.

Many of the definitions you'll find in these pages come from my years of writing, editing, and teaching. Some were not quick to come; I had to ask friends who are writers or who are associates in publishing. Sometimes I was forced to discover the information through my studying of the published fiction I admired, other times through editing the manuscripts of students and authors I hoped to admire. The result is over three hundred fifty sturdy and vivid terms and concepts I've seen at work.

Now you'll ask, what's so different about this book? Why do writers or, for that matter, readers need what some might see as a "dictionary" of literary terms? My literary agent asked straight off; so did my publisher. Here's what I told them:

I'm bored with books on how to write and how to read that begin with explanations that sound canned and glib. The good stuff is often buried, too anecdotal, way too one-size-fits-all. I wanted to produce the book I needed when I was setting forth as a writer, a book you could pick up at any page and be led by your own needs and curiosity rather than the logic pattern of a development editor. I wanted a book that made me believe someone had given away the store. I wanted a book that showed the connective tissue between the tools of storytelling instead of telling me how to construct separate damned chapters. This book, I told them, will inspire writers to take chances and cause readers to want to come along for the ride, all the way to surprise and enjoyment.

So here we are.

Instead of a table of contents, you'll find a *list of entries*. When you consult these articles and see a WORD rendered in SMALL CAPS, you'll find an article of definition for that word or phrase.

I hope in the following pages to have the same effect on you as I continue to have on my friend, the prolific writer Barnaby Conrad, when some years back I gave him a copy of *The American Heritage Dictionary of the American Language,* fourth edition, unabridged, for a birthday gift. Even now I can tell whenever he looks up a word because he invariably leaves a message on my answering machine complaining about the time he spends with that book. This is due to the way the AHD leads him relentlessly from one article to another, and he has come away from his reading feeling as though he's been led delightfully astray.

Most of these definitions and connections are mine, aged in the vaults and recesses of my own experiences with teaching, editing, and writing. On occasion, you may hear other voices as well—some Barnaby Conrad, to be sure, but also the remarkable inventor-head writer of *Laugh-In,* Digby Wolfe, and the writer of mysteries set in Elizabethan England, Leonard Tourney, both of whom I've taught with as well as argued with. And there is the ongoing resonance of my mentor, novelist Rachel Maddux, who answered questions for me with her writing and her own opinions when I had no one else I could trust to ask.

And so, on to the mystery...

Shelly Lowenkopf
Santa Barbara, CA

Preface for Writers Who Are Absolute Beginners

If you follow this book closely, it can and should take you to the point where you will have one or more completed manuscripts. This book can also prepare you to do the necessary work to make your manuscript ready to be sent out into the world with some expectation of publication.

You're about to meet nearly four hundred of the terms and concepts related to the craft of telling stories. As you get to know them, you'll also see the family tree connecting these terms.

Every time you come across a word in SMALL CAPS, you'll see a reminder of how related the aspects of story are.

Open the book anywhere, read an article, then follow the trail of links as far as it takes you. Once you've done that, you'll see the intent and purpose in a dramatic way. Now, you're ready to begin.

Read the article "First-Draft Strategy." Check out all the SMALL CAPS definitions. Set this book and any other writing book aside. Now write as complete a first draft as you can of a short story or novel.

Set your draft aside, then read the article "Revision." Now apply what you've learned to your first draft. After you've applied these changes, reread your rewrite, adding, subtracting, rearranging, changing point of view. Set the revised manuscript aside for a week. Now read the entire manuscript aloud, noting any place where you stumble because of construction or where you notice a glitch you want to fix.

You're ready to begin showing the manuscript to your writing group or someone whose reading judgment you trust. Close family and/or non-readers are out.

The closer you can bring yourself to producing a minimum of two thousand words a day, reading at least two books a month, and revising a completed work eight to ten times, the closer you will come to the place where your story or novel being accepted for publication is less an accident and more a certainty.

Acknowledgments

The realization by a WRITER that authorship is not a one-person activity; there are too many dedicated and talented individuals who gave friendship, advice, support, and that great intangible, presence, for this writer to buy into the conceit of having done it alone.Among these are my two mentors, the writer, Rachel Maddux, and the actor, Virginia Gilmore; writer pals Barnaby Conrad, Brian Fagan, J. F. "Jerry" Freedman, Leonard Tourney, and Digby Wolfe, along with those blazing comets William F. Nolan, Chris Moore, Charles "Sparky" Schulz, and Bob "Batman" Kane I picked up during my editing and teaching ventures.There is some nod to family in the dedication, but not to forget Jake and Pennee, dad and sis. Now that all these are gone, there are nieces, Kathleen and Marianne, who put me back into family big time with their own families.There is Lizzie, hunkered down in her beloved L.A. with her beloved Australian Cattle Dog, writing provocative blogs and taking pictures that break hearts.

Literary agents are topics of lively, sometimes acrimonious debate at writers' gatherings. I've had some of the most notional and controversial in the business, thus the smile creeping across my face like stealthy Navy Seals when the subject of agents comes up.Toni Lopopolo. *Dove andro senza il mio agiente?* Toni knows how tough it is out there, but she's tougher—and smarter—than they are.

No small nod either to COPYEDITORS and the good ones who do so much more than delete misplaced commas; Carol Fuchs, armed only with the *University of Chicago Manual of Style* and a keen eye, aced the vagrant spelling, whimsical usage, and random authorial mischief.

Let's talk about design. Inside and out, text and cover, Deborah Daly. Who'd've thought Garamond for the text? Deb would. Deb knows.

Not to forget publishers. Christopher Meeks of White Whisker goes back to the USC days when the Professional Writing Program was turning out a steady stream of professionals. Chris turned pro not only as a writer, but a publisher, to watch as the latest incarnation of that amazing entity, the American book trade, unscrolls.

Acknowledgments are not complete without GUILT; thus, for all the times a certain black herd dog named Sally was shorted on walks that should have lasted at least a half hour longer while this book was being written. After all, *The Fiction Writer's Handbook* was written on her watch.

THE
Fiction
Writer's
HANDBOOK

~A~

act

The noun, not the verb. An orchestrated, contrived performance given by one or more persons while pursuing some AGENDA; hence the judgmental,"a class act": a person or group whose behavior suggests quality and substantial grace of approach; or "a tough act to follow," meaning an extraordinary performance; or "getting one's act together," an orchestrated routine of behavior intended to produce a desired effect.

An act is a component of a stage play; it contains one or more SCENES in which CHARACTERS simultaneously pursue AGENDAS and through their ACTIONS reveal relevant individual traits. The act is the thematic framework that sets STORY in motion, then advances as the characters, attempting to be true to their intentions, confront OPPOSITION, REVERSAL, and SURPRISE.

The act is a useful reminder to the WRITER of a SHORT STORY or NOVEL, functioning as a checklist of events that have happened, that should have happened, that might happen, and/or are being actively hoped for by one or more characters and by all READERS. An act is a larger petri dish of smaller segments and scenes that have some temporal or thematic hierarchy. Many short stories can be transformed into a one-act play. Many longer novels are reduced to the equivalent of a short story before being transformed into a motion picture. (William Styron's novel *Sophie's Choice,* for example, undergoes transformation from a great number of acts to fewer as a motion picture.)

As to structure, Act I, of course, grounds the story and, ideally, grips the reader, but this grounding and gripping can be accomplished by the use of several different techniques. Act I, Scene II of *Richard III* by William Shakespeare sets forth characters and their agendas in immediate and irresistible motion. Act I, scene I of *St. Joan* by George Bernard Shaw establishes a political climate, introduces the BACKGROUND of an as-yet unseen major character, all the while evoking the ambiance of a time in the distant past. Act I, scene I of *Entertaining Mr. Sloan* by Joe Orton presents an immediate agenda, which foreshadows a bold, arresting CONCLUSION, ironic in its Solomon-like logic.

As a verb, act gives us the movements, plans, and decisions of individuals who assume or take on agendas, ATTITUDES, and entire modes of behavior that are not necessarily their own. In most stories, this acting is apparent to the reader if not to the other characters, forming a double bind with IRONY; the author has conspired with the reader at the expense of the characters to produce this effect.

action IS character

An observation made by F. Scott Fitzgerald in his unfinished novel, *The Last Tycoon;* a reminder that DRAMA is a medium that EVOKES rather than describes.

The best way to convey a dramatic image of a CHARACTER is through the movement the character makes in the STORY, showing AGENDA, BACKSTORY, and emotions released through interaction with other characters while striving to achieve a GOAL against OBSTACLES and REVERSALS (also known as TURNS).

The READER takes more cues from character behavior than from a description of the character's physical traits. Some deft AUTHORIAL INTERVENTION may help a reader form a physical picture of a character, but having a character stoop to get into her car suggests some of the ongoing challenges in her life thanks to her height.

Some of a character's actions are subliminal, not noticed except by the WRITER and the character who is, after all, appearing as an active rather than passive participant in a story. Things may happen to a character, but then a character responds to them and to other characters as well, even to characters who are off stage and nearby or who are off stage and dead, yet still exerting some form of influence, and it is this response that gives away the stuff the character is made of.

actioning

Means finding an ACTION for a particular EVENT in a STORY. This means translating AGENDA or GOAL or perhaps FEAR or revulsion into a CHARACTER'S response at every opportunity, resorting to mood only as a secondary tool. Once the writer understands this concept to the point where it becomes muscle memory, characters will emerge from a story with greater clarity and purpose. The CONCEPT involves knowing, in addition to who the character is, what that character wants, what that character is willing to do or not do to attain the goal, and how the character feels about all the other characters in the story.

Actioning is often thought of as an interpretive concept for actors, but it is useful for providing WRITERS with STRUCTURAL insights and a technique for establishing authentic spontaneity in a character's response to a stimulus, whether from another character, a DRAMATIC condition, or an inanimate object.

Hint: For writers, DIALOGUE is also part of actioning. For READERS, look to what the character *does* in context with what the character *says.*

This last attitude—how characters feel about each other—is of particular importance when one character speaks to another. Does that character admire, distrust, resent, perhaps even hate the other character? And what are the social boundaries surrounding their relationship? Suppose Mary can't stand her mother-in-law. How would she, in a family gathering, inquire if her mother-in-law wanted tea? And suppose the mother-in-law thinks her son could/should have done better in his choice of a wife. How would she respond? "Whatever led you to think I drank tea?" Nice, maybe. What if the inquiry were answered with a stern warning: "This time, remember the lemon." Or a dismissive, "I'll get it, myself."

Dialogue is not conversation; it is an exchange of dramatic action. A simple line of dialogue such as "I'm not hungry" may be read in a number of contexts. Your character should not say "I'm not hungry" (a plausible thing to say under many circumstances) unless, being said, it hovers between the speaker and the hearer—and the reader—with a meaning that extends well beyond "I don't require food." For instance, suppose the speaker of that "I'm not hungry" line is met with the response, "But I went to great effort to make this for you."

Additional hint: Create active verbs for your characters. He wants. She lusts. He envies. She detests.

The writer has the advantage over the actor of being able to use MOOD in NARRATIVE, but to action-ize narrative, imagine the character thinking thoughts *at* as well as *to* a particular character or group. "I should tell them all," she thought, "to take their offer of a vice-presidency and shove it." Thinking that, what does she do next? That's actioning. That's also story.

In much of today's modern theatrical productions, the director and cast meet early in rehearsal to action the script, creating the bonding chemistry among the cast that will inform their interpretations of the lines before them and making it easier for the director to BLOCK out each scene, defining where each character should be. Even for writers who like to proceed with no game plan—and there are those hearty souls who disdain outlines—detailing the feelings for each character to all the others is a flotation jacket in a sea of chaos.

adversary

A front-rank character whose AGENDA and/or interests is in direct CONFLICT with another front-rank character; an opponent in a STORY.

Characters with GOALS provide the CATALYST for story. We see dramatic motion occur when individuals appear who are adverse to the PROTAGONIST's goals and INTENTIONS. Think cowboys and Indians, Indians and the cavalry,

Earthlings and extraterrestrials, cattle ranchers and sheep ranchers, rural and urban, the youthful and the elderly, laborers and management. Often resting between these two sides is THE PRIZE, the status or power or reward striven for by each. All these and additional pairings have the potential for good relationships, which is splendid in real life but dull in fiction. READERS enjoy the potentials for rivalry; they expect (see GENRE PROMISE) rivalry to blossom into adversarial relationship when they pick up a story.

Even if the primary character is going up against a philosophical or social clash, both sides of the argument must be rendered with a human representative. Walter Scott's *Ivanhoe* presented the clash of cultures between the Saxons and their Norman invaders, which was adversarial enough, but Scott appropriately heeded the call to have representatives of each opposing force on stage, if only to glower at one another. When the clash involves addiction, the adverse position—failure to quit the addiction—must be demonstrated. If the clash involves two or more contestants of notable ability, the adversarial position must be represented as some competition among candidates for a position. The winner, for instance, might become a surgery resident, a tenure-track professor of history, or an artistic endowment recipient. (See Arthur Koestler's *The Call Girls,* wherein academics in competition for foundation grants are seen as high-class hookers). If the clash involves Man and Nature, both sides must have representatives. This is demonstrated in the adversarial relationship between Captain Ahab and The Great White Whale, and even there Melville left a human survivor, Ishmael, to tell the story of the clash and to interpret its outcome. When encounters between individuals and a particular culture or ZEITGEIST are concerned, it is more generous and interesting storytelling to have characters representing both sides of the opposing forces.

The most effective way to produce an adversary for a front-rank character is to produce a character who in at least one way has an admirable ability. The more effective and invincible the adversary, the greater the likelihood the protagonist's ultimate victory seems convincing and satisfying. In contrast, it will appear to the reader that the deck has been stacked if one of the contestants is one-dimensional, evil personified, while the other is Sir Galahad writ large.

aftertaste
    The feeling or vision EVOKED after reading a SHORT STORY or NOVEL in which the READER takes up the CHARACTERS and dramatic situations, giving the characters and their circumstances life off the page; a resonant impression triggered in the reader by the EVENTS, circumstances, and personalities in a DRAMATIC NARRATIVE.

Some novels and stories are so evocative that they seem to continue in a reader's mind long after the ENDING has been resolved. How many of us have considered what would happen next to Jake Barnes and Brett Ashley after Barnes has delivered his famed closing line in *The Sun Also Rises*:"Yes, isn't it pretty to think so?" Or, still with Ernest Hemingway, this time *A Farewell to Arms*—Catherine Barkley has just delivered a stillborn baby, then died of a hemorrhage; Frederic Henry stays with Catherine until she dies, attempts to find ways to say farewell, realizes he cannot, then walks back to his hotel in the rain. The endings of both novels, as written, leave no doubt that the story is over, but the characters are drawn so well that they do not fade from the imagination.

Aftertaste is the emotive awareness in the reader of the entire narrative, the literary equivalent of the aftertaste of a particular wine or ale, the lingering effect of the process by which evocation works, the affect and effect a skilled actor produces when portraying a character.

How to achieve aftertaste? Consider the GOALS of each character and the ACTIONS the character takes to achieve those goals. Consider how each character responds to FRUSTRATION and REVERSAL. Consider the endings of stories as dramatic moments of THEME rather than explanations of their significance. Think about the way Anton Chekhov ended his stories. (See AMBIGUITY.) Look for ways HINTS are introduced to pique the reader's curiosity. What further conversations or actions might Fortinbras and Horatio have had at the conclusion of *Hamlet*?

A story that lingers in the reader's sensitivities has a life of its own, a life that will draw the reader back to hear more, because readers want aftertaste.

agenda

What a CHARACTER wants; an achievement, GOAL, or status that propels the character's behavior throughout the ARC of the STORY in which the character is involved. As the story develops, the READER and other characters in the story gain an understanding of what the individual with agenda is willing to do in order to realize his goal. Agenda is like the magnetized cards substituting for keys at hotels and motels: without them, the character doesn't get entry into a SCENE, much less the story.

Even minor characters have agendas. Major or minor in status, each character has a strong sense of entitlement to his or her own agenda and is impacted by the hoped-for result of achieving it. Agenda is the armature about which character is wrapped.

Before considering such details as physical appearance or relationship to other characters, a WRITER will do well to consider the why and wherefore of the agenda that character carries. Then the writer can consider the relative importance of what that character was doing before making appearances in various scenes. *Then* come the EXPECTATIONS that character had in entering the scene. Next would come the character's relationship (if any) with the theme of the story and/or the other characters. Only when these are established may the writer consider physical attributes.

A postal service worker, taxi driver, or deliverer of a pizza or take-out Chinese—more or less faceless, throw-away characters—nevertheless preserve the vital atmosphere of PLAUSIBLE REALITY if they are allotted agenda. The mail delivery person has the agenda of wanting assurance that the recipient gets the intended letter; the taxi driver has perhaps a political agenda or wants an agent for his screenplay; the pizza delivery person is an actor, awaiting discovery by a casting director. The extra line of dialogue or gesture provided by such individuals is another layer of reality painted onto the story.

Whether the story is GENRE or LITERARY, agenda is an essential presence. By checking agenda, the READER is drawn into a greater understanding of the INTENT and scope of the story. Additionally, the writer is given CLUES for the ENDING, and the characters are given clues for idiosyncratic behavior that yanks them, kicking and screaming, from the comfortable shadow land of CLICHÉ.

Some characters of necessity hide their agendas; their behavior is controlled to conceal their overarching intent. Thus one of the more useful tests applied to persons in reality and to characters in story is this: Does this individual's behavior hint at a hidden agenda? The result of behavior intended to conceal an agenda is an entire layer of IRONY. (Imagine the delicious irony in a character hoping to conceal an agenda with a range of behavior that ultimately convinces him of the wrongness of his agenda and the moral correctness of his subterfuge.)

One of the many reasons for the popularity of the MYSTERY or suspense story is the opportunity for the reader to match wits with the author, the detectives, and the cast of characters in the examination of agenda (MOTIVE).

Agenda in fiction does not have to be any more rational than it is in real life. Ahab had intellectual reasons for wanting revenge on the whale, but seeing his tortured physical appearance becomes enough for the reader to suggest validity to Ahab's quest.

agreement

A dramatic condition where CHARACTERS appear to hold the same opinion, or share the same AGENDA, the operant word here being "appear."

The appearance of agreement between characters becomes a signal to expect the CONFLICT of disagreement, exacerbated perhaps by the "I changed my mind" defense. Characters who are comfortable with SITUATIONS in which they find themselves, thus in agreement with the status quo, are seen by the READER as a ticking time bomb prior to the explosion of rebellion. In STORIES where leadership and loyalty are significant issues, a PROTAGONIST may come to suspect too much agreement from his or her underlings.

Agreement is a force that brings dramatic narrative to a screeching halt (see STASIS) unless it is used in a manner that provokes TENSION, as in how long the agreement will continue. Agreement also provokes IRONY as a result of some characters seeing it as a much-desired GOAL, only to discover later how being in a relationship of any sort that relies too heavily on it provokes SUSPICION of unrest or tension.

When characters agree, watch out.

alternate universe

In FANTASY, SCIENCE FICTION, and SPECULATIVE fiction GENRES, a universe other than the one we inhabit exists, is visited, or may be visited by individuals from this universe.

The laws of physical behavior may be the same in alternate universes or they may, at the WRITER'S whim, be entirely different, as may be their histories. An alternate universe (AU) could in theory exist in which the Secessionist States won the American Civil War (see *Bring the Jubilee,* Ward Moore, 1953), The Axis won World War II (see *SS—GB,* Len Deighton, 1980), and not to forget the iconic trope of double speak and eternal war in George Orwell's *1984* (published 1949).

The alternate universe concept pushed into a shotgun wedding with the young adult genre is found in Philip Pullman's *His Dark Mysteries* series, in which two young protagonists move back and forth between parallel worlds; a more classic SCIENCE FICTION from the Golden Era, Frederick Brown's *What Mad Universe,* features a science fiction editor who is thrown into an alternate universe constructed by a teenaged letter writer; and, in addition to C.S. Lewis's well-liked *Chronicles of Narnia* series, in which children are transported from this world to another populated by animals, there is also Lewis's SHORT STORY, "The Shoddy Lands," in which the READER is transported to the "alternate worlds" of the minds of other individuals.

Most alternate universe stories have some portal through which CHARACTERS move from point A to point B, not the least of these portals the rabbit hole through which Alice fell, or the eye of the tornado through which Dorothy Gale was transported to Oz.

There is extensive AU literature from which to choose, including the highly skilled work of Stephen King as well as many of the first- and second-generation science fiction/FANTASY writers, offering twists of humor, politics, psychology, and terror.

Reading at least one such work in this category will help the writer ratify the notion that all FICTION is alternate universe, each STORY being a particular writer's LANDSCAPE and world view, his or her characters emerging to work out problems that affect their sense of individuality and their individual sense of conscience.

ambiguity

An essential ingredient in CHARACTER-DRIVEN FICTION, where INTENT and OUT-COME are left vague; MOTIVES and SUBTEXTS may be interpreted in differing ways by READERS; a quality of meaning in dramatic writing where the reader is allowed some say in the interpretation.

Was the Billy Budd of the eponymous novella a naïve narrator or, to use contemporary PC tropes, intellectually challenged? Surely Herman Melville had had enough seafaring experience to open the possibility of the unspoken SUBTEXT of a sexual hang-up by Claggart over Billy, but did he intend the reader to infer a sexual conflict between the two characters?

Was the governess of *The Turn of the Screw* in fact seeing the ghosts of Miss Jessel and her lover, Peter Quint? Or was she merely delusional? If that were so, how do we explain the fact that the governess's young charges, Flora and Miles, may have been seeing the ghostly appearances? You might also ask, as some readers and critics of *The Turn of the Screw* have asked, if the most recent governess had frightened young Miles to death.

Was Spencer Brydon merely delusional in Henry James's SHORT STORY "The Jolly Corner," or was he seeing a ghost? In even more mischievous fact, has Brydon died at the end of the story? Because the story continues for a bit, was he experiencing a moment in the afterlife from which point he could look back at his earthly self, just as he had in fact done at the beginning of the story when returning to his old family home?

Did Jane Eyre hear or sense Rochester as he called to her across the moors in his moments of need and peril, or was her awareness the intuitive process of a woman in love with Rochester?

Did Hamlet see his father's ghost on the battlements of Elsinore Castle, or was Shakespeare anticipating the arrival of Sigmund Freud?

It is a wicked feeling to have readers arguing over the PLAUSIBILITY of events in one's work, to know that readers have taken one's work away with them, off the page, after the work had been completed. One such way to achieve this status is through the process of ambiguity. Call it CHEKHOVIAN if you wish; the process involves not spelling things out with too much clarity, not explaining too much, removing from one's work the same sorts of details characters in stories would remove.

Call it ambiguity. It is a welcoming country with no officious border guards or entry restrictions, although it does have a suspicious nature when it comes to the excess baggage of explanation and no sense of humor.

antagonist

A front-rank character in a NOVEL or SHORT STORY, cast in opposition to the AGENDA of the PROTAGONIST. Sometimes a force of nature (see Jack London's story, "To Build a Fire") becomes an antagonist, working against the protagonist; in similar fashion, a condition (such as age) can work against a front-rank character (see Jack Schaeffer's *Monte Walsh*), but more often than not, such antagonistic traits reside in one or more CHARACTERS, who accordingly become MESSENGERS or REPRESENTATIVES (Arthur Miller's *The Crucible,* Margaret Atwood's *The Handmaid's Tale*). The antagonist deserves as much attention and complexity as the protagonist. It can't hurt if the READER likes the antagonist as much as the protagonist; this fact alone makes the protagonist's ultimate victory more momentous.

When the antagonist is a force of nature, it is sound dramatic wisdom to have at least one human in the NARRATIVE who reminds the reader of that force of nature, perhaps from that character's own experiences with the force of nature.

anticipation

The visualization of a future EVENT or condition by a CHARACTER, often accompanied by an EMOTION; an intimation of a forthcoming emotional and/or political climate; anxiety over potential CONSEQUENCES as exhibited by a character; a READER's expectations about the fate of characters, the turn of PLOT, and critical SCENES within a long STORY.

Characters come into scenes with anticipation and INTENT; readers come into story and longer works with concerns and hopes, which are massaged by the WRITER; writers come into story with anticipations as well, with expectations of how the story will develop. Thus anticipation becomes a metaphoric presence in an equation involving REVERSAL OF FORTUNE, fortuitous turns, dumb luck, and a protracted campaign against some character's AGENDA. More so even than the characters, readers expect persons in a story to experience FRUSTRATION, defeat, disappointment, from which point they reorganize, set forth once again to accomplish a cherished GOAL, mindful of all the successes and failures to be found in literature.

A character who has no Plan B has given up the right to have readers care; a character who anticipates an easy go in a venture, then proceeds to have a stress-free time is robbing the reader of such sensations as SUSPENSE, CONCERN, and FEAR.

Some characters have as a trait the anticipation of success in every venture, while others have been led by EXPERIENCE and propaganda to expect nothing. The anticipation of success, so says one philosophical side of an argument, passes along a greater burden; he or she who has neither anticipation nor expectation has nothing to lose.

Anticipation livens up a character, animates and motivates him, sets him up to go forth into some further scene and venture, there to meet the future which, in fiction, is sure not to contain the expected.

anticlimax

Is a shift away from a matter of heavy, relevant CONSEQUENCE to something entirely trivial, producing a bumpy, undercutting effect; a comparison of something high-minded with a matter of little or no consequence; it is also overkill on the PAYOFF of a STORY (the delivery of a death sentence when a reprimand would have sufficed). When done with deliberation, the result may be amusing, even considered satiric, but when done unintentionally, not only does the reader suffer, so does the WRITER'S reputation.

Anticlimax is a feeling of impatience forced upon READERS when an author overstays or over embellishes the dramatic effect of a satisfying CONCLUSION. Why, oh, why, for instance, did Alfred Hitchcock think it necessary to add the Psychoanalysis For Dummies ending to *Psycho*? Look for studio pressures, their rationale being to make sure the viewer "got" it. Novelists such as A.S. Byatt, Alice Munro, and Cormac McCarthy, among others, write as though they respect the intelligence of their readers. Often brought about by a writer's unwillingness to allow readers to draw their own conclusions, anticlimax arrives with baggage in tow when the author, in what can nearly always be reduced to a show of distrust for his readers, intervenes through one or more CHARACTERS and insists on explaining critical events by offering BACKGROUND for them or explanations.

Anticlimax undermines an effective conclusion. However managed and emphatic his endings were, Beethoven understood the dynamics of anticlimax in his compositions. Many writers of the past whose works are still being read today—notably Anthony Trollope, Joseph Conrad, and Jane Austen—seem to have found the boundary between the precision of an effective, memorable ending and ornate excess, then observed that boundary, giving some critics the opportunity to note that eighteenth- and nineteenth-century authors made sure their readers got their money's worth.

More recent NOVELS and SHORT STORIES end on a note of AMBIGUITY, prompting the wisdom that writers looking for a VOICE, a THEME, and an audience are well advised to err on the side of understatement.

Unconventional wisdom: if you leave a party too soon, everyone wonders what happened to you; if you stay too late, you get stuck with helping to clean up.

(See DEFENSIVENESS.)

Antigone

A memorable young woman CHARACTER in a play by Sophocles (442 BC), later by the French playwright Jean Anouilh (1942), and later still by the German dramatist Berthold Brecht (1947). She is the sister of two brothers who fought on opposing sides in the civil war of Thebes and is the niece of Creon, new ruler of Thebes.

Antigone as a character bears comparison with the cartoon character WILE E. COYOTE because of the way her embodiment of moral choice leads her to become an unrelenting force, triggering behavior in every direction, throughout her family and in her fiancé and friends.Antigone's opposition to a contemporary convention of respect and honor put her in danger of losing her life and indeed does provoke an unintended death, which further provokes a sad but valuable understanding.

Sophocles, a general who fought in the Theban civil war, eschewed propaganda as did Anouilh, from his position in German-occupied France, and as well Brecht who, although a German, held no brief for German militarism, much less fascism. In any of these versions of the drama, the character of Antigone would do what a character should do: represent a believable individual visited with a conviction and mission that leads her forth regardless of CONSEQUENCE.

As Hamlet typifies one form of young male character driven by a goal, Antigone is archetypal in her representation of a young woman of dramatic integrity.

Any of the three versions of Antigone's story could be successfully presented today; a fourth version, focusing on the recurrent issue of torture and enhanced interrogation techniques, could stand shoulder-to-shoulder with them.

anti-hero

A male or female front-rank character in some or total lack of such classic heroic virtues as honesty, morality, and/or social conscience; a PROTAGONIST for whom the reader roots even though the character is lacking admirable qualities; a male lead as exemplified by the character Joe Buck in James Leo Herlihy's *Midnight Cowboy,* or a female lead as exemplified by the character Becky Sharp in William Makepeace Thackeray's *Vanity Fair,* or the gifted con artist, Addie Loggins in the film *Paper Moon;* a protagonist whose traits are chosen to counter propagandist overkill that hard work, virtue, and empathy with fellow mankind will be rewarded.

Both the hero and anti-hero have resumes that will get them cast in PLOT-DRIVEN and CHARACTER-DRIVEN stories; each is bigger than life, which is a significant requirement to get beyond audition stage, the next requirement being they need to have some quality or be in some existential situation where the reader will begin to root for them.

Yet another example of anti-hero from *Midnight Cowboy* is Joe Buck's eventual friend, Ernesto "Ratso" Rizzo, a seedy, amoral con man. Many front-rank characters, male and female, in Elmore Leonard's novels tend to be anti-heroic, their behavior often the result of self-protection from some vulnerability rather than essential mean-spiritedness.

In many cases, the anti-hero is the idealistic paradigm evolved to reflect the symptoms of actual reality as opposed to fictional reality. The contemporary male anti-hero is a conflation of those two exemplars from King Arthur's Round Table, Gawain and Galahad, morphed into twentieth- and twenty-first-century vets returning from disastrous wars, looking for jobs, coping with marital stress, parenting, and the betrayal of seemingly inherent promises of their social class. The contemporary female anti-hero exhibits the outlook and behavior that reflects the conflicts of a sacrifice of roles in a notably sexist society, the need to live her creative life during the naptime of her children, and the growing suspicion that she may have been chosen as a mate for all the wrong reasons.

The appropriate degree of anti-hero-ness required in a character is discovered through the trial and error of many drafts and/or a story construct where dramatic requirements help to define the need. A splendid series of examples is to be found in the suspense fiction of Walter Mosley, in general, and in the character of Lionel Essrog in Jonathan Lethem's *Motherless Brooklyn*.

apocalyptic fiction

SHORT STORIES and NOVELS framed on the premise that civilization, as it has evolved until the time of writing, has been traumatized by some natural or man-made catastrophe; narratives dramatizing the CONSEQUENCES of severe trauma to earth and its denizens; the evolutionary UNTHINKABLE, COME TO PASS. Whether it is a nuclear holocaust, tidal waves, epidemic, eruption, greenhouse effect, or some politically-inspired pandemic, the story of apocalypse begins with the consequences writ large, dramatizing its effects on the lives and status of the survivors. No matter if the catalyst is a metaphoric result of the SORCERER'S APPRENTICE, atomic rockets fired by insurgents, or a worldwide flare-up of mutant salmonella, the story is about what the CHARACTERS do next and how they accomplish what they do. The apocalyptic novel thus begins with the literary equivalent of Mr. Dickens telling us, *It was the worst of times.* The English writer H. G. Wells (1866-1946), with his frequent ventures into the medium of science fiction, is often thought of in connection with the apocalyptic genre, although Mary Shelley's much earlier work, particularly the 1826 novel, *The Last Man*, is a place to draw the historical if not the dramatic line.

Like Wells, the American writer Jack London had strong socialist beliefs and they wrote about them throughout their careers. In his apocalyptic mode, London produced *The Scarlet Plague* in 1912, depicting a San Francisco of 2027 after a global plague pandemic has killed off enormous chunks of the population. No stranger to her own political extrapolations, Margaret Atwood added another dimension to her speculation, overlaying *The Handmaid's Tale* with the overtly apocalyptic *Oryx and Crake* (published in

2003), which builds on extrapolations of genetic engineering and bio-technologies to produce various species who can then be exploited. Earlier, in 1954, Richard Matheson's *I Am Legend* posited a bacterial pandemic in which Los Angeles resident Robert Neville is the only survivor. The symptoms resemble vampirism, to which Neville, having once been bitten by a vampire bat, is immune.

Apocalyptic novels involve Earth being struck by asteroids and comets; there are cultural and political wars and, in John Wyndham's *The Day of the Triffids* (1951), an invasion by plants with aggressive behavior who are able to communicate with one another. The triffids are fond of feeding on humans. Nevil Shute's 1957 novel, *On the Beach,* tunes in on Melbourne, Australia, dramatizing the effects of the survivors of an atomic holocaust as they await the effects of death from the radiation. Walter Miller's plangent 1960 novel, *A Canticle for Liebowitz*, remains one of the archetypal novels of apocalypse and reconstruction. Cormac McCarthy's 2006 novel, *On the Road,* is yet another example of the flexibility of the apocalyptic novel; things were worse than bad: a cataclysm (probably nuclear, but not specified) has wiped out most of the population of the earth, leaving an unnamed father and son, who undertake a journey toward the sea.

There are hundreds of apocalyptic novels readily available for study, many of them from experienced and prolific SCIENCE FICTION writers, just as many others from men and women who have turned from more literary pursuits, driven by their individual senses of concern and politics, to this GENRE. The apocalyptic story begins with some worst-case scenario—the worse, the better—impending or having taken place. One or more characters are selected to sort through the wreckage and remains, then set forth to do something about making a contribution to the continuation of the human race (which is at RISK). Although many readers have built-in faith in the viability and continuation of humanity, the apocalyptic novel tweaks in some way at the center of complacency and a growing conviction that, somewhere, seeds of destruction are already planted and growing.

arc

The Magic Marker of STORY; it is the path story takes once it is set in motion. This useful term, its origins in geometry—a curved segment of a circle—help it serve as a mnemonic device. The concept of "story line," also a traced path of the progress of a story, suggests the moment in medical thrillers when the patient dies and his vital responses flat line; thus a story line connotes a thin, even episodic progression of EVENTS, but a story arc suggests LAYERING, dimension, an orbital path, all constructs reminding the writer, the reader, and CHARACTERS that story is multidimensional, multifarious, filled with implication, surprise, and the anarchic energy of impulse.

By its very shape, arc implies movement, the story being nudged, dragged, pushed, in some direction, both chronologically and in terms of PACE. Helpful to writer, reader, and characters, arc allows each to see where the story has been, where it needs to go, and what further impediments may cross its path or, indeed, collide (see COLLISION) with it.

Two of the most important individuals in the writer's professional life, the LITERARY AGENT and the EDITOR, will frequently inquire about the arc of a story, by which they ask, "Where is the story going?" Story arc is MOMENTUM informed by volition; it is EPISODE injected with "because" or "as a consequence." Arc is a record of things done in past, in present, because of, and as a CONSEQUENCE.

arena

A place where STORY is the featured event; a locale for a SCENE or the entire STORY, its LANDSCAPE never neutral, in fact frequently inhospitable. In some stories, the CHARACTERS may not know they are in an arena, content to think of it as a place—perhaps not the optimal place nor even a good place, but not a bad place. READERS, however, understand the unspoken irony. Why did Bobbie Ann Mason's iconic SHORT STORY, "Shiloh," take place on the park grounds that were once the arena for one of the most fierce and bloody battles of the American Civil War? Was it mere accident that Allison Lurie named her protagonists the Tates for her dark, funny novel, *The War between the Tates*?

Arenas in story are located in bedrooms, offices, law courts, tennis courts, front seats of automobiles, back seats of automobiles, hospitals, supermarkets, Roman coliseums—anyplace where characters gather to explore and exploit their AGENDAS.

Writers should consider the settings for their scenes with the same care and deliberation they use in selecting characters. If there is some plausible reason for including a particular scene in a story, its venue should be chosen with as much purpose as the cast of characters is selected, allowing its personality to have a tangible effect on the characters, whether a sneeze of allergy, a memory of a painful experience from the past, a sense of discomfort and unwelcome—or a sense of familiarity that causes one or more of the characters to relax, lower their guard, and thus become vulnerable to the CONSEQUENCES.

Arena is a good mnemonic for the fact that characters take their cues and hints from one another—differences of opinion may emerge from contact, AGENDAS may clash, INTENTIONS may be misunderstood.

attitude

An emotional presence often coupled with a state of mind resident in a

WRITER and, subsequently, in CHARACTERS, serving as a pole star for the writer, actor, and READER; the resident timbre of a story or portion of a story; the prevalent trait or personality in a story or character.

Attitude is like STYLE—it happens as a result of choices made by the writer and, in subsequent ways, by characters, reflecting an overall view of the circumstances in which characters find themselves, their approaches to coping with these circumstances, their regard for one another, and their regard for themselves.

Writers such as Jane Austen (1775-1817) and William Makepeace Thackeray (1811-63) showed their attitudes toward individual characters and the classes they represented through a NARRATIVE VOICE that was admiring, critical, or patronizing, depending on their intent, yet each was able to engage READERS without making the reader feel he was a target. In more recent years, W. Somerset Maugham (1874-1965) followed this path, using his narrative skills to take the reader into his confidence, the better to reveal the spectrum of human foibles to them through the prisms of his SHORT STORIES and NOVELS.

Attitude emerges from the writer's feelings and beliefs about a subject, whether the topic is political, sexual, or philosophical. One of the first things the reader notices in discovering attitude is the overall tone of presentation, followed by the behavior and relative flexibility or lack thereof among the characters. In some of his work, D. H. Lawrence emerges as if a schoolboy seated in the front row, waving his hand to get the teacher's eye because he, Lawrence, is so enthused by the information he wishes to present. In his short stories, Lawrence was so assured of his technique that his voice was more restrained, allowing the characters to step closer to the front of the stage.

A writer's preparation for executing a story could well begin with her checking in on the resident emotions that push the events of the story to the surface of the imagination. Begin with the notion that the story is like the toothpaste in a tube. The strength of the squeeze is directly related to the amount of toothpaste that comes forth. Attitude resides in the writer's grip: I'll show them, or, This will amuse you, or, I can't believe people still think this way, or, I didn't realize what a good thing I had until I lost it, or...

attribution

The means of identification of who is saying, thinking, feeling something relevant to the STORY at hand, but it is also a quality possessed by an animal, a person, place, or thing in a story; the most common use of this term is as a direct distinction of who is saying what, perhaps even with the adverb or adverbial clause attachment of how the thing being said was spoken.

Even at the risk of repetition, the identity of the speaker or performer is uppermost, beginning with the READER knowing for a certainty who the NAR-

RATOR of a given SCENE is and at all times who the speaker is, who the listener is, who the one who acts is, who the one being acted upon is.This important standard prevents such awkward, difficult-to-unravel locutions as "She knew she would go with her no matter what she did or when she did it because it was her basic instinct to help her whenever she felt she needed help."

The reader becomes so grateful as to forgive repetition of names, although this gratefulness does not extend across the board to careless, unintended repetitions, which do nothing but make the reader cringe (if the offense gets past the editor in the first place).

In the matter of attribution in DIALOGUE, the verb "said" has demonstrated over a long history its neutrality, thus Jim said, John said, Fred said will not raise any reader hackles that might have been raised if Jim said but John remonstrated and Fred averred.Thus, do not keep at hand a list of synonyms for said, in particular avoiding "expostulated," "admonished," and "uttered."

Verbs that convey feeling are welcome in all other places as synonyms for said. Do not, however, let CHARACTERS bark or growl; ululate is also a no-no, the main reason being that the word may appear to be an authorial judgment rather than from a character.

Unless the string of dialogue between two characters goes on for some time, it is not necessary to continue with the "said." If there are more than two characters on stage, the writer might consider burying the "said" in mid-action or mid-sentence: "This is not going to work," Fred said, standing, stretching."We need another approach."

In such scenarios, the WRITER will do well to pick a dramatic (SUSPENSE producing) place to break up the sentence. "This," Fred said, standing and stretching, "is not going to work.We need"—he looked about him as though tracking a fly unseen by the others—"another approach."

Yet another way to tack an attribution to a line of dialogue is with a sentence immediately following that contains action."This is not going to work." Fred stood, spotted a roving waiter, and motioned him over.

au

An abbreviation for alternate universe on manuscripts and proofs, in upper case (AU) or, in lower, shorthand for author; on occasion au qy is used to mean author query, a question asked the author by CONTENT EDITOR or COPYEDITOR.

audience for story, the

As in, "Who is the audience for this story?"—a question WRITERS need to ask themselves about their work before it is sent off to a publisher, because the publisher is certain to ask it.Thus, audience: a group of students who are assigned the text of a particular narrative; a collection of individuals who read for pleasure or information; a number of friends and relatives of a

WRITER; a team of publishing professionals who are on the look out for something; a writer who is obsessive in his compulsion to relate a sequential series of EVENTS; a writer who is bored with the prospect of having nothing interesting to read; a writer who has just finished reading a remarkable and compelling work by another writer; a writer who is pissed over some racial, social, intellectual, or scientific injustice; a reviewer who likes books; a reviewer who does not like books.

More specifically, is the ARENA of your story a circus? What audience might have a natural affinity for stories that are about a circus? Does your story revolve around a group of women who like to cook together? What age are the women? In what era does the story take place? What sort of food do these women like to cook? Do they get their recipes from the Internet, or do they attempt to cook all of Julia Child's recipes from *Mastering the Art of French Cooking* in one year's time? Who do you think might read a story about a contemporary woman who tried to do such a thing?

authorial intervention

A NARRATIVE condition arising when the WRITER usurps the POINT OF VIEW from one or more of the CHARACTERS, telling the READER how the characters feel and even going so far as to tell the reader how he should feel.

My message is simple: (1) writers, keep out—let the characters experience the STORY; and (2) writers, exercise care with vocabulary, word order, and dramatic action to provide a strong picture of the intended dramatic action and the motives behind them. Nevertheless, readers can and will persist in attaching their own interpretations—and this persistence is part of the desirable, wonderful mystery.

~B~

backpack

The tools, history, emotions, and baggage a CHARACTER carries when setting forth into a new SCENE.

Characters may or may not behave like tourists in a new setting, craning their necks to look at the sights or being blasé to a fault. An actor may show up for a performance, thinking he knew his lines but this time, in this scene, there is doubt. A housewife may return home from grocery shopping, thinking she has three hours of free time to work on a SHORT STORY before her son returns from school, then notices her husband's car in the driveway. Or an ambulance. A businessman leaves his afternoon AA meeting to attend a client party at which he knows there will be several bottles of champagne.

The operant question for characters at all times: What are you carrying?

backstory

The relevant personal history shaping the behavior, outlook, and EXPECTATIONS of each CHARACTER in a STORY; the relevant events and understanding inherent in a character before that character steps into a SCENE. In some cases, the character may be unaware of backstory events, have a flawed or romanticized vision of them, leading the character to search for the truth. In other cases, the character may be in a state of DENIAL over events that may have taken place. And in what has become a sub-genre, the major goal of DISCOVERY for a character suffering from amnesia is the search for his or her backstory. (Check Richard Powers's remarkable *The Echo Maker* for an investigation of how backstory informs identity.)

For conventional and practical purposes, a story is deemed to be taking place in the immediate present. In the case of historical narrative, the story is seen as transporting the reader back to a specified time, then taking place as though in the immediate present. In both cases, backstory is the past information the reader needs to know about the life of one or more characters. As an extreme example, the reference "Mary and Kitty had been roommates as undergraduates at Smith" qualifies as backstory.

Additional convention: Based on the construct of backstory being past history, more than fifty percent of a story should be in the present, otherwise the WRITER is well advised to begin and perhaps end the narrative in a different place. Not all narratives require backstory as a necessary condition, but just as we assume every person we meet has a backstory, we will assume that every character, even the unfortunate protagonist in Jack London's short story "To Build a Fire" has emerged on the page with a backstory.

beat

A useful term signifying a dramatic moment, activity, or deliberate pause; a convergence of action and timing within a SCENE of a NOVEL or STORY; a dramatic expression of time through the filter of portrayed activity.

At most concerts performed in the Western world, the concertmaster arrives on stage with a pre-tuned violin, a particular tuning fork or, in more recent times, an electronic device which sounds the Concert A, the A above middle C, which vibrates at 440 cycles per second. The orchestra then proceeds to tune their instruments on that Concert A.

In many motion pictures involving men in the midst of war, some individual of leadership role makes a countdown with his watch, directing all others to synchronize their watches NOW.

Both rituals are signals: some concentrated and coordinated form of behavior is about to take place.

Scenes in short stories and novels are as concentrated and coordinated. Some concert conductors will set the level of the Concert A at 442 cycles per second when the work to be played might profit from a sense of faster PACE. The Concert A may be dropped to a 438, as well, to suggest a subtle adjustment to tempo.

The writer is more or less the literary equivalent of the concert conductor, apt to use length of sentences, choice of words, and details or their lack thereof to set a tempo. Timing—pacing, if you will—is an important element in a scene, and a musical composition is a nice analogy to have in mind.

By the time we've finished writing the scene, we have a fair idea of how long in virtual time it covers, how much action, how many exchanges of DIALOGUE, how many REACTIONS, how many pauses are part of the recipe. The one ingredient most often overlooked is the pause. Another way to express this situation is to say that there is never nothing going on: no PACE, tempo, ACTION, or movement. Rather there is the coordination of CHARACTERS reacting to their surroundings, to one another, to the unexpected circumstances that emerge between them, and this coordination is complicated, perhaps even inhibited or driven by their individual agendas and their fears of being found out.

These moments of drama are called beats. A character doing something is a beat. A character not doing something produces a beat, which is the equivalent of a return volley in tennis, an arcing lob or a forehand smash. A scene begins when characters do something or do not do something. And then someone responds. And then someone reacts. And then....

It is not always necessary to have unrelenting action. Too much action can cut off the emotional responses of the characters, responses which, according to the rate with which they take place, can inform the tenor of the scene. Fast action can remind the reader of those iconic film clips of The Keystone Kops, erupting forth in lock-step idiocy; slow action can project lugubriousness or its first cousin, careful concern.

Some scenes need to have the author removed from them, in particular those where the author seems to be embarrassed by the pace, the pauses between words or kisses or looks. One way to look at a scene is to consider it as a complex series of reactions between characters who can't get a complete grasp on what's happening to them and who are trying to accommodate to events as well as possible. They are individuals who are facing examinations, performance reviews, legal trials, declarations of love, desires to perform or not perform, called upon under extreme circumstances, certain of success or failure, wanting to be somewhere else. They are us, and we have put them there because we had to out of curiosity and a wish to know.

beating a dead horse

Pursuing a CONVERSATION, line of inquiry, or AGENDA that has been overcome by EVENTS; a CHARACTER endlessly blaming himself or others for the CONSEQUENCES of some previous ACT or decision; taking a HAD-I-BUT-KNOWN trope to an even greater extreme of recrimination; not only crying but sobbing over spilled milk.

The worst example of animal abuse or beating dead horses comes when a character flails himself on the breast, bemoaning some missed opportunity or some previous seduction, either as perpetrator or victim, that seemed like a good idea at the time. Even the rule of three—three repetitions—can be one or two kicks too many. Try a scene in which a character recalls such a time. Or try a scene in which another character chastises the beater of horses of record with, "You're not still blaming yourself for that, are you?"

CUTTING material is an art of its very own, and difficult to learn, but one good place to start is with the kicked horse. Another way to approach this matter is to ask during the REVISION process, "How much does the READER need to be reminded of?" Of equal importance, "How much do you—the writer—trust the reader?" It is, after all, a two-way street. How can the reader follow your suggestions if you—the writer—failed to convey them in the first place? The safest strategy when confronting a dead horse is not to beat it, but rather to move on ASAP.

beginnings

Important places for WRITERS to consider because READERS set such great store by them; they are hot spots where STORY becomes dramatic; moments of NARRATIVE inertia; onsets of EVENTS that assume dramatic form.

The longer the story is, the greater the likelihood it will have more than one optimal beginning point. The beginnings you see on stories that resonate for you have involved deliberation and choice on the part of their WRITER. The same choice and deliberation are owed your own beginnings. Optimal beginnings are places where ACTION is already in motion, where action is about to begin, where a CHOICE has just been made, or where a CHARACTER is confronted by DISCOVERY or event that knocks him or her from everyday routine.

READERS are less likely to care about a story that introduces itself with BACKSTORY or some other form of explanation or footnote. Example: You are at a gathering—a party, or, if you insist, a soiree—when, of a sudden, an individual you do not know by name approaches you, telling you with convincing sincerity and sobriety, "Please help me. I've got to get out of here. There are two people in the next room who are after me."

When such a thing happens, you are immediately engaged. Your mind is already filled with such questions as *Who are you?* and *Why me?* Both these questions will and should be answered, but if this is to be the beginning of a story, now is not the moment for the DETAILS. We want more details that force the issue, which happens to be the issue of the beset individual's actions, convincing you, perhaps even against your will, to become involved, caught up in an ever slippery slope of dramatic event. Conversely, think of how differently you might react if that same stranger approached you with the opening gambit, "Hello, my name is Mark. I'm an insurance agent. It's a family business; my father left it to me when he died in 1993, and I've made a bit of a success of it but, all in all, I can't wait to retire and take up my hobby, which is building birdhouses, full time...." You see? Already, your eyelids are growing heavy....

The Scottish writer, Ali Smith, has it down perfectly in her story "The Child," where a protagonist who is never named is using her lunch break to buy her "weekly stuff" in a supermarket. Shopping carts in Scotland and England are called trolleys. "I left my trolley by the vegetables and went to find bouquet garni for the soup. But when I came back to the vegetables again, I couldn't find my trolley. It seemed to have been moved." In the trolley's place was someone else's shopping cart, with a child sitting in the little child seat. This is all in the first paragraph.

By the second paragraph, the narrator realizes the shopping cart with the child in it is indeed her cart. Events quickly proceed to the point where everyone in the market thinks the child is hers. We are "in" the story; we do not question the narrator's resolve to take the child to the nearest police department; much less do we question the fact that the child has now begun to speak, delivering its lines in the manner of a second- or third-rate stand-up comic. What it says is a stream of racist and sexist commentary.

Even though we do not know her name or where she works or what she does or if, in fact, she is in a romantic relationship, we share with Smith's narrator a sense of being caught up in a swirl of event that demands a solution.

Beginnings yank us into SITUATIONS that need coping; they lead us onto the path where we search for some kind of conclusion or, at the very least, a settlement. Ever the deft craftsperson, Tom McGuane yanks us right into story in "The Good Samaritan" when its protagonist, a man named Szabo, starts by not liking "to call the land he owned and lived on a ranch—a word that was now widely abused by developers." This is all we know of Szabo, and yet we are already rooting for him.

Beginnings are indications some stasis has been or is about to be destabilized. We read to see what and how.

being right

Being plunked into an existential sense of certainty of DECISION and GOALS expressed by a CHARACTER in a STORY; a belief supported by relevant ACTIONS exercised by an individual or group; a conviction of moral certainty.

One of the few exceptions to the rule of all characters believing in the moral high ground their actions occupy is the absolute sense of their inability to restrain themselves from acting toward a particular goal they know to be wrong. Example:"I knew it was wrong to compromise my position, but I was desperate for the money."Another example:"I knew it was wrong not to tell her the truth about my past, but I so much wanted the relationship with her that I remained silent."

For WRITERS who claim to have trouble with PLOT, the FORMULA of each character arriving on stage with an absolute sense of being right is formula enough; it insures a clash of AGENDAS. In addition to their dramatic goals, characters in stories want to inhabit the moral high ground of being right, especially in matters related to the ARC of the story; they will go to great lengths to support their DECISIONS and the rightness of their cause, using imaginative stratagems to avoid awareness of any responsibility for wrong-headedness or wrongful behavior.The great rallying cry of the tyrant, whether a household, organizational, or national tyrant, is,"I did what I did for your own good."

Even though most serial killers tend to see themselves somehow as victims, they nevertheless justify taking lives by an elaborately argued sense of being right, a position one hundred eighty degrees away from the course of the heroic man or woman who uses a refined version of The Social Contract as a pole star.

Hint to the WRITER: Major characters want major things, are defined by them, wanting the objects of their desire to the point of initiating rituals such as home fires, novenas, fasts, charms, and spells to enlist supernatural agencies in the rightness of their cause; they also invent rules or bend already invented ones. Macbeth was blown off course a few times, troubled by his conscience, but the mood passed, and he reasserted his rightness at the expense of Malcolm and, of course, his own conscience.

Hint to the READER: Look for some DISCOVERY a character experiences, convincing him he is right, trying to get you pulled into the same slipstream of rightness.

bigger than life

A quality often attributed to CHARACTERS after the fact of their having been read about; a sense of an individual having a combination of traits, qualities, GOALS, and strategies that make him or her memorable for individuality while at the same time representing a particular type, thus the adjective "quixotic" as it represents Don Quixote, who left an indelible reference guide of the adjective.

Not to be confused with implausible behavior, the concept of bigger than life reflects a vision of an individual that radiates either a single quality or warring internal qualities. Consider Pat Conroy's bigger than life Lieutenant Colonel Bull Meecham, from his novel *The Great Santini.* By all accounts an argumentative, bigoted, bullying sort, Meecham was a dazzling aviator, a man who in metaphor was king of the clouds, a man who, when the choice unexpectedly fell on him, risked then gave his life to save others, causing readers to feel shock and grief at his death.

Another bigger-than-life character that is a splendid example is The Wife of Bath from *The Canterbury Tales*, a portrait of a woman with attitude, goals, and grace, who has remained an out-of-the-ordinary paradigm for five hundred years.

It is possible to track bigger-than-life individuals from the distant past, when characters were either of noble rank or forged on the field of battle, or in the castle drawing room; otherworldly, but effective drama now is about remarkable men and women from more modest stations in life, performing in ways that belie the limitations that go with their situations, men and women who sense talents and obligations that they—not being able to afford horses or cars—walk to greatness.

Bigger-than-life characters are made of the clay of ambition, responsibility, love, devotion, and vision necessary to seek and then affect change. To render them with good effect, the WRITER needs to know who his characters are, what his characters want, what they are willing to endure to get what they want.

READERS will recognize them by the way they stand out from the dramatis personae in which they are cast. *Hint:* Watch for ways writers sneak flaws into them, giving them even more to overcome than the rigors of plot and circumstances.

Bildungsroman (also coming-of-age novel)

A NOVEL about the growing-up process of a young person seeking admission into the hallowed chambers of adulthood and supposed maturity; a youthful journey through painful experiences and idealism to a more pragmatic awareness of conventional behavior and ethics, often rendered in FIRST-PERSON, autobiographical point of view, such as Dickens's *Great Expectations,* Twain's *Huckleberry Finn*, and Bellows's *The Adventures of Augie March*, but of equal effect in THIRD-PERSON point of view such as Joyce's *A Portrait of the Artist as a Young Man* and McCullers's *The Member of the Wedding.*

Although some WRITERS have deliberately set forth to write a bildungsroman, most have done so through the simple expedient of choosing an interesting, talented, or energetic young person as a PROTAGONIST, then following an ARC of CONSEQUENCE in that person's life. (See *Queen's Gambit* by Walter Tevis and *From Here to Eternity* by James Jones. In the former, Beth Harmon is an orphan with a remarkable gift for chess. In the latter, Robert E. Lee Prewitt is a former boxer, now in the army, growing into a gift as a musician.) Some scholars, critics, and reviewers will call such a novel a bildungsroman. If said bildungsroman appears to be a cautionary tale or one with a strong

dose of moral choice, then said scholars, critics and reviewers will be showing off their knowledge of the original intent of bildungsroman, which was
to give young readers a means of measuring their own goals, behavior, and
responses against some topical paradigm.

One American author, Horatio Alger, Jr., Americanized the Germanic construct of bildungsroman to "rags to riches" in a series of inspirational and hor-
tatory novels, a hobby horse he rode to fame well beyond his death in 1899,
inspiring generations of young men to work their way to the top. All these
many Horatio Alger stories could be thought of as bildungsroman.

WRITERS do themselves no good when they allow themselves to be
reined in by a catchall term or concept, regardless of how conventional the
CONCEPT has become, nor how trendy and accepted it is. Accordingly, let the
story come of age with the character, reaching its own, articulated destiny
rather than by way of the author trying to earn gold stars on some critic's
checklist. The story was, is, and shall be everything.

block

An important CONCEPT, linked to a DEVICE, expressed as a verb: Let's block
out your STORY; let's figure out where your characters are standing/ sitting/
jumping/dancing in the ARENA in which the story is taking place. As a concept and device, it is vital to the storyteller's success in keeping the NARRA-
TIVE alive and in motion.

As a concept, block goes to work mapping the setting of a particular DRA-
MATIC landscape, dramatizing it with the details and sensory attributes that fit
the author's intent and contributing to the comfort and potential discomfort
of the CHARACTERS. A SCENE that has been blocked out is a Google map that
shows the reader who is positioned where and what shifts in position take
place. How the characters move within the space the writer has allotted to
them illuminates how they pursue their separate AGENDAS, how they respond
to other characters and, at the same time, suggests the SUBTEXT of the truthful regard each character has for all the others.

A blocked scene also contains relevant information about temperature,
time, smell, taste, relative states of light and dark, and color, as well the perceived sense of openness of space or the pressure of a closed-in space. As an
extreme example of this construct at work, imagine a claustrophobic character and an agoraphobic character in the same setting, first a small, cell-like
enclosure, then in a commodious locale with a breathtaking vista.

Storytellers who do not at some point in the writing process block out
each SCENE and every bit of narrative connection will run the risk of having
the work appear one-dimensional or confining. Knowing where everyone is
or will be in a scene helps determine, as one example of the benefits to be
had from blocking, whether the characters can whisper to one another or
must shout in order to be heard.

As a device, blocking can become a presence or condition that prevents a character from pursuing a stated AGENDA; it may also be a condition having its effect on a large number of individuals who are rendered fearful of acting or frustrated that they cannot act as they might wish, or resentful that they have been issued an order not to perform a particular ACTION even though they may have ardently wished to do so. Thus blocking becomes an OBSTACLE which makes itself felt by a character whose options to keep the story alive are direct opposition, seething resentment, disappointment, immediate embarkation on a counter offensive, or abject surrender. FEAR is another exceptional dramatic obstacle; so is CONSCIENCE. Macbeth is quite prepared to kill Malcolm as a necessary step to further his goal. Screwing up his courage to commit the murder, Macbeth observes a servant carrying a dinner tray to Malcolm, a bit of blocking that allows for a BEAT in which Macbeth's conscience steps in to block him, to become an obstacle. Macbeth cannot for a time bring himself to kill Malcolm.

The obstacle creates dramatic tension, building to suspense. In this sense, story is like the bait-and-switch of advertising and retailing technique: a desirable product is shown at an attractive price, but when the customer appears to claim it, he is either told it is no longer available, or he is shown another, more expensive product. In either case, the customer is diverted from his original intention. READERS not only want to be baited and switched, they expect it.

The writer who knows his characters well enough to see and manipulate the obstacles for each character remains in control of the need of the story to be shoved, driven, propelled against obstacle. This knowledge will lead the writer to understand how vital blocking is for the reader.

As a story develops, the reader begins to take sides to root for particular characters to achieve their goals. But if the characters achieve their main goals too soon or too easily, the story is seen as a cheat or, worse, a dismal failure. This understanding of block-as-obstacle produces the useful dictum: Never take the reader where the reader wants to go.

buyer's remorse

A condition achieved by a READER when it becomes apparent that the WRITER has let story slip through his grasp; a situation in which the writer begins to rue having taken on a particular story or the mentorship of a particular CHARACTER; a time when the reader feels himself the victim of too much promise and not enough delivery.

The term may also refer to one or more characters who are suffering from the CONSEQUENCES of past actions that may have seemed like a good idea at the time but now serve as reminders of disaster. Making the most of a bad situation is the sort of ACTION a character can take to make us admire the individual's ability to innovate.

~C~

canary in the mineshaft, the

A sacrificial testing device used to warn against gasses potentially injurious to humans, thus a CHARACTER involved in a tenuous or perilous situation, used to signal similar danger to front-rank characters. If the READER sees the canary character falling victim to a danger, the reader will become apprehensive when a front-rank character appears to be placed in a similar spot.

Captain Ahab

Major causal CHARACTER in Herman Melville's novel *Moby-Dick,* a man so bent on REVENGE that he becomes the instrument for the death of all but one seaman aboard the whaler Pequod; a sworn foe of the great white whale, Moby-Dick; by extension a metaphor for an individual so focused on his GOAL that all perspective becomes lost. (See also *Don Quixote, King Lear,* and Wile E. Coyote for other examples of memorably fixated characters.)

For all its enormity and discursiveness, there is little specific information in *Moby-Dick* about Captain Ahab; he is a follower of the Quaker faith (an enormous fact given his vengeful mission), has a young wife and son, is somewhere between his late fifties and early sixties, has spent most of his life at sea, is named after a biblical king. Using this scant information, Sena Jeeter Nasland has written a novel, *Ahab's Wife,* which further investigates his conflicting humanity and desire for revenge. (The mere existence of the Nasland novel is a fine example of cultural AFTERTASTE.)

While it is possible to read *Moby-Dick* as an adventure, the characters within it engage in existential and moral questions to a degree that causes the novel itself and many of the characters within it to take on the dimensions and whale-like aspects of metaphor. (Ahab's first mate, Starbuck, for example, is a well-read intellectual, also a Quaker, who is able to discuss and argue with Ahab from a similar background.) Add to that calculus the fact of the whale, which clearly is making statements of its own with a considerable intelligence of its own. The interesting question arises: Did Melville deliberately or by artistic accident happen upon the American equivalent of John Milton's *Paradise Lost?* A pursuit of the answer to that question could lead, for the appropriate seeker, to thematic insight at a comparable level to Nasland's curiosity about Ahab himself and the woman who married him.

Ahab's attractiveness for all WRITERS of fiction begins with the unyielding strength of his purpose—to track down and destroy the whale. A Quaker whose moral code speaks to pacifism, Ahab's ACTIONS and determinations are encouraged by the inner voices of hatred and loathing in the face of the whale's supposed representation of pure evil. Even were he to have won, Ahab would have had to face the CONSEQUENCES of his CONSCIENCE.

Over a hundred fifty years after the publication of *Moby-Dick*, it is no spoiler to observe that the whale is directly responsible for the sinking of the Pequod and the death of all aboard except Ishmael (who survives in order to render his FIRST-PERSON account of what happened). Does this absolute sense of doom that begins with the very first line," Call me Ishmael," make the reader aware that the events are any less tragic than, say, *King Lear*?

Is it such an unfathomable jump for a writer to see connections between the character of Ahab and DON QUIXOTE and WILE E. COYOTE in a landscape haunted by the imperceptible divisions between revenge (Ahab's), illusion (Don Quixote's), and humiliation (Wile E. Coyote's)?

Ahab is a gritty reminder of the ways a character's goals become the interior decorator for the SETTING, PACE, and ultimate EFFECT of story.

catalyst

A CHARACTER, social unit, or organization in a STORY that causes a CHANGE to take place; an EVENT that transfers energy to the point of shifting dramatic inertia from STASIS or status quo; a story point that tilts the LANDSCAPE toward a POINT OF NO RETURN.

Characters frequently self-catalyze to get themselves out of a perceived rut; they change jobs, move to different cities, join the Peace Corps, abort or switch romantic relationships, adopt dogs or cats. Characters also accept opportunities, which seem to them to be steps advancing toward some long-cherished GOAL. Catalysts are often neutral but, depending on the nature of the character responding to them, can be seen as Cosmic, Fate-driven, and certainly Golden Opportunities and Lucky Breaks. As such, the character responding to the catalyst may see some guiding hand or THROUGHLINE in an essentially chaos-filled universe.

A catalyst represents a dramatic unit of energy, which may come from a chance meeting, an unanticipated discovery on Craig's List, or a connection between elements not usually associated. Remember Ishmael, as early as the first paragraph of *Moby-Dick*, wanting—needing—some catalytic agent:

"Whenever I find myself growing grim about the mouth; whenever it is a damp, drizzly November in my soul; whenever I find myself involuntarily pausing before coffin warehouses, and bringing up the rear of every funeral I meet; and especially whenever my hypos get such an upper hand of me, that it requires a strong moral principle to prevent me from deliberately stepping into the street, and methodically knocking people's hats off—then, I account it high time to get to sea as soon as I can." Luck of the draw for Ishmael was choosing the Pequod; nevertheless, his wanting a catalyst to change his humors drew him into an adventure of a lifetime.

Many characters have resident within them the first cousin to HIDDEN AGENDA, the SECRET DESIRE. When a character becomes aware of a catalyst that could bring about advancement to achieving the secret desire, the WRITER will have created a conflict of wrenching intensity.

Hint to READERS *and* WRITERS: Make a list of ten favored characters in ten favored books. Identify the catalyst that propelled them into action. Now you have a profile of your own favorite types of catalyst, which you can enhance by putting one of them to work in your next STORY. It can also help you decide the next book you will read. Adventurous sort that you are, you can also reach within yourself as so many fine actors do, where you will identify a catalyst that is contrary to your standard preference. From such adventures come interesting characters, doing interesting—and perhaps scary—things.

causality

The INERTIA of STORY; CHARACTERS behaving as they do because they are driven by their emotions, their beliefs, or their responses to dramatic EVENTS and other relevant pressures within a story.

In many ways, the defining concepts of story and the American legal system are similar: each is propelled toward a DECISION, solution, allotment of judgment by some relevant precedent. The rules of procedure are based on what happened before—past events, past thinking, past behavior. In the law, this reliance on the causality of precedent is referred to as *stare decisis.*

In dramatic narrative, the effect of precedent resides in BACKSTORY—and the BACKSTORY is foundation for the steady condition of clash in which the CHARACTERS and CONCEPTS coexist. It is not enough, however, for two characters to confront one another with disagreement; each must reek and sound of his AGENDA to the point where the reader can sense its presence. Even if a character does something "Because I felt like it," the reader must be able to sense the plausibility of that character doing so. No amount of simple action for its own sake can cover up the lack of causality. Story with event but no causality is mere episode, inviting the disparaging adjective "episodic."

A helpful mnemonic device for causality is the word "because." Story happens because someone wants something to happen, because someone doesn't want something to happen, because in some field somewhere an ox is being gored and because its owner is not going to let the matter pass.

Causality is a partner with CONSEQUENCE; things are caused to happen by actions, the results of which produce consequence.

chaos

A dramatic condition in which there is no apparent order; a CHARACTER behaving without a PLAN or DESIGN; a multifarious state of being in which there is no seeming thread that connects individuals or EVENTS.

Chaos is the world without STORY, its purpose random and unstructured. The WRITER enters the landscape of chaos, imposes a structure or plan, then steps back to watch the characters as they respond to attempts at DESIGN. Chaos is also the world without specific individuals being assigned starring roles; as it continues to unfold, the condition of chaos levels the playing field of AGENDA so that all agendas are of equal importance. When beginning a story, the writer chooses a LANDSCAPE, which may be pure invention or FANTASY or extrapolated SPECULATIVE FICTION but which nevertheless becomes a tangible place for the READER. The writer then adds characters, whose goals help define their prominence and focus.

STORY, PLOT, DESIGN—they are all a purposeful rearranging of furniture, the *feng shui* equivalent within DRAMA, allowing some procession or ORBIT of EVENT, the totality of which eases the passage of energy from the beginning point to the RESOLUTION. Chaos appears at first to be all the distractions a character or group of characters may face, but as the reader grows interested in the characters, chaos morphs into "things that could go wrong," which is a sort of reverse *feng shui*, a negative energy that arrives in unanticipated increments.

Chaos is a series of LAUNDRY LIST events, awaiting the writer's hand to organize them in some more deliberate form.

chapter

An arbitrary division in a NOVEL; it may contain a number of SCENES or as few as one; it may feature a group of scenes taking place within a particular timeline (day, week, month, year) or present a number of scenes from the POINT OF VIEW of one particular CHARACTER.

Although chapters tend to suggest their own individual organization, it might be a convenient rubric to consider the chapter as a shelf in a particular room in a house. Information, EVENTS, points of view, and time lines are "stored" according to their relevance.

Let's look at William Faulkner's *As I Lay Dying,* a novel with a chapter arrangement that's worth an entire university course in construction and its effects on the READER. There are sixty chapters of varying length, narrated by fifteen characters, which add delightful layers of richness to a story that bursts on our senses like a French Impressionistic painting—even the chapter that contains only five words.

Each chapter begins with the name of a CHARACTER. Through their commentary, we learn their relationship to one another as well as which character narrates from the coffin. We are first introduced to the narrative of Darl, who we learn is the second son of Addie Bundren, who is given her own chapter to narrate as well as several secrets to reveal, not the least of which is that she is a control freak. Yes; it is Addie who tells her story from the coffin we see and hear being built for her. Chapter two is Cora, a neighbor of the Bundrens, who is with Addie when she dies. Cora is highly religious; her husband, Vernon, who also has a shot at a chapter, is a farmer and is more or less content to let Cora do all the religion for the family. After several chapters, it becomes clear that Darl is the most articulate of the characters and the most reliable. It is also clear that Addie was messing around with Reverend Whitfield, resulting in the birth of Jewel. Yes; Jewel has a chapter of his own.

This is not intended to précis the story line but to suggest the imaginative, inventive ways Faulkner used chapters to introduce us to the characters to the point where we have pictures of them and what it was like to live the rural farming life in Mississippi. We also see ourselves being pulled into the reading of the novel by its artful construction. A close inspection of what Faulkner accomplishes in each chapter will guide writer and reader to a deeper understanding of the dynamics of MULTIPLE POINT OF VIEW.

Hint: After close examination of *As I Lay Dying,* compare it with Wilkie Collins's *The Moonstone* for a more conventional and even more suspenseful dramatization of how useful it is to assign entire chapters to different characters within the same novel.

Further hint: Dan Brown's *The Da Vinci Code* overcomes its intrinsic puerility with a dazzling use of chapter placement to suggest story movement. In many ways, Brown's use of chapters is worth study to see how he gets characters not only from place to place but from feeling to feeling so that, just when we are growing impatient with them or losing our interest, they will respond in a way that causes us to grant temporary absolution for another chapter. Then, invariably, something will happen to keep us on board for yet another chapter.

character-driven story

A NARRATIVE in which EVENTS progress because of the effects of CHARACTERS on one another; dramatic entities where behavior appears to generate from responses and reactions as opposed to the scavenger-hunt mentality of the PLOT-DRIVEN STORY.

In real life, parties and gatherings, particularly sit-down dinners, are planned on the basis of comfort and familiarity between individuals or at least in the sincere belief that guests who are strangers will have friends, interests, and talents in common. In STORIES, characters are invited to gather with the understanding that there are already manifest differences of background, opinion, goals and morals; equally possible is the understanding that dramatic differences will soon emerge, sending these characters into a defensive or a combative mode, or a combination of the two.

Character-driven stories are predicated on the notion of disagreement, literal or perhaps figurative strange bedfellows. AGREEMENT causes stories to screech to a halt unless the READER is led to understand that the parties in the story have agreed to things that they do not obtain.

Most of the short stories of Annie Proulx are character-driven, even though many appear to be wound about the armature of the TALL TALE, notably "The Half-Skinned Steer," in which a character successful in business ventures is driven to investigate his past, with fateful consequences. No less character-driven in its own way is her "Brokeback Mountain," in which two young men in the contemporary American West are forced to cope with unconventional sexual tension against an unforgiving landscape.

characters

The individuals in dramatic NARRATIVES about whom the STORY revolves; persons who, by their ACTIONS and responses to events, drive the story beyond its point of engagement, toward a RESOLUTION.

Front-rank characters are PROTAGONISTS, who cause things to happen, and ANTAGONISTS, whose AGENDAS collide with and oppose the protagonists. Messenger characters are those who bring information on stage, anything from "The red coats are coming..." to "Guess who the high school hunk has a crush on?" Pivotal characters are present as backup and support for the protagonists and antagonists, possibly switching sides during the course of the story. Exemplary characters appear to have things happen to them that serve as warnings or examples to the protagonists and antagonists. In a teenage ROMANCE, an exemplary character becomes pregnant and serves as a warning to the protagonist. In a MYSTERY NOVEL, perhaps an individual from the same organization as a front-rank character is found murdered—perhaps making the front-rank character fear now for his life.

Characters at all levels come on stage with some degree of EXPECTATION, which will affect the AGENDA, and vocabulary—words the writer uses in dealing with the character, the way the character speaks and behaves. Even the lowest-level walk-on has some agenda, even if it is just to get home from work or from Oz. All characters come on stage fresh from where they were previously, imparting a history of behavior and, thus, a greater reality to the READER and to the other characters.

Shadow characters are those whom the writer needs merely to open a door, clean a room, deliver a pizza, or get a signature for a package. The shadow character may be on stage for a matter of seconds, but may come to visible life with, for example, the difference in a verb. Did the shadow character walk in the scene, or run into it; the speed of her entrance can help determine or underpin the pace of a scene.

All characters have some features, the front-rank characters having the biggest TOOL KIT of all. Important *hint:* giving any character too many details, whether descriptive or motivational, signals the reader to expect a greater role from that character. Thus the details for each character should be thought out, then managed with care.

One argument for developing characters of all levels has its origin in television. With so many dramatic television shows being presented, the emphasis on type becomes more prevalent, thus some notable clichés—Soccer Mom, Battle Axe Nurse, Dumb Blonde, Catholic School Girl, Hero, Hired Gun, The Nerd, Fall Guy, The Insensitive Spouse. Characters, even seemingly peripheral ones, who are on the trail of some tangible goal, are less likely to fall into the slough of archetype or cliché.

Another safeguard for producing characters who emerge from the shadows: hit them with a combination punch of internal and external conflicts.

character arc

The developmental path a CHARACTER follows in pursuit of a STORY-related GOAL. In long-form NARRATIVE, all front-rank characters undergo change, depending on how well or ill their AGENDAS fare. This developmental arc reaches exemplary texture and subtlety as seen in the quirky resolve of Ava Bigtree, the thirteen-year-old principal narrator of Karen Russell's *Swamplandia.*

In her own way, Samantha Hughes, fifteen-year-old narrator of Bobbie Ann Mason's first novel, *In Country,* takes character arc to yet another plateau. Samantha's father, whom she scarcely remembers, died in the Vietnam War. Her attempts to get a better understanding of him through his letters and diaries put her on the same THEMATIC path as Huckleberry Finn, who was effectively tasked with defining the state of race relationships at the time of the Civil War. Sam's attempt to understand the U.S. involvement in Vietnam produces a character arc worth study for its thematic potential.

Tony Webster, the narrator of Julian Barnes's 2011 Man Booker Prize-winner, *The Sense of an Ending,* demonstrates an imaginative way to present character arc from the point of view of a middle-aged man forced to examine events of his youth, only to be told, "You still don't get it."

Characters in the SHORT STORY are not on stage long enough to undergo the upward evolution of Frank Money in Toni Morrison's *Home,* or the downward plummet of Dick Diver in F. Scott Fitzgerald's *Tender Is the Night,* but their shorter arc can well represent a change of attitude, as Pam Houston's characters in *Cowboys Are My Weakness* do.

See also NARRATIVE, NAÏVE NARRATOR, and UNRELIABLE NARRATOR for additional implications of how character arc may be bent back on itself or otherwise manipulated to create such effects as AMBIGUITY, naiveté, and THEME.

Chekhovian

A useful term meaning similar to or EVOCATIVE of the plays and SHORT STORIES of the Russian WRITER, Anton Chekhov, it refers to materials linked by an underground or less visible CAUSALITY than conventional drama. These NARRATIVES seem AMBIGUOUS, informed by the emphasis on SUBTEXT and internal responses of a CHARACTER. They are stories that lack any appearance of being PLOT-DRIVEN.

Chekhov is best known among writers for his assertion that a gun appearing conspicuously in Act I must be pointed and fired by Act III, opening the door for discussions about FORESHADOWING and CAUSALITY. The statement may also be regarded as a FRAMEWORK in which characters use the tools at hand. Many of Chekhov's stories deal with the inability of CHARACTERS to communicate with one another until a) it is too late, b) a sudden insight emerges, and c) THE ELEPHANT IN THE LIVING ROOM becomes visible to one or more of the characters, each of whom may have a differing interpretation of said elephant. This last possibility links James Joyce and his stories to Chekhov.

Chekhov's major plays and later short stories invite investigation by READERS and WRITERS for his use of such techniques as INTERIOR MONOLOGUE, INTERNAL CONFLICTS, and subtext. His work has inspired twentieth- and twenty-first-century actors as well as writers, guiding them to find non-verbal ways of expressing emotions and INTENT. If there were to be a literary equivalent of Mount Rushmore, Chekhov would certainly qualify as such an image, along with Franz Kafka, George Orwell, and, with some debate, Miguel Cervantes. The names of all four have become adjectival forms in the literary language: Chekhovian alerting to AMBIGUITY, Kafkaesque evoking apparent CONSPIRACY THEORY or dead-pan satire, Orwellian implying Big-Brother supervision, and Quixotic suggesting extravagant ROMANTICISM and idealism.

Hint: Major things to be learned from Chekhov: 1) let the reader work at the story to adduce its meaning and 2) give the reader sufficient but not extensive tools.

Additional hint: The ending of his famed short story "The Lady with the Dog" has a payoff that is not only essential Chekhov, it leads you back to rereading the story to see how he did it.

chemistry

The tangible, measurable result occurring when two or more CHARACTERS interact; an effect that seems to emerge and transfer into ACTION when characters get along to the point where their every exchange of dialogue flares with its own pace and intensity, or they develop an enmity or such disdain and tension that the READER is on tenterhooks, waiting for that one big explosion. Chemistry becomes a palpable aura of reality, emerging from the manner in which characters respond to one another often with non-verbal signals that draw them into friendships, alliances, or mutual distrust.

Chemistry is the unspoken glue in FICTION, producing its own inexorable logic and the resulting CONSEQUENCES of that logic. Often coming as a SURPRISE to the WRITER, particularly when it threatens to shift the predetermined direction of the story, chemistry is a jump-start to MOTIVATION and ACTION.

Sometimes the chemistry between characters is accepted by the writer and the reader on a non-verbal level, "just because it is." This very quality helps project a greater sense of reality and believability because of the way it overrides logic. Readers will probably have some sense in their own life of disliking or liking someone on sight, without any good reason; they probably make judgments as a direct result of such non-verbal signals, picked up by the sensory receptors of the social animal humans are.

One of the many great chemistries in American fiction emerges between Tom Sawyer and Huckleberry Finn, each drawn to the other in ways that make sense only after they are considered in light of the activities shared by the two. To Tom, Huck represents the freedom and anti-convention that runs rampant in a young boy, the ability to come and go as he pleases and the "worldly" knowledge such freedom brings. Huck, on the other hand, has come to accept Tom's views of conventional behavior, a slap-dash view of chivalry as seen by Walter Scott, and the classroom view of the way the world worked at that time. Tom was social, Huck wasn't. Into this primordial ooze came their boyish desires for adventure, and from this came the chemistry that bound them.

In real life, Harry Longabaugh and Robert Leroy Parker met while in prison, each jailed separately on horse theft charges. The chemistry between them brings the Tom Sawyer-Huck Finn chemistry to mind. Longabaugh morphed into the Sundance Kid, an appellation doubtless hung on him by Parker since the name of the prison in Wyoming Territory where they met was the Sundance Prison. Parker, of course, was known as Butch Cassidy.

Yet another version of chemistry between characters emerged in the lengthy series of mysteries featuring Robert Parker's investigator, Spenser, and the unorthodox operative, Hawk, often retained by Spenser as a consultant. Hawk brought his own sense of justice into play, a scrupled-but-wary witness to the bigotry and unnecessary force of POWER brought to bear on the weak. In a real sense, Hawk is Spenser's GOLEM, brought out when the odds against Spenser need a bit of evening up.

Not to forget Sherlock Holmes and Dr. Watson.

The important fact for writers to consider takes in the reaches of partnering (say Dashiell Hammett's Nick and Nora Charles in the *Thin Man* series, and Dionysus and his slave, Xanthias, in Aristophanes's play, *The Frogs*) and leaving one character alone on stage for too long. When two characters appear to get on well—or, as in Louise Erdrich's short story, "Saint Marie," plucked from her novel *Love Medicine,* a young Native American girl in a convent school forms an explosive relationship with a nun—run with the energy. Follow the trail. Exploit the chemistry. READERS love the chemistry, often spotting it before the characters and WRITERS do. (See FUN.)

chick lit

A literary form often patronized and dismissed without giving it a closer look. It is intended for women and young girls; NOVELS and SHORT STORIES intended to appeal to feminine tastes and issues; a separate genre from romance where the ultimate goal is focused on marriage.

In relative terms, chick lit is a new kid on the block, an equivalent for feminine readers of the adventure stories aimed at male readers. As adventure stories run the gamut in voice from a drill-sergeant gruffness to a knowledgeable attention to the details of engines, motors, calibers of bullets, and the specific terrains of bull rings, chick lit reflects a full-bore enjoyment of professionalism, fashion, dating, sexuality, and relationships in general. The chick lit voice strives for and often achieves a tone of HUMOR, with all the EDGE and potential for pain and the sadness understanding that humor implies. In other cases, the chick lit PROTAGONIST tends to be self-effacing, but by no means embraces victimhood.

It is not so much a case of men being barred from writing chick lit as it is a case of the potential for a male writer of chick lit sounding a few degrees too ironic, which becomes sarcasm, which is no fun for anyone to read. Nor is it a case of chick lit being the emergence of revenge fantasy writ large for women writers; chick lit is an emerged and evolved attitude about the conditions and problems of life that follow women about as though these problems were stalkers.

The works of Candace Bushnell are apt targets for studiers of chick lit; so also are the works of MYSTERY writers Martha Grimes (*Fadeaway Girl*) and Alan Bradley (*The Sweetness at the Bottom of the Pie*), each of whom has introduced a young mystery-solving protagonist into the literature. Although their lead characters are a bit young for chick lit, their voices are worth study for understanding characters who will quickly grow into chick lit age and attitude.

On balance, chick lit may be thought of as serious literature for READERS and WRITERS, which means its endings are often of a piece with *Thelma and Louise* and, to mix the gender metaphor, of Huck Finn taking off for the territory ahead, fleeing from civilization. Some endings of chick lit novels are happy in the plausible sense. Others are reminiscent of Yossarian in *Catch-22*, taking off in a small boat for Sweden, hoping to flee the consummate madness that is war.

Chick lit is pushing envelopes of convention. To write it, the writer must remain abreast of the tide. The best way to do this is to read at least one hundred chick lit novels published within five years of setting pen to paper (or opening up the words "chick lit" on a computer search engine).

choice

A momentous decision is inflicted on front-rank characters, resulting in a rapid movement toward STORY. A forced or self-induced DECISION made by an individual that will have relevant CONSEQUENCES is another direct route to a story. Some overt form by which a character takes a stand will, as most READERS already know, necessitate a PRICE to be paid, something to be gained or lost. Resident in this lovely word and its value for WRITERS is the fact that while they were still emerging, they were readers who had access to The Classics, where so many legendary men and women of heroic stature were confronted with the anxiety associated with choice—the anxiety and the suffering it cost them.

In his Nobel Prize acceptance speech, William Faulkner described FICTION as "the agony of moral choice," a vivid way of illustrating the importance and variety of potential choices in any given story. A character may chose to ignore something, take a stand on some issue, commit a particular ACT or, after deliberation, not perform another; the character may stay, go, protest, smile outwardly and seethe inwardly. These and other similar acts are the individual BEATS a character performs during a story—they all have relevant CONSEQUENCES, and, if the writer puts the choices his characters make to good use, they will have some effect, such as provoking a recognizable emotion in another character.

One of the Newtonian Laws appropriate to fiction understands the effects of physical action by observing that each act has a consequence that is equal in effect and opposite in motion. In fiction, acts bring forth consequences, some of which are quite wonderful and positive in their nature; others are painful, inducing regret. A character faced with choice stands the risk of VULNERABILITY, which may make that character more sympathetic for a time. The Newtonian product of choice is consequence and, of course, consequence may lead directly to subsequent actions and—no surprise here—more consequences.

If Daisy had accepted Jay Gatsby straightaway in their courtship, the world would be missing *The Great Gatsby*; if Juliet had thought Romeo a dork, they would likely have gone on to marry others, living entirely different and considerably longer lives. If Sophie had not been forced to make her aching choice, William Styron would not have had nearly so plangent and moving a novel. If Nora Helmer had less spine, that door would not have slammed at the end of Act III of *A Doll's House*.

Thus the paradigms are presented, the lines drawn in the literary sands: You're either with us or you're against us. In or out? Yes or No? Coming or not? Are we going home yet? I can't do this any more.

Choice allows the READER to see large and small moments in the lives of characters, moments in which they set sail on a causal sea of events that leads them through the white waters of CONFLICT and its RESOLUTION; characters who are confronted with choice become inoculated against the one condition that renders them ineffective in fiction—PASSIVITY.

choking Doberman, the

READERS are particularly vulnerable to the "bite plan" of this literary dog device, calculated to arrest attention through the OPENING PAGES of a STORY, holding the reader well into the story's development, but WRITERS may be caught up by this paradigm of an opening concept for a PLOT-DRIVEN story.

Consider: A woman returns home from grocery shopping to find her pet Doberman racked by a severe choking fit. She rushes the gasping dog to a vet, who examines the dog but sees no reason for the breathing difficulties. He decides on a tracheotomy, telling the worried owner that the procedure wasn't anything she'd want to watch, suggesting the woman go home and leave the Doberman there overnight.

But when the woman arrives home, her phone is ringing. When she answers, she is surprised to hear the vet. "Get out of the house immediately! Now! Go to the neighbor's and call the police."

Who could fail to be intrigued by such an opening?

Very few, it seems, because what started as an exercise in arresting beginnings in a creative writing class ended up as a post on an Internet site that deals with debunking urban myths. But beware: This intriguing concatenation of events, classic in its allure and promise of story to come, can ultimately shoot itself in the foot by the very qualities it sets in motion. After such a fine beginning, take care that the payoff has somewhere to go other than a downward spiral. In this case it plays out with the vet having discovered two human fingers lodged in the dog's throat, a result of the Doberman having attacked an escaped killer who was attempting to hide in the house of the unlucky dog and its owner. When the police arrive, the escaped killer is found unconscious, in a state of shock, and somewhat the bloodier for wear.

The concept was so good that it gained the kind of repetition and currency momentum common to the urban myth. In much the same way that a successful movie or TV series begets imitations, the choking Doberman began appearing on urban myth Internet sites as having originated in numerous Canadian and U.S. locales. It was so successful that it even made the jump from website to book, *The Choking Doberman and Other Urban Legends*. During his tenure in the Department of Theater at the University of New Mexico, Digby Wolfe frequently invoked the Doberman as a splendid example of the opening velocity needed to get a story underway.

The medical thriller, *House, M.D.*, alive and running with over six seasons of TV exposure at this writing, begins each episode with the equivalent of a choking Doberman, in which an individual suddenly begins acting out the bizarre, life-threatening behavior of some unusual symptom, often placing the eponymous protagonist, Gregory House, M.D., at risk of breaking some moral code, civil law, medical ethic, or a combination of all three.

Admonition #1: Although there is nothing artistically or morally wrong with the plot-driven story, its side effects may include a weakening sense of reality, diminished PLAUSIBILITY, and CHARACTER development left to fend for itself.

E. B. White, the *New Yorker* writer, children's novelist, and co-author of a legendary STYLE guide, once wrote, "Whoever sets pen to paper writes of himself whether knowingly or not." In similar fashion, writers who attempt to fashion a compelling opening to a story, pushing at the outer limits of plausibility, write of the choking Doberman, whether they know it or not.

Admonition # 2: the choking Doberman reveals itself for what it is—a device. While effective, it is no substitute for characters the reader has been made to care for.

chronology

The arrangement of EVENTS in a timeline, beginning with the earliest, so the result is a chronology, a sequence of activities or BEATS set forth at the time of occurrence; tracking a person, place, or process by its age and subsequent growth. Chronology is to time as alphabetizing is to the alphabet, leading to some urban mythology among WRITERS that biography and STORY must be set before the READER in time sequence, beginning with early, then working its way toward the present. Perhaps because they have been bored by strict chronology, readers have come to expect a severe stirring of the pot. Abraham Lincoln may well have been born in a log cabin in Hodgenville, Kentucky in 1809, but most of the multitude of his biographies begin elsewhere, say as a young lawyer or congressman or even as President of the United States.

NOVELS often begin IN MEDIAS RES—smack in the middle of things—working their way forward and backward at the hand of dramatic whimsy. It is probably a good idea to know when and where CHARACTERS were born so that a plausible BACKGROUND can be constructed for them, but the entire subject of chronology raises the better issue of the information a writer needs to know about a character as opposed to the demonstrable and implicit facts the reader knows and deduces. Entire mythologies have been created around such ICONIC CHARACTERS as SHERLOCK HOLMES and Sam Spade, but the original venues in which these characters appeared—dramatic narratives— do not rely on the mythology, they depend on the story. Begin with a character's birth or some other significant rite of passage, if you must, but do not expect the reader to be as interested as you are, perhaps because the reader has not yet seen the character under stress or in thrall to some agenda, but equally perhaps because the mere fact of a birth, bar/bat mitzvah, christening, graduation is not of itself dramatic.

The character George Amberson Minafer illustrates this point. George is a principal character, you might even say a spoiler, in Booth Tarkington's

novel *The Magnificent Ambersons.* Named after his maternal grandfather
(thus his first and middle name), "At the age of nine, George Amberson
Minafer, the Major's one grandchild, was a princely terror, dreaded not only
in [the] Amberson [mansion] but in many other quarters through which he
galloped on his white pony.'By golly, I guess you think you own this town!'
an embittered laborer complained, one day, as Georgie rode the pony
straight through a pile of sand the man was sieving.'I will when I grow up,'
the undisturbed child replied.'I guess my grandpa owns it now, you bet!'And
the baffled workman, having no means to controvert what seemed a mere
exaggeration of the facts, could only mutter,'Oh, pull down your vest!' 'Don't
haf to! Doctor says it ain't healthy!' the boy returned promptly. 'But I'll tell
you what I'll do: I'll pull down my vest if you'll wipe off your chin!'"That is
George's introduction to us, from which point we move well back in time to
the point where George's mother was engaged to a man other than the one
who became George's father. A chronology is most useful for the writer
when the work at hand involves the activities of a number of front-rank characters, some of whom may or may not know one another. In such cases, it is
a useful guide for planning the order of SCENES and, thus, the possibility of a
particular character being able to appear in two successive scenes.
Chronologies often provide ALIBIS for suspects in MYSTERY NOVELS and for stories in which sexual jealousy is a motivating factor. But let us be clear: the
writer often has to know much more about the chronology of a character's
life than needs to be laid before the reader, who might well become restless,
or even bored, with too much non-essential information.

circumstances

Conditions motivating or surrounding persons, places, things, and events
in STORY are circumstances leading to the READER'S DISCOVERY of the ARC of the
narrative—reason enough for the WRITER to watch them with great care. Circumstances are nothing less than the status of behavior related to a CHARAC-
TER, that character's AGENDA and/or VULNERABILITY, and the likelihood of a
predictable behavior manifest in the ACTIONS or the failure to act in a particular character.

Mysterious or ambiguous circumstances surrounding a character impart
an atmosphere of menace and uncertainty. The SUSPENSE grows as the circumstances become volatile, leading to the growing apprehension that such a
mysterious or ambiguous character will be driven to the point of COMBUS-
TION, whereupon he or she will reveal a true self of incredible awfulness.

Familiar, even predictable circumstances advertise a growing sense that a
SURPRISE explosion is building, some unanticipated demonstration that will ruin
the STASIS, nudge it unceremoniously over the edge into chaos and discomfort.

Thus the mysterious and the familiar combine to FRAME events and the persons who participate in them, raising suspicions wherever possible. These suspicions translate to TENSION, which, lacking actual SUSPENSE, is excellent glue for holding story together. READERS wonder what new circumstances will bring to the equation of characters, bent on pursuing an AGENDA, meeting FRUSTRATION and REVERSAL.

All a PROTAGONIST or ANTAGONIST needs in order to set a story in motion is to hear the repetition of the familiar mantra, "Under no circumstances…"

cliché

An overused meaning or rhetorical device; a stock CHARACTER or dramatic situation that precludes or at least stifles any potential for originality; a form of literary shorthand that presents a person, place, circumstance, or thing in such a commonplace way as to avoid any further need for description or individuation; a deliberate or unconscious statement from the author that all is vanilla.

One of the more persistent clichés is a four-to-five-hundred-word feature composed of as many clichés as possible—The long arm of the law reached out and nipped Al Capone's cavalcade of crime in the bud…—demonstrating DRAMATICALLY how what was once fresh and original has now become trite and predictable. Another is the easy-as-pie Internet cliché finder. Most clichés were at the time of their origin a visual or descriptive trope that became overused because of their clarity and have become irritants through overuse.

Clichés do not stop as catch phrases. They extend to characters such as the absent-minded academic, the hit-person-for-hire who is kind to animals, the Irish cop, the Jewish pawnbroker or banker, the Italian criminal, the lazy Mexican, the red-neck Southerner, the effeminate male homosexual, the butch female homosexual, the bored housewife, etc.

The acquisitions editor confronted with an engaging story is apt to begin with a higher tolerance to an occasional cliché, growing more alert to these infractions if they persist. The cliché joins the COMMA SPLICE, indifferent spelling, and questionable usage as mechanical causes for rejection. The dedicated WRITER makes a search-and-destroy (probable cliché here) anti-cliché mission a part of every revision, starting with word usage then moving to an examination of each character who makes an appearance, finishing with any characters who may be mentioned but not brought on stage, thus coping with the built-in writer's hubris of writing cliché-free prose. If the writer does not do this, a seasoned READER is apt to do it for him—an act that will not benefit the writer.

cliffhanger

A major suspense-generating device in which the immediate welfare (if not the life) of an individual hangs in the balance; a ticking-clock artifice at the end of which a CHARACTER runs the risk of death; severe JEOPARDY left unresolved at chapter's end.

Most seasoned READERS are aware of the concept of the tales of Scheherazade in *One Thousand and One Nights,* in which a young queen extended her life for yet another day by telling her executioner/husband stories that left individuals in PERIL so great that the husband, driven by curiosity, had to hear the outcome. This was SUSPENSE with a VENGEANCE. Newspapers and magazines picked up this technique for telling stories in installments, each one ending with an impending disaster of considerable impact. Giving the device its name, Thomas Hardy, in 1873, published a novel, *A Pair of Blue Eyes,* which had been serialized in *Tinsley's Magazine.*

Against a background of restoring ancient church architecture on the craggy, desolate southwest coast of England, *A Pair of Blue Eyes* features young Elfride, a vicar's daughter secretly engaged to a young architect, the young architect, and Henry Knight, older, unaware of Elfride's secret engagement, and, oh, so interested in Elfride himself.

Sitting on a high cliff above the Bristol Channel with Henry, Elfride is hopeful of a telescope view of the ship returning the young architect from India. They are pelted by a gust of wind, which blows Henry's hat toward the edge. He scrambles for it, but finds himself unable to scramble back to the spot where he sat with Elfride. Trying to help him, Elfride makes things worse. "From the fact that the cliff formed the inner face of the segment of a hollow cylinder," Hardy wrote, "having the sky for a top and the sea for a bottom, which enclosed the bay to the extent of nearly a semicircle, [Henry] could see the vertical face curving round on each side of him. He looked far down the facade, and realized more thoroughly how it threatened him."

Henry Knight is now suspended by his arms from the side of a cliff where, "opposite [his] eyes was an embedded fossil, standing forth in low relief from the rock. It was a creature with eyes. The eyes, dead and turned to stone, were even now regarding him. It was one of the early crustaceans called Trilobites. Separated by millions of years in their lives, [Henry] and this underling seemed to have met in their place of death."

Readers of *Tinsley's Magazine* had to wait a month to see how Hardy would extricate Henry from this place where "the Trilobite was the single instance within reach of his vision of anything that had ever been alive and had a body to save, as he himself had now."

Well, you argue, Elfride could go for help. But where, and how long could Henry hold on?

Thus was the cliffhanger born.

Particularly in a NOVEL, a cliffhanger ending of one CHAPTER presents a splendid opportunity to shift to another POINT OF VIEW, another time frame, another situation, playing the waiting game of SUSPENSE, where so much hangs in the balance.

cock-and-bull story, a

Any NARRATIVE or STORY that on its face becomes of doubtful provenance; a narrative suspected of being contrived, embellished, or a deliberate fabrication; a deliberate attempt at deception, hence the cock and bull, both examples of overdone male swagger.

A cock-and-bull story is built in the first place to deceive, divert, or delay: the dog ate my homework. If the deception has as its purpose an amusing payoff and/or a moral purpose, such as those told by Mark Twain, we are often the better for it, refreshed, our critical senses laundered and hung out to dry in the sunshine of reason and self-examination. If the deception is to tighten the grip of fear and control, the believer becomes in time as much at fault as the perpetrator.

For those of us who are book-oriented, it becomes pleasing to think of an anthology, perhaps even a lofty *Oxford Companion to the Cock-and-Bull Story.* Imagine the fun and clamor. The anthology is to be divided into two parts; no, not Cock and Bull, but rather For Fun and For Real.

The aforementioned Mr. Twain would be a welcomed addition to the fun side, as well as one of his modern embodiments, Kurt Vonnegut. See also Chris Moore, who ingeniously adds what Twain would call "stretchers" to overall credibility and to such off-limits topics as the Bible.

Imagine the mischief and consternation and competition for inclusion in the For Real side, those men and women who promulgate C & B as though they had come down from the mountain top, bearing an engraved slab of granite:

Phyllis Schlaffly
The Rev. Jerry Falwell
The Rev. Pat Robertson
Number Forty-three and his Vice-president
Charles Krauthammer
Ann Coulter
William Kristol

True enough that none of these are fiction writers, but in the long run, what they do is bend reality as fiction writers do, hoping to convince us of their vision and their reality. As did POTUS number 42, famous for not inhaling and not having sex with "that woman." Though he left us a balanced budget, he also left an open door to the ALTERNATE UNIVERSE of political reality via his signature approach of triangulation. How much fun would Philip Pullman of the delightful *His Dark Materials* trilogy (*Golden Compass* being the first book) have with such nuanced triangulation?

As the late, lamented Mr. Vonnegut would have said, "So it goes."

The cock-and-bull story can be a lovely learning experience or a one-way ticket to the worst kind of convention of all. It is the forerunner of the TALL TALE in the grand tradition of the American West. One place to look for its origins is in that idiosyncratic romp about origins and reality, *Tristram Shandy*, in which a character says, "It is a story about a Cock and a Bull—and the best of its kind that I have ever heard."

coincidence

The incidence of two or more EVENTS taking place at the same time in a DRAMATIC NARRATIVE, by happenstance, and the READER suspects the WRITER of being lazy, sloppy, or both. In real life, coincidence is unplanned simultaneous occurrences that can seem to cast a meaning of predestination; events in STORIES that happen without being planned and which appear to affect positively the outcome of the story.

Accidental pairings of events may add COMPLICATIONS to stories. Dick and Jane may be forced by coincidence and a full house to share a table at a restaurant, whereupon in subsequent meetings, they fall in love, because that is a complication. Coincidences should not, however, play a major role in providing the OUTCOME. The outcome is the result of some decisive and planned ACT on the part of the PROTAGONIST; the reader will feel cheated by any other scenario. Similarly, if Bill Villain, arch bad guy, winds up being repaid for his evil ways by having a landslide bury him, Bill Galahad, arch good guy, will have in some way caused the landslide to tumble.

collision

An accelerated impact of two or more objects, two or more persons, an unlimited number of persons and objects/bodies. A vital dramatic verb—you might even think of it as an intransigent verb—collide refers to the very clashes of individuals, AGENDAS, and conventional behavior that informs and buoys STORY. Collision is conflict living in the immediate moment, so much so that you can hear the clink of body armor, the sighs of exasperation, the grunts of frustration.

In everyday life, individuals bump into one another, mumble a brief apology (for they are truly sorry), then move on. In story, individuals who are already late for some significant event do not merely bump, they collide. Tempers flare. Frustration sprays about, rampant as a dropped garden hose turned at full power.

After CHARACTERS and VOICE, collision is such an essential ingredient in story that the merest hint of it will arouse reader anticipation; the results of it will send characters spurting forth like toothpaste out of a tightly held tube. STORY, however, cannot be explained only in terms of collision; it is set in motion by the impact of CONFLICT.

Imagine the long building known as a linear accelerator, in which minute particles are caused to move about at unimaginable speed before being sent down these long corridors to—you guessed it—collide with other minute particles, which then behave in a multitude of idiosyncratic ways, not the least of which is that they are never the same as before the collision.

A young woman, already a tad late for an interview where she will be considered for a position in a prestigious law firm, collides with a distinguished looking man in the lobby of the building housing the law firm's offices. Of course this is a ROMANCE, of course he is the man who is to interview her, of course she thinks he is insufferably rude. This is how characters collide in romances.

They collide in differing ways in the various genres; in LITERARY STORIES they collide out of conscience and lust and jealousy and accident and... what have you.

Collision is what happens on Black Fridays in front of Wal-Mart Stores and again on Boxing Day, where the after-Christmas Specials collide with those wanting to return gifts for credits. Collision is the consequence of conflict; its side effects remain like pesky guests who stay to help with the clean up but invariably fall asleep on the sofa.

combustion

The point in a SHORT STORY or NOVEL where dramatic elements collide with sufficient force to provoke ACTION leading to a CONCLUSION; the aggregation of forces prior to DENOUEMENT; the literal and figurative boiling over of story.

A useful metaphor: story is a crucible into which such elements as CHARACTERS and their AGENDAS, opposing forces, SURPRISE, REVERSAL, and shifts of POWER have been added and the heat of plot inertia is applied. The pressure becomes so great that the story combusts, explodes, boils over, leaving the characters to clean up the mess, which is to say effect some kind of resolution, however permanent or temporary.

Most stories, long form or short, have combustion points; those that do not have them can profit from them. An excellent example of the combustion point in a short story occurs in Tobias Wolff's "Bullet in the Brain," where Anders has already been introduced as the POINT OF VIEW through whom the story is told, the bank robber is introduced, and the animosity between Anders and the bank robber set in motion. One combustion point comes when the bank robber fires a gun.

A combustion point in a longer work occurs in the film, *The Third Man*, written by Graham Greene. Holly Martens, the protagonist, meets his old friend Harry Lime in a gondola car of a large Ferris wheel in the Vienna amusement park and Lime delivers his now iconic disquisition: "Don't be so gloomy. After all, it's not that awful. Like the fella says, in Italy for thirty years under the Borgias they had warfare, terror, murder, and bloodshed, but they produced Michelangelo, Leonardo da Vinci, and the Renaissance. In Switzerland they had brotherly love—they had five hundred years of democracy and peace, and what did that produce? The cuckoo clock. So long, Holly." As a result of this cynical observation from Lime, a line is drawn in the moral sand between the two friends.

Each combustion introduces the element of CHANGE into the respective stories cited here, nudging each to its unique CONCLUSION. The combustion causes change which forces outcome.

Hint: Aggravate, drive, tease, torment the characters to a point where one or more of them moves beyond what he or she appears able to take, causing the behavior that will make some things irrevocable, sweeping safer options off the table. Characters who are always in control ultimately tire the reader. Characters who appear to have breaking points concern the reader. Characters who either discover or are driven to an interior place they did not know they had become permanent residents in the reader's mind.

comedy

A more physical, even rowdy adjunct of HUMOR, characterized by exaggeration, deliberate management of events, pratfalls. These circumstances seem to snowball before the READER'S eyes, gaining a momentum that leads to COMBUSTION, as in the stateroom scene in the Marx Brothers film, *A Night at the Opera*; a set of circumstances building to a conclusive PAYOFF.

Comedy, by its very nature, seems BIGGER THAN LIFE, consequently producing the laughter of relief that it is not us to whom the physicality is happening; humor, by its own nature, is just the right size for life, ordered out of a J. Crew catalog, provoking in us the sad laughter of recognition. Humor is DRAMATIC but comedy is situational and EPISODIC; once the laugh is out, it needs to be wound up again. Comedy is like the cup in which Dunkin' Donuts coffee is served. After one use, it is thrown away. Humor is the growing awareness that we have been holding on to this old paper cup out of sentimentality.

In some of the old Restoration comedies, mistaken identities and lovers hiding under beds or in closets were staples, exaggerated by there being numerous mistakes of identity or so many hiding lovers that they could not all fit in one closet or under one bed. In humor the payoff becomes the awareness that one CHARACTER does not recognize or remember another, that there was a need in the first place for a lover.

Comedy is the antic surprise of the pie in the face, followed by the victim's revenge of returning the favor with another pie and another; it is the anarchy of forced politeness, the convention of rules, the backyard dog digging an escape hole under the gate. Laurel and Hardy are piano movers, lugging a large piano over a narrow rope-and-vine bridge spanning a steep chasm. Midway across, they meet a gorilla coming the other way.

In FICTION, comedy becomes the revenge fantasy acted out, its target humiliated by the forces of destiny as represented by slapstick.

comes to realize

A type of SHORT STORY or NOVEL in which a front-rank CHARACTER is affected by EVENTS or an insight to the point of becoming aware of something not previously known to that character; a dramatic point, often the DENOUEMENT, in which a character experiences an EPIPHANY that guides subsequent, story-related behavior.

One such epiphany or coming to realize visits Gabriel Conroy toward the payoff of James Joyce's short story, "The Dead." Events at a gathering earlier in the evening have prompted Conroy's wife to revisit a long-ago romance with a young man now dead, causing Conroy to realize there were things about his wife he'd never considered, causing him also to reflect almost in an aphorism about the nature of life and death.

Most of the fourteen stories in Joyce's collection, *Dubliners*, have some form of epiphany, making for a convenient source of comes-to-realize narratives. Although originally a religious/mystical insight, the epiphany or comes-to-realize moment is a discovery of the solution to a puzzle, the answer to an enigma that has been troubling a character and is now made clear to the character because of some INTENT or INERTIA on the part of the character.

But beware the sudden appearance of a character gaining AWARENESS or DISCOVERY without having had to work for it or experience some significant blast of emotion; sudden appearances of such dramatic material have the deus-ex-machina effect of being a cheap convenience (see also READER FEEDER). Even if the epiphany experienced by a character brings painful awareness, it must be relevant to the theme of the story or the character's goal for it to have resonance with the READER.

Some twenty-first-century epiphanies or arrivals at understanding come as the PROTAGONIST is about to achieve some sought after GOAL, status, or DISCOVERY, only for the character to realize the goal is no longer of any consequence.

coming-of-age novel
(See BILDUNGSROMAN.)

commercial story, the
Dramatic NARRATIVE in which the PAYOFF is a direct product of the PROTAGONIST'S ingenuity; a STORY in which there is some tangible PRIZE or reward achieved or at the very least strived for; a PLOT-DRIVEN NARRATIVE; a story in which the promise of a particular GENRE is paid off either as a prize won or

as a surprise, IRONIC REVERSAL; a story in which the ingenuity of plot and deployment of events trumps the complexity of characters and their moral choices.

Another view of the commercial story: the problem with which the characters cope or the choices they must make emerge as being larger than the characters themselves, more or less directing the READER to the cadences of plot elements falling into place.

The commercial story is any story that appears in a mass publication platform, meaning that a literary story may have enough of the qualities listed above to give it entrance to a larger audience.

Hint: Read Dashiell Hammett's *The Maltese Falcon.* Now, decide for yourself: Commercial? Or not?

complacency

The feeling of smug sureness and being in control you get as a WRITER, when you think you've almost finished a project, or as a READER, when you think you've figured the design intent of the work at hand. Complacency is a dramatic fulcrum for CHARACTERS who are about to be tipped into the froth of STORY either by ACTION or INACTION, a delineation between characters who believe they have sufficiency to suit their needs and characters who are hungry for change.

When the reader encounters a complacent character, said reader receives the literary equivalent of Blue-Screen-of-Death computer warnings; something earthshaking is about to happen, be it a palace revolt or an innocently voiced "Hey, what's for dinner tonight?" being met with a "Get your own damned dinner because I'm outta here for good."

Into the story come those commandos JEALOUSY, GUILT, and GRIEF, their faces blackened, their knit watch caps pulled down low, invading and occupying the terrain, driving the circumstances and responses. Complacency is metaphorically the best laid schemes of which Robert Burns wrote, and we know what comes after that, they "gang aft agley," and do so big time.

Show us a complacent character, F. Scott Fitzgerald might have written in his longish short story, "The Rich Boy," and I'll show you a story in the making. A complacent character is astride his or her high horse, vulnerable to the low-hanging branch. A complacent character might ride that high horse thinking to make a romantic conquest or achieve a dramatic promotion in professional or academic status, only to be met with the reality of the leveling effects of falling unselfishly in love or being forced to recognize that there are others of equal or perhaps higher qualifications.

Hint: Take an interesting male or female character. In one paragraph, establish him or her as being on the cusp of an easy achievement of a relatively significant GOAL, say chairman of a department or starring role in a stage play of extraordinary range. Paragraph two presents the character striding into the CRUCIBLE. Paragraph three presents the enthusiastic response the respective characters are accustomed to experiencing. Paragraph four introduces the SURPRISE of reality: in recognition of the professor's good work, the dean is keeping him on, serving as a minor assistant to the new department chair; the woman is eagerly recruited to play the role of the maid to the female lead. Now, the story progresses.

Additional hint: A universal theme is the awareness that life is not fair. (See, for instance, the last few lines of Shirley Jackson's short story, "The Lottery.") How about a story in which a complacent character (as opposed to a truly competent or talented individual) wins. How about it?

concept

A pattern of situations, EPISODES, or ideas that wants to be a STORY but doesn't yet know how.

A concept is an amalgamation of CHARACTER, MOTIVE, and EVENT, but be sure to read the label closely. When, for instance, you see a food label advising that protein is contained herein, the first question that comes to mind should be, Is it a complete protein? Which is to say, does it contain all the essential amino acids known to reside in a complete protein? Then ask what the source of the protein is. Soy protein may well be a complete protein, but it is plant based. If you want plant protein, no biggie, but if you don't get what you want, you're going to be disappointed, perhaps even feel betrayed when you discover what you did get. The analogy holds for concept, which is the literary equivalent of protein without all the essential amino acids.

A concept lacks some catalytic agent, which would transform it into a STORY. A private detective sitting in his/her office, waiting for a client, is not yet a story; it is a PREMISE, which is one step down the food chain from concept. A woman who has been dating three men, all of whom suddenly propose marriage to her, is a concept because we know something based in history or action about the woman in question. However intriguing it is to see a dog sniffing appreciatively at a steak that has just been removed from the grill, then set aside for a moment's cooling, that intrigue is only a potential for some great mischief to follow, which is to say there is concept sizzling away but no story yet.

So, OK, then, concept is resident potential for story. One way to turn the private detective premise into a concept is to introduce a character who may not be a potential client. The detective, avid for income, persuades the newcomer to allow some investigative or bodyguard work to be done on his behalf. Now, we have a concept. To turn a concept into a story, let's introduce a character who offers the detective $5000 not to take the assignment that will be offered by a lady claiming to be from Pittsburgh, who will arrive within the next half hour. Story can be made from the concept of the woman with the three suitors by having the woman remove herself with no advance notice to another locale, where she takes a job under an assumed name and begins to lead a completely different lifestyle. We could enhance this story by having the woman, within the next week or ten days of her arrival in her new home, be asked out by three different men. The dog with an appreciative interest in the freshly grilled steak can cause story to erupt by nudging a chair close to the table on which the steak now resides. In all three examples, concept is transformed into story when the protagonist is forced to take some action or make some choice.

concept-driven story, the

A type of DRAMATIC NARRATIVE that focuses on THEME; a NOVEL or STORY whose PLOT appears to emphasize a particular subject such as revenge, redemption, or poverty while still providing dramatic structure.

Novels such as Victor Hugo's *Les Miserables*, John Steinbeck's *The Grapes of Wrath* and *Of Mice and Men*, and Upton Sinclair's *The Jungle* may be seen as examples of the concept-driven story, and although at home in the categories of speculative fiction and cautionary fiction, so, too, are Margaret Atwood's *The Handmaid's Tale*, George Orwell's *1984*, and Philip Roth's *The Plot Against America*. Each of these deals with burning political and/or social issues to the point where they have become more than snapshots of a particular era but rather have assumed the status of museum-quality prints, hung in galleries.

Hint: Unless a concept-driven story has more to it than the potent dramatization of THEME, it runs great risk (as many fictional PROTAGONISTS do) of being caught in the bog of disaster, which is to say it forgets its debt to STORY.

Alisa Zinov'yevna Rosenbaum, she who became Ayn Rand, is an unfortunate example of this forgetfulness, beginning her career with *The Fountainhead*, which took on the theme of art for art's sake to great popularity and, to many critics, to great extreme. Her magnum opus, *Atlas Shrugged*, a thirteen-hundred-plus-page NOVEL, articulated her Objectivist philosophy in extraordinary detail, allowing her to express anti-communism, anti-fascism, and anti-welfare-state views in unbridled gallop, reaching a full, Libertarian crescendo in which she deplored any kind of state at all except a state she may well have considered enlightened anarchy.

In this regard, Rand may be regarded as the right of Upton Sinclair's left. Although they were contemporaries, Rand is probably the better—and more favorably—known, but the reputation comes from her philosophy and argumentative skills rather than her dramatic skills.

Story is the Fed-Ex device for the message. For the concept-driven story to have an audience in the first place, it must have CHARACTERS who become memorable not because of the smirks they produce but because of the heart tugs. Compare, for instance, George and Lenny from *Of Mice and Men* with

Howard and Dominique from *The Fountainhead* or John Gault from *Atlas Shrugged* and you will immediately see my point.

conflict

A clash of AGENDA between two or more forces within a STORY; the internal argument of conscience versus desires raging within one character, as well as the differing views of appropriate behavior among opposing sides.

Conflict is opposition with a big ego, the duel between dream and reality, between age and youth, between conservative and liberal. Conflict emerges from two wellsprings: 1) the desire of an individual to survive, and/or 2) the sense in story that every CHARACTER believes he is right. Conditions that stand in the way of survival represent conflict. Conditions that emerge when opposing forces insist on the aptness and correctness of their positions are also representations of conflict. Since its appearance and subsequent evolution, the human species has struggled against the conflicts of weather, starvation, illness. Since its reemergence in the middle of the twentieth century, Israel has been in one form or another of conflict with its neighbors, each side convinced of the validity of its position.

Story often begins with a character being propelled by a GOAL. (Shakespeare's *Macbeth* and *Richard III* present sumptuous examples. Saul Bellow's NOVELLA, *Seize the Day*, begins with its protagonist having an immediate goal. The goal-enhanced character then collides with one or more OBSTACLES, REVERSALS that cause FRUSTRATION and possible HUMILIATION. These obstacles often take the form of other characters with contrary agendas, but the obstacles may be emotional or philosophical forces within the principal character. In either case, the principle character must seek a way through or around the labyrinth of obstacle to some degree of settling the claims of the original goal.

Real life characters who identify their goals, then set forth to achieve them are admirable, often becoming role models for emulation. They represent progression, but they do not represent story. A woman who strives to accomplish something rarely achieved by a woman is story because of the presence of obstacle, which in story becomes personified, even objectified.

Conflict begins in story with an individual who wants something to come to pass or who wants something not to come to pass. The conflict is engaged when the individual moves toward the goal. The conflict becomes tangible and irreversible when another person or persons react to the individual acting on his goal.

Conflict always has CONSEQUENCES (if it does not, the narrative effect becomes reminiscent of the boy hollering wolf).

conscience

A societal barometer consulted with varying degrees of frequency by

CHARACTERS in pursuit of their daily AGENDA; a mediating device between *want* or *desire* and *ought I?* or *Is this ethical?*; a behavior fulcrum.

Conscience plays a major role in FICTION, its very composition an effective analysis of a character, particularly when compared to that character's sense of self and that character's NEEDS. If conscience is seen as a societal lens through which social and ethical behavior may be judged, the reader will automatically form opinions about where a character is placed on an ethical scale, much in the manner of charting the growth in height of a young person with pencil marks on some communal wall.

READERS are given frequent opportunity to assess characters and, in consequence, they form judgments based on the character's conscience-based responses to previous actions. By the end of chapter one of Thomas Hardy's *The Mayor of Casterbridge,* the reader has seen the immediate consequences of a severe trial of conscience by Michael Henchard. To call the response guilt is to put it in mild terms. A good deal of the arc of Henchard's response to that first-chapter lapse will cause many readers to root for him and his apparent redress of the enormous occasion of guilt, but Hardy piles more travail on Henchard, bringing him face to face with yet another moral quandary. The human attribute of conscience appears in the novel almost as though it were a person itself, seeking another quality that may be interpreted differently among an array of readers: atonement, redress, REVENGE.

Thus does endowing a character with a large conscience or, arguably, no conscience at all, set the stage for DRAMA. Every bit as compelling as the first chapter in the Hardy novel is the payoff scene in Eugene O'Neill's *Desire Under the Elms,* when the full force of what Abbie Putnam's need for love has done to her husband and stepson leaves its mark on her conscience.

Like a full-frame sensor in a digital camera, the conscience is a receptor site, taking in INTENT, FANTASY, CONSEQUENCES, IMPLICATIONS; it may deliver a RESPONSE of guilt or self-justification. Even with murderous and vengeful intent full upon him, Hamlet cannot bring himself to kill his intended target, King Claudius, at least not at the particular moment the king is at prayer. Macbeth, having made the decision to murder King Malcolm, momentarily relents when he sees a servant carrying a tray with a meal to Malcolm. Macbeth's conscience calls out to him, in a sense, with the reminder that this tray carries what will be Malcolm's last meal, from which trope he is reminded of the Last Supper, which, to say the least, puts a damper on his murderous ambitions.

Conscience causes some men and women to refuse participation in armed conflict; it can motivate their behavior relative to birth control and eating products derived from animals. Conscience makes its appearance in ways that may also add a note of wry, off-the-wall humor, as in Frank Pierson's opera buffa, *Dog Day Afternoon,* which begins with three men deciding to rob the bank at 450 Avenue P, Brooklyn. No sooner are Sonny, Sal, and Stevie in the bank, guns drawn, shouting instructions to startled customers and bank employees, than Stevie decides he can't go through with his part, whereupon he leaves. In medias robbery.

Back to Hamlet for a moment because of his observation that "conscience doth make cowards of us all," a reminder that many people fear to act on their agendas for fear of the ransom guilt will require of them. It becomes a fair question for the writer to ask of all his characters, *How little or how much conscience does this character have?* To which can be added, *And what effect does that have on the character?*

consequences

The results of a prior EVENT, thought, deed, decision, or accident; they represent the price that must be paid or the fine assessed for a previous ACT. Consequences are the guiding principle of storytelling—things happening because of things that happened that were responded to or not responded to, to some degree.

As a consequence of A, B came into being; this is the force that holds EPISODES together as STORY, that ties CHARACTERS to tethers of relationship or commitment.

Characters believe they are right, behaving as though they are. As a consequence, they perform or do not perform acts that then become the CAUSAL or triggering force in story. A NARRATIVE without consequences is the literary equivalent of a body without blood; neither supports life.

content editing

The process WRITERS experience as a direct link to publication; editorial intervention focused on the logic, chronology, plausibility, accuracy, and dramatic intensity of a STORY; a structural oversight, usually performed by someone other than the author, with the goal of optimal presentation of the dramatic incidents in a NARRATIVE; not to be conflated or confused with COPYEDITING, which is mechanical in nature with a goal of uniformity of usage conventions.

Manuscripts are conventionally subject to content editing first. The content editor's goal is to enhance the writer's VOICE, removing unnecessary repetition and the literary equivalent of throat clearing. Once any anomalies are addressed and queries are answered by the author, the manuscript moves to the copyediting stage.

contingency

An EVENT that has potential for occurring; a possibility without being a definite certainty; something liable to take place as a CONSEQUENCE of a previous ACTION.

The behavior of a CHARACTER in a STORY is contingent on 1) the character's

REACTION to another character, 2) one or more events in a character's past, 3) a character pursuing an AGENDA, 4) a character suffering a REVERSAL.

Contingency is the excitement of story, mixed with AMBIGUITY and PLOT design to create a simultaneous atmosphere of CAUSALITY and uncertainty in any given NARRATIVE. A splendid example of contingency in operation is Iris Murdoch's first novel, *Under the Net,* the net in the title mischievously referring to the net of language and the potentials therein for misunderstanding. One of the lead characters, Jake Donaghue, is a WRITER who has just produced a NOVEL, *The Silencer,* from which comes this contingency-describing quote, "All theorizing is flight. We must be ruled by the situation itself and this is unutterably particular. Indeed, it is something to which we can never get close enough, however hard we may try as it were to crawl under the net." Many of Jake's actions are IRONIC in nature; they reflect his being driven from place to place by his inability to interpret facts and CHOICES presented through the reactions of other characters.

Some modern critics have made names for themselves by linking CLOSURE with contingency, a useful way for a writer of stories to link the PAYOFF of a story with the writer's personal take on the ZEITGEIST or ambiance of a historical time. For examples of this useful equation at work, consider Thomas Pynchon's huge romp of a historical venture, *Mason & Dixon,* Joan Didion's *The Last Thing He Wanted,* and Philip Roth's *American Pastoral,* each of which has a historical overview against which characters are driven to choices that are defined by contemporary forces.

SCIENCE FICTION and the subgenre of FANTASY dealing with ALTERNATE UNIVERSES are providing a contingency for readers as well as for the characters. Contingency ranks high as a forceful factor in the writer's mind because it allows the writer to simultaneously deal with the structured necessity of DRAMA and the seemingly anomalous plausible SURPRISE offered by the very ways and means contingency is used. Although tightly plotted, Philip Pullman's *His Dark Materials* trilogy provides contingencies that further define the various characters and their GOALS, bringing the TENSION of impending CRISIS into collision with delightful surprise in the crucible of dramatic event.

In the framework of contingency, *Moby-Dick* reflects a search for the nineteenth-century American psyche, and in Mark Twain's often-neglected *Pudd'nhead Wilson,* the author literally and figuratively reverses black and white.

Hint: The message of contingency is to keep presenting characters with junctures, points at which they will have to make choices. These points of choice are where the contingency-based story begins.

controlling idea

The substantive downstream effects of the major GOAL as it influences a

STORY; a thematic presence linking the behavior of CHARACTERS and determining the content and VOICE of SCENES.

The controlling idea of L. Frank Baum's *The Wizard of Oz* is getting Dorothy Gale home to Kansas, from where she has been displaced by a tornado. Dashiell Hammet wound the complex and devious narrative of *The Maltese Falcon* about the armature of a fabled statue of a jewel-encrusted bird. In the short story "The Things They Carried," Tim O'Brien used as his controlling idea the various personal items carried by a platoon of American servicemen as they were deployed in Vietnam.

The concept of a dramatic controlling idea is another way of approaching THEME; both aspects demonstrate the ironic trope of the tail wagging the dog. Writers often do not discover the theme of their work until they are well along in REVISION toward a final draft. Those who do begin with a specific theme in mind, say loyalty, or ideals, or conventions, often discover the characters and PLOT are not the only things to undergo change.

convention

Convention represents an agreement among publishers, WRITERS, and READERS for mechanical usage such as punctuation, spelling, and abbreviations; an accepted common wisdom relative to acceptable norms and understandings.

The conventions for use in most books produced in the U.S. is *A Manual of Style,* 16th edition, published by the University of Chicago Press, referred to with affection as CMS (Chicago Manual of Style.) Newspapers and journals often have their own style guides or use *The New York Times Manual of Style* or *The Associated Press Style Guide.*

As to accepted common wisdom, let us turn to peas. The convention for eating them generally suggests the use of a fork or perhaps chopsticks—but not a knife. The convention for POINT OF VIEW in a SHORT STORY was FIRST-PERSON or THIRD-PERSON, shifting to include OMNISCIENT after the significant contribution of William Trevor in that area. The convention for verb tense in fiction was based on the cultural agreement that past tense represented the present moment, with past perfect indicating completed past action, and the imperfect tense—used to, or would—being action occasionally but not habitually done in the past. These conventions apply to Indo-European languages and are not in immediate danger of changing or shifting, but along about the time Bobbie Ann Mason's short story "Shiloh" appeared in the *New Yorker*, a convention had been developing that allowed Ms. Mason and any other writer to use the present tense—Fred gets up—to indicate events supposedly taking place before our eyes.

It is possible to determine the ZEITGEIST of a century by reading works published during that century—the use and organization of language being a literary dipstick used to measure the oil therein. For some time, the conventional wisdom was that the three things not to be written about, particularly with humorous intent, were sex, religion, and politics. In the twenty-first century, it has become impossible to write about politics without mentioning sex and religion; there are clear-cut politics in discussions of religion and sex, and there are at the very least gender politics in discussions of sex, but just as often there are religious connotations. Just ask D. H. Lawrence…or read his take in *Lady Chatterley's Lover* and his nonfiction treatise, *Studies in Classic American Literature,* where he expounds on all three—sex, religion, and politics—as they relate to the individual. Convention has become the elephant in the literary living room; if a particular convention is taken on merely for the sake of being contentious, the result is apt to become polemical, evangelical, or screed-like, and we all know how these sound. If the taking on of a convention makes for a more illuminated story, the result is apt to become inspirational. Unfortunately, there is too much of the former. In mitigating the inspirational heavy hand, the writer might use HUMOR.

conversation

A degree of communication and discussion among two or more individuals; possibly meaningful exchanges between friends, family members, coworkers, extending to complete strangers; sometimes mistaken for DIALOGUE.

Conversation should not be mistaken for dialogue. Although conversation may have some THEME or AGENDA—Eat in or go out, What movie shall we see, What'll I wear today?—it is more an expression of momentary feelings, ideas, questions. Conversation can and often does edge into discussion, which moves toward argument in the theoretical or moot court sense before tipping over into argument in the argumentative sense.

Dialogue, on the other hand, exists more in the territory bounded by contention, clash of agenda, and the SUBTEXT of the space between what a character says and does and what the character thinks and feels while doing it. Use of too many conversations in a story leads to STASIS, which is the point at which the READER becomes all too willing to set the book down.

copyediting

Another procedural process on the way to publication; it involves checking a MANUSCRIPT for consistency in usage conventions; a mechanical intervention made on a manuscript, usually by a person other than the author or CONTENT EDITOR, to insure standardized use in matters of abbreviations, use of numbers, acronyms, punctuation, etc.

The avowed intent of copyediting is consistency of use, the ultimate goal of which is to suggest authorial and PUBLISHER accuracy and reliability. Most trade book publishers in the U.S. follow the conventions set forth in CMS, THE CHICAGO MANUAL OF STYLE, published by the University of Chicago Press; magazines, journals, and newspapers are more eclectic in their usage or style guides, *The New York Times Style Guide* and *The Associated Press Style Guide* being basic models on which most in-house guides are based.

Much is made of a fictional CHARACTER's reliability to the point where unintentionally UNRELIABLE NARRATORS are regularly exposed by critics, in classes, and reading groups. It is not a great leap to consider poorly copy-edited manuscripts as unreliable narrators because of the reflection such a manuscript casts on the author.

In the usual procession of publishing events, an accepted manuscript is subjected first to CONTENT EDITING, which relates to meaning and clarity of authorial intent. After author approval and REVISION (if any), the manuscript is sent to the copyeditor who may have queries, which are fact-related but not content-related. Even though many publishers employ in-house or freelance copyeditors, the process still conventionally assumes the primary responsibility is with the author.

The Modern Language Association Style Manual and Guide to Scholarly Publishing is a key copyediting information source for schools, academic publications, and universities.

counterpoint

The dramatic play of two differing, possibly even opposing THEMES within the same STORY; the overall relationship between two VOICES or AGENDAS in contour and pace; a blending of two seemingly disparate POINTS OF VIEW resulting in some added dramatic effect such as IRONY, SATIRE, HUMOR, or PATHOS.

Two of the three most obvious examples of thematic counterpoint in literature were composed by Jane Austen (1775-1817); these are *Pride and Prejudice* and *Sense and Sensibility.* The themes are not only sounded in the titles, they are given full orchestration in the thematic use of the CHARACTERS. Who can forget Elizabeth Bennett as she responds to the chemistry of Fitzwilliam Darcy, each in turn battling against the inner CONFLICT of romantic interest and social position? Another English writer, Aldous Huxley (1894-1963), has a title right on the mark, *Point Counterpoint*, its opposing themes being reason and passion. Notable among the array of characters in what could be thought of as a run-up to the talky and pretentious 1981 film from Louis Malle, *My Dinner with Andre*, Huxley presents himself in *Point Counterpoint* as a novelist who is not very good at getting characters down on paper.

Yet another, wickedly inspired example of counterpoint is found in *The Rebel Angels,* by the Canadian writer Robertson Davies (1913-95), which appeared in 1981. Long interested in myth and mythology, Davies's interests gravitated toward the psychology of Jung. His contrapuntal *The Rebel Angels* appeared to be playing the themes of pure academic research and the effects of mysticism and magic against one another. A significant character in this novel is Maria Theotoky, a graduate student researching Rabelais. The theme of academicism is set in motion against the likely prospect of Maria's stern discipline being overrun by the overt sexuality and emotional gormandizing of her subject matter. Davies does not stop there. Maria, through her Gypsy heritage, leads the READER into the murky areas of concert-level violinists having their prized instruments temporarily buried in horse dung to impart the true clarity of the instrument's voice.

Any disparate subjects can be employed, provided the characters have sufficient dimension to support the investigation. Of the four examples given, *The Rebel Angels* outshines the iconic *Pride and Prejudice*, suggesting that novels of ideas must have more weight to them than the sense of talking heads in serious discourse. Indeed, Davies's story has HUMOR and SATIRE bordering on the blasphemous.

Academic, college-based novels have an open-door policy to thematic counterpoint, the novels of David Lodge and *Lucky Jim*, the one venture into the medium by Kingsley Amis, added examples of how effective the medium can be. Saved for last is a strong candidate for the most sublime example yet of the effects of counterpoint in story: D.H. Lawrence's *Sons and Lovers*.

Sons and Lovers engages the theme of a woman of breeding, education, and sensitivity, who meets a rough-and-tumble coal miner at a Christmas dance, falls into a sensual relationship with him almost immediately, then marries him. Together, they produce two sons, each of whom contributes in his way to the counterpoint. The character of Paul Morel has become synonymous with D. H. Lawrence, who was a living example of the unharmonic conflicts visited on him by his mother and father. Watch Paul Morel's relationship with each parent, and then watch his urgent need to leave the atmosphere of the coal-mining village and its stifling effect on him. Now you will have seen and understood counterpoint, the better to use it as a tool in a work of fiction, seeing characters for what they represent through articulation of their needs and the circumstances they have built for themselves.

critical reading

The focused gleaning of technical and emotional tools the WRITER may use to strengthen his own work; the things a writer looks at and for when reading the works of other writers. In other words, it is how a writer reads— or ought to read—fiction.

Even when it becomes apparent to the writer who is reading for more than the transportation of enjoyment and enlightenment that a particular

STORY or NOVEL is a disappointment, there is still value to be had. The writer-reader should pause to delineate specific complaints: Is the story line too simplistic? Are the movements of the CHARACTERS PREDICTABLE? Do the MOTIVES feel appropriate? Does the DIALOGUE crackle with the intensity of complex individuals? Are there distractions?

Reading the work of another becomes an exercise at the level of REVIS-ING one's own work. Are there unnecessary elements? Are the elements arranged properly? Do the characters aspire to attain a connection with the READER? Could I have done this more expeditiously, and if so how, and if not, what have I learned?

The writer-reader becomes anxious at first, as all readers are, to determine if the NARRATIVE VOICE is agreeable, then goes on to wonder what the story is about. What, the writer-reader asks, is the GOAL of the story? What are the resident emotions? What are this author's strengths? Weaknesses? Then come the heaviest questions: Do I care? What made me care or not care? If I did care, when did I begin caring? If I did not care, what could have made me? What could I have done to make this story matter more? What special use does this writer make of the senses?

The writer-reader then goes on to ask some of the questions a literary critic might ask. What is the THEME? What social, moral, and political issues does the writer appear to be engaging? But even these questions and their answers have storytelling at their heart; it is well and good for a writer to observe ways Jane Austen used the dialogue and behavior of her characters to make fun of then-contemporary social structure, but to gain technique from these observations the reader must be able to experience the prejudices and humiliations of the characters. This awareness comes from the reader's need to appreciate on an emotional level the sense of social condition and obligation of the characters, then to observe how these behaviors are demonstrated in the text.

A simple approach to employ while reading the works of other writers is to imagine *you* being cast in the role of one or more characters in a particular novel or story, noting the chemistry and constraints of each character for all the other characters. Another informative approach is to use marking pens to note places where a character's AGENDA, whatever it might be, finds expression in particularly precise narrative description, dramatic action behavior, and/or in dialogue.

CRITICAL READING is the meeting point between readers and writers, as indicated in the Preface of this handbook.

crucible

A metaphoric journey into dramatic intent and intensity, the crucible becomes either a SCENE or series of scenes in a NARRATIVE in which PLOT and

CHARACTER elements collide and boil over to the point of dramatic CONSE-QUENCES; the narrative sense of increasing TENSION, building toward pressure; a bowl- or cup-shaped laboratory container, designed to heat chemical compounds to extreme temperatures.

Hint for the WRITER *of a scene:* think of your work as a container of volatile elements to which the heat of dramatic pressure has been applied. To extend the metaphor from the physics of chemistry to the dynamics of DRAMA, the notion of the crucible extends to the results of the heat, hurrying along the inevitable arrival of CHANGE that is a part of STORY.

cutting

A vital editorial activity requested of WRITERS by LITERARY AGENTS and EDITORS; a process in which writers are asked to pare words, sentences, even SCENES from their MSS; removal of DETAIL that does not make direct contribution to the overall EFFECT of a story.

The writer begins work on a story with a detailed OUTLINE or with a CONCEPT that has been stewing for some while to the point where the CHARACTERS have names and vague shapes, agendas, and attitudes. In either approach, this outlining and/or stewing process is the fiction writer's equivalent of a nonfiction writer doing research. The first intent is to get everything down. What pleasure to writers of a particular age to see photographs of a first draft by such a gifted storyteller as Colm Toibin, done in ink in a bound composition book. What a sense of intimacy to see the spidery handwriting of Rachel Maddux for her magnum opus, *The Green Kingdom.* What a pleasure to see the direct-to-computer-screen MSS of Leonard Tourney's mysteries set in the times of Elizabeth I and, later, of James the VI of Scotland as he became James I of England. In some form or another, the writer must get the material down in some manageable format; then begins the process of REVISION (one result of which is that the work may not begin where the writer imagined nor end where the writer supposed it would).

Into this calculus may come the literary equivalent of moving furniture, expansion of some innocent aside remarks, combining of two characters into one, and reformatting exchanges of dialogue into narrative. Perhaps none of these is enough, singularly or in aggregate. Now comes surgery. Cutting. Removal of repetitions, of the obvious, of the overly descriptive, of the boring.

It is the nature of some writers to resent any suggestions for cutting, even when these suggestions are made by the writer's literary agent, who sees the pared manuscript as a better candidate for publication, or even when these suggestions have been made by an editor who agrees to issue a contract, once suggested surgery is done.

Then there are writers such as Tobias Wolff who believe in removing from the early drafts of the manuscript any details that would prevent most enlightened readers from making decisions on their own, without authorial nudge.

When is enough? Better still, when is too much? It is no comfort to answer that both questions will obtain with each new work. There is no formula, no rule. Some literary flare-ups, as persistent as fires in Southern California, leave the public with implications that a particular writer might not have been published in the first place if a particular editor had not wielded the scalpel in the second place.

One reasonable approach to the matter of how much to cut from early drafts and where to do the cutting: Trust the characters. Do not describe what a key character already knows unless it is to show how he or she is presented with new information that warrants change now, in the immediate present.

Another reasonable approach: Don't tell the READER what the reader already knows, either from INFERENCE, direct experience, or information from other characters. Thus if Bill and Roger both report to Fred that Phil is not reliable in repaying his loans and yet Fred loans Phil money, readers are going to make a number of assumptions—whether the author gets in on the discussion or not.

~D~

deadline

The time by which one or more CHARACTERS in a STORY have to make a DECISION; the time by which a character was to have completed an assigned task. It is the CONSEQUENCE now to be experienced, the time for accounting, the end of some portion of or, in fact, all the previous story ARC.

Often a moment of exquisite TENSION, the arrival of the deadline is a threat even in the abstract sense of the main characters in a story being reminded that the meteor will strike in one day, the dam will burst by noon tomorrow, the planet Earth is doomed in two years if scientists cannot determine a way to shift the tilt of it on its axis, a patient in an episode of *House, M.D.*, is being consumed by her own immune system and only five minutes remain in the episode, a wrongly convicted man faces lethal injection in six hours unless.... Thus time running out: the guttering candle, the remaining grains of sand in an hourglass, the needle flickering even on a hybrid auto's fuel tank.

Deadlines are stress situations spray painted on the walls of your PLOT; they infuse story with a necessary sense of inevitability, which is, after all, one of the ways story takes an alternate route from life.

Also, WRITERS are all too aware of deadlines as dates specified in written agreement when a promised MANUSCRIPT is due in the publisher's hands; the thing to remember about such real world deadlines is that a publisher's entire seasonal schedule, as well as the investment they have already made in terms of cover production and advance publicity, are put in jeopardy when an author misses a production deadline. The other thing to remember is that no one actually dies.

deadpan

A form of NARRATION or delivery in which a CHARACTER relating opinions and dramatic material appears to be neutral and nonjudgmental, but perhaps the READER knows better; a means of conveying material bound to have some effect on the audience without betraying any hint of its implications or explosive nature.

Deadpan delivery is an enormous play on the role of the NAÏVE NARRATOR, a pretense that what is being revealed is nothing out of the ordinary. One of the more legendary deadpan deliverers in American letters is Samuel Langhorne Clemens, who recast himself as the storyteller Mark Twain and who used himself as an apparent butt in order to bring down sundry targets of his outrage. Twain often affected the role of the bumpkin or, as he referred to himself in the title of one of his books, an innocent. (See *The Innocents Abroad* for a classic example of deadpan travel writing.) After achieving one or two laughs at his own expense, Twain strode forth, his overall intent becoming ever more apparent (see the opening pages of his *Christian Science*).

Another style of deadpan writing is seen in the work of an individual whose life span extended a scant fifteen years beyond Twain's—Franz Kafka. His mordant settings were the backdrops for individuals who, at first blush, represent victims of conspiracy or repressive social mechanisms, extending into bureaucracies and families. In some of his works (see *The Trial*) he seemed to be saying that the individual had no choice, was at the mercy of whatever Fates happened to be in power at the moment, had no hope for raising his status. Seen as a deliberate invoker of the understated and a sly precursor to Woody Allen, Kafka and his work take on a richer meaning than a more literal reading would provide. Thus may Kafka be thought to join Twain as charter members of The Satirists' Club.

Yet another, more nuanced gloss on the deadpan approach to the release or revelation of dramatic material comes from the mind and pen of Steven

Colbert, who often seems to provoke the support of his actual targets. Like Twain and Kafka, Colbert can be experienced on a literal basis, from which a set of assumptions may be made. Thus each of these three deadpanners and all those who choose to provide individualized paths of their own are asking the reader to look under the surface for hidden intent. Twain, Kafka, and Colbert have mischievous senses of humor for those who look for the true serious intent that lurks beneath the apparent serious intent.

Imagine the greater effect Ayn Rand would have enjoyed had she regulated her rant to the point where it became more deadpan.

Warning: one of the consequences of deadpan delivery, in live performance or in writing, is to limit the audience and, in the case of the actor, Sasha Baron Cohen, who presented himself as the entity Borat, to not only limit the audience but to give it serious offense as well. Thus does deadpan as a prism of dispensing information become partners with IRONY, which by its own nature implies conspiracy (often of the sort Kafka wrote about), and irony's hard-to-manage cousin, sarcasm. Deadpan also relies heavily on a not-too-distant relative, AMBIGUITY, as in *What did the writer really mean?*

Don't forget: In many of the visual and performing arts, the intent of the composer is to disturb. Disturb from what? Disturb from complacency.

For extra credit: Read the opening two pages of Twain's *Life on the Mississippi,* his love letter to the great American river, which had captured so big a place in his heart. After reading those two pages with their straightforward sincerity and offering of statistics, can you say for an absolute certainty that Twain was dead serious in his facts and not having us on?

decisions

EVENTS are the outcome of the CHOICES of NARRATIVE VOICE, CHARACTERIZATION, SETTING, and other dramatic considerations an author must make when composing a STORY; they are courses of ACTION a character in a story must take after being boxed in an emotional corner or when planning a strategy to achieve a GOAL.

The WRITER is faced with decisions related to where to put things in, when to leave them out, how to render them, and at what length. Characters are— or should be—driven to the wall in developing and implementing strategies that will lead to achieving some GOAL, even the survival-oriented goal of seeking a minimum-wage job as a stepping-stone to something other. The operant word is *other*; characters who are comfortable or fulfilled are not petri dishes for the growth culture of story. Indeed, story only begins when such a character comes face to face with a SITUATION that proves the opposite.

Writers are sometimes overwhelmed with decisions, causing their LITERARY AGENTS and/or PUBLISHERS no end of concerns. It might be argued that writers who are comfortable with their characters are less likely to get maximum performance from them, while writers who are uncomfortable with their characters and reach within themselves for extra measures of EMPATHY and restraint are more apt to produce ICONIC CHARACTERS who remain in the reader's memory long after the very details of their particular stories are forgotten.

The decisions writer and character must make represent the common denominator between the two. One instructive example has the word choice in its title, the pain of it radiating out through its pages like a torn heart muscle: William Styron's memorable *Sophie's Choice.*

Dithering characters often wander into the dangerous verges of stopping the story dead in its tracks with such internal wonderment as, *Where had it all begun?* Or, worse, *How had she let herself get into this situation?*

Hint: Both writer and characters have SECRETS. Since both are linked by decisions they must make, why not have them exchange secrets? Writers are often accused of betraying the secrets of family, friends, and professional associations. Why not make an even four by having the writer accused of betraying the secrets of his or her characters? And just to play fair, think of ways characters can rat out their creators.

Additional *hint:* The key to dramatic writing is to bring characters to the awareness of a decision point from which position they will decide as their nature directs them, from which point they will become aware of consequences or will already have foreseen the consequences. This stream of events was true in *Don Quixote*, in *Hedda Gabler*, in *Lonesome Dove*, and in *Lush Life,* spanning dramatic writing from at least the sixteenth century to the very present.

defensiveness

The literary equivalent of "I did not." Defensiveness is a quality that runs from the apologetic to the insistent, often found in NOVELS and SHORT STORIES, emblematic of the author's need to explain or justify ACTIONS, ATTITUDES, or EVENTS portrayed; an often unnecessary footnote-as-text used to justify a behavioral or moral position taken by the author or one or more CHARACTERS.

Defensiveness begins with a WRITER'S response to critical reaction, said response often rendered as "but it really happened that way," then extending to lengthy explanations in support of what should not have required defense. This quality may be seen as the literary equivalent of a youngster trapped in a fib or lie, extending the flawed trope with even more extensive justification. It is "The dog ate my homework" expanded into *Atlas Shrugged*.

Often the product of a mountain goat leap of logic in the MOTIVATION or BEHAVIOR of a character, defensiveness becomes a good argument for less being more. The more logic is attached to a behavior or condition, the more likely the READER is to question it. The best approach for explaining or inserting behavior attributions: Let the characters do it. The reader is less apt to question the behavior of Character A if Character B questions it first. Thus Character A didn't trust Character B carries more weight than the

author telling the reader how A was trying to convince B of his trustwor-
thiness.

Reminder: A STORY is a procession of EVENTS and interactions, not an argument or harangue.

defining moment

A major point in a STORY, with an emphasis on inertia, where one or more
CHARACTERS becomes committed to a course of ACTION that will bully those
characters and the story ARC they carry to a CONCLUSION; a TIPPING POINT resulting in accelerated story INERTIA; a dramatic POINT OF NO RETURN where one or
more characters can no longer resist the conditions and forces that set the
story in motion.

A story may have more than one defining moment. *Romeo and Juliet*
has at least two: the scene in which the two first meet and, later, the scene
in which they take the sleep-potion. The latter scene is so key to the story
definition that it could not have happened without the meeting; thirty-six
hours later, both characters are dead. Had they not met and been attracted,
both may well have had greater life expectancy. The latter is a DEVICE as defining moment, its consequences causing one of the two partners to believe the
other dead. The defining moment comes early on in *Hamlet*, when the ghost
of the murdered king appears to secure from the young prince a promise to
avenge his death. Bored with their life of semi-retirement, Gus McRae and
Woody Call decide on the adventure of rustling a herd of cattle from nearby
Mexico, then driving up to Montana, where it will be sold, setting *Lonesome
Dove* into motion.

Many ACTION-DRIVEN NARRATIVES force a character into the corner of having
to take sides in an argument. ("You're either with us or against us.") In the
memorable "I coulda been a contender" scene from *On the Waterfront,* one
brother, Terry, realizes his brother, Charlie, was the architect of his being "a
punch-drunk palooka" instead of a serious contender for success as a prize
fighter. Terry's awareness becomes a defining moment when Charlie,
charged with insuring that Terry does not testify against the longshoreman's
union before a Congressional committee, becomes overwhelmed by guilt
and remorse to the point of not being able to carry out his assignment, a
dereliction that leads directly to his own death.

Defining moments may come at any point in the NARRATIVE. They may be
such innocent presences as an anniversary or birth date, the more accelerated trope of a ticking clock, or the rising tension of a DEADLINE come due.
When they appear, their effect on the READER should be of an enormous boulder, poised on the lip of an escarpment, ready to roll, then slowly tumbling
forth. Their effects on characters will be to enhance, modify, speed up, or in
some other manner affect their behavior.

Can a story exist without a single defining moment? Any "No" spoken in reference to fiction is just as likely to provoke from some WRITER a dramatic riposte which in itself is a defining moment, thus the best answer to the question is "Probably not," with this reminder hovering: A close examination of the more oblique MODERN STORIES, vignettes, and sketches will reveal the artifacts of defining moments. Even Chekhov, likely candidate for fatherhood of the modern short story, for all he discarded the moral finality of his narratives, will reveal defining moments (see "The Lady with the Dog").

As a practical matter for the WRITER, defining moments may be regarded as platforms for the necessary presence of evoked EMOTIONS. An effective defining moment or set of them will have the effect no writer can find fault with—characters and situations who remain in memory long after the story has been read.

(See POINT OF NO RETURN.)

degree of intimacy

A standard that measures the extent of awareness and connection between CHARACTERS; it shows an implicit or explicit recognition between characters of status and recognition available as well to the READER.

Characters who are childhood friends, college roommates, lovers have a greater awareness of the details in the life of each other, have shared experiences, a mutual understanding of likes, dislikes, philosophies, etc. Such characters will speak in a kind of shorthand, where common experiences need not be explained. It is unlikely that Mary, married to John for ten years, will serve John a steak for dinner, knowing he is a vegan. This scenario obviates the narrative strain (and READER FEEDER) of John saying, "As you know, Mary, I do not eat meat." On the other hand, there is some opportunity for dramatic energy were the same vegan John to come home hungry after a day at work, only to see a steak on his plate. "Are you," John might say with a touch of IRONY, "making some sort of statement here?"

Strangers are more tentative and reserved with one another, although a character might properly betray suspicion toward a complete stranger who affects great concern or loyalty.

Imagine yourself on the receiving end of a telemarketing call, being greeted by a complete stranger, called by your first name, then asked how you are feeling today. Your immediate suspicion is that the individual wants you to buy something.

Just like real people, characters behave and speak toward one another according to their AGENDAS, their degree of intimacy, their expectations; they respond to strangers in accordance with their social prejudices, their ambitions, and their cautiousness, until they have a better sense of who and what the stranger is.

denouement

A term signaling an arrival at the stage in a STORY directly before the RES-
OLUTION begins; moments in a story when the PROTAGONIST appears to be overwhelmed by conditions and forces contrary to the main GOAL and relevant
interests; the equivalent point in a prose NARRATIVE of the end of act two in
the three-act play format.

The denouement is the critical zenith in a story where the outcome is
uncertain, although the clues and prompts leading to its resolution have
been set into the narrative. Taking the Latin and French origins of the word
into consideration, denouement is the unknotting of COMPLICATIONS and OBSTA-
CLES and, now removed or ameliorated to sufficient degree, the ENDING can be
set in place. The remaining questions: will the resolution please the CHARAC-
TERS and, if so, how do they show it?

Denouement in NOVELS is more detailed than the resolution of a SHORT
STORY; there is more at stake in a novel and some change in ATTITUDE, fortune,
and worldview are often considered necessities by readers. For better or
worse, Charles Dickens felt the need to return to his memorable novel *Great
Expectations,* changing the attitudes and worldviews of two of the major
characters. Why? Dickens and, later, Conan Doyle, published their works first
in monthly magazine installments. Both were subject to significant numbers
of READER complaints about the denouement of their work, sending each
back to the writing desk to produce more agreeable results.

description

The communication of salient qualities of a CHARACTER, place, or thing; the
briefest gloss without distracting from STORY on how an organization or tradition works; relevant details in a STORY; a series of adjectives, adverbs, and
evocations that convey personality, sense of place, or sense of atmosphere.

When you choose words to describe a character, a locale, an institution,
even a room at a Motel 6, they should come from a menu of emotion-friendly
words, words that help transport the feeling of being in Character A's presence,
the patience needed to overcome the ambient awfulness of Locale B, the fussy
bureaucratic wrangling within Institution C, the no-holds-barred torture to the
back and neck experienced while sleeping or otherwise on a Motel 6 bed.

And yet.

Words of description are not like the words of political conventions,
intent on mobilizing crowds to cut back on thought and open up the spending of rabid emotion. Words of description are like the evocations of champagne, rascally pinot noir, single malt whiskey, the hoppy promise of a pale
ale, the piquancy of a homemade pesto; they lead us to the experience, then
turn us loose to experience it rather than lock us in the closet with it. If it is
important enough to the story to include the breakfast menu at a particular

meeting, we should be able to have our impression of each character enhanced by what he or she orders, and how it is eaten.

The best descriptions of a character come from the way he or she *does* things; a locale has a particular personality that is conveyed by the way things within it appear and behave; organizations reflect the personality of a leader or of individuals trying to imitate said leader; rooms in any given Motel 6 smell like mass-produced disinfectant, cheap furniture, and indifferent pizzas delivered by distracted drivers who despair of reasonable tips. To inhale the atmosphere of a Motel 6 is to inhale the pathology of the American dream, then be numbed by the experience.

We should be using description to convey personality; at all costs we should not use description to display our ability as a writer. READERS understand this to the point of being put off by WRITERS who don't know the difference.

Hint: Novelists Willa Cather and Richard Powers, generations apart, use the descriptions of the same geographical area—the Nebraska prairie land—to striking example, each direct and relevant to the story. In Cather's *My Antonia,* the effect of the prairie and the big city on the characters influence their behavior and foreshadow the payoff. In Powers' *The Echo Maker,* description of landscape has direct physical effect on all the characters but also invites them and the readers to investigate their own internal landscape—their identity as individuals.

design

The representation of a DRAMATIC plan or structure; a deliberate manipulation of dramatic elements with the INTENT of producing a STORY; a PLOT or story ARC intended to generate a lasting and memorable effect on the READER.

Design is, in this sense, a noun; it may also be used as a verb in which case it becomes the act of producing a plot line or arrangement of significant dramatic elements that lead to a satisfying CONCLUSION. PLOT-DRIVEN stories are those in which the design may become PREDICTABLE, even though the emotional effects such as SUSPENSE, TENSION, HORROR, anticipation, dread, longing, etc. may vary.

The better of the plot-driven stories, say those of Harlan Coben or Lee Child, implicitly offer a design of sufficient complexity and issues at stake to lure the reader's attention away from the design while producing one or more of the previously listed emotions. In many ways, such stories are the equivalent of Navajo rugs: intricate, colorfully patterned, pleasing to experience. Design is the strategic deployment of all the BEATS within a story.

CHARACTER-DRIVEN STORIES are designed to provide emotional responses as well as moral, intellectual, and aesthetic challenges. Richard Powers's *The Echo Maker,* while superb in its plot vectors, brings characters on stage with issues that call their very sense of self into question, luring the reader well past the notion of mere FORMULA or suspense and into self-examination that could produce uncomfortable feelings.

A conventional approach for producing both types of pattern, the more geometrically structured as well as the more open-ended design, begins with confronting a single character with a choice of behavior or the need to make some choice within a narrow time frame. On a more plot-oriented design, a character may be given a choice between serving out a long prison term and accepting a life-threatening assignment as a ticket to forgiveness for the crime that landed the character in prison. A character may be confronted head-on with the need to choose allegiance between two feuding factions. One possible approach for beginning a character-driven story is to present the lead character with the need to investigate or DISCOVER some relevant information from his own past or from the past of family, a quest that will lead to the discovery of some UNSPEAKABLE information. Jay Gatsby (a bright but poor young man born James Gatz in North Dakota) goes on a QUEST to find his former love, Daisy Buchanan, a quest that brings him into the midst of a complex pattern of love, betrayal, and social collision.

In a longer short story, a novella, or a novel, changing POINTS OF VIEW in rendering the narrative will have a measurable effect on the dramatic design. Nearly any of Alice Munro's longer stories with more than one point of view will present the reader with such choices to make as to which character's memory of a particular instance is the one to be trusted. Wilkie Collins's *The Moonstone,* still memorable after one hundred fifty years in print, uses an ensemble cast, ending chapters on intriguing interpretations or outright CLIFFHANGERS.

desire/secret desire

A dream, plan, or agenda held in absolute confidence by a character; a wished-for outcome with a romantic, career-based, or otherwise political outcome nourished by an individual in a story.

When pushed to extremes, many individuals will readily confess to being indifferent lovers or bad drivers and they will do so well before admitting their secret desire to anyone, making a strong argument that true power over an individual is not related to sexual prowess or financial position but rather to knowledge of another's secret desire. This concealed hankering may very well be sexual or financial in nature. It may also be the ability to perform well at a sport or in a particular art. The SECRET here is, in fact, the secret. Most individuals who wish to act or dance or sculpt or play the B-flat Selmer saxophone are upfront and open about their wishes, but a person who indulges in secret the desire to sing or dance or write or sculpt is setting forth at the very limit of vulnerability. That person would be mortified to have his agenda known, preferring to continue the fantasy life or the secret desire, or preferring the risk of leading a double life in which working toward that secret desire had provided enough inner security for the dreamer to go public.

The argument is provocative: Every character has, in addition to stated GOALS and AGENDAS, a secret desire. Let us, through the magic of projection (which is what many secret desires are in the first place), suppose a number of men whose secret desire it was to have a sexual relationship with a current public figure female entertainer. So far, nothing out of the ordinary, so let's inject the beginnings of combustion positing a male character who is having a sexual relationship with a current public figure female entertainer. He is in effect experiencing the wildest dreams and fantasies of a number of other males. Now we have to wonder who this man has a fantasy desire with or, alternately, what his secret desire is. The same turnabout works with a woman who is in a sexual relationship with a much-desired male figure.

The intriguing question arises, *What would your characters do if someone discovered the very secret desire held by another person?* To add a note of irony and complication into the equation, suppose Character A's security has been breached; someone now knows her tightly held secret desire. Character A is aware of this breach. What does she do to protect herself? And then there is this related scenario: Character A's security has been hacked. Someone knows her secret. But the someone who knows doesn't care, isn't the slightest bit impressed. What does Character A do and how does she do it, the goal of this exercise being to keep the progression of events in an arguably dramatic format—do we have a story?

Luis Alberto Urrea's 2009 novel, *Into the Beautiful North,* posits Nayeli, a nineteen-year-old who works at a taco shop in a remote Mexican village and dreams of her father, who has gone northward to Los Yunites—you know, the United States—there to make a better living and a better life. But her dreams are not deep enough or secret enough to be the yeast for a novel. Accordingly, into this calculus, Urrea adds a realization that most of the men in this small village have gone northward, and now a group of drug dealers has noticed the lack of men, moving to take over the village. We're almost there because, one night, when Nayeli is at el cine, watching a subtitled rerun of *El Magnifico Siete (The Magnificent Seven)* her secret desire metastasizes to the point where she must do something about it. Nayeli's secret desire is to sneak into Los Yunites, find her father and six other Mexican males whom she will entice to return to Mexico, where they will, à la *El Magnifico Siete,* take on the nasty drug dealers.

Having one's secret desire made public is one way to get a story going or, possibly, as in Joe Orton's play, *Entertaining Mr. Sloane,* lead to the ending. Even fear of discovery will prompt behavior. You don't have to let the cat out of the bag or the genie out of the bottle, but an array of combustive and original story vectors awaits writers who know this buried secret of all their characters. Doesn't hurt if they know where to dig.

details

One or more portions of a larger vision of a CHARACTER, a PLACE, SYSTEM, institution, or thing; a discreet, identifying trait; pieces of a defining trait; traces of emotional elements in a STORY.

In order to be effective as ingredients in a story, details must have embedded in them a feeling or the POWER to EVOKE a feeling. Details are the useful adjectives and adverbs humming about a narrative like mosquitoes on a summer afternoon, looking for a landing site. Details may also contain facts but they are best presented as though they also bore emotions, which is to say that facts presented only as empirical sources will lead to boredom. READERS want accuracy in their details but when they turn to story, the facts they are after are INSIGHTS and revelations about human and animal behavior.

There is a relationship between the degree of confidence a WRITER has and the control with which that writer deploys details—the more confident, the less the need for details; the more comfortable with the reach of the story, the less likely the writer will feel the need to defend rather than merely tell the story.

Hint: Avoid LAUNDRY LISTS. Use only those details that relate to the narrative point of view (as opposed to the need for the author to intervene). Each character will have thresholds of awareness, sensitivity, tolerance. A character who is a painter or photographer will have an eye for nuances of light. A musician will be more likely to note details of a voice or sound. A chef might have a nose for the subtle smells and flavors of an atmosphere. A prepubescent child will experience details of time in a different manner than a septuagenarian. As the writer "becomes" and takes on the sensitivity of his own characters, the writer will experience a sense of the right impressions and details for each character. More than any use of physical details in her portrayal of her character Patricia "Paddy" Meehan, mystery/suspense author Denise Mina focuses on Paddy's frustrating encounters with diet, the extreme measures she sometimes takes, how she falls off the dietary wagon, and how she dresses, hopeful of effecting a camouflage.

In his novel *Brooklyn,* Colm Toibin allows his Irish characters a different awareness than his Italian characters, allowing readers of both ethnicities a richer vision into their respective cultures. He is similarly apt in his depiction of sports fans, and in the feel of commercial and domestic settings. In her novel *The Shipping News,* Annie Proulx uses detail to produce the sense of cold in the Newfoundland setting with stunning effect. More to the point, neither Toibin nor Proulx overuse detail; each demonstrates excellent judgment and restraint in the amount and the way the detail is brought into context.

At one time—the 1940s and 50s—writers of the so-called Naturalist inclination thought to define their characters through lists of products they used, types of clothing they wore, specific foods they enjoyed or detested. For all their sincerity and devotion to their approach, their characters still stood out for readers in the details of their ACTIONS and ATTITUDES. Indeed, the temptation still amps up in some writers to use relevant and non-relevant LAUNDRY LISTS. Brett Easton Ellis's characters in *American Psycho* are gifted consumers, allowing their author to define by cataloging.

determinism

The literary equivalent of quantum mechanics in which all dramatic events have an antecedent; the causal basis of STORY; a system or philosophy in which chaos or random event is marginalized; a DOMINO THEORY of event. If ever a dramatic concept merited discussion among READERS and WRITERS, determinism belongs at the tip of the pyramid.

By its very nature, story is a series of RESPONSES to a stimulus. An individual experiences an awareness of some emotionally charged stimulus, attempts to interpret it, builds a personalized system about it, then moves on to other tasks at hand. When the emotionally charged stimulus seems challenging in extreme, perhaps even to the point of becoming a THREAT, the individual seeks counsel, choosing from a smorgasbord list of advisers such as friends, clergy, psychologists, psychiatrists, philosophers. This is the analog of going to a dentist on the occasion of a pained tooth. The habit of consulting has a long history in the human condition. That habit is a driving force behind the decision to CONSULT the writer, who has his or her own philosophy and has created an ensemble of characters to dramatize that philosophy.

Readers seek escape, understanding, TRANSPORTATION, identity, and companionship in story, thus they approach story with a curiosity that asks, *Will this narrative interest and involve me?* Writers have the intuitive awareness of how to invite a segment of the reading public into the forum of their story, knowing also that the reader's curiosity will engage to the point of wanting to know more relevant details about the characters in a situation and the SITUATION itself.

By providing some system, some codification of the CHAOS, for himself, the writer provides primal assurances and comfort for the reader even while disturbing him with a dramatization of the CONSEQUENCES that result from story. As sure of the outcome as the reader becomes while reading *Billy Budd,* the reader assures himself that he will behave differently under similar circumstances. By experiencing John Yossarian's sense of futility and frustration with the rock and hard place of war and wartime bureaucracy in *Catch-22,* the reader understands more intimately his own feelings of futility and FRUSTRATION and is better equipped to engage the chaos about him in his everyday life.

Hint: Significant dramatic events in a story cause the reader to be on the alert for the consequences of those events. Lenny's early responses to stimulus in *Of Mice and Men* trigger the ultimate consequence. The poignant execution of Candy's dog by Carlson becomes another causal trigger that has payoff in Lenny's fate. George Milton, the bright, down-on-his-luck PROTAGONIST, becomes a consequential and IRONIC embodiment of the title of the novel, which came from a poem by Robert Burns, warning that the best laid schemes of mice and men *gang aft agley* and leave us naught but grief and pain for promised joy.

Deus ex machina

The sense that EVENTS in STORY did not evolve the way the CHARACTERS wished and were instead brought about by some extraordinary agent, say the AUTHOR. In the most literal sense, deus ex machina comes from the early Greek plays, where gods were lowered onto stage in a basket, tethered to a winch, where they could be seen coming from above to deliver their whim or judgment, or both, on the mortal characters.

The term as used today is meant to alert the WRITER to find a plausible way to make the ACTION, MOTIVATION, or OUTCOME appear to come as a direct result of the planning or interaction of the characters rather than as mechanical intervention. Any hint of COINCIDENCE will cause the reader to begin looking for the lowering basket, and if the coincidence seems too convenient to be PLAUSIBLE, there goes the reader. As the ebook proliferates in popularity, the writer is well advised to see the reader having the same degree of patience as a TV viewer with the tuning wand.

Beware of such introductory tropes as "Just then," "At that moment," "Suddenly," or "Before he or she knew it" as mini-deus-ex-machina opportunities to have a shot ring out, a fateful knock sound at the door, an important letter or email arrive, a cell phone or land line ringing at a gravid moment in the narrative. Close inspection of the text will reveal not only authorial intrusion but, even worse, authorial intrusion in the passive voice.

Suck it up. Events happen in stories because characters have done things or have not done things, producing CONSEQUENCES. Events also develop because someone (see ANTAGONIST) is throwing roadblocks at your PROTAGONIST.

By the nature of the clue inherent in the name, deus ex machina labels any writer who uses it as more a mechanic than a storyteller.

device

Any stratagem, trait, or narrative technique that triggers CONSEQUENCES in a STORY is some form of device; a framing pattern for including one or more STORIES within a longer work; a catch-all word for narrative technique, metaphor, props, mistaken identity.

Although the READER may not see the device immediately, its cumulative effect begins to tell at some point and the reader goes forth, making assumptions about the left-handed individual who walks with a slight limp, causing the reader at the appropriate moment of hearing the sound of a halting step behind the PROTAGONIST in the alleyway to suspect that the protagonist has been betrayed and is about to suffer unknown consequences.

Another such device is a frequent CLICHÉ in low-grade horror films where 1) the PROTAGONIST is specifically warned about going up to the attic, and 2) the protagonist goes up to the attic, where it is quite dark and, 3) steps on something that produces an eerie yowl. The fourth event is realizing that the genesis of the yowl was a cat, identification of which produces the catharsis out of early Greek drama, setting up the protagonist for stepping on something which produces an eerie yowl but the something is not a cat; it is the reason the protagonist was warned against going to the attic in the first place.

Device may also be POINT OF VIEW, particularly if the use of that particular point of view goes out on strike against a CONVENTION, such as having a story or novel narrated by a dead person, as are the narrators of Machado de Assisi's *Epitaph for a Small Winner* and Alice Seybold's *The Lovely Bones*.

See also Mark Twain's *The Prince and the Pauper*, in which two identical-appearing boys have their roles transposed, and Shakespeare's *Twelfth Night*, in which the character Viola pretends to be a young man, in whose guise her love is sought by a woman, a device that could have stopped right there had Shakespeare not recognized the added device of having Viola fall in love with the man she is now serving as a confidante.

See also ALTERNATE UNIVERSE novels such as those of the *His Dark Materials* trilogy by Philip Pullman, in which the device becomes an entire universe, parallel to but slightly different from our own. (See DETAILS.)

dialect

A variant form of a language, often associated with a class, cultural, or regional uses; a distinction given to a CHARACTER to further define the character's social, cultural, and educational dimensions; an attempt to capture a regional, social, or ethnic tendency through spoken language.

Individuals from different parts of the world and throughout history have had different speech patterns, class identifiers, and expressions, and so why not use these in narrative to the same degree that any other relevant detail is used? One argument for moderation in the use of dialect is to observe the way excessive, court-reportorial emphasis on detail leaves dust bunnies, the charming and worthwhile Uncle Remus being one example of how black dialect and speech patterns don't hold up very well, in fact, and even less so when placed in contrast with contemporary tropes from, for example, Walter Mosley's character, Easy Rawlins. The latter holds up and is likely to.

On a more general level, removing the occasional terminal *g* from gerunds might have an evocative effect of a larger dialect or lack of formal education, but removing all terminal g's might call such attention as to point the finger at the device. True enough, upper classes in England once used ain't matter-of-factly in conversation (see Dorothy Sayers's Lord Peter Whimsy detective series), simultaneous with a middle-class American campaign to rid the language of ain't. Thus do dialect, slang, patois, and such coarse depictions of, say, Native Americans through such CLICHÉS as "Ugh!" and "Great White Father" or "him say-um" defeat their purpose by providing self-parody instead of intended authenticity.

Moderation is a good polestar here. So, too, is trying to capture the metrics and cadence of a dialect, using but not overusing regionalisms. Also worth note, the dialect used by the late Boston crime and thriller writer, George V. Higgins, particularly in *The Friends of Eddie Coyle*, in which Higgins had some of his characters speaking in what was represented as Boston Irish working class; it was no such thing—it was Higgins's impression of Boston Irish working class English. Reading it, few would doubt the obvious shift away from Standard English and Boston upper-class usage, and thus the tail began to wag the dog: readers assumed that the Boston Irish spoke the way Higgins's characters do.

Yet another gifted combination of dialect and regionalisms may be found in the suspense fiction of Elmore Leonard. Many of Leonard's characters would not score well on intelligence tests although they often have natural shrewdness, ambition, dreams, and plans reflecting their shrewdness, dreams, and ambitions. Leonard's dialogue and narrative are reflective of his characters; also clear is the fact that Leonard is not patronizing them.

Dialect can be a helpful tool if used with moderation and inventiveness, ever alert to keep respect for the characters as the highest priority, and a watchful eye for racial, gender, and class cliché.

dialogue

The way CHARACTERS in dramatic NARRATIVES communicate among themselves and READERS. What they say is not always of direct relevance to the STORY; it might be an outright evasion. What characters say to themselves and to others may conceal some AGENDA, or emerge as subversive, but of this we may be sure—*it is not conversation.* Dialogue has a notable EDGE, dancing on the boundary of politeness to the point of stepping on someone's toes.

As far back as Jane Austen's notable exchanges of dialogue in such nineteenth-century works as *Persuasion*, dialogue had the bite of SUBTEXT, the impact of what the speaker felt, weighing against what the speaker actually said.

Try Dennis Lehane's *Moonlight Mile* for circumstances where modern dialogue takes us to emotional heights and depths. Read *The Collected Stories of Deborah Eisenberg* to see how dialogue blends with narrative to the point where an exchange among her characters produces the effect of biting into a lemon. Check the dialogue in the sixty segments of the novel-for-television, *The Wire*. Be sure to catch the range of irony, menace, courtly mannerisms, and unsettling edginess in the TV series, *Justified*, where the writers have made a good attempt at capturing the quirky, compelling effects of Elmore Leonard.

Things to look for when reading dialogue:

1. Hidden agenda
2. Unintentional betrayal of motives
3. Unconscious self-mockery and unintended humor
4. Class or status labels
5. Pretentiousness
6. Reliability of speaker and speaker's message

Things to beware of when writing dialogue:

1. All characters sounding alike
2. The need for adverbs to shore up intended meaning
3. Too great a willingness to explain things to the reader
4. Responses such as "Oh," "Okay," and "All right," which have no emotional denominator and thus want to invite adverbs along as a security blanket
5. One character explaining to another what that person already knows
6. Using italics and exclamation points for emphasis when a better choice of words would do the job

Hint: If, after finishing a memorable exchange of dialogue, you wonder if perhaps you'd pushed it a bit too far, you're on the right track.

digression

A movement away from a STORY line; a detail, introduction of CHARACTER, time shift, or DESCRIPTION that calls the READER away from DETAILS vital to the understanding of and immersion in the present NARRATIVE.

Digression is either a DRAMATIC strategy or a literary wrong turn, the former a contrived movement that will have the effect of urging the reader to continue reading, the latter a case of the author becoming impressed with some detail of surrounding, of meaning, or of implication that will have the effect of causing the reader to say, "Huh? What was that about?" The gap between the two poles is rather narrow, hence this question to pose about a digression: *Does the digression directly add a sense of* TENSION *or* SUSPENSE *to the narrative?*

Digressions in NOVELS are easily achieved—merely shift the POINT OF VIEW to another character who is appropriately engaged in intriguing activity. This strategy causes the reader to suspend focus on the previous situation, although keeping it close at hand. A SHORT STORY proposes a more difficult situation because words must be chosen with mosaic precision. Digressions may be achieved and accommodated in short stories by having one or more characters respond directly to the digression, questioning its very appropriateness (which, in all but the most clever cases, is assuredly what the reader will be doing).

A key to understanding the related plateau of ANTICLIMAX is the awareness that digression produces distraction, which in turn yields anticlimax. Digression and distraction combine forces to undercut the dramatic momentum of story. WRITERS need to develop a search-and-destroy agenda for digression and distraction. This agenda begins with the close examination of the digression to see if it will effectively assist the payoff of the story or is placed where it is merely an advertisement for the writer's ability with words. Does it lead to a relevant discovery, or is it in fact merely showing off? If it does contribute to a DISCOVERY the reader and one or more characters may achieve it; if it is merely showing off—well, that will not get us very far: CUT it.

disclaimer

A dramatic ACTION, statement, or combination of the two intended to distance a CHARACTER from real or imagined CONSEQUENCES; an agreement such as a pre-nuptial, in which rights, obligations, and promises to perform are enumerated.

The basic dramatic disclaimer is "I did not." When followed by a response of "You did so," we have the beginning of a STORY in two scant lines. Close on the heels of the former is the even shorter introduction to story, "I already did" or the equally provocative, "I already was." Not to forget, "I thought you knew."

Disclaimers get characters into trouble they seek to avoid by disclaiming in the first place, opening the dramatic stage for guest appearances from the likes of denial, stubbornness, misrepresentation, and outright lies, moving the NARRATIVE into a downward spiral of considerable complexity.

One of the more common disclaimers, offered as a defense, is "I only meant it as humor," which is to say in real terms, "I did or said it in the first place as an attempt to embarrass, humiliate, or ridicule." A close ally, "It was only a joke," has the intended meaning: I didn't really mean it. The most common disclaimer of all is also DEFENSIVE— "It really happened that way."

Disclaimers appear as warnings of potential side-effects on many medications, presenting in their wake the question of whether the cure or relief, with its inherent possibilities of mischief, is worth the risk of the side-effects. This is a good warning for writers who use disclaimers such as, any similarity between persons living or dead is purely coincidental.

discovery

Information arrived at by a CHARACTER after deliberate research, by accident, or the intervention of another character; DRAMATIC details that will have some visible effect on a character's behavior and/or understanding of himself; awareness achieved by a character through a sudden or gradual process that specific conditions need no longer obtain or that previous constraints are no longer necessary.

When a character discovers that he is not obliged to behave in an advisory or subservient capacity, he is able to move forward with the energy inspired by that awareness. Thus a son may part company with a controlling parent, but at what cost or result? When a character discovers that a trusted and revered mentor has been passing off her work as his own, she may well require a measure of REVENGE before being able to move forward. When a married couple discover their shared boredom with one another, they are ready to move forth to counseling, a joint vacation, divorce, or....

In a real sense, characters are making small discoveries each time they enter a SCENE with other characters or, during the course of a STORY ARC, have a conversation with other characters. When going through the effects of a recently dead relative or friend, a character may make discoveries that will change the way in which the departed is remembered. When a character discovers by accident that he is not the biological product of those he'd imagined, his responses will certainly include bewilderment, anger, perhaps even resentment.

A detective may discover a clue that exculpates a suspect in a criminal investigation, an archaeologist may discover a tool or artifact that defines previously undocumented behavior, a child may discover that—assurances to the contrary—not all adults tell the truth, a character in a fantasy may discover a PORTAL leading to a new world, an adult may achieve a long-sought goal only to discover she is far from pleased with the result.

Discovery is the dramatic equivalent of fermentation; with it personalities, situations, and opinions may evolve from one form to another. Discovery may be the awareness of one character of her romantic feelings for another, the dislike of her job, or the shattering of a long-cherished basis of unquestioned faith.

Discovery walks along the path with naïveté and conviction, playing a divide-and-conquer game, imploding to change the psychological landscape for characters and readers. Discovery is forbidden knowledge, the awareness and understanding some characters are at great pains to keep from others. Discovery is the Alka-Seltzer tablet of transparency, dropped into the glass of human history.

Hint: That discovery may overtake a character is a dramatic given, but it often obfuscates the WRITER'S own dramatic discovery when relentlessly pursuing the trail of a trapped story, driving it into a corner from which the writer and the characters learn something about themselves. Actors frequently speak of reaching into their bright side or their dark side in pursuit of the discovery of what that character wants. The writer, too, should feel no compunction about visiting such places.

distraction

A gambit that takes hold when a CHARACTER, EVENT, or DETAIL shifts attention away from the main GOAL in a dramatic NARRATIVE; it is an accidental or deliberate device having the effect of arousing the READER'S curiosity and possibly as well the interest of one or more characters within the STORY; a detail that because of its being noted by WRITER or character has the power to change the direction of the story in which it appears.

Distractions emerge as a result of authorial laziness, AUTHORIAL INTERVENTION into a narrative, or through random accident. Distractions may be deliberate calculations, sometimes no more than a word, much of a piece with a skilled magician using some device to distract the audience from seeing the mechanics of an illusion. The point to be emphasized is that distractions take the reader's attention from the procession of story elements. This may or may not be a good thing, depending on the writer's INTENT. A distraction or digression will raise EXPECTATIONS in the reader and, possibly, within other characters, triggering the READER-AS-MATCHMAKER instinct, causing the reader to make assumptions, to wait for a payoff that might not come.

Even though the writer is as conversant with the necessary elements in a story underway as a director is aware of the THROUGHLINE in a written narrative, the most efficient mental state for the writer at work is the state of being "IN THE STORY," or completely immersed in the movement of events. Unanticipated details emerge from such states. It is a good policy to include them and move on until the next convenient moment for REVISION and possible rethinking.

In other words, do not think about these distractions as they appear, but wait instead for a thinking mode—a revision mode—to decide whether they stay or go. Yes; you heard that correctly: details come rushing forth during the writing mode. Like guests wanting the maitre d' to seat them in the restaurant, they must be given appropriate scrutiny. Do they belong? Do they enhance the story? Or, like the fabled tourists with white belts and loafers worn with green polyester trousers, are they distractions?

domino theory, the

A PLOT-DRIVEN CONCEPT in which story points (see BEATS) are seen as dominoes, aligned to cause one falling piece to TRIGGER another to fall; a dramatic demonstration of determinism, where the present event has been directly caused by past events; a practical demonstration of CONSEQUENCE and CAUSALITY in STORY.

A metaphoric description of a story: a row of dominoes stood on their vertical end, placed in close enough proximity that, tipping the first domino, it will strike and knock over its neighbor, which in turn topples its neighbor, until the entire row has been toppled. Thus the entire row of dominoes stands in its at-rest inertia until a force (OPENING VELOCITY) topples the first domino in the row. From that point until the last domino falls, the story is in effect "telling" itself.

The literary equivalent of checking the air pressure in the tires of one's vehicle is checking to see if the dominoes (i.e. story or plot points) are spaced at the optimal distance. Too wide a gap between events makes for a lurching ride. Too close an interval produces a frenetic, comedic effect, which often undercuts any intended SUSPENSE or seriousness.

Recipe for success: During the REVISION process, select one incident or scene from anywhere in the text that provides unquestioned opening velocity. Move that scene or incident to the beginning of the story, making certain its narrative TIME FRAME makes the event appear to be taking place in the immediate present. Using this repositioning of events, adjust where necessary the time sequence (verb tenses) in recognition of the "new" beginning.

In this domino-theory regard, triggering devices play important roles; the toppling of any domino in the row triggers the fall of the neighboring domino, thus an action has down-the-line consequences. In longer works, the triggering device may skip a few neighbors in delivering its consequential inertia, but it is nevertheless felt as a product of CAUSALITY.

Graham Greene and Eric Ambler, each in his self-described thrillers or novels of suspense, are worth study in this domino-theory regard. In Greene's *Brighton Rock,* for example, a major character visits a coin-operated booth at an amusement pier, where he records a phonograph with what another character believes is a romantic message, which she plays at the very end of the narrative, to a heightened dramatic effect. Ambler's still-radiant thriller, *A Coffin for Dimitrios,* begins early on with the protagonist being shown a corpse whose life he is invited to track. At one time in the corpse's life, the individual used coffins to transport heroin into France. The corpse and the trope of the coffin have downstream consequences every bit as surprising and ironic as the phonograph record in *Brighton Rock.*

don't go there

A response by an individual in real life or a reply from a CHARACTER within a story when pressed for the details and/or CONSEQUENCES of a painful, potentially humiliating situation. Both instances are meant to stop further questioning. When confronting the "don't go there" assertion, the WRITER needs to pursue full on, recording the results.

don't tell the reader what the reader already knows

A needless repetition of dramatic EVENTS the READER has already seen; repetition of DIALOGUE exchanges; belaboring MOTIVATION, CHARACTER flaws, and IMPLICATIONS.

At some point in the equation of STORY, the reader has to be let beyond the red rope barrier to the entrance, allowed to find a preferred seat and participate in the story being told—in other words, allowed to infer. This comes at a price to the WRITER, who is likely to have been stung in other dramatic venues by readers who completely misinterpret, then go forth to make erroneous assumptions about the motivations of the characters and the intent of the author. Writers are control freaks enough as it is to take this challenge lightly, but the fact is that a writer who over-manages to make absolutely sure the reader "gets" his intention is, in fact, dumbing the story down and not taking necessary risks.

Hint: Always risk the possibility that the reader will understand. Information exchanged between two or more characters in dialogue may be summed up tersely in narrative later on. Example, "He told her the details of his conversation with Fred and Willie. She had no questions, seemingly understanding why he'd acted as he had."

You don't need to remind the reader with stage directions that Fred had a furious temper and was likely to fly into murderous rages. Let the reader see THEME, INTENT, and dramatic INEVITABILITY the way, for instance, John Steinbeck did in his depiction of Lennie in *Of Mice and Men,* reminding us through incident of Lennie's unintentional potential for inflicting painful consequences on the very things he found attractive and comforting.

drama

A NARRATIVE having the inherent suggestion and quality of STORY; implicit content of elements that produce CONFLICT, interaction, GOAL search, revelation and REVERSAL; a NARRATIVE that contains one or more CHARACTERS in pursuit of an AGENDA or embarking on an internal or geographical journey; a QUEST which will involve reversal, FRUSTRATION, and competitive exterior forces.

A successful dramatic narrative reflects the goals and intentions of characters set against the COUNTERPOINT of the WRITER'S personal goals at the time of writing. Thus stories may reflect an attitude of cynicism, pragmatism, sadness, bitterness, expansive optimism, and transcendental anticipation. Differing readerships will be drawn to one of these qualities or perhaps even a combination of them. You might liken the physics concept of water, seeking to find its original level, to the literary concept of story: READERS seek to find their target level. One thing all stories have in common is a VOICE or governing personality. The proper goal of the writer is to seek his own level, which emerges from the pressures informing the voice, timbre, and intensity of its persona.

On a basic level, to say of a work that it is dramatic is to say that it is actable, performable, readable. On a more NUANCED level, to say of a work that it is dramatic implies that the work has skillfully designed characters engaged in dealings with the enormous varieties present in life. If these dealings appear piled on or contrived, the LANDSCAPE in which they appear may be spoken of as melodramatic, exaggerated, even operatic. Thus does balance between intensity and realism come into the equation of which dramatic is an integral part.

drunk in the parking lot, the

A performance-impaired individual in a STORY; an individual in a dramatic NARRATIVE who is emotionally or physically challenged to a degree notable to the READER. The key to this trope may be found in actors whose roles call for them to appear drunk or under some related influence: they are seen as exaggerating their attempts to appear sober or normal or unfazed. The drunk in the parking lot may be seen trying to remember where he parked his car, then striding purposefully to it, perhaps too purposefully. The panicked individual is trying to hold onto a shred of control before abandoning it. The key is control, which the character in question has lost or given away and is now trying to regain.

Hint: Whatever flaws and impairments a character has, make sure he or she consistently behaves in terms of them and with awareness of them.

dystopia, the novel of

NARRATIVES in which the ills of society are exaggerated for THEMATIC effect; cautionary tales demonstrating social, moral, economic, sexual, and religious AGENDAS allowed to run wild.

In the storytelling sense, utopias—stories of perfection and accord—are not really STORIES because they lack the major dramatic ingredient of CONFLICT. Thus grace is boring, the fall from grace and its consequences a magnet for interest. If everyone gets along, is his brother's keeper, does not covet, etc., the READER will have little reason to continue reading because, redemption being precluded, there is no big finale to anticipate. If, however, a PROTAGONIST—say Ray Bradbury's Guy Montag from *Fahrenheit 451*—has a gut feeling that there is something wrong about what he is doing, the reader begins to see the inevitability of Montag going up against something quite larger than himself, then in subsequent EVENTS, being forced to deal with it.

Seen as a paradigm of a dystopia that cautioned against the consequences of war, *The Iliad's* most agreeable character—the one we root for—

is Hector. His tragic fate elevates him to a role model for the conflicted protagonist. It was a dumb war to begin with, started when Hector's brother,
Paris, made off with his prize from having judged a beauty contest. Hector's
wife, Andromache, pleads with him to abandon the war they will surely lose,
reminding him that were things to continue, she'd probably be taken as a
prize of war and their son, Astyanax, would be killed. As devoted to his wife
and son as Hector is, even though he agrees with her assessment, he knows
he could not face life, even a life in exile, were he to turn from battle. Nor is
Hector naïve or insensitive. He well foresees the consequences, but feels
obliged to continue, nevertheless.

The backstory condition of the dystopia—see *Brave New World, Logan's
Run, 1984, The Handmaid's Tale*—is the UNTHINKABLE COME TO PASS. The pres-
ent-time narrative of the dystopia sets a protagonist with whom the reader
can identify in motion to cope with it.

In its own idiosyncratic and memorable ways, Joseph Heller's *Catch-22*
is welcomed company in the GENRE of dystopic fiction, offering its modern-
day Hector in the form of the bombardier Yossarian. For all her bombast and
philosophical *sturm und drang*, Ayn Rand easily is awarded membership in
the Dystopia Society, primarily with *Atlas Shrugged* and its driven protagonist, Dagny Taggart, but also Howard Roark of Rand's other *success d'estime*,
The Fountainhead. And not to forget the preternaturally bright Alex, protagonist of Anthony Burgess's enduring dystopic novel, *Clockwork Orange.*

Hints: There are seeds of dystopia in every SATIRE, just as there are seeds
of satire in every dystopia. If you were to look closely at *Tess of the
D'Urbervilles,* and *Jude, the Obscure,* and *The Mayor of Casterbridge,* you
could find cause to think of Thomas Hardy as a writer of dystopian fiction.
Hardy (1840-1928) was a close contemporary of another dabbler in the
dystopic, Mark Twain (1835-1910). The 1950-90 SCIENCE FICTION era is larded
with dystopic visions, one of many reasons why that genre became literature.

~E~

edge

   A feeling of resentment, impatience, or frustration resident within a CHAR-
ACTER, causing that individual to respond accordingly and in unconventional
ways; a resident nature inherent in a character that seems to nudge or shove

that character into ACTION; a notable impatience with any status quo.

Edgy characters are not necessarily negative, merely wanting to do something about a circumstance, condition, or situation. The presence of edge in a character is an implicit promise of heightened responses and activity to the reader, and to other characters.

Examples of edgy characters: Randle P. McMurphy in Ken Kesey's *One Flew over the Cuckoo's Nest*, Bobby Dupea in Bob Rafaelson's film, *Five Easy Pieces*, Paddy Meehan in Denise Mina's *The Last Breath*, Jackson Brodie in Kate Atkinson's *Started Early, Took the Dog;* all have attitudes and behavior reflecting their life out on the margins of the conventional.

effect

The result or CONSEQUENCE of a previous ACTION or CONDITION; a segment of a sequential scheme of events; the product of CAUSALITY.

Effect is the RESPONSE of a CHARACTER to an ethical or sensual stimulus, or the reaction of one or more individuals to a previous stimulus or action. Captain Ahab felt the effect of the great whale; Huck Finn felt the effect of having been a contributor to the escape from slavery of Jim; Jane felt the consequences of her growing attraction to Rochester, acted upon them, and was rewarded by the appearance of additional effects. Dr. Jennifer White, in Alice LaPlante's chilling novel *Turn of Mind,* is not only a skilled orthopedic surgeon, she is aware, from unsettling experience, that she is afflicted with Alzheimer's.

Little happens in a story without some regard to DESIGN; even less happens without an effect on someone, something, somewhere. Relationships, be they romantic, political, or professional, grow in complexity and interdependence or, conversely, withdraw from closeness, then consequently wither. In a broad, sweeping sense, STORY is a record of effect—the effect of a place on a character, the effect one person or character may have on another (see Jack Kerouac and Neal Cassady for the former, see Tom Sawyer and Huck Finn for the latter). This makes effect a record of impressions and RESPONSES that writers are at pains to dramatize and describe.

Characters may be seen as individuals who try to contain and constrain the effects visited upon them by other individuals, by life experiences, and by the physical and social content of places. In his 2009 novel, *Brooklyn*, Colm Toibin demonstrates the complex range of effect a small town in Ireland and the borough of Brooklyn have on the behavior of a young Irish girl and those she comes in contact with, showing by deft indirection how the effects of place are filtered through a character, then have effect on other characters.

The musical *My Fair Lady*, and to a slightly lesser extent its parent, the stage play *Pygmalion*, demonstrate the effects of social class and of physical locale on the character of Eliza Doolittle in an emotional spectrum worth investigating for the writer who wishes to show how places and individuals evoke emotional responses in characters and, if the reader is fortunate, in him.

ego
   The essential nature of a CHARACTER; how a character ACTS, thinks, feels about himself; the part of the character that REACTS to and interacts with the world of reality.
   The ego is the self, out in the CAUSAL world, reacting and interacting, planning, attempting to be effective in personal, professional, artistic, and moral relations. In combination with CONSCIENCE and NEEDS, it is a helpful way to define a character, attributing respective sizes and shapes to each of the elements—CONSCIENCE, NEEDS, and EGO—with the total combination representing the entire character. A statistically normal character would consist of equal parts of each aspect, a warning flag for the WRITER to look elsewhere for an individual of dramatic interest. Dramatic characters tend to have large egos and extreme needs at the expense of conscience.
   Assign a given character a score of 100 points to be divided among this dramatic trinity. A character with an enormous conscience, say a 60 or 80, would accordingly have to give up ego and needs points. How would a large conscience effect the score of the ego, and what would be left over for needs?
   Try ranking some of your favorite ICONIC CHARACTERS, dividing up their 100 points among the three spheres of individuality, then see how helpful this guideline is when it comes time to assess your own creations.

elephant in the living room, the
   A thing or condition noticed by CHARACTERS but not spoken of by them; a significant result of SUBTEXT; a triggering force for the READER; the deliberate THEMATIC presence intended by the author; an armature about which the relevant details of STORY are wrapped. Although often sexual in nature, the elephant in the living room may be political, religious, ethical, or a combination of two in competition, such as science vs. religion.

elliptical orbit
   A condition arrived at when a STORY path veers off from the circular orbit of the conventional NARRATIVE; the oval-shaped path of a story, implying a movement away from tight plotting while still appearing to revolve about a recognizable THEME.
   Conventional SHORT STORIES and NOVELS tend to follow the structure of THE DOMINO THEORY, in which EVENTS are arranged in close enough proximity to cause one dramatic event (a robbery, for example) to trigger another (unanticipated complication for the robber: get-away car stalls, flat tire, traffic jam),

which triggers the arrival of an investigative agency responding not to the robbery but the stalled car, which triggers the appearance of another investigative agency responding to the robbery, which triggers a bureaucratic confusion in which the robbers escape, etc.

As stories and novels evolve beyond the conventional plot formation, the behavior of the CHARACTERS involved becomes more notional, producing SURPRISE and variations on READER expectations. The WRITER'S role in such stories is to provoke questions rather than to insist upon or even suggest answers. Thus do those frequent passengers, AMBIGUITY and SUBTEXT, hitch rides on the traveling sphere, pulling the circular orbit slightly off course and into an ellipse.

Let Poe's "A Cask of Amontillado" represent the uniformly circular-orbit or domino-theory short story, with "The Cat-Bird Seat," James Thurber's more recent version on the same kind of revenge theme, representing the tendency to veer off slightly, and Tobias Wolff's "Bullet in the Brain" representing the elliptical nature of the latest evolutionary step of the short story.

With this in mind, the question to the writer becomes: *What new thing can you do for story while still keeping it a story?*

emotion

The mood, temperament, ATTITUDE, or disposition exhibited singularly or in combination by one or more CHARACTERS in a NARRATIVE drama; a major force propelling the actions of a particular character; a resident setting or mood of a SCENE in a STORY; a dramatic CATALYST that causes characters to behave as they do.

Characters are walking TOOL KITS of emotion, using them or being driven by them to behave as they do. As a contrast between characters and real-life individuals, the individual is guided in behavior by emotions and/or their absence, occasionally becoming preoccupied, then driven, thus making the necessary transition from real-life individual to character. Being in some way driven, obsessed, or compulsive is the transformative energy needed by a character to earn his keep in a STORY.

Characters are often identified according to their GOALS and NEEDS; the thoughtful WRITER has taken this calculus one step farther by identifying the goals and needs as the comet, the attendant emotions as trails of the comet.

Both the NARRATOR and his father in Pat Conroy's *The Great Santini* convey differing types of emotion, each in his every action. An effective means of conveying emotion in characters is through SUBTEXT, which is what the character actually feels in counterpoint with what he says or does.

In her breakout mystery novel, *Case Histories*, Kate Atkinson established herself as a writer who can effectively maneuver emotions by way of her performance of characterizing four separate crimes, each with a different, resident emotion, then setting her PROTAGONIST, Jackson Brodie, to solving them.

ending

The point at which a dramatic narrative delivers its PAYOFF emotion; CHAR-ACTERS in a STORY being led from a precipitous brink to a more comfortable landing spot; the arrival at an offered SOLUTION to the major dramatic issue.

As in all EVENTS where humans are involved, story endings are at best temporary because one or more of the characters involved will quickly become caught up in another strand of activity—even if it is only a return to some old conviction, habit, or pattern, where a new chapter will begin.

Ending is a sense that things are over, but only for the moment. At the final curtain of *Hamlet*, with so many of the dramatis personae dead, only Fortinbras and Horatio are left to deal with the energy of the previous activities, but just as playwright Tom Stoppard saw possibilities for a spin-off in which Rosenkrantz and Guildenstern had their own show, Horatio could challenge Fortinbras after his final tribute to Hamlet, working himself up to wonder why Fortinbras hadn't done anything sooner, to which Fortinbras could have wondered a similar wonder to Horatio, whereupon the two would get into the exchange of blows and a sequel to *Hamlet* would have been in the making.

Huck Finn could have done well in the territory ahead, but Tom Sawyer, fed up with the responsibilities of family life, civic affiliations, and the weight of The Social Contract heavy on his shoulders, could have come looking for Huck and, once again, become caught up in Huck's life style.

Endings should be a sign to the reader that things are over for now—not necessarily solved, but done until the next DEFINING MOMENT settles upon the characters. When a WRITER leaves the READER with such emotional room, the sensation of AFTERTASTE is sweeter, and it allows the reader herself the inspiration to imagine the lives of the characters as they continue after the last page of the narrative.

Reminder: Not ending soon enough—staying on too long—may produce ANTICLIMAX.

epiphany

An emotional moment when a CHARACTER of some importance COMES TO REALIZE something relevant to the STORY in which she appears, and something of equal if not greater relevance to her own growing sense of awareness as an individual.

For READER and WRITER alike, the concept of epiphany made the jump from a religious to a dramatic VECTOR in the early years (1902) of the twentieth century, with the publication of James Joyce's SHORT STORY collection, *Dubliners,* signaling a bold shift in the passage of the dramatic payoff of a story from the writer to the reader.

An epiphany can come as the result of a discovery of some document (letter, email, tweet), an overheard conversation, or a realization such as the one in Dashiell Hammett's *The Maltese Falcon,* where the fabled bird is revealed to be bogus. It may also appear when a FRONT-RANK CHARACTER such as Lambert Strether, in Henry James's *The Ambassadors*, accidentally sees two persons together in a circumstance where he realizes they are lovers, a fact that has enormous effect on the story and on him.

Hint: Most modern stories, including those with highly ritualized FOR-MULA such as ROMANCE NOVELS, deliver at least one major epiphany. Depending on the GENRE in which it appears, the epiphany will allow the reader to fill in more details. In John Banville's novel *The Infinities*, there are several mor-dant, darkly humorous epiphanies emerging one from another like a set of Russian nesting dolls.

Additional hint: Even though it is over a hundred years old, the epiphany experienced by the character Gabriel in James Joyce's short story "The Dead" remains a valuable teaching tool. Others worthy of study can be found in: Katherine Mansfield's "Bliss" and Louise Erdrich's "The Red Convert-ible," each a demonstration that the epiphany does not require a pleasant or even comfortable realization. The epiphany shared by Nicole Warren and Dick Diver at almost the exact midpoint of F. Scott Fitzgerald's *Tender Is the Night* is a disquieting example.

Bottom line: epiphany is discovery with heavy nuance.

episode

A DRAMATIC incident or EVENT that is part of a larger work; SCENES involv-ing CHARACTERS with whom the READER is familiar, being moved to activity if not action by accelerating circumstances of a PLOT design; a separate seg-ment of a published work.

The WRITER is most apt to hear "episodic" used about a particular work as an indication that the tail is wagging the dog—the incidents and moments are distracting the reader from the STORY. A work thought to be episodic is not lacking suspense or other vital elements of drama so much as it is seen lacking the resulting force of CAUSALITY.

In a well-constructed story, characters behave as they do because the cir-cumstances of their AGENDA and of the plot force them to do so or offer them unanticipated opportunities to do so, thus the sense of the presence of causality.

Episodic narratives may be big on activity and movement, but they emerge as not being relevant to the main force of the story. Think DETERMIN-ISM, a concept that says everything that happens is the antithesis of free will and is, in fact, the result of previous events. Stories, while not entirely deter-ministic, remain well guided by the principle of determinism. Think law in the sense of precedent-setting cases informing the rendering of new deci-sions; called *stare decisis* among legal scholars, their judicial reach for deter-minism is visible. No episodes for them.

In past works from other eras, a memorable series of event-heavy tales of rogue-like men and women, living by their wits, was referred to as picaresque. Memorable among these were Henry Fielding's *Joseph Andrews*, which advertised on its title page, "written in the manner of Cervantes," and which traced the adventures of a footman who ran alongside the carriage of a wealthy person, insuring the coach was not caught in ruts or shrubbery or urban traffic.

One of the earliest picaresque novels, *Lazarillo de Tormes*, dates back to the mid 1500s; yet another popular example returns the genre to the 1748 England of Tobias Smollett, with *The Adventures of Roderick Random*. (Earlier, Smollett had translated a version of *Don Quixote* into English.)

Endings in picaresque novels were often impromptu, the result of an episodic construction. Larry McMurtry's 1986 novel, *Lonesome Dove*, although no stranger to plot points, could be argued as episodic, even though there was an abundance of action and a considerable layering of interpersonal relationships.

Worth remembering: If the characters are picaresque enough and the narrative is kept outside the areas of introspection and logical argumentation, episodic will hold its own with a more goal-oriented plot.

epistolary novel, the

A long NARRATIVE related through exchanges of letters between CHARACTERS.

As technology expanded from the handwritten letter to the post card, the typed letter, and telegrams, the epistolary narrative could be expanded to include messages left on telephone answering machines, While-You-Were-Out messages, email, text messages, journal entries, blog posts, and one-hundred-forty-word Twitter entries. In short, anything that could be taken to have come from characters with AGENDAS and INTENT.

One of the earliest examples of epistolary novels came from the printer Samuel Richardson (1689-1761), with *Pamela*, the first of three such works. *Pamela* carried the subtitle, *Virtue Rewarded;* it appeared at a time (1740) when the English reading public was not as used to the concept of fiction, consequently believing it to be a real account involving real persons. It was so successful that Richardson was motivated eight years later to produce another, *Clarissa: Or, The History of a Young Lady,* and yet another, *The History of Sir Charles Grandison,* in 1753.

The most notable contemporary epistolary novel is Marilynne Robinson's *Gilead*, a series of letters written by John Ames, an elderly Protestant minister, to his young son, concerning the delightful surprise evolving from his later-in-life marriage to a younger woman. By 2004, when *Gilead* was published, the reading public was sophisticated enough to understand the concept of fictional characters, applying the standard of WILLING SUSPENSION OF DISBELIEF to it and to any novel they read.

Since *Gilead,* at least one other epistolary novel, *The White Tiger* by Aravind Adiga, appeared to great critical acclaim, allowing the PROTAGONIST to directly address the characters who were subjects of his letters. In between *Pamela* and *The White Tiger* is Ring Lardner's iconic letters from Jack Keefe, a bush league baseball player, published in 1916, as *You Know Me, Al.*

There are enough epistolary and epistolary-like novels in the publishing stream (*The Beatrice Letters* from Lemony Snickett, *Flowers for Algernon* from Daniel Keyes, and Nick Bantock's imaginatively extravagant *Griffin and Sabine*) to suggest that the epistolary novel has a solid footing in the literary landscape—mainstream as well as literary WRITERS (Vladimir Nabokov with *Ada,* John Barth with *Letters,* to name two) have waded into these waters. This form relies, for its effectiveness, on the same elements a traditionally narrated novel uses: intriguing characters, believable situations, SURPRISE, and REVELATION.

Hint: Back in the day, when Richardson was attracting READERS to his seemingly actual characters, his contemporary, the great satirist Henry Fielding, was inspired to QUIT Pamela, which is to say answer it. He did so with *Shamela,* using the epistolary format to show that Richardson's virtuous serving girl was actually lascivious and scheming, using her wiles to effect a good marriage for herself. Accordingly, think of the fun inherent in such possible approaches as *Letters to a Young Screen Writer,* or *Hester Prynne's Guide to Feminist Freedom.*

euphemism

The evasive substitution of a word or meaning and the subsequent substitution of that word or meaning with a word, phrase, or concept that sounds more agreeable and polite; abduction of a word or meaning by inferring a less bold, graphic, or more socially acceptable meaning.

The most common euphemisms in Western culture are those connected with death. Passing, passing on, passing away, and passing over join company with expired, gone to his/her reward, called home, pushing up daisies—this last one at least appears to be making fun of itself—and croaked, also far from polite, seems to draw on the death rattle for an IRONIC nudge.

There are euphemisms for the three widely touted taboos—sex, religion, and politics—as well, just as split-up is used as a euphemism for divorce or a broken long-term arrangement of any sort. In sports, being sent down to the minors may be literally true but it is also a cover-up for being demoted, just as being held back is a euphemism for flunked.

In much of the world, the infamous n-word has been replaced with Negro, black, Black, and, if appropriate, African-American, almost all the euphemisms (including "person of color") enjoying a cycle of popularity before falling off the radar (not a euphemism, but a definite cliché). Thus also does midget or dwarf become "little person," or, as some would have it, "person of challenged height," which opens yet other doors for vulgar, demeaning conditions manifest in individuals suffering from neurological disorders. What to do? Of course some CHARACTERS, by their nature, will use the n-word or any other word that suits their purpose when dealing with certain people, and it is appropriate to show them in full, non-euphemistic action as, say, Ernest Hemingway did when referring to certain of his characters as a rummy, which lets us know that person has a strong attachment to *spiritus fermenti* or, if you will, booze. Other characters whom you intend as an embodiment of PC (not a euphemism for personal computer) will pour on the euphemisms, and yet other characters you conceive of as covert bigots might reveal themselves with their broadcast liberalism by wanting to introduce you to "my Chinese wife." (Of course the appropriate response would be to say how much you look forward to meeting his Japanese wife and perhaps his Polynesian wife, but you decide to hold your tongue—which is a euphemism for not responding.)

Other of your characters will use euphemisms to delineate for friends and acquaintances alike the sexual orientation of other characters, including such euphemisms as light in the loafers, walks with a notable limp, and wears pink handkerchiefs as well as the one euphemism most of us use, gay. Some characters will refer to bisexuals in baseball terms as in he/she swings from both sides of the plate or switch hitter, and to women homosexuals as holding passports from the Isle of Lesbos and the one-size-fits-all lesbo, or perhaps dyke or the throw-away observation, "she tends to ride the clutch on her Harley."

There are risks in using PC euphemisms, just as there are risks in using vulgar, intentionally hurtful ones, and thus the question arises about whether to call characters out in stories that have nothing to do with their sexual, religious, or political orientations, using this information only as it relates to the development of a story.

The answers (for there are more than one) reside within your characters and their intent. If a character brags of having friends who are Jewish, LDS, Catholic, and, say, Lutheran, as well as friends who are Republican and even some who are gay, what does this say of your character? If a character is constantly reminding other characters that little people are not to be called midgets and that the "correct" designation for an Oriental person is Asian, what does this say of her?

And what does it say to READERS, LITERARY AGENTS, and editors if the WRITER chooses, "Dennis yanked the Glock from his waistband, squeezed off three shots at point-blank range, then bent down to see if his assailant had crossed over."

event

An occurrence (off stage or on) in a NARRATIVE; an ACTION or series of actions involving specific CHARACTERS in specific situations, meant to be interpreted by the characters themselves and, of course, by READERS. (Thus, by being called upon for interpretation, the reader is made an active participant in the transaction of story.)

It is no more fanciful to see electricity as a series of electrons, moving past an arbitrary point at a particular speed and density than it is to see dramatic narrative—story—as a series of events as they move past the reader's point of awareness.

Electricity is, in fact, measured by the rate at which electrons flow, including the resistance against which they move. STORY is, at its heart, the number of events that take place in a narrative, the PACE at which they proceed, and the resistance against them. As the SCENE is the basic unit of drama, the event is the basic unit of scene.

evoke

As a noun, to cause a READER to feel a presence, emotion, longing, or association. Made into a verb, evoke intends the reader to feel the same sort of presence, longing, or thematic association. Distinct from DESCRIPTION, which is the WRITER'S equivalent of drawings on the Lascaux Cave walls, evocation is the indirect approach a storyteller uses when conveying information that causes the reader to apprehend the information on his own terms.

Writer A may say of Character B, "She moved about with an air of perpetual sadness," which is a direct description. Writer A may also evoke Character B's perpetual sadness by forcing upon her situations and responses that lead the reader to conclude that Character B is always sad, the latter making the reader a partner in the equation rather than a passive viewer.

Evocation is SHOW, DON'T TELL spelled out in dramatic form. A significant goal for the contemporary writer is to evoke rather than describe, meaning the writer must choose with care which ATTRIBUTE and ACTIONS to set forth, shrewdly nudging but not pushing the reader toward a desired interpretation. A notable example of evocative writing may be found in the novels and shorter works of Stephen King, whose fans read him primarily to experience at close hand the frightening associations and circumstances he evokes.

After rereading scenes and passages that have remained in their memory for years, many are surprised to note how little actual description these narratives contained, and how important the context mattered in which they were placed. Responses often approximate the famed five stages observed by Dr. Elisabeth Kubler-Ross. The first response, akin to denial, becomes, "This must not be the scene I'm thinking of." Then comes feeling cheated by the intensity of the memory. This quickly shifts into the reader's sense of having grown, perhaps having become wiser or more empathetic. But skilled writers know better: Of course we grow, profit from experience, more fully appreciate NUANCE. The secret to the most effective dramatic writing is the use of significant specifics, items that employ one or more sensory triggers.

These triggers evoke memories of sight, smell, taste, and sound, allowing the reader to experience a desired scene through his own sensual memory.

To evoke rather than to describe achieves the effect of drawing the reader further into the dramatic situation by letting the reader fill in the significant details. This process throws the writer back on his own resources or lack thereof. How to evoke rather than describe? Start with the feeling to be evoked, then set forth the minute details that suggest the feeling. Let the reader connect the dots.

Trained actors understand and use these techniques in preparing for the roles in which they are cast. They first read the script to determine the author's INTENT, then begin rummaging through their own TOOL KIT to find sensory triggers that will inform their movements, pacing, and speech cadences to project a sense of their character. The writer, whether consciously or not, uses the same process.

exaggeration

A device in which attributes, EVENTS, and gestures are overemphasized to provide a dramatic effect such as HUMOR or apprehension; a conspicuous situation in which a CHARACTER will demonstrate with emphasis a response one-hundred-eighty degrees in opposition to the resident condition or emotion; an extension of superlative degree to hyperbole; use of hyperbole as an IRONIC comparison to simple fact.

A drunk exaggerates sobriety in movement and speech; a liar who has been caught out exaggerates his protestations of truth-telling, both in tone of VOICE and rhetoric; a self-possessed individual is less likely to resort to operatic flair or DEFENSIVENESS of an opinion or position; a teller of TALL TALES deliberately minimizes astounding or paranormal events.

Exaggeration is the "equals sign" between reality and desired effect. An individual is hungry is the reality and the hyperbolic response is, *I could eat a horse*, making the momentary hyperbole comedic, rather than humorous. A character who is hungry for power has large ambitions and an AGENDA to back them up, the behavior in both cases given a stronger sense of dramatic intensity by exaggeration. The net effect on the READER is cumulative. The reader expects the character's exaggerations to bring the character tumbling down into the pit of HUMILIATION, thus rendering the hunger for power a candidate for HUMOR or TRAGEDY.

The purpose of exaggeration is to remove it from the ordinary, continuing the dialectic between ordinary and extraordinary. Use of exaggeration alerts the reader to expect some revelation, whether in direct PLOT points or through thematic IMPLICATION. Characters who emerge as larger than life broadcast the pheromones of some inner flaw or inability to cope on some level, said flaw or inability a useful tool in producing an end result or PAYOFF.

Characters who exaggerate tend to be unreliable as narrators; characters who rely on hyperbole emerge as less than likeable; characters who are themselves exaggerations, say the protagonist of Annie Proulx's *The Shipping News*, attract our sympathy and interest because of their VULNERABILITY.

exit strategy

Dramatic design for concluding a SCENE in a NOVEL or SHORT STORY, a chapter in a novel, or an entire novel; a purposeful building of EVENT, DISCOVERY/REVELATION, and SURPRISE that will lead to a RESOLUTION in a longer work of fiction, or a significant, reflective pause in a short story.

The two key words for exit strategy are SUSPENSE and resolution. Ending a scene without one or the other tempts the reader to set the work down with limited need (curiosity) or INTENT to return. Ending a scene or chapter with suspense leaves the dramatic outcome unresolved, tempting the reader to remain, hopeful of experiencing further dramatic events, which is to say, how "things" turn out. If "things" turn out well enough to have resolved the major thrust of the story or novel, then the story or novel is ended and there is no pressing need to inject additional suspense.

In eighteenth- and nineteenth-century novels, the easy-way-out exit strategy was the trope "...and they all lived happily ever after." A notable exception, perhaps even a trendsetter exit strategy, was Huck Finn who, unwilling to be civilized, lit out for the territory. This strategy was employed midway through the twentieth century when Joseph Heller had his determined bombardier, Yossarian, set out on a hegira similar to Huck, this one toward the neutral country of Sweden.

For a time, early in the twentieth century, it seemed that all novels moved to some highly structured resolution where the murderer was revealed and justice restored, where true love was finally allowed back on track, and where all teenaged rebellions gravitated toward a sensible maturity. Simultaneously, most if not all short stories ended with a punch line, heavy irony, or a trick. But the effects of WRITERS such as Anton Chekhov, Guy de Maupassant, James Joyce, and in later years, Eudora Welty, John O'Hara, John Cheever, and Alice Munro forged the exit strategy where resolution meant something less finite, more reflective of how individuals in daily life behave as opposed to moral finality.

Thus does another burden fall on the writer, the burden of articulating a life philosophy that attends the characters and story of a given narrative, then structuring the ending to approximate an as close-to-plausible-as-possible payoff before leaving the READER with the unspoken implication that, soon enough, these characters will become involved in yet another story.

Lord Byron, the poet, observed that tragedies end with death, comedies end with marriage. Modern stories begin with the tragedy of death as it evolves into the next step in the lives of the survivors. Modern stories also begin with the humor of the romantic energy of marriage, then evolve to such mile posts as developing relationships, children, career, and aging, to name only a few. The purpose of a well-thought-out exit strategy in any story is to leave the dramatic quality of AFTERTASTE, the recurring appearance of characters after the story is ended, haunting the hallways and battlements of the reader's mind with add-on possibilities for new stories.

expectations

The results each CHARACTER foresees when venturing into a new SCENE, a guiding compass as the character is being borne along on the stream of NARRATIVE within scenes or connecting them. A character without expectations in a scene is the equivalent of the scenic backdrops found at tourist attractions, where one inserts one's head and is photographed as a comic memento.

Every character wants something; this is the passport to cross the border from joke or anecdote or vignette into the more defined landscape of STORY. Imagine such a tourist character, equipped with a fanny-pack right out of the L.L. Bean catalog. Along with that character's desire, rolled neatly and resting on top of history/BACKSTORY, ATTITUDE, and feelings about the other characters in the story are expectations. That character expects the next scene to be an occasion of achievement, boredom, surprise, humiliation, frustration, severe reversal, sexual opportunity, inspiration, or challenge. These will be delivered in such a way and by appropriate characters to send the story forward, leaving as emotional residue an identifiable counterpoint.

Expectations are the qualities that give dimension and life to story, allowing the character to do what characters are intended to do—REACT. The character need not use all the tools in the fanny-pack in every scene, except for expectations and the personal sense of having been in or lived through some situation or encounter before entering the present scene. Without these two possessions, the character is sure to be turned back at the border.

~F~

family

A group of consanguineous individuals; a single- or multi-generational unit of relatives; a non-consanguineous group who have some connective association such as an alumni group, members of a religious group, longtime members of the same work group, a heterosexual or homosexual group who have formed live-in partnerships. A family may also be a group of individuals defined by the group's boundaries. To have legal validity, a group must meet state, tribal, or national conditions, which immediately becomes STORY material, given the arbitrary nature of conditions.

Families are, for better or worse, gatherings of individuals who know one another's strengths and weaknesses, who may know SECRETS or be blind to the potential of one or more members of the extended group. Family is a petri dish for STORY, the mold of AGENDA, INTENT, control, and tradition proliferating at every gathering of the clan. Happy families may be all alike, if one could only find them somewhere, but within every family is an unhappiness that influences behavior and tradition, dictates who from the outside may enter, and what the CONSEQUENCES are of undesirables trying to marry their way in. Even families that affect a patina of happiness and closeness have somewhere within their history an ATTITUDE that leads to a substantial story. (Try Booth Tarkington's *The Magnificent Ambersons* or Philip Roth's novella, *Goodbye, Columbus,* if you need examples. Try your own; don't say you haven't already begun taking notes.)

family history

The chronicle of causal familial EVENTS that helped shape a CHARACTER; the cultural and environmental forces in which a character evolves; generational behavior and the ATTITUDES in which such behavior is viewed from within the family and from external sources.

Family is such a fertile launching pad for the definition of a character, giving TRADITIONS to be applauded as well as traditions to be shunned. A character may become a VICTIM of such tradition or a beneficiary, not to forget a martyr. If a character is informed, "All our family did their undergraduate work at Yale," and the character had hoped instead to attend The Rhode Island School of Design, might not there be a howl of CONFLICT raised? And what about the IMPLICATION that the family did undergraduate work at Yale, suggesting that a graduate school venue may be an option, but graduate school itself was more a directive?

Families are social bands dispensing tradition, learning, social and financial resources, all provided with varying degrees of love or complete lack of love. Characters may be assumed to have RESPONDED in some way—as actors in stage and film renditions respond continuously to one another—to their family origins, but also beyond their family influence in terms of wanting to break from family behavior and set out on a fresh set of responses.

Two widely differing examples of family effects on present-day characters are found in Evelyn Waugh's *Brideshead Revisited* and Jim Harrison's *Returning to Earth*. Each has as a pivotal issue the impending death of a patriarch and its CONSEQUENCES and EFFECTS on the survivors. Told from the point of view of the outsider, Charles Ryder, *Brideshead* is essentially the story of the Flyte family, who own the Brideshead estate. It involves their Catholicism and its effects on them and Charles Ryder. *Returning to Earth* focuses on the approaching death of Donald, a middle-aged man of mixed Finnish and Chippewa heritage, terminally ill with Lou Gehrig's disease. The narrative begins with Donald, who is dictating his story to his wife, Cynthia. Reminiscing on his connection with his Indian heritage, Donald recalls the influence of his father's cousin, Flower, on him. "Flower shook my brain like one of her many rattles hanging from the rafters of her tar paper shack." Each of these authors is remarkable in a specific way, deft in the ability to describe the reverberations of family into the dance the individual members have with life.

Hint: Members of a family might not agree on the accuracy or actual meaning of any family event not of their own writing. This is true in real life, and it is fertile ground for CONFLICT for the WRITER.

fantasy

A NOVEL or STORY in which magical, supernatural, and preternatural elements are presented as though they were real; narratives in which ALTERNATE UNIVERSES, mythic creatures, imaginary worlds, and extraordinary mental and physical abilities prevail; stories involving clashes of power between rival forces who have rival thematic AGENDAS; stories built on the consequences of spells, curses, and charms.

Ever since Alice (of Wonderland fame) fell into the rabbit hole, fantasy WRITERS have capitalized on the PORTAL or entry way into worlds of their own creation, worlds where often enough there may be intended comparisons between individuals, institutions, and places in the real world. These are worlds where magic—abilities that extend beyond the boundaries of reality—flourishes, but just as contemporary pharmaceuticals do, the magic has a known list of side effects: spells do not last indefinitely, curses may exact a reaction onto the curse giver, and such desirable abilities as invisibility have strict time limits. Even in fantasy worlds, rules apply; the writer makes up the rules, but then must adhere to them. To have a character successfully break a magical rule, or to simply make up another rule on the spur of the moment to help a character get out of a jam is to toy with and irritate a READER who has suspended disbelief in a major way to enjoy the fantasy and will rightfully feel cheated.

Portals have led readers and, of course, CHARACTERS to antique shops, restaurants, bookstores, even pawn brokers. The consequence of such visits becomes manifest when the PROTAGONIST of the story attempts to return to the venue of the portal.

Fantasy worlds often parallel the real universe in most details except for those one or two of the author's choice. Thus in Rachel Maddux's short story "Final Clearance," written during the days of Congressional hearings and loyalty oaths, the payoff comes in the form of a recently dead atomic scientist being denied actual death because of a failed security clearance. In one form or another, fantasy has been with us since there was a spoken language; it plays a significant part in, for instance, *Gilgamesh*, which has fantasy themes revisited in *The Iliad* and even more so in *The Odyssey*, where it is often used as a metaphor. The contemporary writer, Ursula K. LeGuin, has written a short story, "Horse Camp," in which two sisters, Sal and Norah, along with a friend, Ev, go to horse camps during the summer and are transformed into equines. In yet another of her fantasies, "The Professor's Houses," there is a thematic COUNTERPOINT between the house where the professor lives and a dollhouse he has made for his young daughter. In her novel *The Language of the Night*, LeGuin has done for fantasy what Stephen King has done for horror in *Danse Macabre*, which is to provide a historical background and rationale for each genre, a trampoline on which wannabe fantasy and horror writers may jump with palpable results.

Just as the historical story has evolved and allowed for the mixing of genres such as historical thriller, historical mystery, historical juvenile, etc., so too has fantasy become a pairing genre, often seen as magical realism (see any work by Alice Hoffman). This mixture easily extends to work that is by any account considered "literature," Robertson Davies's *The Rebel Angels* being a significant example.

Hint: Check out the pulp fantasy magazine, *Weird Tales*. Also of seminal interest to fantasy writers as a source of inspiration, Philip Pullman's *His Dark Materials* series, and the near-iconic Harry Potter books.

Additional hint: Start with a short story in the works, then add to it one magical element, keeping everything else as grounded in realistic detail as possible.

Yet another hint: Do not ever forget *The Wizard of Oz*, which is not only pure fantasy, it is a paradigm for the structure of a novel, as Margaret Atwood points out in an essay in which she shows the connection between Richard Powers's literary tour de force, *The Echo Maker*, and *The Wizard*.

farce

A dramatic subset of COMEDY in which the PACE and physical action intensify to the point of COMBUSTION; plot-driven circumstances which accelerate to the point where CHARACTERS cannot adequately cope with them.

An appropriate analogy for farce is the now legendary stateroom scene from the Marx Brothers film, *A Night at the Opera*. Another good analogy is what results when a professional juggler drops the dishes he has in motion and is now surrounded by broken china. The dramatic BEATS begin to come faster, adding a surreal note to the already comedic, physical atmosphere of the action, causing language and gestures that turn up the heat, leading to one final, uproarious explosion.

Farce may appear in any STORY, coming as a SURPRISE, appearing when the READER least expects it but where, appropriately, the building tension of the story is growing more intense. Depending on the length of the story and the WRITER's ultimate GOAL for the CONCLUSION, the whole NARRATIVE may have the atmosphere of farce. As an example, thanks to adroit use of farcical elements such as one or two OVER-THE TOP scenes, Evelyn Waugh's satire *The Loved One* moves into farce.

Farce may rise above mere jokes, pie throwing, and slipping on banana peels, even while using BURLESQUE settings and techniques. For all its antic, zany humor, Neil Simon's *The Sunshine Boys* has a strong texture of PLAUSIBILITY.

As with its cousin, HUMOR, the intent of farce is to reduce some target by RIDICULE. Just as humor may well appear suddenly within a tragic or lofty narrative, so too may farce slip in the back door to work its effects. The goal of humor is the exposure of some painful truth or awareness. Farce aims further below the belt, wanting not only to destroy or render dignity inoperative but to inflict some damage on the furniture as well.

For the history-minded, Georges Feydeau (1862-1921), the French playwright, is generally considered to be the quintessential modern farceur, *A Flea in Her Ear* being one of the more legible and instructive examples.

Complex PLOTS, mistaken identities, and misunderstandings are salient ingredients of farce, making such diverse examples as Oscar Wilde's *The Importance of Being Ernest*, Noel Coward's *Blythe Spirit*, and yes, even Michael Chabon's *The Wonder Boys* arguable candidates for the farce hall of fame.

fatal flaw

A physical or psychological trait given a CHARACTER; a handicap that informs the behavior of a character in a NOVEL or SHORT STORY; the Ugly Duckling writ large, the more-intelligent-than-others writ small; an often-imagined deficiency experienced by a front-rank CHARACTER that is, in fact, often not noticed by others.

If he'd been fashioned with a nose of ordinary length and configuration, Cyrano might well not have had to enlist Christian to act on his love for Roxanne, but the forces that shaped him (and his nose) also had undeniable effect on his way with words as well as his way with a sword. And to look at the flaw of the inner person, let's suppose Macbeth had been content to accept the promotion from King Malcolm and let it go with being Thane of

Cawdor, or that Miss Rebecca Sharp had not been so, shall we say, upwardly mobile. What then of *Macbeth* or *Vanity Fair?* We could also look at Antigone and her determination to bury her brother, but just as well we can look at her uncle, who is determined that Antigone's brother not be buried. Without the willfulness of uncle and niece, Antigone would not have been put to death, seriously undercutting the impact of the story.

John Steinbeck notably applied the fatal flaw to Tom Joad, a paroled murderer, in *The Grapes of Wrath,* and even more notably to the characters of Lennie and George in *Of Mice and Men.* Lennie is big, powerful, and simpleminded; George is small, quick-witted, a bit of a martyr. He has become Lennie's protector and in so doing has mortgaged his own ambition of becoming a rancher.

The flaw, whether the inner one of psychological origin or the outer flaw of injury or GROWTH or general appearance, literally affects the direction and outcome of the story, and as an adjunct, the READER'S reaction to the afflicted character. From the beginning of Ken Kesey's *One Flew over the Cuckoo's Nest*, we are presented with a self-serving PROTAGONIST, Randle P. McMurphy, whom we see using his feigned mental state to avoid incarceration in a prison. We watch him warily to see where his game will take him, in the process buying into the process of GROWTH. We know from experience in reading that characters in a novel cannot stand still—they either go forward or spiral downward. McMurphy's fatal flaw becomes his compassion, his empathy, which trumps his own self-serving pleasures and extends to his fellow inmates.

Joe Buck and Enrico "Ratso" Rizzo come steamrolling out of James Leo Herlihy's *Midnight Cowboy* with fatal flaws, Buck's being a romantic naïveté similar to Emma Bovary's, Rizzo's a one-two punch of a leg crippled by polio and an incipient consumptive cough. As in the explosive ending of *Cuckoo*, the payoff of *Cowboy* provides a plausible-but-unexpected flash of warmth and light for the survivor and, however uncomfortably, for the reader. The novel is about characters orbiting to resolution, which is defined by growth. The fatal flaws are inertial forces, propelling the characters to their release-through-understanding or their descent into a relinquishing of the POWER to rescue themselves. Writers inflict fatal flaws upon some characters in order to inject the explosive emotions of epiphany and awareness into the STORY.

fear

An essential emotional presence needed to affect the needed vision in writing, acting, music, and visual renditions. Fear comes after the idea begins to emerge, precisely when the executor is poised and ready to execute the words or performance or visions; it is the fear of having overreached this time, not having suitable technique to accomplish the vision. Without fear, the resulting performance would be variously rote, boring, and safe. Without fear there can be no DISCOVERY. Without discovery, writing becomes reportage, acting becomes mimicry, music becomes mechanical, visual renditions become parody.

Fear comes to CHARACTERS when they await the CONSEQUENCES of past ACTIONS or when they contemplate future actions. As all powerful emotions do, fear causes afflicted characters to behave in out-of-the-ordinary ways.

In Pat Conroy's remarkable novel *The Great Santini,* the young protagonist asks his Marine Corps fighter pilot father, "Are you ever afraid of anything when you fly?" The father, Lt. Col. Bull Meecham, replies, "Yeah. I'm always a little afraid when I fly. That's what makes me so damn good. I've seen pilots who weren't afraid of anything, who would forget about checking their instruments, who flew by instinct as though they were immortal. I've pissed on the graves of those poor bastards, too. The pilot who isn't afraid always screws up..."

Be afraid. Fear is a good thing. It encourages writing about unsafe things.

first-person narrative

A form of DRAMATIC NARRATIVE in which an individual using the pronoun I becomes the filter through which the events of the drama are related.

The first-person format represents the author's appointed agent to relate the details of a fictional history. It became popular at a time when READERS believed the NARRATOR was relating actual EVENTS in actual SETTINGS, a belief that resurfaced during the middle years of the twentieth century when a confession-romance literature of I-narratives found MASS MARKET magazine audiences.

The first-person narrator may play a direct role in the STORY being related, in which case he or she becomes the individual in whom the READER invests emotional and psychological capital, a notable example being the eponymous narrator of Saul Bellow's *The Adventures of Augie March.* The first-person narrator may also play an ancillary role in the story, such as Nick Caraway in F. Scott Fitzgerald's *The Great Gatsby,* a presence used to good example by the author as it became apparent that Caraway was being exploited by the major focus, Gatsby.

As with all other points of view, the WRITER must endow the first-person narrator with enough quirks, obstacles, relevant background, and GOALS to provide a distinct personality, including but not limited to vocabulary, a place on the optimism/pessimism scale, prejudices and antipathies, and a history with some relevance to the story at hand.

After constructing the platform of ATTITUDES and GOALS for the first-person narrator, the writer must then quantify a place for the character on the naïve scale, in which the writer assesses how relatively naïve or realistic the character is. The NAÏVE NARRATOR does not see individuals and events the same way as cynical or realistic narrators might, thus does interpretation become an important factor in the forces driving the first-person narrator.

One of the stated technical disadvantages for having a first-person narrator is the need for that individual to appear in every SCENE in order to be able with plausibility to relate the scene to the reader. With a little thought, the writer will see through this limitation by, for example, allowing the narrator to be "off stage" at a particular event, then hear the details of the event from one or more other characters. This limitation may also extend well into the past by having the first person narrator encounter diaries, journals, or newspaper accounts of an event that took place earlier.

Hint: Try burying the "I" in the midst of sentences and paragraphs in order to keep it from popping up at the reader like weeds in a sidewalk.

Two splendid examples of first-person narrative are Charles Dickens's *Great Expectations* and Mark Twain's *Huckleberry Finn*, each of which has survived the Still-Readable-and-Inspiring-After-A-Hundred-Years-in-Print test, and one of the most enduring opening lines in a novel, "Call me Ishmael," had to have been written in first person because Ishmael was the only survivor of the ill-fated Pequod.

Critics, editors, and teachers are divided over the appropriateness of first-person narrative; it is an idiosyncratic call, best answered by listening to the characters, who should have a hand in the decision of their being rendered as I rather than he or she. The true test to be applied to a character is the plausibility that character presents to the reader as narrator.

first-draft strategy

A working gambit for securing a MANUSCRIPT of a project that seems at first blush to be complete; the result of saying what you have to say about a dramatic situation before undertaking REVISION; a deliberate experiment in rendering a narrative through the filter of a particular POINT OF VIEW; the exhaustion of the conceptual energy that brings a STORY or story CONCEPT to mind in the first place.

The primary strategy for the first draft is to realize that other drafts will be necessary, each being powered by its own energy (which is likely to differ from any previous energy). The systematized process of revision may well begin with a decision about the point of view, followed with investigation of BEGINNING and ENDING points. After CHRONOLOGY is decided, the MIDDLE POINT may provide occasion for choice, followed by a review of the CHARACTERS, their GOALS, movements, what they say, and to whom.

WRITERS at all stages of development may find themselves at a momentary brick wall, unable to continue work even though there is available time in the writing schedule. At such a point, if forty-five minutes elapse with no clue emerging, move on to the next SCENE, leaving a simple Post-It note to identify the intent of the unwritten segment: Sex scene goes here; Bill confronts Fred about missing bank statements; Phyllis confronts Fred about getting a job. Subsequent drafts may reveal that the missing scene would not appear for the writer because it was not necessary in the first place.

This approach is for writers who set forth to discover the ARC of the story as they work or who have a particular ending in mind toward which they choose to build.

For the writer who works from OUTLINE, the ideal first-draft strategy is a list of scenes or a set of index cards with a key phrase for each scene, arranged in what appears to be the most fruitful order.

There is a middle ground between the Discoverer writer and the Outliner: Move forward as quickly as possible, without stopping to think. When you hit a brick wall or pause point, think out a new complication, OBSTACLE, REVERSAL, or news of some off-stage event that will have effect on the story. Compose until that point before stopping or make sufficient notes to carry you to that point.

Most writers will agree that a writing session ends best when the text has reached a need for a CHOICE, DECISION, challenge, or review of options. Ending at such a point will keep the writing part of the mind working on the next session through and during sleep, daytime job, and personal to-do lists.

One of the many great myths surrounding writing has it that really gifted writers such as Louise Erdrich, William Trevor, Annie Proulx, and T.C. Boyle are presented with the fully developed idea every time they sit down to write, no assembly required. Only one draft necessary. Read their interviews. Take note of the number of drafts they discuss.

fish in a barrel

A metaphor for removing the need for skill in a contest or competition; tilting the conditions of a confrontation to a degree that insures easy solution; purging the doubt of final outcome from a dramatic NARRATIVE, thus an easy outcome from an endeavor.

This trope is an important one for the WRITER to remember. READERS do not want—cannot abide—results that come too easily. Even now, in the twenty-first century, there are those who think David got off too easily in his "contest" with Goliath, whom they try, in their revisionist history of the legendary sling-shot event, to represent as given over to HUBRIS. Readers respect and admire skill and cunning, but they want these qualities to bring results after some pattern of trial and error. The scientist should not be allowed to come forth with a cure for cancer after spending only a week or two in the lab; she should have some added burden or incentive as a goal or as part of an emotional partnership approaching that of Captain Ahab and Moby-Dick or Santiago and the great marlin.

The actual phrase, "shooting fish in a barrel," has many possible meanings, beginning with the obvious question: *Is there any water in the barrel?* Fish in a waterless barrel would likely be dead, making them a stationary target for the shooter. If there were indeed water in the barrel, discharging a gun into it would probably kill all the fish, thanks to the reverberation of sound. The common denominator in the concept is the absolute ease of outcome. The applicable dramatic denominator here is: Never take the READER where the reader wants to go, which is to say make things such as RISK, misunderstanding, REVERSAL, and SURPRISE exponentially more likely to join the party as the story progresses.

A fish-in-a-barrel NARRATIVE is one in which the GOAL was not exquisite enough or was achieved too quickly and/or too easily, leaving some doubt in the reader's mind whether it was actually a "real" story or merely a SHAGGY-DOG STORY. When a reader comes upon a STORY where some stated goal is achieved early on, the reader intuits the sinister hand of CONSEQUENCES, reaching metaphorically out to bring big-time complication raining down on the protagonist. The reader waits for these complicating consequences and, if they are not delivered, the reader experiences, at best, disappointment.

Thomas Hardy rode into the twentieth century with a number of anti-fish-in-a-barrel novels, most notable among them being *Jude, the Obscure*, in which the protagonist had a specific goal for which he was emotionally and intellectually qualified and which, had Horatio Alger been the author, Jude would have at last achieved. But Hardy was Hardy, and Jude's seemingly reasonable goal met some fatal complications.

Something has to be given up, lost, or at least tempered before the goal is achieved, an observation that can lead to the IRONIC ending comparison between what has been gained and the price paid to achieve it. Not all endings are or need be ironic, yet it is nice to know that IRONY is there, waiting to be invited in.

flash fiction

SHORT STORIES or vignettes of fewer than seven hundred fifty words; preternaturally short fiction pieces, often with an arbitrary word limit; a prose NARRATIVE conspicuously shorter than the conventional short form. Earlier referred to as the short-short story or, on occasion, sudden fiction, flash fiction generally trumps plot over character; thus it is more apt to have an ironic payoff or some observable turn in which the protagonist is blown up by his own device. On occasion such stories can have a resonant frequency that makes them memorable. They are attractive for editors who can then use three or four of these for every story of a conventional length (say 3500 to 6500 words). *The Novel and Short Story Writer's Market*, available in February or March of each year, lists publications that welcome submissions of this word length. At the time of this writing, a Google query for "flash fiction" submissions produced thousands of results.

The downside of flash-fiction ventures is that because of their formulaic overload or their tendency to the punchline type of ending, they emerge sounding like a joke. Much is made of a six-word short story allegedly contributed by Ernest Hemingway, "For Sale, baby shoes, never used." By default it has become the high watermark for the medium, but the greater likelihood is that the story about Hemingway having written such a tale is without foundation.

It may help a WRITER of short stories to attempt to characterize a particular story by its length, and it is a help for the storyteller to have to learn how to use language as though it were a precision tool, but these two factors, even if used in concert, do not guarantee a successful story. The better approach is to write early drafts long, then cut them short.

flashback

A NARRATIVE device that brings the forward movement of a STORY to a screeching halt as the action shifts to a past time, in which a relevant SCENE is replayed. Flashback is a way of using a given narrator's sensitivity to reflect back on a past EVENT as though it were taking place before the READER now.

Largely archaic because of the universal discovery of the two-line space break separating one SCENE from another, the flashback is no longer necessary; the dramatic UNITIES to the contrary notwithstanding, no contemporary dramatic decree or convention argues the need for a STORY of any length running in absolute CHRONOLOGY.

Scene B, directly following Scene A, may have taken place fifty years in the past, a shift the reader can easily accommodate provided the WRITER gives a simple, basic clue of when and where Scene B is in progress.

When in doubt: Action in the contemporary NOVEL or SHORT STORY ought to take place more in the present moment than in past reflections or flashback.

foreshadowing

A technique by which a person, place, thing, trait, or concept is introduced in a casual way for later moments of expansion and exploitation; the deliberate avoidance of bringing up a detail without the need for stopping the NARRATIVE to explain its RELEVANCE to the STORY.

As much as READERS enjoy, even look forward to SURPRISE, they especially enjoy the sense of a smoothly progressing NARRATIVE, one that allows them to proceed without asking, *What blue jacket?* Rather, it is possible for them to agree, Oh, right, Mary's favorite blue jacket, the one she always wears on such occasions. Explanations of key events, objects, or persons seem less likely to have been dropped in conveniently if they have been foreshadowed.

Whenever a particular noun (person, place, thing), attitude, or detail has enough importance in a narrative to support a BEAT, that noun, attitude, or detail is best served by being introduced in a foreshadowing MOMENT. Surprise in this context must be watched to see that it is plausible surprise, one that maintains the WILLING SUSPENSION OF DISBELIEF.

formula

The recipe or pattern for a STORY that becomes a means of linking READER expectations with a plausible outcome; a NARRATIVE device for producing accelerated risk and subsequent resolution.

Some examples of formula in story:

1. A sympathetic CHARACTER struggles against great odds to achieve a worthwhile GOAL.
2. Characters sin, suffer, and repent.
3. Something happens and someone changes.
4. A journey and/or quest produces unexpected results.
5. A stranger arrives.

The operating factor in formula is a degree of predictability that runs parallel to READER EXPECTATIONS in GENRE fiction; if you add element A, the reader will expect element B as a CONSEQUENCE, thus formula makes the READER less vulnerable to the possibility of SURPRISE. When a narrative is spoken of as formulaic it likely means the speaker believes the work to be predictable, suggesting the need somewhere in the process for the WRITER and characters to collude against the expectations of the reader. Narratives that are considered non-formulaic are often those that end with a resolving force that veers sharply from EXPECTATIONS, as in Thomas Berger's *Little Big Man*.

But there is another way to look at formula. Often conflated with PLOT, formula is THEME based, traceable from culture to culture throughout human history. It is myth as discussed in abundant detail by Joseph Campbell, as well as the archetypes that have arisen from myth, including the trickster who recurs in such diverse cultures as Native American and in the persona of Captain Spaulding (Groucho Marx). Other widespread themes: Man against Nature, Man against machinery, Man against convention.

Bottom line: To hear that a story is formulaic is not a compliment, but to use formula in the service of story is cultural.

fourth wall, the

The boundary between READER and CHARACTERS; a conceptual enhancement of the illusion of the audience eavesdropping on characters in the midst of STORY; a convention observed by authors for the purpose of implying that their activity is happening now, in real time.

A character in a NOVEL or stage play who addresses the audience is said to be breaking the fourth wall, which by implication extends the three sides of a stage setting to the remaining dimension, the space between players and audience. The convention of the fourth wall is as old as storytelling, a given that has produced memorable breaches.

As far back in time as Greek drama, characters were breaking the fourth wall by addressing the audience. Even before poems, plays, and STORIES were set in movable type and printed on a press, Geoffrey Chaucer was imaginatively breaking the fourth wall in his *Wordes Unto Adam, His Owne Scriveyn,* by telling his scribe to copy his lines with care, avoiding the skewing of Chaucer's intended meter by using regional spelling and accent marks. Shakespeare would later have his characters break the wall with asides to the audience, including preludes in which a chorus would directly address the audience. In his film version of Shakespeare's *Richard III*, Laurence Olivier had Richard directly tell the audience what his main agenda was. In eighteenth-, nineteenth-, and twentieth-century NOVELS, numerous authors spoke directly to the audience in some manner, examples being Henry Fielding's frequent asides to the reader in *Tom Jones*, Rudyard Kipling actually addressing his daughter in the *Just So Stories,* and James Michener addressing the reader in the opening chapter of *Hawaii.*

The major objection to fourth-wall violations is the argument of broken reality; a broken wall is thought to be an advertisement that the STORY is illusory, distanced from any connection with reality, to which it may be argued that the nature of the story, the manner in which the characters interact and respond to the dramatic situations are all factors contributing to the VERISIMILITUDE or sense of reality the writer strives to achieve.

Use of the intrusive authorial point of view is a constant shattering of the fourth wall. Some of the modernists (Donald Barthelme and Italo Calvino come to mind) may evoke the amusing conflation of Ronald Reagan's exhortation to Mr. Gorbachev, "Tear down this [the Berlin] Wall," with the ghost of the elder Hamlet haunting the battlements to enlist his son in his desire for revenge. Shall the fourth wall come down? Only if it has to.

It is a truth universally recognized that literary conventions arose in the first place in response to some technical impasse but now await artful trespass. If breaking the fourth wall in a NOVEL or SHORT STORY serves a purpose that will make the narrative more effective, then break away with clear conscience. The only valid reason for not breaking the fourth wall or, for that matter, for not breaking any convention is if doing so will seem more an act of anarchy or pretentiousness than a contribution to the artistic, emotional, and intellectual payoff of the narrative.

(See WILLING SUSPENSION OF DISBELIEF, PLAUSIBILITY, and CONVENTION.)

frame

The method of placing a STORY or EPISODE within a larger, organized or thematic format such as *The Decameron* or *The Canterbury Tales*, where it becomes a segment of a whole; to base a new story on the CHARACTERS and PLOT of a previously published work. The "framed tale" concept is an advertisement for a MULTIPLE POINT OF VIEW narration.

James Thurber's memorable short story "The Man in the Cat Bird Seat" is another variation on the device of framing, duplicating the revenge concept that inspired Poe's "A Cask of Amontillado." Motion picture director and novelist Paul Mazursky framed an imaginative modern version of Shakespeare's play, *The Tempest*, while yet another version of that play was framed for television, casting the dramatic events at the time of the American Civil War. Katherine Anne Porter's novel *Ship of Fools* returns us to the stories-within-a-story concept; it bears comparison to *The Canterbury Tales* in its use of a broad segment of national, social, and moral types, bound together in transit from one destination to another.

frame-tale format

A NARRATIVE or series of separate STORIES built about an INCIDENT, a historical moment, or THEME; a single or multiple narrative constructed with recognition of an earlier work; a staging or formulating device for the presentation of a group of stories within a single story.

Thus *Tales of Scheherazade*, or *One Thousand and One Nights*, a series of stories told by a young woman to a misanthropic Persian king who had the habit of marrying a new wife every day while beheading yesterday's candidate. Thus also *The Decameron*, in which a group of young nobles, moved to the country to escape the ravages of The Black Death plague, told stories to amuse themselves. From his awareness of these and other frame tales comes Geoffrey Chaucer's *Canterbury Tales*, stories of individuals on a religious pilgrimage. Off in another part of the world comes the frame tale of the *Rashomon* stories, where a single event is replayed to reflect the point of view of the participants, illustrating, as Chaucer did in *The Canterbury Tales*, a significant view of the human condition from various vantage points on the social scale—a view which, by the way, has remained constant over the millennia.

In more modern times, the frame tale has become ubiquitous; it appears in such forms as James Joyce's *Ulysses*, studiously framed on *The Odyssey*, Clint McCown's short story collection *The Member-Guest*, dealing with a weekend golf tournament in a down-at-the-heels country club in the Midwest, and Pam Huston's achingly hilarious collection *Cowboys Are My Weakness*, which is a variation on the theme of women being drawn to men who are more drawn to a particular lifestyle than to a particular relationship.

Not to forget the memorable cattle-drive theme of the motion picture

Red River, which was framed on the seagoing *Mutiny on the Bounty,* or the Coen Brothers' film *Brother Where Art Thou?*, which shows yet another variation on *The Odyssey.* To return to a prime example used in FRAME above, Katherine Anne Porter's 1962 novel, *The Ship of Fools,* is framed on a 1494 narrative, *The Ship of Fools* by Sebastian Brant; aspects of Porter's novel could also be argued to link to Hieronymus Bosch's painting *The Ship of Fools,* which Bosch admitted to have come from the Brant narrative. It is a likely and lively comparison to argue the connection between Porter's *Ship of Fools* and *The Decameron.*

The frame-tale format adds another layer of thematic connective tissue between the newer version and the original, the two versions becoming linked in the READER's mind—if the reader is aware of the source. As previously pointed out, however, the more recent version of a framed tale must stand on its own dramatic merits, as though the reader had no previous knowledge of the original. The motion picture *Shakespeare in Love* has a richer level of significance for those familiar with *Twelfth Night* and the conditions of the English theater in which young boys performed the roles of women characters. The reader familiar with Shakespeare would know that the character of Viola in *Twelfth Night* was performed by a boy, leading to the conceit in *Shakespeare in Love* of a young woman masquerading as a boy in order to win the role of a woman in a play, "causing" Shakespeare to "see" the inspiration for *Twelfth Night.*

The doors of imagination fly open to admit possible entrants for future frame-tale circumstances. What thoughts were dancing in the mind of Ray Bradbury when he got down to work positing the concept of a tattooed man in a circus—a tattooed man whose very tattoos came to life, each demanding its own story? What thoughts later danced in the mind of Mario Vargas Llosa, whose *Aunt Julia and the Script Writer* becomes another excellent example of exciting ways to tell stories within a larger story by writing about a WRITER of daily soap operas?

frustration
The emotional response to the blocking of an AGENDA or GOAL as a major player in motivating STORY; the awareness in a CHARACTER of the lack of POWER to perform a motivated behavior; a triggering device for aggression or passive-aggressive behavior.

Characters in fiction frequently find themselves with frustration as a pole star, alternately inflicting it and being victim to its CONSEQUENCES. Given the nature of dramatic writing, frustration is the leavening agent in STORY, motivating PROTAGONISTS to take steps to slog through its quicksand-like impediment, motivating ANTAGONISTS to step up their behavior.

If a story line appears to be faltering, add more frustration in the form of

REVERSAL or SURPRISE. Keep the goal to which the main character aspires in sight but just beyond reach. An out-of-sight goal may be forgotten or trumped; a goal within reach may be moved or shattered or stolen.

As an illustration of the far-reaching effects and landing sites of frustration, consider the universal desire to be understood, then recall the comedies and tragedies in which two individuals, believing they have the same goal in mind, begin to act upon that belief only to encounter the reefs and shoals of awareness that they have completely misunderstood one another. Thus dramatic IRONY, the bedfellow of frustration, is brought into the story.

fun

An engulfing sense of pleasure, transmitting itself outward from the CHARACTERS, and then, through their behavior, to the READER; a condition of being transported into a zone of carefree, sensuous, and intellectual awareness by a combination of stimuli; an antidote to boredom, depression, or gloom; what writing should be for the reader and the WRITER.

A number of writers, enormously skilled and well-progressed in the development of their talent, neither suicidal nor given to depression, emerge as serious, argumentative, perhaps even gloomy. Philip Roth and Joyce Carol Oates come to mind. Nevertheless, these writers all continue at their writing efforts because not doing so would produce a sense of disconnect with the inner LANDSCAPE they strive at such effort to achieve. No matter what one may think, they are having fun while they are working.

Writing is hard work, but the mere fact of its difficulty should not and does not preclude the results of its being fun for the writer as well as the reader. Fun appears when an individual becomes interested and involved in the work at hand. In his philosophical treatise, *The Myth of Sisyphus,* published in English in 1955, Albert Camus argued that Sisyphus, given his ordained task, was nevertheless a happy man, a judgment to give us pause. How, we wonder, can an eternity of performing a meaningless task make the performer happy? And if Sisyphus is happy, does that mean he is having fun?

The nature of writing produces FRUSTRATION in the writer, primarily because of the difficulty in translating the vision of the project into words that do it sufficient justice. In a real sense, writers (and artists of any sort, for that matter) are doomed to the frustration of "not getting it right," which is to say not rendering the vision well enough to suit them. This is fun? Well, yes; it is. Like Sisyphus, you take pleasure in lending your skills to a task that appears hopeless from the get-go, leaving you in the same mind set as Samuel Beckett, who said, "Fail again, only next time fail better."

Every time we read a poem, a SHORT STORY, or NOVEL that moves us in some primal way, our exquisite response blazes across the night sky of our imagination like a firefly, intense, brief, and gone. In its place, to extend a mixed metaphor, we are faced with the vision of the ceiling of the Sistine Chapel, handed a packet of crayons, then told, "Go, thou, and do likewise." And yet, some of us will do just that, diving into the project to the point of losing the hopelessness of the task, seeing connections, possibilities, opportunities. The last part of that equation is fun in action. Like the life of the firefly, it is intense and brief. It is the writer's job to keep it from being gone.

Elmore Leonard, a writer who knows a thing or two about having fun, has shone his light into the darkness. "Only write the scenes that interest you," he has said. This dictum could well be studied alongside Camus's *The Myth of Sisyphus* for its implications. But what of practical considerations? There is a particular scene that you don't feel like writing. A literary agent and/or editor *wants* that particular scene in place before the manuscript can progress toward publication. The answer: find a way to make yourself like the scene. Do something to it and the characters within it to make the writing of it become not a chore but fun. What attitudes did Sisyphus need to allow him to take pleasure from what would seem a hopeless, eternal exercise of rote behavior? How could he, of all people, think to fail better next time? Are the Karma Yogis—work as worship—having fun? And what about that remarkable line from the Bhagavad Gita, "To the work you are entitled, but not the fruits thereof…"? Surely there is flat-out fun to be had from adopting such an attitude and taking such approaches.

~G~

genre

A term referring to the various categories of FICTION; specific niche-fiction shelving in bookstores and libraries; defining characteristics of a particular type of fiction.

READERS approach fiction variously for escape, entertainment, inspiration, distraction, and other similar mind- and spirit-enriching reasons. The common denominator for all readers is the understanding that the CHARACTERS and SITUATIONS are invented, products of a WRITER'S imagination. This common denominator extends to include the READER'S FIRST EXPECTATION, that the reader will be given sufficient reasons to suspend disbelief, in other words to forget that the characters and situations are unreal, thereupon to consider them as though they were real and then to empathize with them.

The READER'S SECOND EXPECTATION is that the specific categories or genres will contain but not necessarily be limited to specific circumstances, COMPLICATIONS, conditions, emphasis focus, and formulas.

Here are some of the more prevalent fiction genres and what readers expect from them:

ADVENTURE NOVELS and STORIES: Individuals at accelerated risk and danger.

CHICK LIT: Young women protagonists confronting sexuality, shopping, romance, careers, friendship.

Chivalric Romance: Men on horses fighting dragons, wicked royalty, and their own sexual urges as they pursue Lady Right.

Comic Novel: Imagine Ivanhoe of chivalric romance fame, riding off into the sunset with Rebecca on his horse instead of Rowena. Imagine also Chris Buckley, thanking us for smoking, or of everything that other Chris, Moore, writes.

Crime Novel: One or more murders have been or will be committed—now someone has to find out who's doing it and why. The "someone" occasions subgenres such as private investigators, sworn police officers, little old ladies, large young ladies, park rangers, process servers, innocent civilians, etc.

Erotic Literature: Individuals of both genders attempting to get laid with a modicum of originality, told in evocative prose.

Fables, Fairy Tales, and Folklore: Individuals are portrayed who never actually existed, but they provide a moral or an insight or even a laugh, to repay the time put forth reading about them.

Historical Fiction: Story set in a particular period in time, reflecting the details, manners, and customs of that time. May include actual historical personages, either as PROTAGONISTS or in cameo roles.

Literary Fiction: Story having to do with moral choices, philosophical issues, mankind as a species adapting to the social and ethical challenges that confront it.

Picaresque: A more-episodic-than-plotted story in which a rogue, scoundrel, con-person, deluded or intelligence-challenged person sets forth on a mission (which is usually to seek a fortune, his own or someone else's). You could consider James Leo Herlihy's *Midnight Cowboy* in this category.

Political Novel: One or more of the major players is a politician or an insider watching politicians as they behave. George Orwell's *1984* is political as well as speculative and cautionary, demonstrating yet other genre. Robert Penn Warren's *All the King's Men* is political as well as biographical. Allan Drury's *Advise and Consent* takes its title from the U.S. Constitution and involves a number of U.S. Senators in action.

Romance Novel: A youngish woman who is often more attractive then she realizes is forced to make romantic choices.

Speculative Fiction: Story that portrays an if-things-continue-the-way-they're-going scenario; utopian or dystopian views of as-yet-unrealized outcomes. Margaret Atwood's *The Handmaid's Tale*, George Orwell's *1984*, and Philip Roth's *The Plot Against America* are speculative; so is Robert Heinlein's *A Stranger in a Strange Land* and, indeed, Ray Bradbury's *Fahrenheit 451*.

Alternate History: Story that rewrites actual history, then improvises on what the result might bring. See Len Deighton's *SS/GB* and Ward Moore's *Bring the Jubilee* in which, respectively, Germany won World War II and the Confederate States of America won the U.S. War Between the States.

Fantasy: Story in which magic is a key element. May also involve alternate universes, which are accessed through a portal such as the rabbit hole into which young Alice fell. A subgenre of fantasy has one or more individuals being transformed by magic into an other-than-human form. Yet another subgenre involves a quest for an object which is the power source of magic, such as the sword which only Arthur can withdraw from the stone in which it was embedded.

Horror: The intentional portrayal of events that will seriously frighten the reader. See Stephen King's work for any number of good role models.

Science Fiction: An extrapolation on actual scientific reality, extended to expand the dramatic, emotional, and moral landscape in the world as we know it or in imaginary worlds where most of the conditions we recognize exist in some modified form. Science fiction may use either the "hard" sciences such as chemistry, geology, or astronomy, or extrapolate on the so-called social sciences ranging from anthropology to political science.

Thriller: The clock is ticking, the metronome is hurrying the pace along, and the good guys are, seemingly, in over their heads in a mismatch against a hugely powerful opponent.

Conspiracy Fiction: "They"—whoever they may be—are against "us"—whoever we may be—in a paranoid scenario come to life. See Richard Condon's *The Manchurian Candidate* as a prime example, but see also the screen version of *The Verdict*, David Mamet's screenplay adaptation of Barry Reed's novel in which a down-at-the heels lawyer, superbly played by Paul Newman, goes up against a particular "them." This genre perhaps began with Erskine Childers's still-compelling novel *The Riddle of the Sands*, followed by Graham Greene's *The Ministry of Fear*. Lest the genre sound too pulpy, consider Thomas Pynchon's *The Crying of Lot 49* and Umberto Eco's brilliant spoof, *Foucault's Pendulum*, by way of injecting literary tropes into the text.

Legal Thriller: Bright young attorney goes up against prestigious firm with unlimited resources to tip the scales of justice in favor of an underdog client; fading, possibly alcoholic attorney scores a courtroom triumph, once again proving that justice will out. The deck in legal thrillers is always stacked against the good guys.

Psychological Thriller: Is the narrator psychotic or merely naïve? Are the inmates running the asylum? Will the bright young psychiatrist break through the catatonic seizures of the targeted character? What about Richard Powers's penetrating dive into what an ego actually is via *The Echo Maker*? If ever there were a rich example of a genre, both literary and thrilling in its implications, this is it. Unless, of course, you wish to consult Jonathan Lethem's *Motherless Brooklyn,* in which the private-eye genre and the psychological thriller meet up in a back alley somewhere. The protagonist in *Motherless Brooklyn* is a PI who is afflicted with Tourette's syndrome, a fact that may or may not trump Powers's protagonist, who is diagnosed with Capgras syndrome.

Spy Fiction: Betrayals, double-dealing, and covert operatives being lured into death traps, sometimes by alluring ladies wearing tightly belted trench coats, sometimes by alluring young ladies wearing nothing at all. Is it really espionage if you give vital information to a friend for a worthwhile cause and are not paid for it? Are there moral justifications for spying? Suppose you are a spy for a cause you are willing to risk your life for as in, say, Graham Green's *The Confidential Agent?* Any of the novels by Eric Ambler or John LeCarre set the bar of performance at an appropriate level.

TRAGEDY: Back in the day, when Aristotle was alive to write about tragedy, the genre signaled the fall from grace or power of a member of the nobility, or even the tumble from power of an entire family. Now tragedy has become democratized. *Death of a Salesman* earns its way in the front door of this genre; so, too, do the likes of John Steinbeck's *Of Mice and Men,* Nathaniel Hawthorne's *The Scarlet Letter*, and Herman Melville's *Moby-Dick.* Thomas Hardy's novels, particularly *Tess of the D'Urbervilles, Jude the Obscure,* and *The Mayor of Casterbridge* portray wrenching, tragic events which not only illustrate their own circumstances but remind readers how close at hand the prospect of tragedy is in their own lives. Theodore Dreiser was well aware of the implications of his *An American Tragedy,* wanting to earn recognition as the American, middle- and working-class Henry James. If tragedy is not paced properly, that is to say, if it is speeded up, it tips over into the realm of comedy. Comedy is tragedy on steroids.

WESTERN: First things first—a Western is a historical action novel set in the American frontier some time after 1840. Some of its many potential themes are well dramatized in Jack Schaefer's magnificent *Monte Walsh,* which is an episodic, semi-picaresque novel about the growing up and aging of a cowboy. Other Western themes: Cows vs. sheep; ranches vs. farms; cowboys vs. Indians; Indians vs. the cavalry; the coming of the rail-road; free range vs. barbed wire; cattle drives. Western writers to study for imaginative ways out of the conventional themes include Dorothy John-son, Elmore Leonard, Larry McMurtry (particularly *Horseman, Pass By* and, later, *Lonesome Dove*), Mari Sandoz, and Wallace Stegner. In particu-lar, McMurtry's *Horseman* is a demonstration that the history of the West is still very much taking place now, involving some of the very issues with which it began its life under the hands of Owen Wister (*The Virgin-ian,* 1902) and Zane Gray (*Riders of the Purple Sage,* 1912).

genre promise
    The set of EXPECTATIONS a READER has when selecting a work from a par-ticular CATEGORY of dramatic NARRATIVE; the circumstances and arrangement of PLOT devices a reader anticipates (and a WRITER delivers) when choosing a particular STORY.
    A reader embarking on a ROMANCE expects to root for a youngish woman who is often not aware of how attractive she is, rushing to an appointment of some consequence to her when she is literally bowled over by a man who seems to be rude and unthinking. A reader embarking on a MYSTERY expects to be confronted with a corpse or threat of death, followed by investigation, pursuit, clues, and unraveling of the motives leading to the corpse and/or threat of death. Readers of FANTASY will expect a narrative tale in which fig-ure magic, quests or chores to be performed, and the possibility of a PORTAL through which CHARACTERS from another time or place may enter will pro-vide major structural moments. SCIENCE FICTION promises the reader an extrapolation on an already established scientific principal to provide a QUEST, contest, or dramatic struggle. Science fiction may also promise extrap-olations or variations on such "soft" or social sciences as anthropology, polit-ical science, psychology, and sociology. Young adult (see YA NOVEL) and younger reader genres confront individuals of a particular age with moral, ethical, and physical challenges, the RESOLUTIONS of which lead them to an understanding of how to cope with adult life. Readers of HORROR FICTION expect to be led on a fearful journey where they are frequently confronted with scary events. Readers of HISTORICAL FICTION expect immediate and evoca-tive transportation to a historical time and place where the details, politics, and social atmosphere play integral parts in the development and resolution of the STORY.
    Genre promise in the twenty-first century has gone fusion, at least to the point where historical fiction has merged with such other genre as romance,

mystery, suspense, gothic, horror, YA and so on; doors to other fusions remain open, limited only by the collective imagination of the writing community.

To instill one's self with the sense of reader expectations in a particular genre, read at least five of the first-generation works in that field, verifiable from virtual reference librarians or that quintessential reference librarian, Google. Then read another twenty published within five years of your interest in the genre, focusing where possible on prolific authors.

Clue: The writer's mantra is "Never take the reader where the reader wants to go," which means to keep the genre promise in mind but deliver it later rather than sooner. If the young woman in a romance realizes immediately that the rude sort who bumped into her was Mr. Right, the story would be over. The late delivery of a pizza may cause the pizza to lose some of its warmth but the lateness will enhance the hunger for it. If the delivery is late because of some misadventure or whim on the part of the delivery person, another ingredient from the dramatic menu comes into play.

ghost of Hamlet's father, the

What some editors call a "woo-woo element," a young prince being invoked by his father's ghost to pursue revenge on his murderous uncle. This trope is a metaphor by which a CHARACTER is reminded of some debt from the past, related to a much loved or much feared friend, relative, or mentor, calling upon the character to become an instrument of REVENGE; the forces of GUILT or retribution conspiring to drive a character to exact payback for EVENTS not directly related to him; the long, heavy-handed reach of OBLIGATION, conflicting with a character's personal AGENDA.

The ghost of Hamlet's father wants revenge against Claudius, his brother, for having murdered him and subsequently become the husband of Gertrude, his widow. What better instrument for the ghost than his son? A productive line of inquiry in FAMILY and dynastic narratives, and the squeeze of CONSCIENCE and duty on the present day PROTAGONIST, undercuts his or her own AMBITIONS and recipe for achieving them.

In the traditional ghost story, the ghost has remained in a particular corner of reality, wanting retribution or some related form of justice before moving on to its place in history, reaching across time and cultures for an instrument to represent it in the here and now. Thus haunting is brought into the dramatic sphere as a force that wants something, reminding characters of OBLIGATIONS, debts unpaid, talents undeveloped, justice hanging fire—all of these connective tissue to someone, some ideal, some unfinished business. The haunted character is placed in the exquisite conflict between his goals and those of another, placing the haunted in a position to discover ATTITUDES, qualities, and techniques which will allow him or her to cope on behalf of another.

Not all ghosts rattle chains or moan at midnight; some are subtler, attracting their mortal instruments across centuries, cultures, traditions, drawing complete strangers into their orbit.

Sometimes the instrument of justice is merely an individual who speaks up to insist that Uncle Fred may have liked his peppermint schnapps but he was as well a wise, empathetic, and kindly man. In another such fanciful scenario, the ghost and mortal instrument could easily be as diverse as, say, the iconic but no-nonsense English poet John Milton and a word-loving hip-hop singer from South Philly who happens on an unpublished manuscript in a centuries-old reading room at a college in England, then brings yet one more last and resonant word, perhaps his most important word of all, from the old poet to the world of literature.

A sort of ghost, too, or one who can play the same role, is the genie in the bottle waiting with growing impatience for someone—anyone—to find the bottle in which he has been imprisoned for thousands of years and remove the stopper, which allows the genie to step out for a stretch.

goal

A desired achievement or destination for a CHARACTER; an ability, excellence of performance, or arrival at status desired and striven for by a participant in a STORY; recognition or reward for performance.

Goals cover a wide variety of targets, a reminder that their very existence imparts ATTITUDES and judgments about those who strive; in story, they are particularly visible in their absence. Characters need goals to gain admission into the terrain of story; a character who wants nothing, or who says he has everything he wants, needs to either reconsider or get used to an undramatic life.

In Walter Tevis's *The Hustler*, Fast Eddie Felson set his goal to be acknowledged as the best pool hustler in America. Eric Stoner wants to be the best draw poker player in Richard Jessup's novel *The Cincinnati Kid*. Becky Sharp wanted to rise up the social ranks in William Makepeace Thackeray's *Vanity Fair*. Dorothy Gale wants to get home in L. Frank Baum's *The Wizard of Oz*. All of these goals are completely recognizable, primal in their nature. Walter Tevis's Beth Harmon, in *Queen's Gambit*, wants to become a chess grand master, by many accounts a remote goal, but Tevis has made us care about Beth and about chess.

A character with a goal is a character that READERS can root for or against, either option being a method for drawing the reader into the story and its outcome. The reader may be overwhelmed by Ahab's goal of revenge upon the whale, but certainly the implications of Ahab's vendetta propel the reader deeper into the murky consequences of *Moby-Dick*. The reader of *Les Miserable* is drawn along by Inspector Javert's obsessive goal of returning Jean Valjean to prison, while Caspar Gutman's goal of securing the alleged riches of the statue in *The Maltese Falcon* sets a swirl and eddy of consequences that cause murder, duplicity, and betrayal.

Goal is the capstone of story. What do the characters want? What are they willing to do to get what they want?

goes without saying

A comment left in the margin of a manuscript by a skilled content editor; a matter or issue already made obvious to the READER by STORY points; a RESPONSE so obvious that it does not have to be explained.

Edit this sentence: "If you come any closer, I will shoot," she said menacingly.

The place to cure GWS responses is on the MANUSCRIPT, before it is sent out into the world.

golem, the

A fictional being (thus a CHARACTER), made of clay and other elements, who is called into being in order to correct a moral, social, or social injustice, usually associated with Jewish folklore and tradition; often a servant of a prominent and learned rabbi; a series of servant-beings, intended for a serious, life-affirming task before being deactivated, stored for future use against injustice, should it be necessary.

The best-known golem was a sixteenth-century creature, created by the chief rabbi of Prague, made of clay from the banks of the Vitava River, brought to life with incantations and a seal placed on its forehead bearing the Hebrew word "truth," whose job was to protect the inhabitants of the Prague ghetto from anti-Semitism.

The golem bears an interesting analogy to Lucius Quinctius Cincinnatus, a farmer who was appointed as dictator of Rome by the Roman senate when the Romans were engaged in warfare with the neighboring Aequians. Cincinnatus quickly took control, organized an army and a campaign to defeat the Aequians, after which he returned the powers of dictator to the senate, whereupon he returned to being a farmer. Another comparison might be argued for the creation of Dr. Frankenstein, particularly since the word "golem" in Hebrew slang can also be interpreted as a witless hulk.

Beyond the rural and urban mythology surrounding various golems, a disturbing side effect of their powers indicated a usurpation of power after it was granted them, in some cases resulting in violence, selfishness, and hitting on the rabbi's wife. In most cases the tide of admiration and support for the golems turned to a tide of fear and revulsion. (See similar themes in Kurosawa's film story, *Seven Samurai*, and the Americanized version brought to the Old West as *The Magnificent Seven*. See also Elmore Leonard's story of the Old West, *Hombre*.)

There is a bit of the golem resident in all heroic characters, thus our need to watch them carefully and their need to watch themselves. This vigil is necessary whether they appear as historically accurate representations or manufactured dramatic quantities, leaving them as Napoleonic individuals whose sense of mission is trumped by their enjoyment of POWER for its own sake, thus the need for the writer of heroic CHARACTERS to be on guard for the side effects of power. The golem is a theme found throughout Western literature, from *The Canterbury Tales* and Shakespeare to *The Gunfight at the O.K. Corral.*

Cincinnatus remains over the years as a figure who used power wisely, meriting his choice as its recipient. No less remarkable in his own way was Atticus Finch from Harper Lee's *To Kill a Mocking Bird*; he took up the role of defender with all due seriousness but he also knew his own values and his own sense of justice.

P.S. The Hebrew word inked on the seal of the Prague golem's forehead was "emet," the word for truth. To make sure the golem was decommissioned, the "e" was removed, leaving the Hebrew word for death.

P.P.S. Wasn't Rambo a golem?

growth

Dramatic motion toward change inherent in a CHARACTER, an institution, a place, or a thing; the need for a front-rank character in a NOVEL to advance or retreat in relation to behavior and understanding.

Growth is accretion or erosion, the CONSEQUENCES of a character's participation in a longform STORY, the evolution or devolution of an organization or institution; it is tangible movement in a direction the READER will recognize, a movement to which some emotional weight is attached by the character who experiences it. In the longer dramatic narrative, characters have the time and the need to grow; this is, after all what is meant by development.

Characters change, COME TO REALIZE, or at the very least are held hostage by their CIRCUMSTANCES. Institutions change, arguably for the better or worse, depending on the characters involved in the institutions. The mythical town of Pluto, North Dakota, so vivid with promise in the early pages of Louise Erdrich's *The Plague of Doves,* devolves toward the end of the novel as a virtual ghost town, while in the same narrative, the principal characters age, grow away from or grow into other mind- and heart-sets, while the once thriving Pluto Historical Society, down to two members, disbands.

It is not so much that growth in a longer work must be particularized in detail, as it must be recognized with some hint of what is to happen, allowing the reader to imagine (and argue) about the likely results. Shorter works do not have the CONVENTION or luxury of recording change; they instead play out on the characters being led to a brink and bade farewell, their INTENTIONS not readily known.

As the twenty-first-century NOVEL and SHORT STORY gather traction and personality, it is almost unthinkable that their characters will, as many earlier novels and stories decreed, all live happily ever after, but will instead be buffeted with the whims, uncertainties, and multifarious inducements of life as we have come to know it.

Modern life has evolved in many ways to the UNTHINKABLE COME TO PASS. Future life grows into the yet more unthinkable. If we are realistic, there will always be an ELEPHANT waiting for us somewhere, be it the living room, the Greyhound Bus Station, the supermarket, or the already crowded landscape we like to think of as the soul.

guilt

A critical state of awareness in a CHARACTER, occurring when that individual believes he has violated some moral boundary; an internal sense of remorse at having caused harm intentionally or deliberately to another; anguish for a particular behavior or for a specific lack of performance.

The Holy Trinity of the storyteller's art consists of guilt, JEALOUSY, and GRIEF, any one of which, by virtue of an extended examination, will provide at the very least a short story and quite probably a novel-length narrative. Taken in tandem, the Trinity becomes a richly entwined tapestry of emotional power, well able to maneuver the flintiest characters—say, Llewellyn Moss from Cormac McCarthy's *No Country for Old Men*—through an engaging investigation of human experience.

A character feeling guilt is likely to do something energetic to ease the pangs, creating a CAUSAL equation, A DOMINO EFFECT of ACTION. For his iconic character Leopold Bloom, James Joyce borrowed a concept from a thirteenth-century religious story, transmuted it into "the agenbyte of inwit," by which he meant the self-inflicted wound of remorse of CONSCIENCE. The other major player in *Ulysses*, Stephen Dedalus, was also riddled with guilt for, among other things, refusing to pray for his dying mother at her request.

The READER may COME TO REALIZE, as readers so often do, that the guilt felt by a particular character is inappropriate, an awareness that may cause the reader to identify more closely with the character, feel superior to that character, or consider the character an unnecessary martyr.

Guilt may be viewed clinically as a religious or social tool for imparting values or maintaining control of behavior. It may also be seen as a lever to motivate a character to ACT or, when appropriate, not to act.

All three arms of the Trinity—guilt, grief, and JEALOUSY—may be regarded by writers with some profit as the numerator of a fraction, the denominator of which is Remorse. A character infused with any one of the Trinity feels remorse for his behavior, then sets forth to square the emotional account, producing story. See Nelson Algren's *The Man with the Golden Arm*, in which Francis Majcinek, aka Frankie Machine, driving while drunk, caused an accident that crippled his wife, Sophie. While considering this excellent, noirish novel as an example, consider also the manipulative power of guilt. Sophie may not, in fact, be crippled. There is no questioning the crippling power of Frankie Machine's guilt.

~H~

HIBK

An abbreviation for Had I But Known; a woeful cry coined circa 1908, growing popular, extending to the '40s, indicating for our purposes a CHARAC-TER in a NOVEL or STORY whose past ACTIONS and DECISIONS have produced unwanted CONSEQUENCES; a rueful equivalent of "If I'd known then what I know now..."; often attributed to the Sue Grafton of her day, mystery writer Mary Roberts Rinehart.

HIBK, as it has been used in the past, is like a garden hose running at full pressure, then dropped, at which point it does a manic dance on the lawn; it is a DEVICE. Like any device used properly, it can be useful. After all, regret for past ACTIONS has a significant place in story, often producing more story, as in Thomas Hardy's *The Mayor of Casterbridge*, in which a good portion of the PROTAGONIST's middle years were given over to expiating a particularly awful act performed in Chapter One. Thus does rue nudge a character toward the path of redemption and possibly even restitution, presenting as a lovely OBSTACLE the obdurate refusal of the injured party to accept the remorse and restitution. Oh, how grand it all is, provided the writer does not drop the running hose.

Some novels and short stories, particularly PLOT-DRIVEN ones, use HIBK as a NARRATIVE HOOK to arrest the attention and sympathy of the reader by hinting directly at the emotional and physical morass now engulfing the narrator and threatening to drag him or her even deeper. Along with the sometimes arbitrary admonition to "SHOW, DON'T TELL" is the greater notion of "Let the reader figure it out," which is to say, avoid any tendency of the rueful character to beat his or her breast; rather, the character should take some action to cope with the consequences of the misstep, recognize the buyer's remorse with an appropriate ritual, and the writer should get on with the rest of the story.

Besides, what the rueful character did may well fall into the "It seemed like a good idea at the time" trope, a connecting link with many a reader whose own life experiences have not all been rousing successes. HIBK remains a mnemonic for writers, reminding them of the shift away from the operatic, approaching the nuanced and understated. By all means allow characters to make rash or impulsive decisions, only to have to live with their consequences. Do so without the breast-beating, teeth-gnashing gestures of nineteenth-century opera. Allow the characters to move beyond the scarlet letter, into the realm of picking up the shattered pieces with some remnant of dignity and decorum left.

habit words

Words favored (often unconsciously) by WRITERS who use them repeatedly to the point where they become distractions for the READER.

All writers have habit words; many make a point of a special seek-and-destroy mission during REVISION to root them out or change them. One of the many habit words shared by large numbers of writers is the innocent connective "and." The writer uses "and" with a comma to connect independent clauses, a technique most famously used by Ernest Hemingway and now parodied at his expense some fifty years after his death. Another habit word in frequent use is a tense variation on the verb "to walk," as in he walked over to, she walked by, they walked up to, he walked into.

The verb "said" might seem to be a habit word, thanks to its use with attribution in dialogue, but here things differ in a perspective of IRONY. The need some writers feel to supply synonyms for said, such as averred, opined, intoned, rebutted, growled, barked, shrieked, moaned, etc., help make the point that repetition of said is scarcely noticed. "Said" is considered a blind word, not an obvious repetition, rather than a habit word.

True enough, the reader may misinterpret, gloss over, or take text to have a meaning completely foreign to the author, but the reader is often an amazing computer, able to detect anomalies missed by COPYEDITORS and fact checkers, all too eager to hold these anomalies against the author. Readers are not generally offended by "said" as it is used in dialogue.

What are your habit words?

happy ending, the

An OUTCOME of a STORY or NOVEL in which one of more of the lead CHARACTERS is successful in achieving a GOAL; a PAYOFF or result of a NARRATIVE in which the BEHAVIOR of the PROTAGONIST leads the READER to feel optimistic; characters getting what they want without having to overpay.

One could almost paraphrase Tolstoy with the observation that happy endings are all alike, then qualify that observation with the added observation that the happy ending is the one where most of the characters achieve some measure of success after having competed for it. One could also consider the number of such endings that were dictated by publishers after having read the original endings produced first by their authors. Charles Dickens, who knew his way around endings, comes to mind with his original ending to his most superbly realized novel, *Great Expectations*. Dickens's publisher was not happy with the ending, asked for and got an alternate where things produced a greater glow of home, but at what cost?

In some noteworthy cases, publication seems to depend on the trope of the greater good rather that what works for a single character. The ENDING, which is to say the PAYOFF of *Lolita* had to have a justice-is-served ending because the stakes were—and still are—so high. Conventional morality wants Humbert Humbert to have suffered more than he already has. Conventional morality wants to forget that Dolores-Dolly-Lolita might have been sophisticated and aware enough to have read Humbert and his intentions and to have "been there" for him.

Two notably happy endings that bear heavy IRONY are found in *Huckleberry Finn* and *Catch-22*; each novel ends with the protagonist fleeing from an intolerable situation. Both these happy endings deserve consideration and study. Each one has the protagonist faced with an untenable fate. Readers join them in that escape and, as a consequence, experience the happiness of the ending. Humbert Humbert, on the other hand, is in a no-win situation. Even if he'd been able to ride off into the sunset with Dolores, we know she'd probably have grown tired of him soon enough and, indeed, he would have grown tired of her because she was already on the verge of outgrowing his range of interest.

As in other relevant matters, the WRITER must be the arbiter of what constitutes the happiness part of the happy ending. The better way to look at the happy ending is to see it as a "justice served" moment, when the time has come to cash in the characters' and the author's chips for dramatic currency.

Annie Proulx's short story, "Brokeback Mountain," written to expose what she felt was the resident homophobia of most rural areas, can hardly be said to have a happy ending, but given the characters and the author's stake in them, the payoff of the story speaks to the issue of justice and the double standard in its service.

Happy endings and sad endings are opening hands in the metaphoric poker game of the contemporary story; the true ending, the literary ending, comes with the reflection on the fate of the characters involved as it is measured against justice, served or not served.

hard-luck story

A NARRATIVE which intends through its telling to EVOKE sympathy and compassion for the teller; a STORY in which one or more CHARACTERS collide with an ever-worsening pattern of setback and misfortune.

All stories have some kind of end-game GOAL, some intended effect on the hearer/READER. Is it laughter? Perhaps the author's intent is education, or IRONY, or REVERSAL. Perhaps the narrative is offered in self-defense, or the adjunct of self-defense, excuse. As long as we're dwelling on the conditional, might the intent of a story be to make the teller sound modest—*moi?*—or resourceful?

Surely one of the more plentiful among dramatic narratives is the hard-luck story or its close relative, the SOB STORY, where the purpose is to evoke or elicit sympathy for the teller, both in the nature of troubles piled on and in the way the load is borne by the forces of Nature and natural disaster.

You could say that *The Book of Job* is the classic hard-luck story, not only because of the trials visited upon Job but because of the capricious nature of the way the visitation was set in motion. Job happened to be in the wrong place at the wrong time, when those polar representations of The Cosmic Forces got into a bragging and betting mood.

hidden agenda

A secret plan, initiative, or desire nourished by a CHARACTER while professing loyalty to another cause; self-interest disguised under a veil of piety or moral superiority; a battle between the id and super ego of an individual, the splendid protagonist of Sinclair Lewis's novel *Elmer Gantry* serving as an example.

By asking of a character what that character wants, and doing so with the persistence of an investigative journalist, the WRITER may well discover a valuable commodity—the character's hidden agenda. This is not to argue that *every* character has a hidden agenda, nor is it to argue that most characters don't; it is to argue that characters who appear in stories are larger than life; they have about them an explosive or impulsive tendency to act on desires. You have to watch out particularly for the repressed ones, who may all along have been fighting an increasingly losing battle of ignoring what they truly want. Similarly, the sybarites may secretly yearn for a moment or two of sincere renunciation. Go figure. But don't pass up opportunities to bring the hidden agenda forth. The censor, tollbooth guard, or other border cop should reside within the character—not the writer, which is to say the writer who wishes to be as effective as possible needs to ignore threats of personal discomfort in pursuing the motives of his or her characters.

Dumas's *The Count of Monte Cristo* portrays, if with a bit of melodrama, the hidden agendas of those who wished to frame Edmond Dantes, thereby having him out of the way while they executed their individual plans of romantic and financial profit. The narrator of Poe's "A Cask of Amontillado" begins with the announcement of Montresor's vow of revenge on Fortunato.

The hidden agenda may be temporarily—but not indefinitely—concealed; it is the cat in the bag, a catalyst for the combustion inherent in the UNTHINKABLE COMING TO PASS, because it is at this point that the STORY gains an irresistible momentum.

historical novel, the

A NOVEL (this will also apply to a SHORT STORY) set in a specific historical era, often involving actual historical EVENTS and personalities; an increasingly popular choice among GENRE WRITERS and READERS for the mixing of genres (for example, historical romance, historical mystery).

The historical novel absorbs details of SETTING, customs, and mores; readers not only want to be transported to a particular time and place—they want to experience it. So the obvious question arises: How much detail? The answer: Enough to move the story along, but not enough to impede it. The historical novel has a strong enough foundation to stand on its own as pure history. Jean Auel researched the Ice Age people known as Cro-Magnon, then detailed their activities in a series, *Earth's Children,* dealing with individuals who populated the Danube River Valley some 25,000 years ago. In *The Clan of the Cave Bear,* she provided a Cro-Magnon orphan who'd been raised by a band of Neanderthal.

Mary Renault took us back to ancient Greece in *The King Must Die,* using historical background and archaeological research to trace the young years of Theseus, an attractive mythological CHARACTER. The work was well received, motivating her to a sequel, *The Bull from the Sea,* in which Theseus's life is expanded to the time of his marriage to another well-known character, Phaedra.

A serious rival to Renault's output was Mary Stewart, particularly her version of the Arthurian legend, *The Crystal Cave.* By the time the English language version of Umberto Eco's novel *The Name of the Rose* was published in 1983, the novel had reached bestseller status in Europe. Set in 1327, *The Name of the Rose* takes us to a monastery where a murder has been committed, thus showing how historical and mystery genres are natural allies. Moving a bit forward in time, Leonard Tourney moves us to Elizabethan England when the husband and wife team of Matthew and Joan Stock began their career in *The Players' Boy Is Dead.* Tourney used his Shakespearean literary background to set the scene for whodunits. In 1959, James Michener published yet another of his enormous histories, this one a replication of the background of Hawaii. Some forty years later, Thomas Pynchon found enough material to fill 788 pages of his historical postmodernist romp, *Mason & Dixon,* a celebration of the two iconic surveyors for whom the Mason-Dixon Line is named, and an awareness if not understanding of the cultural division that line represents.

While all this was happening, another kind of historian was producing work that still draws new readers as well as re-readers—that sturdy band of men and women who contributed to the dimensions of the American West: A.B. Guthrie (*The Big Sky*), Mari Sandoz (*Old Jules*), Dorothy M. Johnson (*The Hanging Tree*), Larry McMurtry (*Horsemen Pass By* and *Lonesome Dove*), and Elmore Leonard (*Three Ten to Yuma*). (See THE WESTERN NOVEL) In addition to standing firmly on its own—say *I, Claudius* (Robert Graves) or *Hadrian Remembers* (Marguerite Yourcenar)—the historical novel mixes as well with YA, fantasy, science fiction, alternate universe, and political; all it requires is imagination, research, and a willingness to take RISKS.

horror novel, the

A GENRE in which the READER seeks the anticipation and experience of fear and possible revulsion; NARRATIVES which exploit the hidden menace in ordinary characters and details.

Just as HISTORICAL FICTION has morphed into a convenient hybrid force when combined with the likes of ROMANCE, MYSTERY, FANTASY, and SPECULATIVE FICTION, horror fiction has proved equally flexible. So long as one or more CHARACTERS is placed in chilling, frightening circumstances, horror stories are appropriately set in past, present, or future surroundings in which other generic categories may play supporting roles.

The quintessential late-twentieth- and early-twenty-first-century horror WRITER is Stephen King, whose prolific output of fiction might cause the reader to overlook his textbook-perfect publication, *Danse Macabre* (1981), a personal-but-highly evolved history of horror fiction and, via the frontage road of subtext, an excellent resource for horror writers.

The primary goals of horror fiction include frightening the reader and unsettling, disorienting, and bombarding the reader with potential conspiracy theories that often involve supernatural elements. Haunted houses are so plentiful in horror fiction that they have become a sub-genre. Ditto vampires, with zombies and werewolves representing yet other forks in the road.

Robert Louis Stevenson's novella *The Strange Case of Dr. Jekyll and Mr. Hyde* certainly fits the category, as does Oscar Wilde's *The Picture of Dorian Gray.*

Another contemporary writer to consult for insights into the medium is William Peter Blatty, whose *The Exorcist* uses the extreme vulnerability of a twelve-year-old girl as a host for invasion by a malevolent, demonic force and allows a natural match-up between dark forces and religion.

Henry Farrell (1920-2006) produced instructive examples of horror fiction with *What Ever Happened to Baby Jane?, Hush, Hush, Sweet Charlotte*, and *How Awful About Alan*. In each case, there was a revelation of a secretive character with a hidden past, and a push-the-envelope revelation.

In *Danse Macabre*, Stephen King credited Ira Levin's 1967 novel, *Rosemary's Baby*, a progressively more horrifying novel in which a vulnerable protagonist is impregnated by a demonic force, as his early inspiration.

Not to forget Howard Philips Lovecraft (1890-1937), whom Stephen King has also called out as the greatest practitioner of the classic horror tale in the twentieth century. Lovecraft was a brooding cynic and pessimist, the polar opposite of his contemporary, C.S. Lewis, with his religion-based optimism; he relentlessly took on such major icons as Romanticism and Enlightenment, producing major dramatic thrusts, almost as though he were Cyrano de Bergerac in a sword fight against Christian humanism.

Until Stephen King's popularity became established, horror fiction was more likely to be shelved in libraries and bookstores as weird fiction or weird stories. Indeed, a major pulp magazine published between 1923 and 1954, and which featured stories by Lovecraft, was called *Weird Tales.*

Hint: If the explanation for the horrific or supernatural elements in a story is too rational, the work is more likely SCIENCE FICTION or at least SPECULATIVE FICTION than it is horror.

hubris

A display of pride or entitlement that becomes so vast in nature it overrides an individual's more sensible behavior; the resident sense within a CHARACTER of being right, to the point where the character's behavior intentionally or unintentionally HUMILIATES other characters; a near evangelical course of behavior from a character in service of a belief and/or GOAL.

Hubris drives many characters in the dramatic and literary arts, leading the READER to suspect that eventually such a hubris-driven character will have to pay a huge price. Was Achilles being hubristic in *The Iliad,* particularly after he had slain Hector in battle, then paraded his corpse about? Was King Creon showing hubris when he exacted his directive against his niece in *Antigone?* Was Ahab showing hubris when he gambled and lost against the whale? Was Dr. Frankenstein showing hubris when he believed he could take on Nature by creating life? What began as indifference to or a disrespect for the Gods and Fates (who knew a thing or two about retribution) became as democratized as other aspects of social and moral behavior to mere humans who, impressed by their own self-interest, began to believe it was their due to get what they want. Consider Charles Foster Kane, of *Citizen Kane* fame, as a modern force of hubris, forcing his wishes upon those near him and extending to individuals he might never meet. Thus consider all these larger-than-life characters made in part what they are because of a complete lack of empathy. A guiding definition of a hubris-driven story is: How the mighty are fallen, the powerful led to humiliation, all pushed along the road by hubris. Bringing the nature of hubris into tighter context, we examine how anyone with an overarching position of pride is brought down into disgrace and humiliation or, as Jane Austen did with the representational characters of Elizabeth Bennett and Fitzwilliam Darcy in *Pride and Prejudice,* the characters undergo an acceptable shift toward *empathy*. Although, since Austen is known for her keen wit and satire, perhaps she is saying that the payment for the positions of pridefulness and prejudice is—marriage. Under most literary circumstances, there is some payment necessary for having lived at the level of hubris.

humiliation

The stripping away of the self-esteem of a CHARACTER who has been parading on the moral high ground; a significant GOAL of HUMOR, in which some posturing individual or organization is brought to the extreme public ridicule of laughter; the modern equivalent of placing a character on display in a stock and pillory.

Much is to be learned about a character from the way he or she deals with a humiliating situation; the individual who brandishes humility is often arranging the stage for his or her own undoing. The character who becomes the deliberate prosecutor of his own humiliation earns the READER'S admiration.

Humiliation, or public exposure of the emperor's nudity, is seen by many readers and WRITERS as the ultimate argument for the presence of cosmic justice. In his short story "The Cat-Bird Seat," James Thurber double downs on the famed Edgar Allen Poe icon "A Cask of Amontillado," making his revenge by humiliation seem even more effective and, in the process, more a public affair. In a remarkable display of the understanding of humiliation, Jack London presents a character who inflicts humiliation on an adversary from beyond the grave in his short story "A Loss of Face."

humor

The sudden, painful awareness of exposure or VULNERABILITY; a force aimed at an individual, institution, or tradition with the intended goal of ridicule and possible destruction; a view of reality and a redemptive philosophy for dealing with that view; a sense of justice in which the emperor is revealed to have hand-me-down clothing but nevertheless insists it is Ralph Lauren.

First principle: there is no such thing as victimless humor.
Second principle: the target of humor always believes he has the moral high ground.
Third principle: the moral high ground in humor is mortgaged for more than its actual value.
Fourth principle: when someone tells you "That isn't funny," it probably is.

Humor is explosive, irreverent, undemocratic, a splendid example of the UNTHINKABLE COME TO PASS. Suspicious and anarchistic in nature, it asks the wrong questions, makes the wrong assumptions, creates a shambles of disorganization; the only thing left standing is the truth for all to see—not the truth you are told to see, but the only truth that remains after the dust settles.

Humor is separate from COMEDY in that humor is situational and dramatic—a punctilious food snob being caught using ketchup, then trying to explain his way out of it; comedy is more physical—the snob being caught with the ketchup, trying to hide it, and having it conspicuously leak on his clothing.

How to initiate humor:

1. Select a target, which may be any institution, profession, or attitude, also an individual who thinks or feels entitled, justified, or merely right.
2. Place that institution, profession, attitude or individual in a situation where it/he/she feels it appropriate to behave as usual, then apply pressure in the form of a question, challenge, or time constraint. And then push the subject to defend it/him/herself.
3. Watch for the results.
4. Think dramatically, along the lines of the three-act-play format of old where Act I presents the challenge, Act II presents the attempt(s) to cope with it, and Act III brings the venture to a COMBUSTION that blows up in the target's face.
5. Remember Wile E. Coyote. The reward is HUMILIATION, which the target may not yet be able to see—but the audience can.

Hints:

1. A major goal of humor is humiliation.
2. Memorably successful humorists often used themselves and their foibles as targets (see Mark Twain, Robert Benchley, Dorothy Parker).
3. Even though the goal is humiliation, don't kick the target unnecessarily when it is down, lest you bring a backlash onto yourself.
4. Ignore the warning that a particular subject is not fit for humor.
5. Remember, humor is not jokes; humor is exposure of facades and hypocrisy, REVERSAL of positions.

~I~

iconic characters

Individuals who exert transformative influence on the STORIES in which they appear, outweighing the PLOT; persons who are simultaneously focused on a GOAL and imbued with stoical good humor and empathy, should either be needed; persons whose responses under stress create a lasting impression with READERS.

Whether they are of the ilk of Cormac McCarthy's sociopath killer, Anton Chigurh, from *No Country for Old Men*, the squeaky clean moralist, Sir Galahad, of Arthurian legend, or the rather plain-appearing Jane Eyre, iconic characters' eyes are not cast on their immediate problems but are seemingly fixed in intimate gaze with the reader. Appropriately enough, readers carry with them the images of such characters long past the time when their exploits in dealing with the entanglements of their PLOTS are remembered. Even Pinocchio, the puppet who wanted to become a real boy, is iconic not because of the CHOICES he made but because of his goal.

What the character wants and the path he or she pursues in order to achieve such ends are often the most magnetic qualities for readers. Each goal becomes a pole star for the character, influencing direction and behavior. A good approach to examining the qualities of these icons, male and female, young, middle-aged, and old, is to start with the more simplistic ones: Dorothy Gale, wanting to get back home from Oz; the Horatio Alger shoe boy in the eponymous *Ragged Dick*, wanting to work his way upward toward success and self-esteem; the quintessential male free spirit, Huckleberry Finn, wanting to get away from an abusive father and an overly structured social environment. From there, move on toward stories in which the moral landscape is grayer, the issues less likely to be settled with one last-chapter speech from the likes of Tom Joad in *The Grapes of Wrath*.

Some notable icons and what they want:

1. Randle P. McMurphy from Ken Kesey's *One Flew over the Cuckoo's Nest*—avoidance of hard physical labor, access to drugs
2. Nora Helmer from Henrik Ibsen's *The Doll's House*—equality
3. Pacote from Barnaby Conrad's *Matador*—reputation
4. Jeffrey Spaulding from *Animal Crackers*—lunch
5. Ratso Rizzo from James Leo Herlihy's *Midnight Cowboy*—an angle, any angle
6. The Wife of Bath from Geoffrey Chaucer's *The Canterbury Tales*—a husband who values her
7. Madame Arcarti from Noel Coward's *Blythe Spirit*—a spell that actually works

8. Anton Chigurh from Cormac McCarthy's *No Country for Old Men*— people to play by the rules
9. Hester Prynne from Nathaniel Hawthorne's *The Scarlet Letter*—a good life for her daughter, Pearl
10. Florentino Ariza from Gabriel Garcia Marquez's *Love in a Time of Cholera*—Fermina Daza
11. Heathcliff from Emily Bronte's *Wuthering Heights*—Cathy Earnshaw
12. Antigone from Sophocles' play, *Antigone*—respect for her brother

There are hundreds of icons to study, the better to assess what it is about them that causes them to stand out in readers' memories.

Hint: It is not necessarily their professional goals so much as it is the way they go about achieving their aims and their emotional responses to other characters, thus their empathy.

Additional hint: It is often the way they behave when they are feeling the most VULNERABLE—and make no mistake about it, they are vulnerable at various times, every one of them.

Final hint: Make two lists of iconic characters, the first including all those you see as being conventional icons, the other list being entirely your own favorites, which may include both living people and favorites from stories you encountered in any medium. This exercise helps validate your choices, ratifying the sound of originality living in your VOICE. The persons who are your heroes, anti-heroes, and antagonists become role models for your characters.

imitation

A process followed by BEGINNING and intermediate WRITERS in which they sedulously copy the STYLE, concept, and ATTITUDE of established writers whom they admire or whose success they envy.

Imitation is useful in terms of education, but only up to a point. Once that education is achieved, the writer needs to move on to the risky business of discovering the writer inside of herself who awaits activation. As the sale price of an individual hardcover title increases, it becomes particularly apparent that the reader is looking for the original rather than an imitation. Some publishers are in fact on the lookout for voices that sound like their big sellers, but unless you are content always to be thought of as the generic rather than the authentic, you will follow the guidance of your own writing voice. It is not only possible but admirable to learn from other writers, living or dead. The time comes, however, when this learning must be recast into the writer's own words and feelings.

Intermediate- and experienced-level writers, having discovered their voices, THEMES, and lines of dramatic attack run the risk of self-parody when they begin imitating themselves, the ideal being that each new project is a launching of the ship of discovery on the vast ocean of enthusiasm.

Hint: The READER can spot imitation because, while writers are busy writing, readers are busy reading, keeping mental if not actual notes. The reader has a long memory.

implications

Meanings or qualities expressed by indirection or DOUBLE ENTENDRE; ATTRIBUTIONS attached to a CHARACTER by demonstrations of how that character performs or does not perform; markers or signals placed in a STORY to cause the READER to make assumptions about the INTENT of a character and/or subsequent EVENTS in a narrative.

Implication resides at a considerable distance from—but still in sight of—SHOW, DON'T TELL, allowing the reader to see, to suspect and, when she does see and suspect, confirming that she has bought into the characters and their story. This is the polar opposite of the WRITER describing character traits. Under the circumstances of a proper SET-UP, the reader will assume two characters have some romantic destiny or that, were they to continue as they have, they will evolve to a serious conflict. The more the writer allows the characters to proceed on a VECTOR of (a) each pursuing his AGENDA or GOALS and (b) each responding in some way to the others in a particular scene, the more implications will be broadcast for readers to pick up and, accordingly, make assumptions about. The reader is not only a natural matchmaker; as mystery writer Leonard Tourney has observed, "Most readers fill in their own descriptions and images of characters. Readers enjoy thinking and feeling things about characters, waiting for their personal portraits of them to emerge."

Thus are the variables of assume and assumption introduced into the calculus of story to work their way on the reader.

Hint: As the writer, you know the tendencies and attitudes, even the secret desires of the characters, allowing you to write *at* them—or in their general direction—but not directly *to* them. This is how one sets his toe in the pond of implication.

Additional hint: As the reader, notice how deft your favorite author is, embedding these implications so that you take them in almost without realizing it.

in medias res

Literally "in the middle of things," a reference to dramatic works that begin with a good deal of BACKSTORY having already taken place; a dramatically convenient way to expose the READER to the main CHARACTERS; a potential opportunity to FORESHADOW characters and events to come later.

One of the older, more enduring narratives with an *in medias res* beginning is *The Iliad,* where the Trojan War has already been raging for six years. It begins with a relatively minor incident in which one of the major players, Achilles, feels he has been insulted and consequently decides to stop fighting, indeed removes his Myrmidon warriors from the forces attacking Troy, a decision that could turn the tide of battle. Some of the other major players try to talk him out of his decision, during the course of which readers get doses of backstory.

In medias res openings begin at some dramatic point that sets opposing forces in enough motion to engage the readers before taking a dramatic pause to fill in relevant DETAILS, DESCRIPTIONS, STAKES, and ISSUES. No less popular now than they were back in earlier centuries, these openings become a valuable tool for WRITERS to study. They support the removal of chronological constraints and guide the writer into beginning with situations where characters are actively engaged in conflict, making it difficult for the writer to spend too much time on description or backstory the reader has not yet been prepared to accept.

There is nothing toxic or wrong with telling a story in more or less strict chronology. Tobias Wolff's memorable SHORT STORY "Bullet in the Brain" is a compelling example. "Anders couldn't get to the bank until just before it closed," it begins, "so of course the line was endless and he got stuck behind two women whose loud, stupid conversation put him in a murderous temper. He was never in the best of tempers, anyway, Anders—a book critic known for the weary, elegant savagery with which he dispatched almost everything he reviewed." From this beginning, it proceeds in close chronology to the dramatic PAYOFF.

In medias res openings often come as a result of a REVISION tactic in which the writer reviews the entire narrative, searching for the most ideal place to begin. Sometimes moving the furniture about for a better arrangement will transform a story from the ordinary to the memorable.

"in the story"

A condition in which the WRITER is actively immersed in the activities and details of a STORY to the extent of engaging in the PROCESS without thinking; being in the emerging, creative details of a NARRATIVE.

However well planned things may be in the beginning or however much in the moment the developing story stands, inside the story is a place on an emotional map for the writer. Being too thoughtful, too mindful of readership or audience removes the writer from a precise place on the emotional map, opening the door for too much DETAIL, too much explanation, too much self-justification from the various CHARACTERS. All of this contributes to the writer being evicted from the story, in a state of being "out of the story" and her fertile, creative ground, and needing to sneak back inside if anything more is to be done.

Time enough during the REVISION process for critical thought, rearranging of scenery, meddling with TIME LINES.

How to get "in" the story? Find out what the characters want, then set them free to secure the GOAL, watching to see what ruses they will employ, what depths they will to go to gain an advantage, and the CONSEQUENCES that emerge, demanding payment.

inevitability

The story-governing certainty that something will go wrong; a presentiment that CIRCUMSTANCES surrounding one or more CHARACTERS will worsen; the likelihood that a character who is given a menu of CHOICES will select the one most probable course for disaster.

Fred has decided to attend a ten-year reunion of his college graduating class. Still smarting from the painful break-up of his marriage, Fred is thinking the reunion might be a place to reenter the relationship market. By the time the evening is over, Fred has been given four email addresses of former classmates, all of whom he considers attractive, all of whom have hinted their willingness to let him take her home. They are all attractive, each in a different way. They are all bright, each according to her particular interests. Aroused and lonely, Fred makes his CHOICE. Most READERS will recognize the landmine Fred will have stepped on as a CONSEQUENCE of his choice. Most readers will know that the one Fred chose would be afflicted with a rusted-out Honda and have at home a cat with a urinary infection. Moreover, she will cry loudly at unexpected times and want to know from Fred why people cannot learn to be more respectful to one another. Not that any of these qualities are of themselves disastrous, but to Fred, they are COMPLICATIONS he does not think he needs. As such inevitability goes, Fred will have subsequent contact with the other three former classmates who signaled their availability, finding each in her own way borderline remarkable. But the added inevitability is that Fred is drawn to his first choice and is last seen advancing to her apartment with a large container of rust remover and a copy of *Cat Care For Dummies.*

Inevitability makes no distinction in gender. Nicole, herself still uneasy from a painful break-up with a man who was compulsive to the point of arguing with her about the only proper way to allow toilet paper to spool, has gone to the same reunion as Fred. She has urged herself to go, thinking the experience will be good for her, even though she knows in advance that she will leave that night with the one man in the entire gathering who will be the most disastrous. Indeed, the individual Nicole chooses can't wait to get her to his place in order to show her his collection of breakfast cereal boxes, including his prized Wheaties box with the still florid image of Duke Snyder smiling forth. The evening ends with her moodily watching him as he pours bowls of corn flakes for both of them.

Although inevitability takes human psychology well into consideration, dealing as it does with such tropes as VICTIMS, compulsions, EGO, avocations, and the very nature of individual identity, inevitability is CAUSALITY and consequence in Costco quantities. It is the dramatic distillation of forces observed in reality but often buried under an array of distracting signs and misinterpreted biological responses to stimuli. All it takes to trigger awareness of inevitability in the reader is for one character to ask another, "You'll wait for me, right? We'll be married as soon as I finish grad school." Not to mention one of the most famous of all lines, the all-purpose, one-size-fits-all "Is this safe?"—which could relate to robbing a bank, initiating a sexual encounter, crossing the street in the middle of a block, risking savings on a business venture. And the inevitable, "I'll be right back," and "I'll call you."

Why, oh, why did Colm Toibin's character Tony, so deeply in love with Eilish in *Brooklyn,* plead with her to marry him in a secret civil ceremony before returning to Ireland for a funeral? Why, he did it to add considerable depth to both characters, and to introduce the worm of inevitability into the apple. Who among Toibin's readers did not suspect that Eilish would experience a heavy pang of temptation while away from Tony?

Inevitability is like the black keys and the white keys on the piano; the composer knows which to designate to produce the most resonant results.

inference

A game-changing assumption or conclusion reached by a CHARACTER in a STORY or by a READER; a REACTION or DECISION which is possibly correct, made without direct, unassailable evidence; a conclusion formed by a character or a reader based on past experience; the use of circumstantial evidence; arriving at a conclusion or decision based entirely upon a character's experience and subsequently based on the reader's experience.

As the twenty-first century shifts into gear (see PATHETIC FALLACY), one highly visible fork in the NARRATIVE road is the inferential one, in which the reader is left with more leeway to assume such matters as AGENDA, INTENT, and volition of characters as well as what actually happened in a narrative. Did they or didn't they? Were they or were they not? Such words as AMBIGUITY and elliptical come forth, particularly in the SHORT STORY.

A highly prolific and versatile WRITER, Elmore Leonard has often been quoted expressing his working approach to story, which in essence is to write only the parts that interest him, while leaving out the "other" parts, it being understood that "other" means DESCRIPTIONS and SCENES that don't directly involve him. By extension, Leonard could be interpreted to advocate as a part of the revision process the removal of anything he considered unnecessary explanation, whether in narrative (which includes description) or DIALOGUE. Studying any of his recent works, we can see him at his craft of EVOCATION, deliberately leaving the reader room to infer.

Contemporary writers as diverse as Alice Munro, Margaret Atwood,

Tobias Wolff, George Saunders, Jhumpa Lahiri, and Haruki Murikami may be argued to write with the inferential less-is-more approach, yet none of these is arguably a minimalist. There is among them a common thread of trust. The interesting questions to consider are the applications of the trust: Do they trust the reader? Themselves? The reader and themselves?

An emerging storyteller is well advised to read these writers, keeping in mind choices the individual writer will have to make about how much the reader truly needs to know.

Hint: Some writers of nonfiction are often seduced by the need to use all their research in a particular project, resulting in their project telling the potential reader more about the subject than the reader wants to know. In similar fashion, some writers of fiction may be tempted to explain more about their characters and the MOTIVES of those characters than the reader wants to know.

Additional hint: Because of its subjective base, the result of fiction is greater than the sum of its parts; the goal of storytelling is the evocation of that greater effect. Evoke rather than describe. Encourage the reader to infer. The reader would rather discover his misapprehension in the face of surprise behavior from the characters than be told he was wrong by the author.

information dump

Literary equivalents of landfills and trash bins placed by WRITERS throughout manuscripts to serve as dump sites for the unused research materials assembled for a particular NOVEL or SHORT STORY. Research takes time, effort, and considerable discretion. Whatever it is you are researching, your GOAL is to make it fit seamlessly into the narrative without calling attention to itself. You want to make it seem to belong in the same way your CHARACTERS belong.

Alas, some writers can't resist the temptation to use all nine yards of it when one or two feet would have been sufficient to keep the READER in the story.

Hint for WRITERS: EDIT your research with the same vigor you apply to editing your story. You do not have to invent the wheel to let your CHICK LIT protagonist drive off in a huff or even a hybrid.

Hint for READERS: Feel free to take a wide detour around information dumps. Once writers get the notion you're skipping portions of their narrative, they and their EDITORS will devise ways to get you back. The good news is that the ways they devise will relate directly to STORY.

injustice

A CHARACTER'S sense of having been dealt with unfairly, a rip or tear in the fabric of social accord or justice; a person or system inflicting on another individual or group of individuals a behavior or treatment extending beyond civility; encroaching on another person's or group's defined territory; any thoughtless or bullying oppression or harassment.

Injustice may be real or imagined, either case being a strong beginning potential for STORY. The actual VICTIM may not feel the unjustified invasion but a close friend or family member, observing the circumstances, might see the occasion and then attempt to urge the actual victim into recognition of the injustice. What a splendid motivational force for fiction. Injustice may breed resentment, which in its turn motivates IRONY, which gives way to SARCASM, which becomes the CATALYST for REVENGE. Injustice is a prized motivation because it so frequently begets DRAMATIC ACTION, which is, of course, the life's blood of STORY.

One of the more notable victims of injustice was Edmond Dantes of *The Count of Monte Cristo* fame. In Dumas's epic tale, Dantes becomes the victim of a conspiratorial web of injustice to the point of considering suicide in his helpless despair. Through a dramatic SHIFT OF POWER, Dantes is able to embark on a pattern of revenge, which, once exacted, allows him the luxury of getting on with his life.

Another victim of injustice, the near-iconic Montresor of "A Cask of Amontillado," has suffered injuries (never specifically detailed but assumed to be countless HUMILIATIONS) in the past but has now been insulted by Fortunato (also not detailed but through implication presented as sufficient to merit revenge). The story ends with Montresor having sufficiently played upon Fortunato's overweening pride to the point of luring him into a fatal trap, during the course of which Montresor is given cause to cite his family's motto, "Nemo me impune lacessit" (No one insults me with impunity), which is a tell of the outcome. Montresor's ultimate revenge for the injustice suffered appears to satisfy him, but since the story is a FIRST-PERSON narrative, it is possible to read it with the interpretation that this is merely one of many retellings of the story, that Montresor has literally been dining out on the tale for some years and that in doing so, he has become as overweening in his pride as he felt Fortunato to be in his.

There are also victims of circumstance, in which the target has had no direct part in his own misfortune. Such stories often present patience or discipline as being the dramatic force that helps overcome the roadblock.

Fiction abounds with characters setting forth to undo injustices. Happily, there is room for more.

inner critic, the

That awful voice that repeats and repeats in the WRITER'S ear, "You can do this better;" an interior conviction that a particular WORK under way is doomed because of its inanity; a self-inflicted editorial wound; setting the FIRST-DRAFT bar high enough to guarantee failure.

The inner critic's most powerful hold is on the EGO of the writer, reminding the writer of all the gifted storytellers the writer must outperform in order to be noticed in the first place. The inner critic's second most severe hold is with the incessant warning that one must not proceed until all the previous work done on a project is in glowing condition, resonating access, success, and transparent clarity of artistic intent. Simply put, the inner critic thinks too much, is allowed too much critical leeway and, all the while insisting on his desire to make the work as perfect as possible, managing to render the work beyond completion.

Whatever the work wants to be—haiku, SHORT STORY, trilogy-level NOVELS—the most effective means of heeding its call is to get it down on paper or computer screen as quickly and expeditiously as possible, comforted all the while with the notion that it can and will be REVISED.

The most effective way to reach that point is to turn off the thought process, trusting that you are building your individual muscle memory for reaching as far as possible.

Somewhere out on the myriad urban myths web pages are the descriptions of "real" writers, "natural" writers who are distinguished from amateurs and wannabes by the fact of their being able to "get" a work down pat by the first draft, a few crossed-out words, perhaps, but not many. These literary elect are not plagued by inner critics because they already know the worth of their project and simply do not require inner critics, but were, in fact, born without them. Thus did inner-critic-less Mark Twain approach the end of his mortality with the belief that his best work was a biography of Joan of Arc; thus also did Twain frequently stop work on his most remarkable and honest work of all, *Huckleberry Finn,* losing several battles with his inner critic until the work was finally finished.

To get the better of the inner critic, listen to the tone of the inner voice that prompts a particular work, then carefully note that tone, whether humor, tragedy, romance, adventure or irony. The next step is to set forth with the GOAL of defining to yourself what that particular emotional compass means to you. Mark Twain made an effective comparison that bears repeating here: "The difference between the almost right word and the right word is really a large matter," Twain said. "It's the difference between the lightning bug and lightning." The difference between defining the intended tone of a work of your own and the close-enough tone is the difference between locking out the inner critic or inviting him in with the sure knowledge that he will steal the silverware.

intensity in language

Dangerous territory; it covers the use of italics, exclamation points, all-capital-letter words to emphasize DRAMATIC points; the use of "very" and other intensifiers that visually signify emphasis.

Mommy doesn't like it when you do that.

Mommy wishes you would stop doing that.

Mommy is tired of having to remind you not to do that.
Mommy is very tired of your behavior.
Will you please stop doing that?
How many times do I have to ask?
Stop it.
Stop!
I said, "Stop, damn it."
What is it you don't understand about "shut the fuck up"?

It is neither fair nor an intended slight to suggest that mothers alone are driven to the use of intensifiers in language. John Lardner, in a reminiscence of his father, Ring Lardner, told of a time when the family was out for a Sunday morning drive, the auto being driven by father (RL) who was suffering the effects of last night's drinking spree with his newspaper chums. After a number of wrong turns, muffled curses, and roads being driven in reverse gear, one of the Lardner youth ventured to query, "Are we lost, Daddy?" The younger Lardner immortalized the now classic reply, "'Shut up,' he explained."

It is encouraging to note how CHARACTERS frequently blow their cool, over-respond, lose composure, and experience other lapses of equipoise. How to represent these moments? The best way is through DIALOGUE in context, which is to say with words, expressions, and accompanying gestures that do not require italics or exclamation points or all-cap lettering in order to convey the exasperation and/or frustration being experienced at the moment. The second best way is with some bodily response, the blink of the eyes, a tilt of the head, a flinch, a muffled grunt, a shift in stance, and, yes, the sudden attempt to drive the human fist through the inhuman wall. The third best way is through an IRONIC combination of the first two, say pinching the bridge of the nose and saying, "I see," particularly when it is clear that the character doesn't see—not at all. Any other way, such as exclamation points or AUTHORIAL INTERVENTION are "tells," clues that the author doesn't know how to bring off the intensity or is afraid the reader won't get it without Las-Vegas-like displays of emphasis.

Imagine a spoken response to an incendiary disclosure of information. For instance: "I am very disappointed in your behavior." Now imagine an intensified response. "And I am very disappointed that you were so very disappointed in my behavior that you couldn't see the necessity for me to do what I did." The response obviates the need for such adverbs as "retorted defensively," or "sneered sarcastically," or the use of the over-used exclamation point. The response is in what the characters say rather than the way the writer uses Microsoft Word applications.

intent

A significant purpose for performing or not performing an ACTION; a governing MOTIVE or reason for a CHARACTER doing something in a NOVEL or SHORT STORY; the desire to do or become; the planning and performance of an ACT or the planning and performance of an OPPOSITION to an act or behavior.

A character such as John Russell, the blue-eyed Mexican-American raised by Apaches in Elmore Leonard's *Hombre*, may step forth without intent, until a crisis point is reached and a DECISION—you're either with us or against us— is required.

A character such as Detective Dave Robicheaux, in James Lee Burke's *Swan Peak*, may step forth with intent, only to have that intent abruptly and directionally changed.

A character such as the gunfighter, Shane, in Jack Schaefer's eponymous novel, may intend to remain neutral through some crisis point, only to find the position of neutrality beyond his grasp.

Each of these examples places a character in STRESS, which may evolve into JEOPARDY. Each example also places the character well within the LAND-SCAPE of story.

Characters are measured by the intensity and complexity of their intent.

interior monologue

The soliloquy/conversation a CHARACTER has while engaged in a DRAMATIC NARRATIVE; relevant sensory and thought process from which a READER may adduce and deduce a character's INTENT, MOTIVATION and, if necessary, doubt; a supplement to narrative from any point-of-view character, simultaneously advancing STORY and developing the reader's familiarity with the narrator.

Unless the design of a story allows or calls for AUTHORIAL INTERVENTION or comment, all narrative is seen as originating with the point-of-view character. The simple sentence, "John was waiting at the mailbox for at least a half hour before the mailman arrived," becomes translated by the reader to extend beyond mere stage directions, spilling over to reflect John's eagerness to get what he anticipates will be included in today's delivery. To add an intensifier of interior monologue to the narrative, the WRITER might render, "Was today the day it would arrive, John wondered." And to nail it all down with dialogue, John might well greet the mailman with the spoken observation, "You're running late today."

Interior monologue is thought process; in order to be successfully dramatic, it must be made to seem ACTION-based. The best way to accomplish this step is to tie the can of CONSEQUENCE to the tail of the thought. Would she ever get here, he wondered. Would she recognize him after all this time?

A handy tip for the writer: Consider all narrative as originating from a particular character's of point-of-view focus, using his or her vocabulary, biases, blind spots, range of sensory awareness. If that character is a particularly thoughtful person, the door is open for that character to think consequence-related thoughts. Would this work? Would she truly see the intended affection in his gift of daisies, or would she turn out to draw the line at roses? The hell with it. He liked daisies. If she couldn't see the beauty in them, what future was there in a relationship with her?

Readers appreciate internal monologue because it gives them a window on what the character is thinking and how the writer is able to keep dramatic tension riding shotgun with the character.

Caveat: Make sure the internal monologue is relevant to the story. In the case of the daisy-offering suitor, the choice of flowers relates to courting the girl who is, after all, the GOAL. If our suitor had interior thoughts about things unrelated to the goal, he'd be doing the same thing the character of Sonny was doing in the film *Dog Day Afternoon,* taking hostages.

Hint for readers and writers: Do not be put off by the use of such terms as "free independent speech" or, worse yet, "free independent discourse" by critics and teachers of literature or writing; they mean interior monologue; they also mean presenting the reactions and internal questions of characters without the need to resort to the "she said/he said" tags of attribution. When a character asks, "How had she let this happen?" she is talking directly to herself. If it is presented in an artful manner, you'll come away from reading it with the belief that you're eavesdropping on her personal thoughts.

internal conflict

The torturous battle between two or more opposing forces within an individual, a culture, or a society; choices a CHARACTER makes that impact his behavior in a STORY; the agony of moral choice as dramatic issue.

The key word in an internal conflict is "but," which translates as "except for the fact"; *but* is the tin can tied as a prank to the rear bumper of a car, the conditional divide between the two warring forces that tug at the character. *But* is the fulcrum, the CONTINGENCY with which the afflicted character lives. Sound dramatic principle dictates an internal conflict step forth in front rank characters: Mark Antony the soldier and Mark Antony the lover. Cleopatra struggling through the emotions of the lover and the duties and responsibility of the queen.

A PROTAGONIST may be a natural leader, except that he freezes in arguments; a scientist may be devoted to the pursuit of her research but feels compromised for once having managed the OUTCOME of one of her more significant studies. Huckleberry Finn may admire and respect the runaway slave Jim, but feels his CONSCIENCE being conflicted because, after all, Jim was his master's property and Huck has effectively helped Jim escape from his rightful owner.

The conflict may be essentially internal, particularly in the SHORT STORY, but it will have an effect on the way significant characters behave and in the way the READER feels.

intrusive author

An anomaly of irritating proportions in the modern NARRATIVE, where the WRITER intrudes on TEXT, upstaging one or more CHARACTERS; dramatic equivalents of footnotes being wrenched into the text; muddying the waters of narrative voice by allowing the author to appear in SCENES with characters. (See FOURTH WALL.)

Unless there is some contextual or stylistic reason for the author or authorial spokesperson to appear in a STORY as, say, the Stage Manager does in Thornton Wilder's *Our Town*, or in a deliberate and managed BACKSTORY, as in Junot Diaz's opening chapter to *The Brief Wondrous Life of Oscar Wao*, the message is clear: author stay out. Delegate messages and devices to characters. Spend time considering what things you want to bring on stage; then spend more time considering ways to dramatize those messages. NB: *dramatize* means that the author provides for the reader to INFER.

Writers such as Aldous Huxley, Ayn Rand, D.H. Lawrence, C. S. Lewis, George Sand, and William Makepeace Thackeray, although wildly diverse in their political and social attitudes, have remarkable and distinctive voices, enhanced to a degree but undercut to a greater degree by their incessant asides and obsessive commentary on what their characters happen to be doing at a given moment.

Writers such as Elmore Leonard, Louise Erdrich, Philip Roth, Cynthia Ozick, Tobias Wolff, Christopher Moore, and Joyce Carol Oates do not steal scenes or upstage; they become prisms through which their trained and vivid imaginations cast a spectrum of color in which the beam of Reality is refracted. The reader is allowed to discern, to see without being yanked by a chain, argued into compliance.

Hint: You have a favored author who is booked into a local venue to speak on his or her approach to storytelling. You have purchased a ticket for the event, arrive early to secure a strategic seat, and now await your anticipated pleasure only to discover that there are immediate, disagreeable complications. Your author is to be introduced by a local literary wannabe who is by no means your favorite person. The program begins with this wannabe confirming many of your reasons for disliking him; he spends a good ten minutes explaining how out of the ordinary it is for him to appear on the same stage with your favored author, then lurches through another ten minutes of describing how his own work fails to rise to the level of tonight's guest, then perhaps another ten minutes of description of the favored author's work. The introduction is now well on its way into an hour's duration, during the course of which you see the favored author, perhaps sipping nervously from a bottle of San Pellegrino, beginning to look as uncomfortable as you feel. Will you ever get to hear your favorite author?

This is the feeling the reader will most likely suffer if you intrude in your story. There are, however, novels and short stories told as if from the author's point of view— *Heart of Darkness,* for example, in which the character Marlowe could be argued to be Joseph Conrad's spokesperson. These are done with great deliberation and are not meant to be considered as authorial intrusion. The opening chapters of James Michener's *Hawaii* and *Centennial* are unabashedly (and successfully) told from the authorial point of view. The opening chapter of Junot Diaz's *The Brief Wondrous Life of Oscar Wao* is seen through the authorial point of view—or perhaps not; perhaps it is through the character Yunior, or perhaps Yunior is Diaz's spokesperson. In none of these cases does the reader feel the frustration of being lectured to at the expense of the story waiting to be read.

irony

A condition created when a CHARACTER says one thing while feeling an opposing urge; a deliberate, emphatic expression made by a character in the explicit belief that the recipient will conclude the exact opposite meaning; any lurking space between what is said and what is meant.

Irony is the stage manager for most human drama; it is the genome of crossed purposes, misinterpretation, and expressions of things being taken as other than what we intended. The marvelous prank letter inflicted on Malvolio in *Twelfth Night* demonstrates irony in a never-to-be-forgotten manner. Through a ruse, Malvolio, the steward of the attractive young Countess Olivia, is led to believe Countess Olivia has a romantic interest in him. When Malvolio appears before Olivia, dressed as the prank letter suggested, the disconnect plays forth, with irony taking the winning hand, one on which the writer doubles down when Olivia finds herself drawn to a handsome young man, Cesario, who has undertaken the job of commending to her the interest of Orsino. But of course the reader will already know the irony of Cesario not really being Cesario, but rather Viola, who wishes nothing more than the affections of Orsino. Irony truly trumps in this exemplary comedy.

As the inherent condition of a person, place, or thing being opposite to our EXPECTATIONS makes itself known, irony causes us to understand that we are in a rigged game, a drama called Life.

"it's eleven o'clock"

The first part of an iconic advert, targeting parents of teens by asking if they know where their children are at this hour; a call for parents to have greater awareness of where their children are and what they're doing; a relevant analogy targeting WRITERS to be more attentive to their CHARACTERS.

Stories traditionally focus on the activities and attitudes of front-rank characters. Nevertheless, it can be instructive for the writer to know where, at any given moment, all other characters are and what they're doing while the front-rankers are on, being done to, and responding. One extreme example of the usefulness of keeping track is found in Tom Stoppard's *Rosenkrantz and Guildenstern Are Dead*, a STORY in which the primary character is shunted to the background.

Knowing where all characters are at all times in a narrative may not produce a result so witty and engaging as the Stoppard play or as revelatory as Valerie Martin's dramatic point of view shift from the eponymous Dr. Jekyll in her role reversal, *Mary Reilly*, but there may be SURPRISES for the writer, the READER, and, of course, the characters. These surprises might not change the intended course of the story, but they can enhance the texture, which is to say the story becomes more dimensional and vibrant.

It is nearly time for DENOUEMENT. Do you know where all your characters are?

~J~

jargon

Language extending beyond conventional usage to convey hidden or special meanings; terms which openly make fun of gender, race, sexual and social orientation; terms and words used when speakers are confirming a special, insider status.

Jargon is an omnibus word, taking in academic usage, slang, lingo, buzzwords, shop talk, and idiom, representing age, class, and cultural ranges. When used in FICTION, jargon becomes a risky business because of the possibility that it will have gone out of date, dragging the narrative down with it—or, conversely, placing the narrative squarely in a particular time frame that the author may or may not intend. If a character uses the word "groovy," you can be certain you are reading a narrative that takes place in the 1960s—or can you? Is the character using the word ironically? Is the character a 1990s hipster? An aging baby boomer reverting to the slang of his youth? What does the use of that particular word tell a READER?

The other side of that coin is the lengths some WRITERS will reach in order to yank passé words from the vault as a means of presenting a verbal ZEITGEIST. A reasoned approach is to concentrate on the NEEDS, ambitions, and INTENT of CHARACTERS; those qualities will suggest the degree of jargon or lack thereof a particular character uses.

jealousy

A major dramatic emotion producing anxiety and possible fear of LOSS of status, romantic commitment, or ABILITY; concern about ability to maintain a status quo, triggered by the presence of rivals or potential rivals; insecurity over anticipated loss of a tangible thing once securely owned.

Jealousy is a major dramatic motivational force, emphasizing a CHARAC-TER's insecurity and triggering responses that contribute to deeper dramatic holes for the character in whom it resides. One of the more plausible and enduring cases of literary jealousy is seen in the unquestioned attraction between Heathcliff and Cathy Earnshaw, later to become Cathy Linton in *Wuthering Heights.* Even though she loves Heathcliff, Cathy sees Edgar Linton as a step toward a social status she aspires to. Heathcliff's loss of Cathy to Edgar provokes a PLAUSIBLE if melodramatic train of CAUSALITY that plunges into the supernatural. Jealousy as a motive in MYSTERY and detection NOVELS needs no justification as a motive.

Novels set in college/university settings frequently use jealousy as a driving force applied to members of a particular academic department, and novels with medical backgrounds may bring jealousy and/or rivalry between doctors and administrators or other doctors in similar or competing departments.

Jealousy and rivalry are splendid, yeasty dough for the WRITER to knead. And even successful writers are not immune to it in real life. Witness Mary McCarthy, who said of Lillian Hellman, "Even when she uses the word 'and' she is lying." Edmund Wilson and Vladimir Nabokov, once great friends, fell into a jealous squabble over Wilson's belief that he could render a better translation from Russian into English, even though Russian was Nabokov's birth language. From reading the journals of the gifted short story writer, John Cheever, the READER learns of his jealousy of the meteoric success of fellow writer Irwin Shaw, who admired Cheever and continuously sought his company.

The jealous individual fears the loss or diminution of something—including a personal relationship—already possessed; envy is the result when one character covets a quality, ability or relationship possessed by another.

jeopardy

A danger, risk, or peril existing as potential for a CHARACTER; the state of VULNERABILITY a character experiences before, after, and during the making of a DECISION; enhanced possibility of COMPLICATION or danger a character lives through while navigating toward SOLUTION of the problem that landed him in the STORY in the first place.

The jeopardy may be the internal one of losing faith in a person, discipline, plan, even a philosophy; it may also be the RISK of falling in love, getting into further complications, causing more damage or being caused more damage; it is the CONSEQUENCE of trying to move through the literary equivalent of a minefield while wearing snow shoes. Richard Stark (pseudonym of Donald E. Westlake) opens his Parker novel *The Outfit* with bravura jeopardy for Parker: "When the woman screamed, Parker awoke and rolled off the bed. He heard the plop of a silencer behind him as he rolled, and the bullet punched the pillow where his head had been." Only two sentences and Parker is already in jeopardy.

The more productive characters never know better, rarely know enough beyond maintaining the status quo before being mired further in some activity or ATTITUDE where they become even more firmly stuck without traction. In many ways, jeopardy is cousin to risk, a state where additional things, worse things, can arise as a consequence of a character having taken some step, whether to avoid a problem, cope with it, or entirely flee from it. A narrative without some front-rank character being in jeopardy of some consequence or in some risky circumstance is yet a story.

Jeopardy becomes the return of the pigeons to roost, the consequences of the thing that should not have been done in the first place. Now it is worse; the character could have opted out (but there would have been no story). Now there is a price to be paid.

journey, the novel of

A longform NARRATIVE in which one or more CHARACTERS embark on a trip involving a QUEST; an extended STORY involving running away from or returning to a locale, or visiting a previously unknown terrain; a longed-for visit to a particular site; may also be a PICARESQUE novel.

In formulaic terms, the NOVEL of journey represents a significant bit of travel that produces some form of RESOLUTION and, if not resolution, some DISCOVERY or awareness—which is why thematic and symbolic interpretations are drawn to the form like ornaments to a Christmas tree. One of the most venerable tales of journey focuses on Odysseus, returning to his homeland of Ithaca after having fought in the Trojan War, a journey in which the PROTAGONIST encounters and deals with a full ensemble of gods, goddesses, monsters, mere mortals, and mortal temptations.

Geoffrey Chaucer's reputation as a storyteller rests heavily on his framework tale of a group of pilgrims on their way to the Canterbury Cathedral, telling stories to pass the time. Jack Kerouac set out on a road journey, ostensibly to capture the warp and weft of the American experience, and, in the process, found the four-lane paved highway of his VOICE and crystallized sensitivity. In *The Grapes of Wrath*, the Joad family, over their heads in debt, their Oklahoma land awash in the dregs of the Dust Bowl storms and drought, set off on a journey to the land of milk and honey, or at least opportunity.

Gus McRae and Woodrow Call, bored in their retirement as Texas Rangers, undertake a cattle drive from Texas to Montana, but first they have to steal the cattle in order to have the cattle drive, thus a brief venture south into Mexico to literally rustle up a herd, and then *Lonesome Dove* can begin in earnest. John Haskell's 2005 novel, *American Purgatorio,* begins with a man whose wife inexplicably disappears while they have stopped at a gas station, then leads to a journey in which the husband tries to find the missing Annie.

Perhaps this quotation will resonate with some recognition: "I am looking for the man who shot and killed my father, Frank Ross, in front of the Monarch boardinghouse. The man's name is Tom Chaney. They say he is over in the Indian Territory and I need somebody to go after him." The speaker is fourteen-year-old Mattie Ross, the principal in Charles Portis's journey-within-a-novel, *True Grit.*

The journey novel is by its very nature a metaphor, the object of which is more or less in the hands of the WRITER.

Hint: Can you be happy with your status as READER or writer if, at some point in your consideration of the novelistic journey, you are not reminded of Joseph Campbell, who gave both camps the gift of *The Hero's Journey?*

Anne Tyler's *The Accidental Tourist* is yet another of the potential ways for the novel of the journey to provide a means of transportation to a destination that by its very nature is electric with surprise and provocative AFTER-TASTE.

justice

A sense of closure to a conflicted outcome; the payoff of a story; the rendition of a negotiated settlement on some moral, ethical, or artistic conflict.

In a legal sense, justice should be impartial, balanced and, if not quite satisfactory to all, at least carry a sense of attempted fairness. In the sense of reality, which FICTION approaches with some degree of IRONIC vision, justice is more likely to reflect blindness or bias or rank unfairness, even to the point of referring to some outcomes as poetic justice. By such reference, we imply that the universe takes care of its own, reality rewards its acolytes, the Cosmos is on our side. Life is supposed to be neutral, but look what we learn about a CHARACTER who complains, "Life isn't fair." We already know that Life is as impartial as it can be; it is POINT OF VIEW that is partial.

One instructive way of determining the ATTITUDES and visions of a particular WRITER is to consider how that writer's stories payoff as related to a scale of justice. (Consider: Evelyn Waugh, Graham Greene, Joyce Carol Oates, Willa Cather.) Another instructive approach is to ask this question after reading any work of FICTION: *Was justice done in this story?* If the answer is "no," you know you are reading a legal thriller.

~K~

Kafkaesque

Murky, conspiratorial CIRCUMSTANCES or conditions applied to CHARACTERS without any apparent reason or MOTIVE; an adjectival gloss on life coined from the name of the Czech writer Franz Kafka (1883-1924); intended to reflect mordant, irreconcilable life forces.

Kafka's own writings contain numerous EVENTS in which characters appear to be persecuted by unnamed social or political forces or from which they feel isolated, even alienated. The adjective derived from his name has become part of a greater language, describing existential events, which are useful for actors and WRITERS in their definitions of characters. To be Kafkaesque in the twenty-first century, a character may well be female, experiencing the cultural gravity of her chronological and social age. A Kafkaesque character or circumstance has come to be for the READER an occasion to question the reliability and/or complicity in victimhood of the character or circumstance.

In his lifetime, Kafka was an ardent follower of the Yiddish theater, which had a strong SATIRIC and irreverent bent, particularly in its hybrid gloss on conventional mores and conventional dramatic icons. Many American writers and actors came from this tradition. Given Kafka's own penchant for the DEAD-PAN or understated humor, it is wise to see such attributes of the Kafkaesque as conspiratorial, alienation, and conventional DETERMINISM in the context of satire, SUBTEXT, and the painful revelations of HUMOR.

Hint: Read Gregor Samsa's plight in *Metamorphosis* for its more obvious payoff of discomfort and alienation, then reread it in the context of its being a burlesque or a more sophisticated satire on family life. Read *The Trial* under the same circumstances. In both cases, note the potential for differences between the first impression, in which the author Kafka emerges as mordant, dour, and possibly paranoid; then consider Kafkaesque as having the same enlightened cynicism of so many of the great ethnic senses of humor. And then consider the delicious IRONY of a contemporary writer/performer such as Stephen Colbert, being taken with dead seriousness by the very targets of his satire.

The dramatic link between Yiddish theater—which had to be performed outside the synagogue because of its potential for profanity and DOUBLE ENTENDRE—and the theater of the absurd is as evident as contemporary stretches of Route 66. But from this now-derelict road come such credible off-ramps to Gabriel Garcia Marquez, Don DeLillo, and Joseph Heller.

The old advertising slogan once proclaimed, "You don't have to be Jewish to enjoy Levy's Rye Bread." You do not have to be ethnic to be Kafka-esque, but a little understatement, a little deadpan—it couldn't hurt.

kicking a character while he or she is down

Authorial judgment and intervention in describing a CHARACTER's attitude or fortune; usually an adjectival or adverbial attribution accorded a character in NARRATIVE, as in "he stood miserably while awaiting his fate," or "he whined piteously when confronted with evidence of his misdeeds," or "she sneaked away from the gathering, shamed by her selfish motives."

All characters have some flaws which, if set forth in a non-judgmental manner, will have the better result of allowing the READER to decide who is strong, who is weak, who is worth rooting for, who is opposing the protagonist.

Word CHOICE in the depiction of a character's behavior can betray authorial animosity, which is a step toward undermining the authenticity of a character. It is wise to avoid such verbs as slinked, slithered, cringed, snorted, barked, sneered, mocked, and all other negatively charged choices, and further to shun attributions in which the WRITER may be seen as trying unduly to influence the reader with narrative argument rather than allowing behavior to speak for itself.

In real life, depending on our index of tolerance, we will eventually call a halt to an *ad hominem* argument directed against an individual we know at first hand or by reputation alone. If a writer transgresses this index of tolerance, directing it against a character he wants the reader to dislike, the reader may very well take up the cudgel on the character's behalf and instead begin to dislike the writer or the characters the writer appears to admire.

~L~

landscape

The physical, moral, political, ethical, psychological ARENA in which a given STORY is set; the lowest common thematic denominator of a DRAMATIC NARRATIVE.

A STORY could be set in Revolutionary France, the guillotine blades still dripping blood, but the NARRATIVE instead is about individuals who had no sides in the Revolution nor cared about the CONSEQUENCES one way or another, thus rendering the landscape one of indifference, ignorance, or perhaps even some form of indulgence. Landscape decor allows the WRITER to show through direct or ironic intervention a sense of what the population of the story was feeling, thinking, doing.

Landscape is a core sampling of ZEITGEIST: the sense of the time, places, and denizens thereof. Landscape cannot—and should not—help itself; it is the writer's personality and attitude, bleeding through the scenery, that makes the STORY. Example: The enormous sprawl that is Los Angeles represents to many writers a Dante-esque version of Purgatory conflated with Inferno, emerging from their writings as a landscape of crowded freeways, drive-by shootings, PhDs and out-of-work actors doomed to waiting tables or delivering pizzas, the faux yogic posture of freedom from arthritis. The characters, settings, and attitudes resident in this landscape will emerge with some sort of cynical tinge. The visions of L.A. cherished by other writers will emerge as eternally bright, undershot with the camaraderie of hope, shared dreams, and the sun-baked sizzle of success at every major intersection. Few caught this more acutely than John Fante with such novels as *Ask the Dust* and *Dreams from Bunker Hill.*

Five hundred words or less: What was the landscape of Spain when Cervantes wrote *Don Quixote?* What was Don Quixote's relationship to his landscape? What were the landscapes of England and Scotland during the writing life of Sir Walter Scott? Compare and contrast the World War II landscapes of Norman Mailer's *The Naked and the Dead* with Irwin Shaw's *The Young Lions.*

Whatever the setting or time frame is for your landscape, do not undercut it with attempts at objectivity or floridity. Just as the READER can tell from the way a CHARACTER walks, speaks, behaves, what that character's internal landscape is, the reader similarly absorbs your Los Angeles, your feudal Spain, your own sense of the ground on which Normans came up against the Anglo-Saxons.

laundry list

A detailed list of CHARACTERS, traits, ATTRIBUTIONS appended to a STORY; qualities, personalities, DESCRIPTIONS deployed at great length in a NARRATIVE; burdensome details of an individual, SCENE, or setting.

Laundry lists had their widest use during the time of Realism, where the things a character used or wore or noticed spoke volumes toward their authenticity. The temptation to double-down on adjectives or strenuously and purposefully use duets of adverbs is great, particularly when the characters, places, and objects in a story have outstanding traits or features. The temptation to describe a character's movements in small, precise steps also flares up, particularly if, in a particular scene, the character is performing under the influence of a controlling emotion. The solution is to use as much of the laundry list as possible in the early drafts; this will insure a vivid picture of the individuals and events in which they are engaged. The second part of the solution is to see the laundry list cast as an extra in novels and short stories to convey background and personality, but—ha!—impressed by the exposure, the laundry list wants a starring role.

Anything that calls attention from the story is risky casting.

Remember also that story is EVOCATION rather than description.

layer

A stratum or single element manifest within a STORY; a SUBPLOT, thematic, or character-related motif found in a dramatic narrative.

Stories, even shorter ones, tend to have more than one layer of activity accompanying the main thrust of the story, perhaps extending to a remote past or one possibly not quite as recent as the present moment. Layering often takes form in the interaction between two or more characters, relying on ATTITUDES related to past experience or experiences between them. Results from conflicting or disappointed EXPECTATIONS among characters may also add layers of complexity to a narrative, just as they do in life. It is one thing, for example, for the READER to see in a story that husband and wife don't get along. To see that the husband also has a difficult relationship with his sister adds a layer of texture—and to see that the husband has a healthy relationship with his sibling as a different layer of texture.

The conventional wisdom for layering holds each tier responsible for some enhancement of storyline (PLOT), character development, SUBTEXT, or THEME.

Thus may a story be seen as an archaeological dig in which the reader discovers more about the individuals involved in the narrative, their social make-up, artifacts, and attitudes as each layer is excavated. In general, PLOT-DRIVEN stories tend to have fewer layers than literary, but as with all generalities related to story, the WRITER must take care not to be driven by them to the point where the reader's imagination and inventiveness are overridden.

Lewis (Meriwether) and Clark (William)

Two army officers selected by Thomas Jefferson to lead an 1803 DISCOVERY, mapping, and ethnography expedition through the northwestern corridor of North America.

Although Lewis and Clark did not specifically "discover" or encounter a hoped-for Northwest Passage, they returned with an inspirational amount of useful materials as well as a splendid written record of their travels, in the process becoming an inspiration for WRITERS. Like Lewis and Clark, a storyteller sets forth through a particular LANDSCAPE, often with a particular GOAL in mind. Never mind that more often than not the writer does not achieve the intended goal; mind instead the ancillary discoveries made by the writer, discoveries about the landscape, the characters, and the human condition. Setting forth on a STORY, even one well plotted in advance, may lead to unanticipated discoveries that inform the final result to its betterment.

With Lewis and Clark in metaphoric mind, the writer sets forth in ANTICIPATION of some discovery. Similarly, READERS embark on a story, being led by CLUES and EVENTS to expect in the PAYOFF a satisfying discovery.

likely story, a

A NARRATIVE or tale producing a cynical or questioning response from the listener/READER; an intuitive or logical sense that a narrative is of questionable value; an IRONIC expression of disbelief to a scenario, thus a judgment of information not being PLAUSIBLE.

Whenever we see or hear the words, "A likely story," in response to a narrative, we are coming face to face with audience reaction—and not the good sort. STORIES, tales, narratives, and yes, even accounts are all very much like notes in a bottle, set loose in some river or ocean by someone hopeful of a response from someone else. By its very nature a story is a crafted plea for a response, the worst of which (for the WRITER) is complete indifference. Samuel Taylor Coleridge, a protean and often pompous literary force, set in motion a concept quite relevant to the designation, "A likely story." Coleridge introduced for our consideration the WILLING SUSPENSION OF DISBELIEF, which is to say a deliberate setting aside by the READER of a narrative that its CHARACTERS, their motivations, and the resolution of these motivations are anything less than plausible.

Willing suspension of disbelief is often challenged in the courtroom of the reader's sensitivity. I don't believe that character would do or say such a thing, comes the indictment. To which the author replies, BUT IT REALLY HAPPENED THAT WAY. To which the critic replies, *Doesn't matter; it wasn't rendered in a way that convinced me.* Thus the great divide (which can be wider than the Continental Divide): what the writer of the tale observes, either from reality or imagination or a combination of the two, and what the reader believes. It comes down to plausibility. How plausible is it that the protagonist in Nathaniel Hawthorne's short story "The Minister's Black Veil" actually wore a facial covering? Only as plausible and believable as Hawthorne made it. We believe what we are led to believe, at which point the belief becomes what we want to believe. For some writers, it is second nature to bring politics into this equation as an explanation for what other people believe, views different from the writer, to which could also be added "My Kind." Me and my kind believe or can be induced to believe. The elitism continues to include my kind of truth and other people's, a not-so-subtle variation on the equation that the only real truths are those such as chemical and mathematical formula. Sorry, Jane Austen, but a truth universally acknowledged often ends up on urban myth websites. Listening to a narrative—any narrative— then deeming it "a likely story" is a frontal attack on the narrative's intent of veracity. It is the equivalent of asking, Are you serious? Are you kidding? You expect me to believe that? Saying or thinking "A likely story!" is taking a step toward cynical sanity, a form of questioning that may cause the questioner a great sense of isolation and loneliness, but in the end it causes the writer to examine his or her own unreliability as a narrator.

Some religious philosophies introduce the concept of a mantra, a series of mystically charged words to be repeated and contemplated until the individual begins to take on the very qualities embodied in the formula. Hindu mantras involve *bija* words, words crafted from Sanskrit that have no other purpose than to convey aspects of the ineffable. Our own secular mantra could very well be, "A likely story." Keeping this simple phrase in mind will help keep writers on the path of working at craft and not taking anything, particularly ourselves, too seriously. It will also work wonders to keeping us out of the urban myth casualty lists.

linkage

A useful connection between writing fiction and one or more other crafts; awareness of an outside analogy or philosophy to writing that, when applied, imparts another dimension to writing; a way of placing writing in a context that will result in helping the WRITER implement the originality of his VOICE.

Two obvious links to writing are acting and musicianship. All three are predicated on timing; all three convey emotion; all three have an individual rhetoric, which, on closer examination, addresses the same concepts and techniques. Acting is a moment-to-moment representation of a THEME or AGENDA under development. Musicianship relates to the performance of a particular work with the intent of development and interaction. All three disciplines are built around the same set of notions—relating a STORY.

Writers are more likely to recognize common interests among actors, seeing them as extensions of the CHARACTERS writers have created from whole cloth. Writers are perhaps slower to recognize the fact that their craft (like musicians' craft) uses a system of notation in which time and timing play important roles, complete with notations to represent durations of time, intensity, and meter; rondo, concerto, symphony have thematic patterns and conventions just as do FLASH FICTION, SHORT STORY, NOVELLA, serial, NOVEL.

The Japanese novelist Haruki Murikami openly expresses his fondness for jazz, having written copiously about the influences of the medium on his work, while Jack Kerouac tried to use his understanding of jazz improvisation as a defining template for his own written improv and tempo.

To get his or her work beyond the stage of imitative and philosophical reverence for individuals who are writers, the emerging writer will profit from seeing the discipline in terms of yet another discipline, say astronomy or quantum physics, but also in potential relationships with astrology, mythology, and Jungian psychology. Or baseball.

To writers familiar with the theories of circularity of events as expressed by Giambattista Vico (1668-1744), the structure of James Joyce's *Finnegan's Wake,* not the least of which being the opening and closing lines, will come as no surprise. Nor will the seemingly effortless understanding of seamanship surprise readers of Joseph Conrad, nor the comprehensive understanding of bullfighting to readers of Barnaby Conrad.

Does this infer the need for a writer to have a hobby or avocation or other compelling interest? Yes. Writers need something other than the act of writing. Tony Hillerman, for a fine example, fell in love with the ways of the Navajo people to the point where he became the William Faulkner of a large ramble of landscape in the Southwest, infinitely larger and more complex than Faulkner's Yoknapatawpha County and, as well, created at least two candidates for the Character Hall of Fame—the no-nonsense detective, Joe Leaphorn, and the cop who wanted to be a tribal shaman, Jim Chee. The point is: without passions and interests, you are surrendering necessary dimensions of the writer you seek to become. (Would Vladimir Nabokov have been the same remarkable writer if he had not been an ardent collector of butterflies? Think for a minute about his reach of observation and exquisite use of detail before answering.)

But even when a writer is in possession of a beloved hobby or avocation, there is more to be done. Whatever the "other" interest or discipline, the writer needs to exercise extreme caution against installing READER FEEDER into the work at hand merely for the sake of using the gleaned material. A writer doesn't go fly fishing in order to dazzle her readers with her knowledge of the sport—that would be tedious for a reader who could well buy a non-fiction book about fly fishing if that was what he wanted to learn about. A writer goes fly fishing as a restorative experience, to enrich her life and her grasp of metaphor, her means of articulating the lines of linkage, which in turn enriches her readers' experience of her fiction.

Lionel Essrog

The PROTAGONIST of Jonathan Lethem's 1999 novel, *Motherless Brooklyn;* a private investigator, a CHARACTER with a FATAL FLAW—Tourette's syndrome. What a brilliant flash of imagination it was for Jonathan Lethem to have anointed his lead character with Tourette's, an affliction that could be triggered at any moment, sending his cerebral circuitry off into a karaoke of the mind, his tics and associations gathering momentum like the boulder of Sisyphus on its downhill course, gathering momentum until he was forced to give over to it. Lethem could have chosen other afflictions for Essrog, not the least of which could have been *petit* or *grand mal* seizures; he could have chosen autism or perhaps even bipolar shifts from the manic high to the depressive low.

Lionel Essrog, in the moment of the big bang of his creation, became an ICON. It is not that there were no afflicted characters before him; Willie Ashenden walked with a limp as, indeed, Somerset Maugham, his creator, did; Quasimodo was a hunchback, the eponymous phantom of the opera had a badly scarred face, and Johnny Tremaine had his thumb fused to the palm of his hand when a pot of molten silver spilled. Pre-Essrogian literature is filled with men, women and children who bore a physical fatal flaw and were transformed by it to the point where they made it a valuable commodity. But Lionel Essrog took the fatal flaw to a new height: Tourette's syndrome begins interiorly, then extends outward. Lionel Essrog opened the door for Mark Haddon's Christopher John Francis Boone of *The Curious Case of the Dog in the Night Time,* allowing Boone, an autistic, to do a detective job of his own, recording his adventures in a book that at first blush seems to have a mechanical defect of missing pages until we realize that his adventure is chaptered in prime numbers, demonstrating the quirky, compulsive nature of the narrator and one of the ways by which he holds onto the reality we non-autistics leisurely take for granted.

Jonathan Lethem did for affliction what Hammett and Chandler did for the mystery. Since the appearance of Lionel Essrog, it is no longer merely democratizing to bring the afflicted and unusual out of the closet and into the full light of inquiry; it is a dramatic enhancement by which the character employs his or her transactions with the flaw to make a transformative story. In the early days of pulp magazine mystery and suspense, Frank Gruber's Oliver Quade used his preternatural memory for fact to solve crimes. Quade was known as The Human Encyclopedia, his erudition the cause of the solution. Lionel Essrog succeeds not because of his Tourette's but in spite of it. Read of Essrog in *Motherless Brooklyn* and take notes.

lit fic
The nickname given to literary fiction; STORIES and NOVELS with an emphasis on CHARACTERS as they cope with moral questions rather than following PLOTS dictated by genre fiction conventions.

The ARENA of literary fiction is a confusing but worthwhile one to enter, leaving the WRITER to make individual choices as the ideas arrive—and leaving the bookstore manager to decide where to shelve it. Christopher Isherwood's collection *The Berlin Stories* earns ranking within the lit fic classification because of the way it unifies a group of separate narratives into a single, thematic vision, and because of the way its characters may be seen as representatives of the polarized and cynical German state of the early 1930s. His character, Sally Bowles, has a significant enough role in *The Berlin Stories* to earn her the role of principal narrator when the collection was recast into a play and, ultimately, a film—*Cabaret*. Because of Sally's emotional growth as evidenced by her awareness of the behavior about her, the work could also be classified as a BILDUNGSROMAN.

Any number of literary writers has been attracted to GENRE FICTION, adapting literary techniques to help them explore the potential of the genre. Joyce Carol Oates, for instance, has written romances and mysteries along with her literary work. John Banville undertook a mystery series after having finished a novel that won the Man Booker Prize (*The Sea* in 2005), and Denis Johnson, after having won the 2007 National Book Award for *Tree of Smoke*, published *Nobody Move*, a mischievous take on the noir, hardboiled crime novels of the 1940s and '50s. And remember Graham Greene, who called certain of his novels "thrillers," as though he were abdicating some literary kingship.

Lit fic, accordingly, is the result of the writer carefully and deliberately choosing characters who best represent the issues the writer wishes to deal with, then peeling the onion of DISCOVERY with care.

literary agent

An individual who represents WRITERS with publishers; someone to whom authors are required to assign a limited power of attorney, authorizing payments due the author be made to them; often a former book editor, an individual who may have been the scapegoat (fired from a publishing company) when sales figures sagged; an individual who often becomes a writer's scapegoat when a project does not sell well or at all; an author of form letters suggesting no new clients are being accepted.

The literary agent is the first hurdle the writer must pass; because of his or her expertise, informed judgment, and taste, the agent believes what all CHARACTERS believe—the agent believes the agent is right. Often it will take more effort finding an agent to represent the work than a publisher to publish it.

NB: literary agents are not career coaches, they are not counselors for persons with emotional problems, and they are not supposed to provide motivation for writing; they are skilled editorial workers. Find a good one and take his or her advice.

literary story, the

A prose narrative written to discover a feeling, intent, or meaning; an exercise of the WRITER'S curiosity to see where the problem will lead and whence the solution—if any—will come; a prose narrative in which the writer knows the CONCLUSION or believes the provisional conclusion is, in fact, the conclusion, then retraces in order to clarify the OBSTACLE.

The writer often begins the literary story with a dramatic construct located beyond his ability to see an easy way out, barely able to deal with the emotional impact of the story in the first place, but drawn nevertheless into the void. This ongoing challenge of the boundaries of safety is one reason why many writers are suspicious of everything, why their monsters and misfits may not willingly retire at the end of a day's work. A literary story is a contract made by the writer not to write anything safe. This covenant between the writer and the writer's process has little to do with the usual risky business—the use of language as related to profanity and sexual or racial slurs—but rather with the use of language as a tool to explore layers of observed behavior, residues of speculation, and confrontations with the intransigent parts of the self.

Starting in more recent times with the literary stories of such writers as Nathaniel Hawthorne, Anton Chekhov, Edith Wharton, Katherine Mansfield, and Willa Cather, we can sense an insistent pushing at boundaries of human understanding, the beginnings of a move away from the formulaic, one-size-fits all effect.

There is no formulaic way to produce the literary story; a profitable approach, however, is the Oliver Twist approach, daring to ask for more oatmeal in an atmosphere where doing so was a simultaneous expression of acting on personal need and exposing the self to CONSEQUENCES. Need and VULNERABILITY are great comrades for the writer to have on hand. Also swimming about in the sea of the writer's uncertainty is curiosity, which should also be hauled aboard.

The difference between the literary and the COMMERCIAL TALE is the difference between RISK of the unknown and replicating the established; each tale has a dramatic genome, each produces an emotional payoff, but the point of departure is in the depth and complexity of the emotion, the difference between the shock of awareness and the nod of amusement.

literature
Written information that instructs and prompts study to discover deeper, perhaps even hidden meaning; dramatic portrayals of social, moral, and philosophical issues with a maximum of probing and a minimum of AGENDA or propaganda.

You might be tempted to regard someone else's work as mainstream and your own as literature—the first step toward the actual engagement of the forces informing literature. Whether your work is genre such as, say, Kate Atkinson's mysteries or Chris Moore's mischievous taking apart of contemporary mores and conventions, there is some point of recognition where you felt you were pushing your vision of humanity over some unseen boundary and into an act of daring and audacity, a place where you wrote to explode a niche, caused READERS to wonder why a book such as yours had not been written before. You wanted it to be understood while at the same time you wanted it to be quirky enough to cause the reader to say, "Wait a minute. Does this mean what I think it does?"

While you were writing your MYSTERY or ROMANCE or HISTORICAL, you were still high on having read Jhumpa Lahiri or Katherine Mansfield or Richard Powers, your buzz of awareness spilling over into your own work. For moments, perhaps even pages, you were thinking yours could be literature, too. And for moments, perhaps even pages, it was. You had taken the trouble to track the process of publication from the beginning of the story as it first illuminated the caverns of your mind to the submission of it, through the editor's notes, the changing of your title, and the sinking feeling that you knew less about writing than you'd first thought after seeing the copyedited version of your manuscript. You experienced the flush of finality when your author's copies arrived and the tingle of excitement when you saw your own work in a bookstore, followed by the momentary flash of anger when you saw your book for sale in a used bookstore. All these feelings go with authorship and literature—even the ones experienced in the used bookstore.

loss

The quality of having experienced or possessed something at one time, but no longer; a sense of something or someone being valued then wrested away by CIRCUMSTANCE; an ability, a position or talent once enjoyed and used, no longer accessible either through neglect or a deliberate disassociation; a relationship such as a friendship, mentorship, or romantic connection abrogated by death, neglect, or lack of interest; a prized possession lost or stolen; sums of money or other trade-based media subjected to RISK then forfeited through rules of the risk; the after-the-fact realization of something or someone of value being appreciated in retrospect.

Loss, an important coeval to experience, is a significant means by which a WRITER can convey to the READER a sense of who a particular CHARACTER is; a simple list of things lost begins to supply background, but dramatic focus on such internals as innocence, face (thus dignity), ambition, power, youth, confidence begins to sketch in an inferential picture of how the character will respond under specific circumstances. The focus on such dramatic externals as agility, hair, teeth, eyesight, hearing, and particular abilities associated with performance that do not result in pain or stiffness further define a character and that individual's attitude.

Imagine a particular character, then, engaging the loss of a loved one, a special professional position, or some treasured relic or memento. Imagine as well a particular character becoming aware of lapses of memory. In such awareness and recognition or, conversely, by lack of awareness, a dimension of the character emerges, propelled by loss, by grief, or by the stoic presence of denial stalking the battlements instead of a ghost with an AGENDA. Think about Beethoven, who revolutionized the music of his day, writing some of the most sublime music of his life after his hearing had departed from him, to appreciate how loss can impact character for good as well as for ill.

As in real life, characters will do things with greater purpose in their attempts to regain what has been lost or to attempt to protect what might next be lost, in so doing revealing even greater depths of themselves, embarking perhaps on an ever-widening path of VULNERABILITY.

We can learn so much from a character once we discover what that character has lost. The effect of the learning increases exponentially as we watch how the character responds, tries to regain what has been lost or come to terms with the loss. Even a comic-strip character can "benefit" from loss: B.C. in *Doonesbury* came vividly to life dealing with the loss of his leg in Iraq, his rehab, his getting used to his prosthesis, his eventual outreach to others whom he saw as having been even more wounded than he was.

~M~

macguffin, the, (also mcguffin)

A DEVICE or object that appears germane to the PLOT of a NOVEL or SHORT STORY but which has little to do with the OUTCOME; a DISCOVERY such as a map, a letter, a weapon that serves as a plausible distraction from the THROUGHLINE of a story.

The concept of the macguffin bears striking resemblance to ANTICLIMAX, which starts as an ACTION, EVENT, or thought that distracts from a recently established dramatic high point, quite possibly even an intended conclusion or the PAYOFF of a scene. Anticlimax is a dramatic pull away from the previous effect, leaving both READER and writer bewildered. (See SHAGGY-DOG STORY.)

In a geometry class setting, macguffin could be demonstrated to be congruent to RED HERRING which, one account of origins has it, was actually a dried fish, dragged across the trail of some valid prey such as a raccoon, fox, or badger to draw young dogs in training off the scent, whereupon they would be educated not to be distracted. The red herring has the same purpose as the macguffin, which is to draw the attention of the characters and, if done to good effect, the readers off the true plot line of a story and into a dead end. Red herrings are also used in debate and logic contests to draw the participants off the THROUGHLINE of argument.

A standout example of the macguffin at work is the reputed Maltese falcon of Dashiell Hammett's eponymous novel, a statue that may be a repository for jewels and gold. The Indiana Jones films also come to mind, as does the Alfred Hitchcock film, *North by Northwest*, in which the macguffin was microfilm copies of documents "vital to the survival" of the United States. In much of its use, the macguffin begins with enormous importance, and then, as characters begin to interact and alliances begin to be formed, its significance dwindles, making it possible to argue for the macguffin in a Western being grazing rights for cattle or barbed wire fences interfering with the concept of free range.

The macguffin is a gimmick similar to THE CHOKING DOBERMAN, an armature about which to wrap elements of PLOT and CHARACTER. The more plausible it may be made to sound, the more plausible the related responses of characters involved will seem. An argument could accordingly be made for one of the great macguffins in American history being the Northwest Passage Lewis and Clark were dispatched to find in 1803, an argument that has as collateral the dramatic value of the outcome, once the macguffin has failed to live up to its expectations.

magic

A non-scientific ability to control natural phenomena through charms, spells, ritual, and alchemy; paranormal behavior or abilities exhibited by individuals and inanimate objects; a POWER that allows designated individuals to foretell future events and/or defy known physical qualities; the attribution of unusual traits, qualities, and abilities to real and imaginary beings.

Magic is the basic power in all FANTASY FICTION, its possession and use having an effect on who the READER sympathizes with. Magic often has a time span—a CHARACTER, for example, having the magic of remaining invisible for thirty minutes after which point he will become immediately visible wherever he happens to be. Magic is the glue that holds spells and curses in place; it is a power to be possessed, used, challenged. Just as some ADVENTURE and HISTORICAL stories depict the clash of rival forces, FICTION is often presented as a contest between good and evil, the good or better force triumphing with a little help from some magical friends.

Magic often employs animals, spirit beings, totems, and arcane formula as adjuncts to mystical forces, directed by mortals or imaginary beings who have found ways of manipulating the force. Individuals who become magicians are able to manipulate elements, chemical reactions and human destinies, using them for good or evil purposes, but sometimes merely for selfish reasons.

Attributing magical qualities to a person, place, or thing is also a superlative on steroids, a hyperbole expressing extreme admiration. Describing an individual, a setting, a work of art as magical is the ultimate hyperbole of declaring it too good to be true and thus by implication it can only exist through paranormal circumstances.

magical realism

Dramatic NARRATIVES told from the perspective of one or more narrators who have a vision of reality that differs from the conventional; STORIES in which beings, places, and EVENTS appear as though conventional, their existence supported by the behavior of one or more CHARACTERS and/or the WRITER; narratives which suggest alternate origins, universes, and abilities than those found in conventional literature.

Against a setting most CHARACTERS and READERS would agree is a plausible rendition of reality, the writer of magical realism adds one or more fantastical elements that barely slip under the net of READER believability or are not overtly challenged because everything else seems acceptably real. Accordingly, characters in magical realism are less likely to seem vulnerable than those in super realism, the measure of a writer's ability and popularity ranked in accordance with the degree to which readers believe their characters are subject to harm. Thus the intriguing comparison between two seemingly incomparable couples, Frederic Henry and Catherine Barkley in Hemingway's *A Farewell to Arms*, and Lyra Belacqua and Will Parry in Pullman's *The Subtle Knife,* the former being lovers from an all-too believable wartime reality, the latter lovers in a reality infused with alternate universe topography and magical realism. The argument here is that while the relationship between Henry and Barkley is convincing enough and poignant, the young love romance between Belacqua and Parry is the more memorable because of a greater depth of detail and NUANCE, in spite of being set in a patently unworldly landscape. The further argument becomes: no matter how fanciful the setting, if the details of a commonly felt emotion are strong and nuanced enough, the reader is more likely to suspend disbelief to the point of accepting the magic along with the realism.

Such widely diverse authors of magical realism as Ben Okri, Gabriel Garcia Marquez, Isabel Allende, and Alice Hoffman employ the medium with a significant lack of defensiveness, while the Japanese author, Haruki Murikami, is so deft in his applications that the reader may totally buy into his uses of COINCIDENCE, dream states, and implied symbolism.

A good governing principle for the use of magical realism is to set one magical element into a world of stubbornly exact realistic detail.

manipulation

An arrangement of dramatic elements to produce an emotional effect in a STORY; distortion or exaggeration of NARRATIVE events; the deliberate bending of perspective and/or time in a story; use of IMPLICATION and subtlety to engage readers; use of a RED HERRING to alert or divert READERS' suspicions.

WRITERS are the literary equivalent of chiropractors, adjusting, kneading, articulating; they are looking for a DESIGN pattern to provide the best posture for a story. A basic approach to such adjusting is to rearrange the time sequence. Mystery writer and teacher Leonard Tourney is an advocate of "a slice of the crime," in which he advocates beginning a narrative with a crime being planned or executed by individuals we will meet later on in the text. James Joyce manipulated temporally in *Finnegan's Wake*, beginning the huge, complex novel with the last half of the opening sentence, then, hundreds of pages later, ending with the first half of the sentence. Tim Gautreaux's *The Missing*, narratively acute and suspenseful from the opening line, actually manipulates dramatic convention in the sense of providing a double hit of BACKSTORY before the main issue is introduced.

In addition to time manipulation, the writer may perform narrative chiropractic with POINT OF VIEW, choosing FIRST-PERSON, SECOND-PERSON, THIRD-PERSON, OMNISCIENT, and MULTIPLE POINTS OF VIEW, and in some cases venture into AUTHORIAL INTERVENTION to make commentary on the characters and their doings. This last approach is amply demonstrated in Henry Fielding's *Tom Jones* and William M. Thackeray's *Vanity Fair.* Aldous Huxley often stops a novel in progress to discuss the past, present, or future of a particular character or to offer a brief philosophical commentary.

Characters—their motives and activities—may be manipulated to the extent of influencing the way other characters and readers will respond to them, and indeed, motives may be manipulated to provoke reader SYMPATHY or ANTIPATHY.

Manipulation works best when it does not call attention to itself but seems to be a natural presentation. Such control is exemplified in the entire presentation of *Captain Corelli's Mandolin* by Louis de Bernières.

manuscript

The text of a NARRATIVE, either printed on 8?" X 11" manuscript paper, or as a formatted electronic package which may be transmitted by electronic mail; one or more pages of text formatted in accordance with publishing conventions.

The WRITER's first responsibility in preparing a manuscript for submission is to learn the publishing conventions. Most book publishers in the U.S. standardize on (and copyedit to) the conventions of CMS, The University of Chicago Manual of Style, aka *Chicago Manual of Style.* In addition, most book publishers standardize on punctuation, spelling, usage preference, and word-break conventions articulated in *Merriam-Webster's Collegiate Dictionary* although a wise and useful investment for the writer is the *American Heritage (unabridged) Dictionary of the English Language*. One compelling reason for considering AH is the number of writers on its usage panel, which means the ranking of meanings is vetted by persons who use words as tools rather than objects of scholarly inquiry. Magazine and journal publishers have different usage conventions relative to the use of numbers, abbreviations, capitalization, and punctuation. A handy guide is *The New York Times Manual of Style and Usage*, yet another is *The Associated Press Stylebook*.

The key to the preparation of any manuscript is the consistency of usage.

It is not necessary to concern yourself with COPYEDITING, punctuation, or spelling until you have engaged and completed the REVISION process. Some say that a part of the revision process includes an awareness of usage convention and appropriate application. If you don't "do" copyediting, however, hire someone who does. The professional writer's obligation is to turn in a professional manuscript. Mystery writer Tony Gibbs, himself a former *New Yorker* staffer and son of Wolcott Gibbs, the noted first-generation *New Yorker* staffer, liked to recount stories of when manuscripts from John Updike arrived because the interest in the new work extended beyond the editorial content to the exquisite accuracy of its presentation. The goal of the revision process is to have a manuscript that can be sent forth into submission with no further work, thus any preparation of manuscript is mechanical.

You may have some reason, particularly in longer works, to use different type faces to convey such effects as handwriting, interior monologue, shifts in point of view, newspaper stories, e-mail, Twitter entries, etc. Best bet is to be as simple as possible, making your design-related suggestions to the editor after the fact of acceptance.

Much of the time, we will not have direct personal contact with those on the receiving end of our manuscripts, meaning that the arrival of the manuscript and its condition speaks of its creator to the READER. As you would not appear for a formal gala wearing sweat pants, your manuscript should reflect at first glance, via its crispness and legibility, your having dressed for the occasion. Professional writers tend to prepare their manuscripts as though the words on the pages merit respect and consideration. Think how you would feel if a colleague handed you a business card that had coffee stains on it, notes scrawled on the back, and perhaps a dented corner.

Think of the impression your manuscript will have on the reader, known to you or not; then think of that reader settling into reading your text, formatted, punctuated, and spelled with consistency, your choice of words exquisite, spiraling upward to the authoritative sense of authorship you mean to convey.

marginal

A fictional or critical condition resident in a CHARACTER or CONCEPT; a necessary condition of a person or idea to convey the distance from mainstream; the distance from the statistical mean occupied by a character or concept.

Marginal characters are highly provocative of STORY; they may take on AGENDAS that will further remove them from the mainstream or nurse some desire to move closer to it even as they may provoke envy or discomfort among those already in it. Marginal ideas are equally fecund. Ideas seen as conventional wisdom rise up in status, where they become threats or shibboleths, waved about by such characters as those in the novels of Upton Sinclair, Horatio Alger, James Fenimore Cooper, Tom Clancy, and Steig Larsen, to be accordingly shunned or promulgated.

Many of the characters of LITERARY and GENRE fiction began as marginal; some gravitated to the IRONIC conclusion of mainstream, others continued to enhance their marginality. A diverse array of historical and CONTEMPORARY FICTION addresses the existential condition of marginality—*The Swiss Family Robinson*, for instance, or *Robinson Crusoe* serving to represent enforced separations from the mainstream; *Lord of the Flies* representing quite another result as mainstream characters shift away from their societal armature. The political satire *Catch-22* could be seen as an ironic triumph of the marginal man, and *The Man in the Gray Flannel Suit* could be seen as another commentary altogether on marginality, where individuality is seen as undesirable.

Start with a character who is out of the mainstream, say a high school student whose parents have moved her to a new city where she has to start making new friends. There is a group of students who attract her, but they are tight-knit, jealous of their status. Add to the calculus a member of the in-group who is drawn to the outsider. Result: story under way. One of the more productive dramatic clashes is the formula of the marginal wanting to become mainstream and mainstream envy of the constraint-free status of the marginal.

Mars probe, the

A complex data-assessing instrument sent from Earth to Mars to gather and relay climatic, geological, weather-based data and other measurement-related information about Mars, back to Earth; a metaphor for the individual WRITER's sensory-gathering apparatus, allowing the writer to send a probe into differing cultures, locales, relationships, and emotions, classifying and filing them for later use in creating settings and circumstances.

The expense, energy, and planning needed to get Mars probes to their destination, or in orbital paths from which they can relay photographs, serves to enhance the metaphor for a writer: Often the search for the Big Theme or the Big Story causes the writer to miss entirely the smaller details which, on examination and understanding, provide significant hints to human evolution, history, and emotional complexity.

Each writer has a unique sensory genome, taking in, absorbing and synthesizing for future use the smorgasbord of available experience. This sensory genome contributes significantly to the emergence of the individual writer's VOICE, without which the writer is more a transcriber of events than a teller of STORY.

matchmaker

A READER of a NOVEL or SHORT STORY; an individual who becomes interested in one or more CHARACTERS in a narrative to the point of becoming invested in their activities.

A matchmaker is on the lookout for your characters, regardless of age or gender. The matchmaker surveys likely romantic interests, possible friends, co-conspirators, colleagues. You may have your own AGENDA for your characters, which is not only a good thing, it is a vital thing, but the reader will also have plans as well. This, too, is not only a good thing, it is a vital thing. The reader must care; otherwise the characters you have created will seem only as substantial as the bubble package for throw-away products at the supermarket.

What then to do about this seeming conflict of interest? Suppose your down-the-road plans for Character A involve a comfortable hook-up with Character B, but the reader is thinking maybe Character D or E is a better candidate? Answer: nothing. Let it happen because you can't stop it and because it will add the pleasure of involvement to the reader's experience with your work. Somewhere in every generation of readers, there are those who root for the eponymous protagonist of *Ivanhoe* to cast his romantic lot with Rebecca rather than the fair-haired Rowena. Similarly, readers will consider Anne Shirley of the Green Gables series a natural for Gilbert and others still will be rooting for her to pair up with the mischievous Royal.

However vexing it may be for the WRITER, readers will not only attempt to broker relationships the writer never intended, readers can also become involved with so-called Fan-Lit, in which they compose entire episodes of a work that the writer never intended, sharing these Fan-Lit concepts on blogs and in virtual editions. These add-on episodes are, it is to be emphasized, the product of respect, admiration and—matchmaking.

mcguffin, the

(See MACGUFFIN.)

messenger

A CHARACTER that physically brings news on stage (into the NARRATIVE); an individual who by example becomes a recognizable symptom of a fate that could befall a front-rank character.

Ever since the days when authors not only could but *were* expected to address the reader directly, a persistent opposition to that practice has evolved. Henry Fielding's PICARESQUE romp *Tom Jones* (1749) and Laurence Sterne's rollicking *Tristram Shandy* (1759) led the way toward the authorial aside, a technique that may be yet employed today, provided it is done with an inventive purpose—otherwise editors will thank you for thinking of them and wish you good luck elsewhere. Enter the messenger, appropriately dressed for work in your STORY, bearing some message, INTENT, or example of behavior thought to be of contextual interest to the READER.

Messengers are of primary importance in contemporary fiction because the reader may still have his doubts about the author, but if the reader has gone beyond the first five or six paragraphs of a SHORT STORY or the first chapter of a NOVEL, he arguably believes the characters more than he believes the author.

metaphor

A literary device that makes a comparison between two persons, places, or things (often unseen previously), causing a sudden awareness of relevance.

"Sometimes," Sigmund Freud said, "a cigar is only a cigar." By that statement, we may assume he meant the shape of the cigar is not to be construed as a phallic symbol or even a wand, merely a tightly wrapped bundle of selected aromatic tobacco leaves. Not in FICTION, it isn't. No matter what Freud said or meant, STORY is different; the father of psychoanalysis gives way to Yogi Berra in that, as the former baseball great might have said, "Even when it is only a cigar, it is not only a cigar."

Metaphor is the explosive result of man's presumptuous brain, linking things, comparing them, evaluating them. Thus do all stories become metaphors for something other than what they are. Beginning WRITERS, whose early attempts at story may be misunderstood, gradually come to realize the Zen-like need of letting go of proprietary control of what metaphor their work will convey, a letting go that leads them to embrace AMBIGUITY, from which they take the next significant steps forth in the ARC of their career as writers.

Writers at all stages of emergence need to avoid CLICHÉ in their choice of comparisons; cliché inhibits the growth of metaphor in a STORY. As an example, let's take the hoary idiom, "Turnabout is fair play," undoubtedly itself a riff on "What's sauce for the goose is sauce for the gander." OK. Professional couple, a man and wife in their mid-forties, both well placed. Two young kids. Wife gets the big break, a district manager in L.A., where they live. At the same time, he gets the Big Promotion, but in New York. There are at least two possible ways to go with this story concept—any number of explorations that avoid cliché are possible. This cliché, for example, introduces the potential for theme in a fresh iteration of the gender issue, including what's so awful about a man being a house husband while the wife works, and the added potential for the spouse who gives up the high-profile job to go along with the other stumbling upon a hobby that explodes with such potential that it pulls both characters in.

Mickey Mouse ending

The ending to a SHORT STORY or NOVEL in which justice triumphs with a loud tap of the gavel and the characters act as though they'd just been awarded E tickets to Disneyland; exaggerated all's-well-that-ends-well CONCLU-SIONS, prognoses, or PAYOFFS.

Not all stories require endings in which CHARACTERS are being led to the gallows. Many stories build to conclusions that by their very nature transmit touchy-feely emotions and are to be relished as, say, a frothy cappuccino or a bottle of Sierra Nevada pale ale. But Mickey Mouse endings connote a mindless move toward propaganda that pays homage to cultural decorations. Such endings relegate the PROTAGONISTS of a story to the equivalent of the figures atop wedding cakes, a doughy, sugar-laced concoction colored with vegetable dye.

It is no accident that Mickey Mouse, the iconic nice-guy figure from the second generation of comics in America, has devolved into an adjective for types of music, books, and ad hoc events suggestive of music heard while riding in elevators or while waiting on hold for customer support from large organizations. In a terrible celebration of wholesome excess, Mickey Mouse endings have become associated with the controlling imperatives of the company that owns him via copyright and registered trademark, a formulaic vision of the human condition, fostering a SUBTEXT of cynicism bordering on outright antipathy.

Much about endings of stories can be learned from reading the short stories of Anton Chekhov and James Joyce, adding to this accretion of wisdom the dead-pan wryness of Mark Twain, leavening the mixture with the individual writer's own special view on what it takes to make a go of life in the twenty-first or, for that matter, any century.

Yet more is to be learned from comparing the rules of behavior surrounding Mickey Mouse and his ensemble crew with the rules and regulations governing yet another figure from the animation world, WILE E. COYOTE. From the former "bible," the writer can glean little more than ways to produce Mickey Mouse endings. From the latter, the writer can glean a workable recipe of HUMOR and a GPS of the human agenda.

middle

A point in a STORY after the OPENING VELOCITY of the BEGINNING where CHAR-ACTERS, confronted with problems, needs, threats, or DEADLINES, have engaged their circumstances with some attempt at understanding and solution, only to have encountered a REVERSAL, SET-BACK, or some other form of accelerated complication where things seem even worse than at the outset.

STORY is conventionally thought to have three basic parts: beginning, middle, and ending that are more or less—but not necessarily—of equal length. The information provided in the beginnings and middles provides the characters and, often, the WRITER with possible solutions or endings. The compiler of *The Fiction Writer's Handbook* is fond of describing story in classes and writers' conferences as having three parts: a beginning, a muddle, and a negotiated settlement.

Hint: When thinking of middles, think about adding complications—and then more complications, even to the point of SCHADENFREUDE.

mise-en-scène

A term that covers the visual aspects of a STORY; DESCRIPTIONS or EVOCATION of a place, a time, and a setting; the positioning and movement (but not physical description of CHARACTERS) of individuals in a dramatic NARRATIVE.

The term has been borrowed from the stage and motion picture set where it refers to uses and placement of scenery, BLOCKING, and atmosphere. When used critically or editorially to discuss a particular NOVEL or STORY, it may mask the critic's or editor's desire to make the CONCEPT of setting seem more mystical than it ought to be, thus the warning to WRITERS that terms expressed in foreign words or terms (such as DENOUEMENT and DEUS EX MACHINA) should be made to show their passports at the border: Is there, they might ask, a suitable English language translation?

Mise-en-scène is a valuable tool for a writer, but it is analogous to a power tool in that both must be appreciated and understood before they are used, otherwise they may provide disastrous results that prove to be tedious or harmful rather than instructive. Look to Cynthia Ozick's use of descriptions of music in *Foreign Bodies.* The descriptions of various types of music are vital to our understanding of the characters who make the music and play an active part in the payoff. Willa Cather's descriptions of the prairie in *My Antonia,* particularly the sea-like movement of the grass in the wind, provide insights into the emotional complexity of Jim Burden, the narrator, his feelings for Antonia, and the inevitability of the outcome.

Mise-en-scène, however, can also be mis- or overused, and requires close attention in the REVISION stage to keep it from interfering with the orderly advance of story. At the time of their publication, Herman Melville's South Seas novels, *Omoo* and *Pierre*, were good contemporary examples of successful *mise-en-scène;* today's READER is likely to start skimming for indications that story has resumed. In its more optimal uses, *mise-en-scène* gives the writer of NARRATIVE FICTION an opportunity to provide SUBTEXT, wherein the setting and/or activities of characters provide an unspoken, unwritten feeling or THEME. Richard Powers's novels, *Generosity* and *The Time of Our Singing* do the work of *mise-en-scène* without actually suggesting it, thanks to their deft balance of description and narrative movement.

Consider early on in the first act of Tennessee Williams's play *A Streetcar Named Desire*, where the principal character, Blanche DuBois, appears. Had *Streetcar* been a novel, we might have had some moments of interior monologue, but as the play is mounted, we see Blanche appearing in a brightly lit room, turning down the lights as she appears to be looking for something. Our curiosities aroused, we follow her as she approaches a hidden bottle of whiskey, then takes a bracing pull on it. Not a word has been spoken, and yet we have learned things about her.

What would it say, for instance, about two characters who are watching television in their bedroom? What would it say about the same two characters who were watching television in their living room, each seated behind a fold-up tray on which a dinner dish rested? What else would it say about the same two characters if they were sitting on separate Laz-y Boy chairs which had clear plastic covers on them?

The most effective use of the *mise-en-scène* concept can be experienced by remembering the importance of STORY in the dramatic equation. If *mise-en-scène* contributes to a deeper sensory awareness of story, then it is successful.

moment
An instant of fixed or indeterminate time within a STORY; a cross-section of a SCENE; a point in which CHARACTERS react in one way or another; they may react by each standing ground and refusing to give or, conversely, exchanging the warmth of shared GOALS and purpose, or openly addressing antagonism, or pretending to be in accord while seething with resentment (which is SUBTEXT).

All stories have an ARC of elapsed time; a moment is a segment of that elapsed time which, however brief, should earn its way into the story, either through NARRATIVE recitation or the more specific focus of an exchange of DIALOGUE. There should be one or more reasons for including a particular moment in a story, yet other reasons for allowing the moment to achieve its merited significance—and, of course, the significance of the hint of emotion inherent in a particular moment is found in the overall emotion achieved by the story.

A moment in a dramatic narrative is like a note in a concerto or symphony; the moment is to be experienced at a particular speed, which the WRITER may control by description, confrontation, intimidation, or resolution. A story's PACE is determined by the length of its moments and the intervals of time at which these moments occur.

ms

The common abbreviation for MANUSCRIPT. Plural **mss.**

A manuscript is conventionally thought to be a double-spaced presentation on 8?" x 11" white paper with a basis weight of 20# and an opacity of at least 92, rendered on one side only. With the exception of author information on the title page, all other text is double-spaced.

Most publications are now accepting electronic submissions. Nevertheless, the terms ms and mss, derived from templates and formats designed as though they were paper pages, with inch-and-a-half margins, and a straightforward, serifed typeface delivering approximately 250 words per page, remain standard usage.

MTIWK

A marginal note a WRITER may find on a MANUSCRIPT accepted for publication or, worse yet, a comment on a rejected manuscript; a potential judgment by one or more READERS on a portion of a published STORY; an indication from a relatively reliable source that the indicated passage is More Than I Wanted to Know.

MTIWK has its origins in an undoubtedly apocryphal story of a young boy assigned to prepare a book report on Herman Melville's *Moby-Dick*, who is said to have begun his report: "This book tells me more about whales than I want to know."

The thrust of this entry is to remind the writer of the difference between what he has to know in order to write something and the writing itself. The READER wants to do some work. If the opportunity to contribute to the experience is utterly removed, the result is sure to be boredom.

multiple point of view

A narrative design by which the DETAILS of a STORY are seen and reacted to by more than one observer; a pattern of the same dramatic event or subsequent events seen from the perspective of numerous witnesses.

For a longer work (NOVEL, NOVELLA, NOVELETTE) multiple point of view may be the most felicitous, allowing the WRITER to include widely differing variations on the THEME, extending TENSION and SUSPENSE through the mere fact of the various narrators having differing opinions about the EVENTS the READER has seen and of the CHARACTERS' opinions of what they mean. A significant advantage to the multiple point of view approach is the potential for one or more of the narrators to be unreliable or naïve, the READER being left to discover the results.

One of the oldest extant versions of multiple point of view, the *Rash-omon* stories, relates an incident as seen from the point of view of several of the participants and close witnesses, complete with a trial presided over by judges bent on getting at the truth and including the summons of one of the witnesses (who had subsequently died) from the spirit world to testify.

A splendid, more modern version of the multiple point of view as a source of fresh perspective may be found in Tim O'Brien's short story "The Things They Carried." O'Brien uses a spectrum of American soldiers, engaged in the Viet Nam war, developing their personalities through the contents of their equipment, letters from home, and INTERIOR MONOLOGUE.

Although multiple point of view is most commonly presented with a number of narrators represented by the use of the pronouns he or she, there is no convention or edict against using the pronoun I or, indeed, mixing she, I, he. The major concern associated with the use of multiple points of view is that the reader always be able to identify the immediate narrator. Wilkie Collins has provided a substantial role model for this in *The Moonstone,* in which the differing points of view each get a separate chapter.

mystery

An enigma—a puzzle to be coped with by a single CHARACTER or team of characters in a GENRE NOVEL; an attempt by a WRITER to solve a perplexing condition or circumstance.

Lima, Peru: Friday, June 12, in the year of our Lord 1714. A bridge across a gaping chasm, woven perhaps a hundred years earlier by heathen Incas, collapses, sending five individuals to their deaths. Brother Juniper, a Franciscan monk who was about to set foot on the bridge at the moment of its collapse, wonders why he was spared and why the five individuals who were on the bridge at the time of its collapse were allowed to proceed to their death. He is, in a sense, investigating what could be variously seen as God's purpose, the nature of God, the meaning of life, and mysteries of the universe. Thus *The Bridge of San Luis Rey* by the American novelist and dramatist Thornton Wilder. In an interview conducted some twenty years after the publication of the novel, Wilder was asked if he would have reached different conclusions or ended the novel differently at this later date, to which Wilder observed that he had moved beyond his personal state of curiosity about the elements of the story that had intrigued him earlier. In other words, he had moved beyond his need to write that novel, perhaps even having "discovered" the answers or answerability to his prompting questions.

Dashiell Hammett set forth another kind of existential mystery in his novel *The Maltese Falcon,* where the major issues were who killed Spade's partner, Miles Archer, where was the "real" Maltese falcon, and was there in reality such a prize as there had been in urban myth?

A. S. Byatt has set forth an academic mystery in her novel *Possession*. Did a noted Victorian poet enter an adulterous affair with another poet? Had there, in fact, been a child born of that relationship? In the present day, an obscure American scholar, eager to forge his own reputation, makes a discovery in the London Library that leads him to suspect the connection between the two Victorian-era poets. His discovery leads him into a meeting with and then a competition with an attractive and well-regarded scholar, a distant relative of one of the two Victorian poets. Among the mysteries unearthed, literally and figuratively, is the NUANCED one imparted to the reader: will the modern scholars find a mutual romantic connection?

Mystery is an essential SUBTEXT or direct THEME for all fiction, making the reading of at least one such genre work a necessity for every storyteller. The THROUGHLINE of a MYSTERY NOVEL is its introduction of one or more murders, the discovery of CLUES, and the use of clues as an avenue to the SOLUTION, at which point the STORY is over, with scant room—perhaps a paragraph or two—for an EPILOGUE in which some ironic or instructive commentary is hinted.

Hint: Before undertaking the revision of a novel-length work, read at least one mystery from the time period between Wilkie Collins's *The Moonstone* and a Tony Hillerman Joe Leaphorn/Jim Chee mystery, and one mystery from the twenty-first century. This is standard advice for every genre: pick one or two acknowledged classics from Generation One, and at least one work that is less than five years old to see how narrative techniques, point-of-view use, and other dramatic and social conventions have impacted the genre. The writer pushes the genre, imparting her or his own thumbprint on it; the reader gleans a sense of evolution and personality.

~N~

naïve narrator

An inexperienced, innocent or impaired filter of reality through which dramatic accounts are revealed.

The presence of a naïve narrator is often a signal of ironic intent on the part of the author; in the case of Don Quixote, the naïveté and IRONY are declarations of SATIRIC intent; in the cases of Huckleberry Finn in the eponymous novel, or Scout in *To Kill a Mockingbird*, their naïveté about slavery leads each character to a moral evaluation of that practice and an opportunity to change—an opportunity each takes.

The naïveté of the narrator often has no effect on the CHARACTER being likable to the READER. Sam, the naïve narrator of Bobbie Ann Mason's *In Country*, is old enough to be sexually aware. Her growth comes from her attempts to learn more about her father, who was killed in the Viet Nam war; in so doing, she discovers things about herself, her conscience, and her country and, just as Huck Finn and Scout had done before her, learned to leave her inexperience and innocence behind. Benjy Compson, in Faulkner's *The Sound and the Fury*, cannot change or learn; his brain has limited capacity. Nevertheless, his vision of events in the novel compels the reader to make comparison between Benjy and less intellectually challenged characters in the NARRATIVE, raising significant questions for the reader to ask and comparisons for the READER to make.

The real irony with naïve narration appears when the beginning or intermediate WRITER uses the device to pursue a story about her belief that Daddy and Mommy must be doing a lot of wrestling at night because of the grunts and groans that come from their room; compare this tired CLICHÉ with the seasoned writer using the naïve narrator to take on a serious moral issue that has a grip on the human condition.

For more approaches yet to the naïve narrator, consider George Orwell's *Animal Farm*, in which the narrator refuses to accept the implications of the fable being presented; consider also the narrator of Ring Lardner's extraordinary short story "Haircut" in which we have a barber giving a complete stranger an inside look at a local scandal, apparently unaware of the implications.

narrative

The systematic arrangement of dramatic information for the purpose of relating a STORY; presentation of CHARACTER-BASED activities that involve READERS to the point where they feel a stake in the outcome; EVENTS related with the purpose of keeping the reader alert, anxious, and concerned.

"Narrative" is a lazy term, being used generically to mean any story or tale. Narrative in a novel or short story is the sum of INTERIOR MONOLOGUE, DESCRIPTION, *MISE-EN-SCÈNE*, and ACTION, which leaves only DIALOGUE as non-narrative. A WRITER'S narrative is any FICTION intended for print or web media. A writer's VOICE is the tone with which a story is freighted.

narrative hook

A dramatic device intended to draw or, if necessary, lure a READER into a STORY by placing an interesting CHARACTER in a situation of STRESS or VULNERABILITY; using a MYSTERY or puzzle to intrigue readers; any combination of narrative circumstances and circumstances that arouse interest and curiosity in a reader; an effective SCENE or situation placed at the BEGINNING of a STORY with the intent of building sympathy or an empathetic connection between reader and character.

Some narrative hooks are so simple and straightforward on the surface that they completely belie their subversive intent, almost to the point of daring the reader to set the work down without thought of returning to see what happens next. This observation is made to suggest the infinite varieties of narrative hook, ranging from those of the PLOT-DRIVEN STORY (a man or woman in immediate trouble) to the more CHARACTER-DRIVEN (a character is confronted with an intriguing choice which must be made almost momentarily) story.

Regardless of the genre and appropriate ominous nature of the circumstances confronting the characters, narrative hooks have as their GOAL gaining and keeping the attention of the reader. The key is some form of ACTION or a deliberate inaction in the face of some need to perform, meaning the narrative hook is action-based, often with little or no support by way of explanation or reference to past events which might have some effect on the present moment.

Some narrative hooks are little more than effective opening lines, such as "Call me Ishmael." Having decided to compose a novel based on the merest fact in Melville's *Moby-Dick* that Captain Ahab had a young wife, Sena Jeeter Nasland needed for her own novel, *Ahab's Wife,* a first line that was appropriate competition as a narrative hook. Her own first line is a masterpiece of narrative hookery: "Ahab was neither my first husband nor my last."

Since they are in large measure circumstantial, narrative hooks work best when they explain least, using INNUENDO, IMPLICATION, perhaps even DOUBLE ENTENDRE, certainly more action than DESCRIPTION, emphatically more action than thought. Description often slows the narrative hook from its intended effect, suggesting that the writer is well advised to see a specific GOAL of the narrative hook as the catalyst for causing the reader to have questions, if not outright suspicions, a moment or two before the characters.

After the hook has been "set," which is to say the reader has become engaged to read the work through to the very end, then the writer may begin offering some clues and explanations of what the reader may expect down the road. To do so before the reader is caught up in active concerns for the characters and the outcome misplaces and dilutes the dramatic information. It is always better to withhold information than it is to provide it at times when the reader is not likely to be interested or ready for it.

(See OPENING VELOCITY.)

narrative voice

The interior source from which an individual STORY is told; the sense of a story dictating itself to the writer; the genuine tone and INTENT, driving a story forward.

The narrative voice is the WRITER'S voice, which in turn is the writer experiencing the story, telling it first to himself or herself as completely as possible, and in as unguarded a way as possible, the better to rule out attempts by the voice to sound like someone else. During the course of a day, the writer sees, hears, feels, and remembers things—things read, things imagined, things related by others. Many of these seem attractive. Many of them actually *are* attractive, suggesting situations, conflicts, excellent demonstrations of human behavior, intriguing conundrums. The writer should be free to take them in and note their attractiveness, but should not try to imitate this attractiveness. What the writer sees, hears, feels, remembers informs the authentic narrative voice and is to be cultivated. Hemingway has a lovely way of linking sentences with the connective "and." Good for him. Louise Erdrich exudes a sense of vocabulary, mere words fluttering like a flock of birds taking off on an adventure. Way to go, Louise. James Lee Burke has an inner cadence that could make the drawings of Hieronymus Bosch and scenes of great violence seem like the lace doilies on your grandparents' easy chairs. But these things, however you value them, are not *your* things; they do not inform your narrative voice. It is for you to find that voice in each of your stories. You find it by listening to the story, listening to the way the senses inform you. It is similar to an actor of some stature—a Meryl Streep, a Dustin Hoffman, a Derek Jacobi—searching for the authenticity of a character about to be portrayed, seeking entry into the landscape. For a writer it is listening until the story tells you what it is and what it wants from you.

needs

The personal, professional, intellectual, artistic, spiritual, and financial items a CHARACTER requires or believes he requires; motivating forces that drive a character to attempt to acquire ATTITUDES, information, relationships, goods, or a combination of these things; perceived powers, understanding, or techniques a character assesses as being necessary.

As a CONSEQUENCE of extraordinary NEEDS, a character's EGO and/or CONSCIENCE may be impacted. A character without NEEDS is not likely to produce viable STORY elements.

A character enters any given SCENE with EXPECTATIONS, with INTENT, and with NEEDS. Any time a character in a scene is not pulling his or her weight, the WRITER is well advised to examine the CONSEQUENCES of any or all these traits for vital clues leading to the discovery of what that character will do next, and to whom. Nearly any scene from the last pages of Dennis Lehane's stunning and effective novel *Moonlight Mile* could have been cut entirely or enhanced with unanticipated information being presented to Patrick, the principal investigator, because the last twenty pages were not significant in their contribution to the payoff. The contributions had already been made; the payoff had been achieved.

Even in PLOT-DRIVEN stories, this examination merits consideration because it helps provide plausible reasons for the character's behavior. The knowledgeable reader expects one or more of the NEEDS of the principal character to influence the way the DENOUEMENT is approached, with specific emotion-bearing details, and what effects these details have on subsequent behavior.

novel

A prose narrative of about 50,000 words at the low end, more at the high end, depending on how close you are in ability to Leo Tolstoy and the edge of your editor's patience. The novel is built around STORY; one or more CHARACTERS trigger an EVENT or series of events, which in turn causes CHANGE. The elements of character, event, and change are crucial to the foundation of the story, forming the avenues of MOTIVATION on which the dramatic vehicle of the novel travels.

Novels happen because characters initiate events in a string of CAUSALITY. To understand the inner workings of the novel, it is useful for READER and WRITER to see any such narrative, whether it be the experimental-laced-with-angst of William Faulkner's *Absalom, Absalom,* the more-complicated-than-the-inside-of-a-dog's-ear mystery of Dashiell Hammett's *The Maltese Falcon,* or the no-nonsense romantic stylings of Danielle Steele's *oeuvre,* as a series of dramatic incidents or BEATS. The story is the totality of the beats in it, including BACKSTORY, those relevant events from the past that have impact on this story. The arrangement of the beats for their most dramatic and memorable effect becomes the PLOT.

Another illustrative way of looking at the novel: One or more characters set out on a journey of discovery (see Bobbie Ann Mason's *In Country),* discovering something along the way that causes a precipitous change in plans, triggers an awareness, or both.

Yet another useful approach: A stranger appears in a close-knit community, provoking behavior that suggests a HIDDEN AGENDA.

More often than not, novels are related in SCENES, but there are EPISTOLARY NOVELS, narratives related in letters and, now that we've entered the electronic/digital age, novels related via e-mails and texting.

The more memorable and successful novels develop through the CONSEQUENCES of CAUSALITY, where the dramatic beats provide a continuous movement of dramatic stress. A splendid example of consequences and causality in action may be found in the nineteenth-century favorite *The Way We Live Now* by Anthony Trollope, which still stands up against the likes of Tom Clancy and Dan Brown.

For convenient reference, novels are shelved in bookstores and libraries according to GENRE or category such as ROMANCE, MYSTERY, SUSPENSE, HISTORICAL, FANTASY. This is because each has its unique fingerprint of personality. (See GENRE PROMISE.)

novelette

A NARRATIVE form that runs between 7,500 and 25,000 words; an arbitrarily defined length that is longer than a SHORT STORY and not quite so long as a NOVEL.

All of Alice Munro's short stories have the feel of novels, but this is because her ability to evoke CHARACTERS, SITUATIONS, and SETTINGS is so commodious and accomplished. It may be said of her that she has compressed novels into a shorter form; it may also be said that it is difficult to read one of her short stories without feeling as though it had the TEXTURE and LAYERING of a novel. Many of her short stories have elements commonly associated with novels, elements such as MULTIPLE POINT OF VIEW, protracted time span, and extensive shifts in LOCALE (or at least significant shifts from urban to rural settings).

Although technically a novel because of its THEME, THROUGHLINE, and ensemble cast of characters, George Orwell's *Animal Farm* is often spoken of as a novelette, perhaps as a mild rebuke or patronizing response to the author because of the political views expressed in the work. E. B. White's iconic *Charlotte's Web* is, in spite of its slender spine, rarely spoken of as a novelette and is generally regarded as a novel intended for younger readers (see YA NOVEL). Such length distinctions are idiosyncratic, often political in nature.

For a better perspective, try thinking of the serialized story that once appeared in monthly magazines. These had a reduced length, ensemble cast of characters, possible shifts in point of view, and possible shifts in time frame. Such stories were edited with an eye to CLIFFHANGER episodic endings and overall space considerations. In the 1950s and 60s, *Cosmopolitan Magazine* editorially trimmed such novel-length mysteries as Ira Levin's *A Kiss Before Dying* and Bill S. Ballinger's *A Portrait in Smoke* to make them fit in one edition. These and other novelettes (see NOVELLA) appeared later in full text hardcover and paperback book form.

Because of its word length and the subsequent decision to package it as a part of a hardcover book, Houghton Mifflin presented Philip Roth's narrative, *Good-bye, Columbus*, as a novella. Had it first appeared in a magazine, it could easily have been called a novelette.

In the belief that younger readers are less likely to stick with the 210,000-word length of *Moby-Dick,* or the 600,000 words of *War and Peace,* YA novels such as Gary Soto's *Afterlife* cap at 40,000 words or under. Books for younger readers tend to cap at fewer, with such nineteenth-century titles as *The Adventures of Tom Sawyer, Huckleberry Finn,* and *Uncle Tom's Cabin* remaining as pre-TV anomalies. This conventional wisdom, however, in no way accounts for the Harry Potter or *Golden Compass* series, rather for some of the MBA and other business-related approaches to such issues as final, edited size of a project and indeed the press run for the first printing. Such embarrassing exceptions to the notion that publishers know best occur on a regular basis. The underlying reality is that book publishing is not a rational business, nor are attempts to make it so.

Hints: Write the story for its length. Revise it for its length. Send it forth into the world at whatever length you feel best presents it. Depending where it is sent, if it is under 40,000 and over 200,000 words, expect an editorial argument.

Additional hint: Publishers tend to exhibit more "understanding" of such issues as word length, subject matter, even usage, provided the author's previous works have earned out. Conventional publishers will expect conventional adherence to lengths and format because they have experience dealing with them; shorter or longer works will require greater imagination in placing with literary agents and publishers.

novella

A literary form of greater length and complexity than a SHORT STORY; a prose narrative of at least 15,000 and as many as 40,000 words; a narrative of greater length and thematic structure than a NOVELETTE.

Although there have been some longer short stories with more than one POINT OF VIEW (see Alice Munro or Margaret Atwood for examples), the point of view may be a way of drawing an arbitrary line between short story and NOVEL more deeply; a novella could easily support more than one teller of the tale. A novella could also support more thematic density than a short story, leaving word length as a major boundary between it and the novel, which begins at about 50,000 words.

Novellas are widely believed to have originated in Italy, probably at the hand of Boccaccio, who gave his a SATIRIC bite and thus invested the form with a tradition of EDGE or corrective HUMOR, which passed along to Chaucer, who put the form to work and to rhyme in his *Canterbury Tales.* Given its own edge and relative shortness, CHICK LIT could be argued into this tradition of providing outgoing characters whose reach to readers is based on their non-traditional approaches to the traditions held up to them by a conformist society.

Because of its in-between size, the novella is not a comfortable fit for most book publishers. Ernest Hemingway's *The Old Man and the Sea* first appeared in a magazine. The Roth novella appeared as a book, but the publisher added five short stories to provide greater bulk. As a writer who finds the length of the novella suited to his dramatic visions, Jim Harrison has produced a large number of them, his publishers bunching them in triads for book publication. His most recent collection of novellas were packaged in 2005 into *The Summer He Didn't Die.*

Hint for writers: None of the writers named in this entry wrote to a particular word length; rather they wrote for the STORY, regardless of its length or brevity. Should a novella emerge, it can be bundled with one or more others, used as a feature for a collection of stories, or simply mounted as an electronic publication.

nuance

The use of a particular word, CONCEPT, gesture, or INTENT for the best shade of meaning possible; the right word or concept in the right place in a STORY or NOVEL; the difference offered to the reader between two or more possible interpretations; an opportunity for the close READER to appreciate the intent of a story in greater detail.

Nuance is a major challenge to the READER and the WRITER, a trail of literary crumbs left by the writer to lure the reader onward. Flaubert gained some note of attention because of his preoccupation with finding the right word. Mark Twain played with the same notion, speaking of "the right word, not its second cousin."

Nuance and subtext are not mere second cousins; they are kissing cousins, forcing the reader and the writer to examine the words that will best radiate the intent of the characters behavior and perceptions. Not one character in *The Remains of the Day* would have called Mr. Stevens, the lead, a naïve narrator, and yet the reader knew through nuance and subtext of the numerous instances where Stevens simply did not "get" or properly read the intent at hand. When Lord Darlington asked Stevens if any of his employees were Jewish, for instance, Stevens was unable to read the implications, nor was he able to see Miss Kenton's romantic coming on to him. Indeed, Stevens's new employer, the American owner of Darlington Hall, has to remind Stevens to loosen up a bit, and Stevens dutifully reports to us that he will attempt to do so.

Ford Maddox Ford's breakout novel, *The Good Soldier,* begins with John Dowell, the FIRST-PERSON NARRATOR, telling us, "This is the saddest story I have ever heard." Dowell continues at somewhat of a ramble, seemingly looking for a way to introduce the story of a nine-year friendship he and his wife, Florence, have shared with an English couple, the Ashburnhams. At length, Dowell decides to imagine himself at the fireplace of a country cottage, "with a sympathetic soul opposite," the best way of telling us his story. By this point, it is possible to suspect motives of Dowell, sympathy from us not the least of them. As Stevens does in *Remains*, Dowell presents a scenario of events which, through their highly nuanced nature, suggest an outcome that directly plays off the opening line, "This is the saddest story I have ever heard," but does so with a payoff that has lingering, IRONIC CONSEQUENCES.

Does the title of Katherine Mansfield's short story "Bliss" alert the reader to the potential of its principal character, Bertha Young, being naïve? Ask yourself the same question after reading the final scene.

Hint: Look for the effect you wish the reader to arrive at, then construct a situation in which one or more of the characters can demonstrate that effect. Dramatize, don't state. *Show* by inference rather than *tell* by AUTHORIAL INTERVENTION.

objective correlative, the

An object, situation or EVENT that EVOKES an EMOTION beyond a situation's or an event's common association.

A fountain pen, however attractive, may evoke in a CHARACTER negative memories of a parent who was on his case because of sloppy handwriting. It may also evoke fond memories of the parent, well beyond awareness of the beauty of the pen itself. An office party to which a romantic partner invites you may evoke a sense of foreboding if your own experiences at office parties were dismal. A FAMILY gathering may evoke fond memories or combative ones, depending on the history you had with your family.

Given a resurgence of popularity among academics and critics for an essay, "Hamlet and His Problems," in which T.S. Eliot took on the lack of cohesive motivation in *Hamlet,* the objective correlative is a valuable reminder to STORYTELLERS, suggesting they think of objects, situations, and events as having the power to radiate emotion, first to the characters who experience these feelings, and then, by transfer, to the reader. Understated objective correlative can help the writer fulfill the premise that story must deliver an emotional impact, an explicit reminder that the devil may be in the DETAILS, but specific memories and feelings reside in them as well.

obligation

The duty a CHARACTER feels to perform or behave in payment of an EXPECTATION, a debt to be repaid under specific circumstances; acknowledgment of a favor given and the subsequent expectation that an ACT of similar CONSEQUENCE will balance the account.

Obligations may be established between individuals and groups such as banks, clans, or families; they may apply to complete strangers as well as friends or relatives. In FICTION, obligations may be real or imagined, tugging at the CONSCIENCE and patience of the parties involved. Often felt as duties "owed" an older generation by a younger one, obligations have the power to disrupt lives, cause rebellious behavior, and produce the abrupt consequences of impatience and anarchy.

A character's hackles may rise when he is told, "It is your duty...." The building blocks of duty and, often, guilt become building blocks to STORY as yet another basic element of story is moved into place: the element of resentment may well engender an obligation to extract REVENGE.

The cloud of obligation has hovered over the human species throughout its development; in many cases survival of a prehistoric band or clan depended on it. A traveler accepting hospitality at the home of a friend or someone recommended by a friend was obligated to return the hospitality if the circumstances were reversed. TRADITION placed heavy weights on the obligation of hospitality: if you accepted a person's hospitality, that individual became responsible for your welfare, a circumstantial CRUCIBLE that could and undoubtedly did provide unexpected story elements.

It can be argued that a country in possession of the knowledge of nuclear fission has the obligation to use that knowledge to enhance the prospect of comfortable and peaceful living among nations. An individual with knowledge of a crime has an obligation to take action to the point where JUSTICE will be served. These are just two examples of how obligation can serve to set CONFLICT loose, the basis for a clash of AGENDA.

A 1972 play by Neil Simon, *The Sunshine Boys,* becomes an instructive example of the explosive relationship between obligation and resentment and the impact of this explosion on narrative. Al Lewis and Willy Clark are a one-time vaudeville team who worked together on stage for forty years, during the course of which they attracted a large, loyal following. Trouble is, they grew to hate one another, spoke only when on stage during a performance. Clark, the stubborn one, resented Lewis's decision to break up the act and retire from show business. Now he has to make it on his own, doing commercials for a potato chip maker. The story begins with a television network inviting the team to reunite for a special tribute to the history of comedy. In his superb rendition of the feuding team, Neil Simon has caught the combustive chemistry of the relationship, helping us see the potential for placing obligation and resentment in motion as the embodiment of the two cantankerous characters.

Obligations are like visiting relatives; they drop in unannounced, stay too long, often leave a mess. And those same relatives are always "away" should you ever need a place to stay when you are in their neighborhood. You could smolder with resentment or use the list of personally felt obligations as a starting point for story opportunities.

But characters are not the only ones with obligations in literature. All the various narrative GENRES may be seen as reflecting obligations. MYSTERY readers, for example, expect challenging puzzles, thus the obligation of the mystery writer to make the mystery as intriguing as possible without removing it from the sphere of plausibility. It becomes the writer's obligation to provide elements a reader of that genre has come to expect, and additional obligations include providing those elements with imagination and originality. It may even be argued that at some point a writer is obligated to interest as many readers as possible.

obstacle

An ATTITUDE, FORCE, or condition that prevents a CHARACTER from dramatic movement toward a desired goal.

Obstacles are best friends of the construction of FRUSTRATION, adding to the character's sense of constraint and suggesting to the READER a potential conspiracy. Will the MYSTERY be solved? Will justice be done? Will the good guys win? In CHARACTER-DRIVEN fiction, obstacles are the best friends of the characters because they allow the character wiggle room via memories, self-doubt, sucking it (whatever *it* may be) up, and the greatest luxury of all, the avoidance of taking ACTION. The manner in which a character deals with obstacles becomes a truer definition of that character than any descriptive narrative; it allows the reader and the other characters to witness this individual at work—or avoidance of work.

In his last, unfinished novel, *The Last Tycoon,* F. Scott Fitzgerald noted in capital letters, ACTION IS CHARACTER, by which he meant that the reader is called into judgmental play by being given the power to assess the depth and stature of individuals through observation of their behavior.

This observed response is particularly valuable to ACTORS, who speak openly of "working off" one another, a condition that can translate to chemistry or synergy. Such chemistry defines the difference between modern drama and the earlier, more emotive drama. Characters in modern fiction seem focused on "playing off" one another, uniting against common obstacles or regarding one another as obstacles to be coped with on an immediate and ongoing basis.

Obstacles may be internal or external, a pang of conscience (as in Macbeth, losing his resolve to murder Malcolm) or a tangible disappointment (the eponymous statue in *The Maltese Falcon* proving to have been cast in lead rather than gold). Obstacles appear with regularity in reality, earning them appropriate venue in story. One such obstacle is time-related; there is never enough time. Another obstacle is money; there is never enough of that either. Having enough room is often an obstacle, as are crying babies, noisy neighbors, allergies to cats, sullen teenagers, vegan relatives, visiting relatives, romantic exes, in-laws, stinginess, and departmental meetings.

Obstacles stalk us, cling to us like limpets, slip ransom notes under the door, insist on having the last word.

Occam's razor

A useful concept of logic for the storyteller developed by a medieval English Franciscan, William of Occam; it is an injunction against the logical construct of unnecessarily expanding universes (by which he meant arguments); best known among non-philosophers and critics for his "razor" which he applied to any argument:"The simplest solution is the best solution."

The message in the razor for the FICTION WRITER: AMBIGUITY and complications are enhancements—until they proliferate beyond the READER's ability to keep track of them, at which point, they become albatrosses. Saddling a character with claustrophobia, as Dan Brown did to Robert Langdon in *The Da Vinci Code*, helps to give the character an interesting BACKSTORY, and an intriguing, even endearing personality quirk. The same goes for Indiana Jones's aversion to snakes. Each had one personal OBSTACLE to overcome in their adventures—their writers wisely did not attempt to afflict them, however, with too many quirks. When it comes to proliferating story points, try, for example, to render an outline of the plot of Dashiell Hammett's novel *The Dain Curse*. Then, for instructive fun, try fitting a description of it into the brief descriptions of novels found in the bestseller lists in the Sunday *New York Times Book Review.*

Rich, ornate detail has its well-deserved place in fiction, and so does the work of such minimalists as Raymond Carver and Tobias Wolff. What course to take? As you write, imagine hearing the flapping of wings, your mnemonic for the flight of the albatross about to roost in your prose.

occupation

A plausible reference to the profession, occupation, artistry, and state of career development in a CHARACTER; a convincing sense of the agenda occupying a character's INTENT.

In many NOVELS OF MYSTERY or SUSPENSE, private investigators or security persons have had some career as sworn police officers, sheriffs, or as federal agents, while others have come to their work with a history in military police. Lawyers have attended various types of law schools and have been admitted to practice in specific locales through the gatekeeper of the bar exam. Hairdressers, barbers, manicurists, and stylists are required to obtain licenses before they can perform in many states. A head chef, interviewing a subordinate, will probably want to see the subordinate's knives and how they are cared for. Before assigning a profession, occupation, artistry, or experience to a character, the WRITER needs to check plausible standards the character must possess before setting the character to work. This understanding may provide the writer with an entire dimension of behavior for the character, having a direct effect on how that character thinks, feels, and behaves. As an exaggerated extreme, imagine a butcher, having gone through apprenticeship and risen through the employee ranks in a high-profile market chain, developing an aversion to the meat and organs he or she must deal with, to the point of becoming a vegan.

For further extremes, imagine all minor characters who are service oriented (wait persons, delivery persons, janitorial persons) with walk-on roles in stories as wannabe actors, photographers, painters. Imagine possible conflicts between psychologists (with PhD degrees) and psychiatrists (with M.D. degrees). Imagine potential rivalry between a Freudian psychiatrist and a Jungian psychiatrist. If you needed cosmetic surgery, would you consult a "mere" surgeon or one who was board certified in cosmetic surgery? If your character is a classically trained musician, for whom did she audition and fail to please? If your character is a jazz musician whose instrument is a reed, how did he keep his reeds moist before appearing at work?

Actors carefully research the working habits of characters they are to portray, often learning such arcane things as how to throw a curve ball in baseball, how to get a tone out of a bag pipe, how to do things as a doctor or nurse would do them; their research brings a quality of reality and plausibility to their performance. Writers need to do no less in assigning an occupation to a character. They must study the job for the details that will bring the job to the page and past the READER's warning radar.

old wives' tales

Data purporting to be accurate information, passed along by an elderly generation of women or taken without authentication by moderns as valid; a hearty mixture of what may have once been common sense, home cures, myth, recipe, superstition. Also known as *bubbe meises.*

In many ways and in many cultures, old wives' tales are operatic warnings, direct from the communal super ego, examples of dire fates that befell those who did not follow the conventional wisdom of the time and place. An effective way to write off suggestions offered in a helpful spirit is to call them old wives' tales though some advice is shrewd and turns out to be effective if followed. Amusing dramatic ironies take root when old wives' tales, contrary to conventional logic and wisdom, prove out in their accuracy. In other ways and cultures, old wives' tales are seen as prescient and inspirational. Although they suggest what might be seen as sexist derogation, it might be wise to consider old boys' tales as yet another way of getting facts, INTENT, and ability all jumbled up, their consequences leading directly to STORY. In any case, their very mention as well as their use is a reflection of the writer's view of a particular culture and the individuals who inhabit it.

Omar Little

A front-rank character in the HBO novel-for-television, *The Wire*; a gritty, magnetic character who is openly gay and whose major source of income is robbery; a man who has, in fact, killed in defense of his beliefs. Omar Little never robs from people who are not directly involved in the drug trade, has a strict code of ethics; he emerges as one of the few uncorrupted characters in the MISE-EN-SCÈNE of the series and remains likable, even admirable throughout his tenure in the sixty episodes.

When presented with moral quandaries, Little can be seen considering them as a prelude to determining his course of ACTION. His senses of HUMOR and IRONY are manifest; he is the only front-rank character who does not use profanity nor does he in any way suffer from not doing so. On occasion, Omar Little's purposeful focus is reminiscent of Wile E. Coyote, although Little is more apt to use irony instead of becoming its victim; Little and Coyote represent polarities in character force that merit study. Omar Little is a reminder that dignity is a major factor to consider in the creation of character.

omniscient point of view

A NARRATIVE technique that filters the essential goals and sensations of STORY through the lenses of more than one CHARACTER in the same scene; it is a vision of story simultaneously seen by numerous perspectives. A major effect of the omniscient point of view is its suggestion of a crowd—even if there are only two characters on stage at the moment, they appear to be speaking and thinking and behaving at the same time, which, in fact, they are. An omniscient SCENE with three or four points of view evokes the sense of being at a party or gathering, with voices clamoring to be heard.

One of the resident difficulties accruing from the use of the omniscient point of view, particularly in shorter narratives of five to six thousand words or less, is the problem readers will have determining whose story it is, then subsequently what that character's goal is.

The omniscient point of view is the least used of the narrative spectrum; its shifts from person to person may produce a bumpy narrative ride unless managed with care. The WRITER who uses this approach is well advised to spend time in revision checking for a seamless switch from character to character, making sure the reader has a reasonable clue who the next narrator has become.

The significant modern writer to observe for his use of this technique is the Irish writer William Trevor, who uses it exclusively in short stories, midrange narratives, and novels. Omniscient point of view is not an easy technique to control; reading Trevor makes it appear that it is. Caveat writer.

An ideal situation for an omniscient point of view narrative is a family or group event in which a number of front-rank characters gather to celebrate, mourn, or render a necessary decision, each bringing to the gathering a different agenda. Trevor has managed to expand on this trope by bringing romantic, filial, or sororal relationships into the tent.

on the nose

A theatrical term that indicates an ACTION, behavior, or DESCRIPTION has become too literal; it is a reminder of the need for greater EVOCATION of a desired RESULT in all dramatic STORYTELLING.

In a larger sense, being told a particular interpretation or scene is too "on the nose" is to be alerted to the absolute moral, white or black of meaning, of the operatic nature of one's drama. Human behavior tends more to gray than white or black; it is rich with shading and shadow. The judgment of "too on the nose" is a cry for greater complexity, depth of CHARACTER and enhancement of the MOTIVE of character.

one character on stage alone

A lone CHARACTER, in most cases, is a dramatic train wreck in progress. One version of it has a single character reviewing past relevant EVENTS prior to making a CHOICE. Another such moment comes when one character waits for one or more associates to show up. Another is the dramatic crossroads where a character lays out plans for a future event as a means of FORESHADOWING the event and its consequences.

Characters in film, TV, or stage dramas have recourse to the device of voice-over, in which the audience can hear them "thinking" aloud. The danger here is for the thoughts to seem READER FEEDER, "thought" for the convenience of the audience, undercutting the realism of more literary work in which characters do not do favors for the audience so much as they appear to be propelled by their own AGENDAS.

A film, TV, or stage actor is often an exquisitely tuned instrument, able to convey feelings and impressions with mere gestures, inflections of posture; characters are not necessarily so well tuned and must be nudged, even prodded by the weight of EVENTS. A character left alone for too long has only one way out—in thought, which leads to one of the great clichés of written story: "She began to wonder how it had all begun," followed in rapid succession by the second great cliché, "...how she'd let herself get into this mess in the first place." (See HIBK.)

One of the safer ways for a character to be alone comes when the character is somewhere he or she should not be, a situation enhanced by the accelerated risk of DISCOVERY. "What are you doing here? You're not supposed to be here."

Shakespeare addressed the problem by keeping his soliloquies short, bringing them in at about thirty seconds, before another character came on stage. In one of his most famous soliloquies, Hamlet is considering a serious act with a serious consequence, his friends Rosencrantz and Guildenstern on stage at a distance all the while.

opening pages

The first three or four pages of a NOVEL, usually the first page of a SHORT STORY; these contain the OPENING VELOCITY of a story. (See NARRATIVE HOOK.)

Before a novel is published or a short story has any hope of finding its way into book or periodical publication, it must pass the watchful eye of the LITERARY AGENT and/or the ACQUISITION EDITOR. To accomplish this goal, the narrative must present an interesting CHARACTER in a situation of confrontation, danger, DISCOVERY, or emotional quandary of significant enough degree to trigger some measure of concern—and he must do this within the opening pages. The WRITER who refuses to consider this calculus or who feels unable to execute it is at high risk of receiving a note declining the MANUSCRIPT on the grounds that the READER had not been sufficiently made to care.

As observed by such PLOT-DRIVEN writers as Louis L'Amour, Frank Gruber, and Elmore Leonard, many novels and short stories, sent forth into the world as eagerly as hand-waving students wanting to impress their teacher with their knowledge of the right answer, do not always begin at the right place. As an ideal, the opening pages plunk a CHARACTER into a spot where there is some physical vulnerability, such as the opening of Karen Russell's *Swamplandia*, where the narrator, a teenage girl, is watching her mother dive into a pond filled with hungry alligators. Sometimes emotional vulnerability works as well as the physical, as in J.D. Salinger's *The Catcher in the Rye*, where we first meet Holden Caulfield in the act of trying to tough out the emotional breakdown already chasing after him. Whichever the vulnerability, the opening pages also include some implicit promise, writer to reader, that the character will get back up and try again.

Often the true opening pages of a story are buried within BACKSTORY or other explanations, which come forth more as unwanted-but-necessary DESCRIPTIONS rather than emotion-based circumstances. The net result is to present the reader with textbook-style NARRATIVE rather than dramatic engagement. The solution is often found in the REVISION process, wherein the true opening pages present themselves. How are these pages to be recognized? They are spare on description and backstory, sparer still on auxiliary verbs such as "had," which yank the chronology from the present to the past. Wherever opening pages are in the story's CHRONOLOGY, they are more effective if they appear to be happening in the immediate present. If they actually took place, say, ten or twelve years earlier, the reader will quickly adopt to the manipulation of the time frame. No convention requires fiction to be in strict chronology. The key is to place the reader immediately in some compelling situation—some circumstance that grabs him by the lapels and says, "Hey, now, look at *this*."

opening velocity

The momentum and pacing of EVENTS surrounding CHARACTERS should be immediate and palpable or a STORY moves into dramatic inertia; the conditions, forces, and desires resident in characters that should become apparent to READERS at the onset of DRAMATIC NARRATIVE; the TIPPING POINT between STASIS and story.

Life, before the story begins, is static; as some animals are said to sense the beginnings of earthquakes, readers begin to sense the arrival of story. They become concerned for the safety of the characters, or curious to see how they will respond to the conditions in which they find themselves. Opening velocity is the gathering of inertia that propels the story forward into its labyrinth of REVERSALS, regrouping, and subsequent plans.

How to achieve it as a functional matter? Try an unexpected DISCOVERY, or the delivery of an intractable deadline, some likable character being given an odious choice. What you are after is an event or series of EVENTS that produce a CONSEQUENCE that may be felt on an emotional level.

Opening velocity is not always achieved in a first draft, but it should emerge from within the text during the REVISION PROCESS because it is required in some way by the story itself. The opening pages of Marilynne Robinson's EPISTOLARY NOVEL *Gilead* may not have the same type of velocity a Harlan Coben or Lee Child opening has, but for the thousands of Robinson's readers it evokes the inevitability of the sweet ride ahead.

More often than not, successful opening velocity comes with a character on the cusp of recognition of a potential problem. One immediate variation resides in the character proceeding to ignore the problem; another variation is seen in the character overreacting, while yet another has the character underreacting.

The experienced reader is used to eighteenth-, nineteenth-, and twentieth-century conventions in STORY BEGINNINGS, is respectful of them, and may even have a preference for an older, seemingly more leisurely build up to the events that define the conditions of a story and provide clues to its outcome. As a novelist, Thomas Hardy fell on the cusp of the nineteenth and twentieth century, easing the longform story toward modernity. Most if not all his novels begin on a country road, where one or more characters move along a landscape on their way to some event or condition, allowing the reader to become gradually immersed in Hardy's social, ethical, and conflict-laden scenery. A splendid example is *The Mayor of Casterbridge,* which is extremely slow-starting by twenty-first-century standards, but which remains one of the most stunning openings of all time. Nevertheless, a twenty-first-century version of the same novel could become equally effective simply by rearranging the CHRONOLOGY to the point where one of the front-rank characters, Michael Henchard, was already the mayor of Casterbridge, a well-loved politician with a secret—the secret of the original opening chapter—that would not be revealed until later.

The modern STORY more often than not begins in the present moment, long enough to define its characters through their behavior and goals before pausing to spoon in background.

orbit

The path taken by a STORY as it moves about a set of CHARACTERS is its orbit. Just as a story has an ARC instead of mere linear progression of episodes, it also moves through its dramatic universe like a satellite moving about a planet. Some story orbits, particularly those of a PLOT-DRIVEN nature, are circular, seemingly well balanced between ACTION and INTENT. Other story orbits are more elliptical in their paths, giving no hint where they will go next, seeming to end on a note as ambiguous as reality often is.

Once the story is in PROVISIONAL DRAFT, the WRITER will have a better sense of the shape of its orbit, making it easier to enhance a particular flavor of the story. A perfect demonstration of the orbital nature inherent in story brings us to consider *The Iliad.*

If we were to retrace all the dramatic BEATS associated with this narrative and start in absolute chronological order, we'd begin with the moment a bunch of bored goddesses—Venus, goddess of love, among them—approached that handsome but super ditz Paris, asking him to judge a beauty contest to determine which of them was the most attractive. Then we'd move to some behind-the-scenes maneuvering, where the contestants are offering Paris inducements for choosing her. Minerva, for instance, as goddess of wisdom, offers Paris unrivaled smarts. Although this gives us pause to reflect how much Paris could have profited from accepting Minerva's offer, he accepts Venus's bribe, which is possession of the most beautiful woman on Earth. Gotta have that, Paris concludes. And to show how better he'd have been served by accepting Minerva's offer of intelligence, as well as illustrating the perfidious nature of the goddesses, Paris judges Venus the most beautiful, whereupon he is rewarded with Helen of Troy.

One little problem Venus hadn't mentioned: Helen was married. By starting the narrative here, we'd have a completely different take on *The Iliad;* it would seem more on a level with *Sex and the City.* Where do we start instead? We begin with the war well into its sixth year. What war? Why, the Trojan War, of course, the war that was waged over—wait for it—the attempt to get Helen out of Troy and back to her husband.

Beginning the story in the middle of a war (see IN MEDIAS RES) is a great way to attract an audience as Homer did in *The Iliad*. What was Achilles so pissed about? The affront to his honor, of course. One of the honchos of the army attacking Troy is Menelaus, who is, among other things, Helen's husband. The biggest honcho of all is Agamemnon, Menelaus's big brother, who is having marital difficulties of his own, and who is becoming more and more impatient with Achilles' showboating and scene stealing. Achilles is irate because Agamemnon has pulled rank and taken away one of Achilles' trophies of war, an exotic concubine. Now you see why Achilles was pissed and why *The Iliad* begins with a dramatic moment in which Achilles can refuse to remain in the fight and withdraw all his troops. This means that the next scene, naturally, is a gathering of the heavy hitters in this ensemble cast to talk Achilles back into the fray, to pump up his ego, and to introduce us to Odysseus—and the sequel narrative, *The Odyssey*. Not least, beginning *The Iliad* in the midst of war allows the author a chance at foreshadowing, by the mention of Paris's brother, Hector, whom many readers consider to be the true hero of *The Iliad*.

Considering the length of time *The Iliad* has been "in print," and the enormous success of the sequel, the author appears to have made a brilliant choice for his use of OPENING VELOCITY.

The author could have also begun with the touching scene where Hector takes a few moments away from battle to visit his wife, Andromache, and child. Andromache pleads with him to run away to somewhere safe for all of them, detailing the inevitability of what will happen to her and the child if Troy is taken. Hector knows she speaks the truth and actually believes he will die in battle, but his duties and obligations require him to return to the field of war.

Any close reading of this story, taking all its dramatic beats into consideration, demonstrates how the one or more writers we have lumped together as Homer have picked the optimal moment in the orbit of the story to let us see the characters in the richest detail, where they emerge as considerably more than mere stick figures.

Most stories have orbits of dramatic action that allow for a BEGINNING at any of a number of places. The task of the writer is to choose the existing place in an orbit to produce a desired result or to extend the orbit so that another beginning will work better. Stories may begin at any point of the orbit—the ideal place is a moment where there is enough relevant action to preclude lengthy physical descriptions or extensive BACKSTORY.

order of awareness, the

The things noticed—or not noticed—by a character in a dramatic situation.

When a CHARACTER enters a SCENE, a SENSUAL priority list kicks in. Depending on the age, gender, social rank, and purposeful agenda of a given character, that person will tend to notice conditions, surroundings, and individual traits in a ranking related to the type of STORY being told. A member of Gang X, for instance, on discovering he is out of his turf, is going to be particularly watchful for males who are potential members or allies of Gang Y; a racially prejudiced white male might find himself looking for possible escape routes when he notices an approaching group of young blacks on the same side of a narrow street. A young man out on the prowl for meeting women will, upon entering a bistro or neighborhood tavern, be struck by the presence of nubile females. A group of women friends, out for dinner and a movie, will be likely to note the bothersome (or welcome!) presence of a group of predatory males. Further, characters recognizing strangers, possible threats, or anomalies will have cause to wonder what each of these types might want from them.

Characters already located in a setting will probably classify newcomers in terms of their gender, height, and clothing, but not necessarily in that order. Knowing your characters will make it easy to have a director's feel for what they notice and when they notice it. Some men, for instance, note the sexual viability of every woman who enters the place, age being a third- or fourth-place factor in that calculus, behind body type, height, and hair color. Women are more likely to note the posture, height, and dress of a new male addition to a room.

What are your characters going to notice first when they enter a room? Decor? Airiness? Number of persons present? Their height? Perhaps their age. How do your characters enter scenes? What are they looking for? What qualities or presences make them ill at ease? How do these responses help define who the character is?

Hint: A character's individual reaction to persons, places, and things speaks directly to who they are and how the reader may expect them to behave.

Additional hint: an endangered character is more likely to focus directly on the immediate source of danger rather than what tune is playing in the background or what two other characters in the background are arguing about.

Characters are in a sense like the Hubble Space Telescope, sent out to gather images of events. Understanding the psychology of each character, along with his or her strong and weak points of observation, helps to render them as individuals rather than types, and we know what F. Scott Fitzgerald said about characters and types in his novella *The Rich Boy*.

"Begin with an individual," Fitzgerald's narrator says, "and before you know it you find that you have created a type; begin with a type, and you find that you have created—nothing. That is because we are all queer fish, queerer behind our faces and voices than we want any one to know or than we know ourselves. When I hear a man proclaiming himself an 'average, honest, open fellow,' I feel pretty sure that he has some definite and perhaps terrible abnormality which he has agreed to conceal—and his protestation of being average and honest and open is his way of reminding himself of his misprision."

organization

The divisions and sections of a work, mindful that in shorter works such as stories, SCENES are separated by a two-line space break, advancing to the long form where, after the scene break, the most significant division is the CHAPTER.

A constructive way to look at the chapter is as a collection of relevant scenes, meaning the rudder could be the simple matter of chronology or POINT OF VIEW or THEME. It may help to regard a chapter as a mini three-act play, in which there is a beginning, a middle, and a resolution: the presentation of a problem and/or goal, a muddle of clangorous expectations, and an apparent goal in hand which results in a significant abeyance (which causes the READER to look at yet another chapter before setting the STORY down for the night). Chapters are often presented with a number, which serves no real dramatic purpose and is little more than the literary equivalent of a mile marker on a map. Chapters are just as often presented with a date line, much as newspaper stories, followed by a city: September 1985, Los Angeles. Chapters in multiple-point-of-view novels often begin with a tag line reminding the reader who the narrative focus of the following events will be. "Fred," for example.

The next potential division is the Book, a collection of relevant chapters in which the rudder could be chronological or, back to Fred, a particular point of view.

other shoe dropping, the

An emotional PAYOFF, resulting from a previously FORESHADOWED clue; the literary equivalent of the aftershock following an earthquake; a degree of CLOSURE achieved from an earlier ACTION.

The well-known trope of the other shoe dropping comes from the theoretical supposition of an individual preparing for a night's sleep in a cheap hotel or rooming house. As the individual settles down to sleep, a guest in the room one floor above is similarly preparing for sleep when he hears his upstairs neighbor's shoe fall to the floor with a thud. The individual of our focus is wrested from the brink of sleep by the sound above him; he waits for the second shoe, the famed "other" shoe to drop so that he can return his concentration on achieving sleep. Of course, he cannot. The wait for the sound of the other shoe dropping has claimed his focus. It could well be that the guest in the upstairs room has realized the consequences of letting the first shoe drop. Out of consideration, he has resolved that the other shoe shall be set down quietly. But the expectant one cannot achieve sleep until he has heard the second shoe drop.

The other shoe dropping may be an actual physicality, such as the lodger in the upstairs room removing his shoes; it may also be an ASSOCIATION made by one character or a REALIZATION achieved by a character. Oscar Madison, one half of Neil Simon's dramatic odd couple, is used to getting verbal suggestions and written notes from his roommate, Felix Unger, any of which serve to intensify the growing irritation Madison feels toward Unger. But as the narrator of Poe's "A Cask of Amontillado" puts it, "when he ventured upon insult, I vowed revenge." In this case, Felix Unger's venturing on insult is not at all intentional but is nevertheless seen by Madison as having crossed a line, of having gone too far. What is Unger's step over the line, his dropping of the other shoe? Why, leaving a note for Madison signed merely with his initials. How would you feel if you were on the receiving end of a note signed FU?

ANTICIPATION is a cherished dramatic force, whether the drama is comedic or tragic. Simplistic as it may sound to offer the council that the READER is in a constant state of expectation, it is virtually unthinkable not to mention anticipation.

Hint: At some point during the REVISION process, see if there are any shoes being dropped, any event that would cause irritation or consternation to visit a character, perhaps even an EVENT that refuses to go away. Then exploit it.

outline

A template or design for a dramatic NARRATIVE; a SCENE-by-scene breakdown of an intended STORY; a thematic riff intended to lead the WRITER through the development and orchestration of a CONCEPT through its conceptual stage into viable story; the first step in a process that is completed with REVISION.

Some writers will not consider beginning work on the text of a story without some form of road map to guide them in varying degrees of detail through the development and enhancement of a story. Other writers will argue that such an approach precludes SURPRISE, an essential ingredient not only to the READER but also to the writer. The late, prolific suspense and thriller writer Dennis Lynds (aka John Crowe, Michael Collins, Carl Dekker) developed a mid-range outline in which he sketched a situation where a character became engaged in a fast-growing COMPLICATION, "wrote" his CHARACTER to the edge of the complication, then stopped writing to expand the outline to cover the next forty or fifty pages before returning to text. Lynds did this until the final resolution, at which point he began revision, looking first for anomalies in the plot/motivation structure.

The jury is expected to be out for some indeterminate time on the outline-or-no-outline question. There is no evidence to show that working with an outline makes the work easier or if, indeed, writers who outline are more prolific than those who do not.

Hint: How many of your last five stories (of any length) were written from outline? What does your answer to this question tell you?

Additional hint: Try outlining in some detail your next novel, keeping opinionated notes about your progress to writing text. What does this tell you?

Yet another hint: Try outlining a novel by using index cards, one for each proposed scene, using as few as one or two sentences to describe the intended scene.

The major points to be made here: (1) an outline is not a *sine qua non* of a story or NOVEL; (2) there is nothing "wrong" with you if you choose to outline; (3) there is nothing "wrong" with you if you choose not to outline; (4) the decision to outline or not is one of the choices you will have to make on your journey toward becoming a writer; (5) any notes, however sparse or *ad hoc*, may be considered an outline. Editors will not ask whether you outline, nor will they ask to see one, particularly if they have the entire manuscript before them.

over the top

An expression meant to imply an ACTION or concept that has been overloaded with THEME, SYMBOLISM, and perhaps even verbal excessiveness; ACTIVITY done to the extent that the reader will resent its DETAIL; a DRAMATIC BEAT performed as if the CHARACTER were auditioning for a new position as an evangelical minister.

Over-the-top material may, depending on the heaviness and operatic nature of the load it carries, be considered—you guessed it—ON THE NOSE.

pace

The momentum at which a STORY progresses; the cadence in which dramatic BEATS appear for the CHARACTERS and READERS to respond.

Dramatic writing is the result of characters reacting to stimuli. Even a character on stage alone is responding to past events, making plans for future ones—perhaps even by playing a waiting or delaying game. Stories that move too slowly will make the reader impatient for something to happen. Stories that move too quickly take on a jerky, frenetic quality that turns moments of potential poignancy or suspense into FARCE. How then does the WRITER approach pace? Begin by considering the dramatic situation at hand. If it is a disaster such as an earthquake or a sudden heart attack, there is no time for nuance or reflection, but rather the need for quick, reflexive action. If the narrative involves some issue with serious downstream CONSEQUENCES, the pace needs to accommodate necessary deliberations. If the NARRATIVE is built around a DEADLINE, the pace should suggest the element of time running out by supplying constant reminders of time slipping by.

Hint: Listen to the story for pacing clues. Take its pulse. An action adventure story will be snapping its fingers, urging you to "Hurry up." Romance will want a slower pace, some recognition of sensuality.

paper or screen?

The choice of medium in which a WRITER composes; variously, lined legal pads, three by five index cards, computer screens.

If you are of a certain age, the implications of the title of this entry will provoke an animal-like noise resembling exasperation. How dumb is that? No one writes on paper anymore. Paper is something you stack into a printer to print words you have composed on a computer.

If you are a certain other age, an age where you can still remember preferences among Remington and Olivetti and Underwood, you may well remember when the print ball on the Selectric was still a novelty. You wrote on such instruments because your handwriting was so terrible, and because everyone who wrote to be published worked on one of these whether they could use the so-called touch system or, like you, had to be content to live with rows of X's used to block out unwanted lines.

If you are yet another certain age, you probably remember DOS and WordPerfect. Even though your printer was dot matrix, with a draft and a final copy setting option, you felt the surge of progress inherent in the move away from the typewriter, along with a sense that writing was going to be transformed into something easier, something that would allow you a more direct contact with your material. Being of this age, you can identify places on your body and psyche attesting to the fact that computerization did not make writing any easier; you were simply giving up typewriter ribbons and those rascally thin Mylar tapes associated with the early electrics and the Selectric, and now had to deal with crashes, freezes, diskettes, or such words and practices as burning or ripping.

Writing not only did not become easier, you were discovering, thanks to modems and printers, even more remote sites on the planet of frustration.

Nevertheless, all these potential or actual memories dance around the issue of why anyone with today's equipment and gadgetry at hand would want to compose on paper in the first place. Paper is so New York publishing, which is to say tanking—at least the way they are going about it as of this writing. Nevertheless, if you are of a certain age, there is the heft and smell and convenience of a book because that was what got you doing what you do in the first place, writing things on paper to preserve the material prior to shipping it off to its fate, which also involved paper.

Thanks to Microsoft Word, iPages, and the no-nonsense new kid on the block, Open Office, it is theoretically possible to get your words down on the screen, save them, submit them, have them edited via the Track Changes tool, accept or reject various edits as you will, and not touch paper until your author copies arrive in the mail. It is also possible to indulge your early, pre-computer muscle memory by doing your first draft on a lined legal pad before you begin the REVISION process, at which point you'd do the actual keyboarding onto your very own hard drive.

There is no correct answer to the question posed here. Sooner or later, you'll want to capture the keystrokes (notice how easy it is to pick up the lingo), thereupon to back them up on your Time Machine if you're a Mac person or the likes of Mozy or Novastor for the PC user. Until the sooner or later arrives, you can use a flash stick to save each day's increment, email it to your gmail or Yahoo account, and/or download it to your Lacie external hard drive.

A new workday begins and during the course of it, you experience a mild disillusion with your chosen POINT OF VIEW or your entire TONE. You simply save everything you've done under the heading of version 1, save it to your hard drive and/or other storage vault, then head off in another direction you might enjoy more. You could not do this with mere paper, not unless you photocopied, color-coded your drafts, and set about an enormous process of merging that would still require you to spend more time at your keyboard.

Whichever way it is—paper or screen—get it down as quickly as possible. Writing remains as difficult as it ever was, and inspiration ever as elusive.

parody
The use of ridicule, exaggeration, and ironic imitation to undercut the INTENT and relevance of a work of art; the use of broad, comedic imitation to make fun of a literary work and/or its creator.

Parody is, in effect, a weapon fired at close range; the most important result is the identification by the READER of the target work and/or the creator. The target often provides the name of the parody. A noted American parodist and satirist, Peter De Vries, took on William Faulkner's often-convoluted prose with a parody, "Requiem for a Noun." The English parodist and humorist, Digby Wolfe, took on a well-known popular song by adding a mere coma to its title, "What is this thing called, Love?" Some instances of parody were so successful that they outlived the work and creator they attacked, a notable example from history being John Dryden's "Mac Flecknoe," used to parody the poet Thomas Shadwell, his work and his attitudes. In contemporary times, the newspaper and website *The Onion* parodies politicians and political news by exaggerating their seriousness with a DEADPAN humor of their own, reducing the target to ridicule.

Parody is an invitation for the READER to collude with the WRITER against a target. Unlike SATIRE, parody rarely goes unrecognized, does not offer so much a solution to a problematic individual, work, or convention as a parting shot to the head. Some writers who refuse to take on new artistic and thematic challenges emerge as unintentionally making fun of—or parodying—themselves. Let the writer beware.

partner

A co-worker or confidante with whom a PROTAGONIST can exchange ideas and BACKGROUND; a relationship between protagonist and ANTAGONIST suggestive of a dramatic symbiosis if not an actual partnership; a love-hate relationship between two CHARACTERS.

One of the earlier partnerships, the master and the slave in *The Frogs* by Aristophanes, sets the potential for dramatic symbiosis in motion. The lead player is Dionysus, accompanied by his slave, Xanthias, who is clearly the more pragmatic and gritty of the two. The major GOAL of the STORY is to repair the state of TRAGEDY in drama. As Dorothy Gale would do some time later when she traveled to Oz for information from the wizard, Dionysus must travel to Hades to bring the great tragedian, Euripides, back from the dead. In discussing how best to begin their task, Dionysus and Xanthias engage in what has become known as the buddy system, reminiscent of the comedy teams who followed them over the millennia: Abbott and Costello, Martin and Lewis, Rowan and Martin, the Smothers Brothers, Burns and Allen.

Partnership of some sort in STORY is too much a CONVENTION to be considered merely an interesting coincidence. It was absolutely essential for Sherlock Holmes who, had he been allowed by Conan Doyle to go it alone, would not have got far, thanks to his ATTITUDE and tone. Captain Ahab could have ruminated to Starbuck about the way his life had been shattered by the great whale, but the story would not have achieved its stature without the actual presence of Moby-Dick, a partnership made in the hell of Ahab's psyche. Nor would Santiago, the protagonist of Hemingway's *The Old Man and the Sea*, been complete with only the presence of Manolin, the young boy apprentice, or Santiago's friends who are mentioned but who do not appear in person. Santiago needed the huge marlin, arguably the biggest catch of his life, as a partner, just as Ahab needed the whale.

To extend the METAPHOR of partnership in yet another direction, imagine

Macbeth as unmarried, a middle-aged soldier who'd focused entirely on his military career. With no Lady Macbeth in the story, several dimensions fall away, leaving the mere carcass of a powerful drama.

In the modern setting of Boston, private investigator Patrick Kenzie and his girlfriend-partner Angie Gennaro provide a moving thematic thread to the investigation of an abducted four-year-old girl, moving Dennis Lehane's *Gone Baby Gone* from being merely an intriguing puzzle into the landscape of deep moral inquiry. The partnership succeeded so well that, fifteen years after their debut, Lehane brought the pair back, gave them a daughter, and once again set them in motion with *Moonlight Mile.*

The danger of not having a partner takes the writer directly into the murky landscape of ONE CHARACTER ON STAGE ALONE, having nowhere to go with dramatic information but the INTERIOR MONOLOGUE, which often gets reduced to: *How had it all begun?* and *What would she do now?*

Such remarkable fiction as Jonathan Lethem's *Motherless Brooklyn* (in which the protagonist has Tourette's syndrome), or Mark Haddon's *The Curious Incident of the Dog in the Night-Time* (where the fifteen-year-old protagonist suffers from severe autism and, in a sense, "communicates" with his favorite character, Sherlock Holmes) are notable exceptions because of the way they use the FIRST-PERSON POINT OF VIEW to move them beyond the need for a partner.

When appropriate, the MULTIPLE-POINT-OF-VIEW narrative format can substitute for a specific partner. Take Mark Schluter, the twenty-seven-year-old protagonist of Richard Powers's *The Echo Maker*, involved in a near-fatal accident that causes severe brain trauma, inducing Capgras syndrome. Victims of this affliction tend to question the authenticity of those closest to them. A perfect partner for Schluter is his older sister, Karin, who gives up a good job to care for him, all the while aware that her brother does not believe she is really the person she claims to be.

passivity

A condition involving lack of will, of not being in motion or operation; grounded in the inertial state of rest; inert; lacking AGENDA or GOAL, consequently reliant on outside energy or influence; having little or no motivation.

As a quality or characteristic, passivity is an ATTITUDE a CHARACTER can least afford. Except for brief moments when a character may be stung by defeat or grief or fear, passivity precludes the energy and directed motivation toward GOAL that a character needs to sustain STORY. Dramatic NARRATIVE cannot proceed without a tangible VECTOR of goal or a plan set in place to implement a goal. Characters have to want something; they need to want something with enough passion to be driven toward achieving that goal— either that or they need to be shown as they respond to the frustrations preventing them from working toward that goal.

A frustrated housewife is one kind of story, finding significant numbers of readers. Add to the housewife-as-Sisyphus the element of that housewife's being a musical genius, capable of extraordinary composition and concert-level performance ability on an instrument, and the inherent story takes on even more dimension and significance.

The Golem of Prague represents an example of a mythical character that was created from mud, given a mission, which it achieved, then was deactivated or rendered passive. Lucius Quinctius Cincinnatus (approximately 520 BC 430 BC) is best known for the episode in his life where he was yanked by circumstances from relative passivity to the supervisory operation of maximum leadership to accomplish one goal, whereupon he retired from his leadership position, returning to a passive, contemplative life. Each of these stories ended when the goal was achieved and passivity entered the picture.

Characters are best identified by their goals. Those who seem to lack ambition or drive do not inspire empathy from the READER—unless the reader experiences the revelation that a seemingly passive character has shifted inertia for a particular reason, a reason that immediately is seen as an OBSTACLE to be overcome.

One of the best obstacles to set before a character is FRUSTRATION (another is GUILT); the unquestionably worst obstacle to confront a character is passivity.

Compare and contrast: *Oblomov* (1859) by Ivan Goncharov and *Ragged Dick* (1867) by Horatio Alger. The eponymous Oblomov was an affluent member of the Russian landed gentry, a nice enough fellow who was given over to sloth and procrastination to the point where he remains in bed for the first hundred fifty pages of the novel. Goncharov was clearly using him to make a statement about nineteenth-century Russian nobility. The protagonist of Alger's novel is also a metaphor. Dick is a poor shoeshine boy who, through unceasing hard work, clean living, optimism, and determination, rises from the ranks of poverty into the middle-class status held forth as The American Dream. An immediate point of difference: Oblomov was passive; Ragged Dick was the exact opposite.

pathetic fallacy, the

A literary device or tendency toward written or spoken exaggeration by which inanimate forces and objects have life-like qualities attributed to them.

This term, yanked into the literary sphere by the Victorian-era critic, John Ruskin, a staunch advocate of Realism in writing and the visual arts, the pathetic fallacy has spread like kudzu grass, reminding Julie Andrews that the hills are alive with the sound of music, fires dance before our eyes, brooks babble merrily in their courses, and mountains are moody and somber in the sunset.

Pathetic fallacy is an addition to the list of commandments and injunctions addressed to WRITERS: Thou shall not split the infinitive. Thou shall show rather than tell. Thou shall not begin sentences with "and or "but." Thou shall not use one-word paragraphs. These commandments and injunctions appear in the works of critics whose work is alive with the sound of textbooks.

What arbiters and critics fail to note is that successful writers have been getting away with pathetic fallacies and other crimes against boring writing by giving the language at hand a fresh way of looking at the human condition or at our remarkable universe. Go for it; it is like getting a last shave out of a shaving cream bomb or a last brushing from a flattened tube of toothpaste. The best approach to take with an inventive use of language is the Do No Harm Rule, which unequivocally supports tropes that clarify a condition, person, place, or thing to the point of causing the READER to say, "Yes! I have felt that way myself but was afraid of saying so for fear of being thought out of the mainstream."

John Ruskin did not like the idea of liberties being taken with art, nor was he a fan of sentimentality. But there are times when a wind comes up at sundown and the aspens seem to be sighing or laughing as the wind courses through them, and if you listen closely enough, the result does have music to it.

The risk of relying overly on the pathetic fallacy for effects in fiction is the projected sense that you or your CHARACTERS are talking up the case of the human effect on Nature, saying, in effect, that Nature owes everything to us and that we, in turn, owe nothing to Nature.

The careful storyteller will investigate the intent of the story, its setting, its characters, and the way the story is rendered to make sure that the methods of telling do not reveal more than the actual content.

payoff

The orchestrated result of the ENDING of a SCENE, a SHORT STORY, or a NOVEL; the outcome of a DRAMATIC NARRATIVE after the DENOUEMENT; the target for which the writer aims and the characters strive.

Scenes, stories, and novels, unlike the slot machines at a casino, have some payoff in the coin of EMOTION. If an ending does not produce some clue to what the author wants the READER to feel, the ending is sending forth a 911 call for rescue. Readers, of course, love to see CHARACTERS caught up in any or all of the potential puzzles of the human condition, their delight increasing exponentially as the puzzle becomes more complex, potentially volatile and threatening.

picaresque

A form of NARRATIVE, usually EPISODIC in nature, featuring a male or female PROTAGONIST who is of uncertain origins or from a lower social ranking and who is not motivated to a work ethic but rather earns his keep by skullduggery, wits, and deception. Often SATIRIC and IRONIC in nature, the picaresque form allows a close look at a type of society that is, by comparison with the protagonist, even lazier and more corrupt.

The protagonist of the picaresque tale—the *picaro*—is usually seen to be more upright and moral than those in whose company he is cast. He (or she, because Defoe's *Moll Flanders* certainly fits the picaresque rubric) emerges more victorious and with greater integrity at the DENOUEMENT, a dramatic demonstration that too much virtue is unbearable. Consider Huckleberry Finn, whose behavior is put in constant question, by himself and by others, causing him at the end to pretty much write off the societal norms and potentials he sees about him as he lights out for the territory ahead.

The Horatio Alger novels sold extremely well in their day, their prototype protagonist becoming a secular saint of grit, good cheer, hard work, and politeness. Equally true, such gritty individuals as Joe Buck and Ratso Rizzo from *Midnight Cowboy* attracted their share of devotees, largely because READERS can recognize the nobility in these CHARACTERS—and, so, in themselves

The *picaro* or *picara* may appear to be short on wit or incentive, as in Jaroslav Hasek's *The Good Soldier Schweik,* and thus more vulnerable. Such a character nevertheless emerges ahead of the game, the winner by a narrow-but-discernible margin over "them," the characters representing the less marginalized segments of a society. For all practical purposes, William Goldman's screen version of *Butch Cassidy and the Sundance Kid* is an EPISODIC journey of two bank robbers and the woman they both love, dancing picaresquely across the American West and parts of Bolivia, meant to convey the message that individuals at that historical time didn't have many opportunities for advancement and adventure. Similarly, the book and the screen version of *Monte Walsh* presented an episodic romp about a man whose primary ability in life was his talent for managing and breaking horses.

Picaresques have appeared in times of war and peace, in such specific locales as the American West, branches of the military (in war and in peace), and in the academic world such as the one portrayed by Kingsley Amis in *Lucky Jim* and the more extended worlds of academe as set forth by David Lodge in his NOVELS. The underlying formula might be expressed as: Roguish character makes good in spite of himself. It is in many ways a thumbing of the authorial nose at the Horatio Alger or "virtue rewarded" tale. An underground legend of such a picaresque character persists in Richard Farina's compellingly antic *Been Down So Long, It Looks Like Up to Me,* featuring Gnossos Pappadopoulis, who rides in—and then out—on a motorcycle.

Picaresque novels are deceptive because they seem to rely on the COMEDIC, which is by definition one or two steps removed from HUMOR because of its physicality. Such tales deftly move beyond the physical into the visceral, the intensity of the sad revelations of humor taking us by SURPRISE to the point of burning the characters and the story into our memory. A number of *The Canterbury Tales* make this segue from the comedic to the more deeply felt, notably *The Pardoner's Tale* and *The Knight's Tale*, each of which pays off in revelations of self-awareness in the principal characters at the expense of their self-esteem.

plausibility

A condition that features the DRAMATIC sense of a CHARACTER, deed, or EVENT being believable to the READER; a depiction of a character's AGENDA, MOTIVATION, or desire being an appropriate, life-like expression; a quality of realism and trust in a NARRATIVE and its denizens that helps the reader maintain a sense of belief.

Because an event portrayed in a narrative actually happened in reality does not automatically grant it a license for plausibility; the WRITER must believe the event and the characters and must write about them in a way that renders them as dramatic forces, considering what they want and what they are willing to do to get what they want. A good portion of plausibility is found in the VULNERABILITY of characters; when a reader sees a defect or longing in a character, it becomes easier to forget that the character is only a smudge of someone else's imagination.

plot

A design or floor plan for the placement of dramatic furniture; a *feng shui* of emotional obstacles, arranged to produce STRESS, ACTION, and either some degree of SOLUTION or recovery.

In order to qualify as STORY, the most opaque and elliptical of NARRATIVE ARCS requires some plot design to give the READER the sense of having entered at one point and experiencing the PROCESS of being transported to another. The narrative arc must draw two or more CHARACTERS into a situation where events such as CHOICE, HUMILIATION, understanding, exultation, FRUSTRATION, or successful achievement are within sight. Plot means someone is vulnerable to something, whether the ticking clock of time elapsing, romantic or artistic rejection, or the awareness of failure looming like the marine layers of mist and fog off the California coastline.

Used as a verb, plot means to arrange a plausible set of OBSTACLES for one or more characters and then track those characters as they attempt to work themselves free. For characters to feel that others are plotting against them, they must be aware of an organized plan or INTENT to frustrate their stated GOALS. Not all antagonistic plotting has malicious intent; it may be merely a doctrinal or philosophical placement of obstacle. When a character senses that the plotting against him is malicious, the READER senses an enhanced dramatic presence.

Most memorable plots are wound about the armature of a single basic emotion such as revenge, fear, love, ambition, or jealousy. These emotions are widely recognized across cultures and time, powerful enough, each in its way, to hold the most determined character in a stubborn grip.

Hint: For a textbook demonstration of plot, form, flexibility, and resolution at work in the most agreeable manner, study Louise Erdrich's *The Plague of Doves.* The payoff and resolution are deftly hinted at on the first page, then brought to bear with a dramatic flourish at the last moment, producing the kind of surprise that comes when we realize how prepared we were for its possibility and how deftly it was hidden.

plot-driven story

A NARRATIVE experience in which the intricacy and persistence of PLOT appears to take charge of the behavior exhibited by CHARACTERS; it is a STORY in which the domino theory of SCENE and EVENT holds priority over behavior by individuals.

In plot-driven stories, characters respond to the placement and removal of obstacles more than they respond to their feelings about another character or their reactions to events. Some plot-driven stories do approach high levels of character revelation and investigation—some, indeed, are so artful as to make the READER overlook the plot-driven nature of events. One such example is Richard Powers's unsettling NOVEL, *The Echo Maker.* On close examination, Richard Price's novel *Lush Life* also fits the definition of plot-driven—both examples being offered here as refutation of the belief that plot-driven stories are necessarily inferior to stories in which characters and their responses seem to dictate behavior.

The plot-driven story serves as a challenge to the mature WRITER who is able to moderate between the mechanics of goals and obstacles and the inventive discovery of dimensional characters.

point of time

The instant when any given moment of the STORY is taking place.

POT is identified by verb tenses. The preterit or immediate past tense is conventionally represented as now. "John woke up early this morning" is used to convey to the READER, Here is John, waking up now. If we want to suggest that John has already been up for a while, we'd introduce the auxiliary verb had and say, "John had been up earlier than usual this morning." Using the "had" form indicates action completed in the past. The so-called present-tense form of NARRATIVE renders action through the lens of the "now" of all CHARACTERS, thus "John gets up early this morning," conveys, Here is John, waking up now. Using the present-tense approach, you'd indicate past action with the direct past tense. "John got up early, remembering he has to be at work before the Boss, but even so, he has to rush to get ready."

All POINT-OF-VIEW filters (persons) may be rendered in the present to suggest the immediate moment; the conventional past tense may also be used to suggest immediate present moment.

Whatever verb tense the author chooses, the contemporary narrative convention requires more than fifty percent to take place in the now; upwards of forty percent (BACKSTORY, past influences, memories) may take place in the past.

point of view

The CHARACTER or characters in a STORY through whose eyes and other senses the READER learns and intuits the dramatic action; the teller of the tale; the biased, human filter through which the dramatic information is transmitted.

The WRITER achieves a significant part of WILLING SUSPENSION OF BELIEF from the reader when dramatic forces cause the reader to forget that the story is emerging directly from the writer and that, in fact, the story is pure artifice. This WSOB is well achieved by artful introduction of one or more characters who are telling the story, ASAP. As in: "My father's family name being Pirrip, and my Christian name Philip, my infant tongue could make of both names nothing longer or more explicit than Pip. So, I called myself Pip, and came to be called Pip."

The first sentence would actually fit as a Twitter entry. The second sentence pretty well nails the character and his point of view in place, where it remains, a resoundingly successful example of a writer assuming the persona of Pip and his traits and experiences in order to relate the details of his encounters variously with his snarky sister, her jewel of a man-for-husband, an escaped convict, a cantankerous old lady, and a spoiled-if-beguiling young woman named Estella. So gifted a public speaker was Pip's creator that he could have chosen to tell the story of *Great Expectations* in his own voice. A writer could profit from considering why he did not.

There is often some practical reason for a particular character or set of characters having been chosen to narrate a story, sometimes as simplistic as the selection of narrator of *Moby-Dick;* Ishmael was the only one who survived the events of the novel. Mr. Stephens was chosen to narrate *The Remains of the Day* because of his position as head butler, but also because of his not "getting it," which is to say because of his naïveté. Thus was the writer, Kazuo Ishiguro, constrained to keep Stevens's naïveté in mind at all times and to constantly be aware of the need to render it plausibly.

Who is telling your story, and why?

Benjy Compson was chosen to narrate a portion of *The Sound and the Fury* because the wiring of his intellectual and reasoning processes were some degrees away from the intellectual and emotional outlook of other POV characters. No doubt about it, at some point during his writing of the story, William Faulkner recalled the Shakespearean line from *Macbeth*—"…it is a tale/Told by an idiot, full of sound and fury/Signifying nothing." But Faulkner knew the need to have larger fish to fry than the mere perception of Benjy as an idiot; Faulkner wished the reader to compare Benjy's vision of reality with that of the other characters in the novel. Benjy is then by no means a case of a writer thinking merely, *Aha, I'll tell a story from the point of view of an idiot.* The novel is a complex comparison of ATTITUDES, sensitivities, and behavior in which Benjy emerges as an IRONIC symbol of the most admirable sort.

Once again, why have you selected a particular person or combination of persons to relate your narrative? What effect will your choice have on the other characters? What effect will your choice have on the reader? (See AUTHORIAL INTERVENTION, FIRST-PERSON, SECOND-PERSON, THIRD-PERSON, MULTIPLE POINT OF VIEW, OMNISCIENT POINT OF VIEW.)

political novel, the

A fictional NARRATIVE constructed to EVOKE political commentary; a NOVEL formulated to level criticism, even ridicule, at a present-day or historical circumstance.

For the politically-minded WRITER, the novel of politics represents an attractive target GENRE, allowing flexibility in choice of historical eras, narrative tone (gravitas, HUMOR, SATIRE, etc.) and the mixing of actual historical CHARACTERS with fictional ones, or the use of the ROMAN À CLEF approach to strongly suggest an actual personality through the portrayal of an invented one (as in Robert Penn Warren's *All the King's Men,* in which Willie Stark is conceded to be taken for Huey P. Long).

The short story writer and novelist Junot Diaz would not be thought of as a political writer at first reading, but even before the appearance of his stunning novel *The Brief Wondrous Life of Oscar Wao,* it would be possible, after considering his shorter work, to conclude that Diaz had a shrewd eye for the social politics of Dominican Republic emigrants to America, the politics of Latino families, and the politics of outsiders trying to establish identity and place within a large social landscape. Although the story of Oscar Wao is highly personalized, its close-up focus transcends into a universal metaphor for COMING OF AGE, even as it details with some imagination, rage, and sophistication the effects the United States has had on smaller countries at a considerable remove from it.

Although associated with political causes in his personal life, Dashiell Hammett was more frequently associated with stories of crime and detection—*The Maltese Falcon,* and *The Thin Man*—thanks to the general awareness of his having been associated with the Pinkerton Detective Agency. Yet Hammett's 1931 novel, *The Glass Key,* plays heavily on political themes, introducing a protagonist, Ned Beaumont, whose association with a crooked political figure leads him to investigate a murder, the trail of clues gradually transforming his views of the world about him and his self. The tenor and scope of Beaumont and the NOIR atmosphere of corruption in politics led to an influence in crime writing that has had profound effects on writers, on crime novels, and political novels. An arguable heir of Hammett and his Ned Beaumont is Sara Paretsky's Chicago PI, V. I. Warshawski.

Political novels are like thermometers: They reflect the temperature of a given era's political symptoms—and may also affect it. Harriet Beecher Stowe's 1852 political novel, *Uncle Tom's Cabin*, is one many critics and historians argue as a significant catalyst. This sentimentalized accounting of the American experience with slavery fueled the Abolitionist Movement, which in turn influenced the American Civil War. Uncle Tom, his family, and slave owner Simon Legree evolved from fictional presences to stereotypical realities that lasted well into the 20th century.

Richard Condon's 1959 thriller, *The Manchurian Candidate,* took the political novel on yet a new vector. In this conspiracy theory thriller set during the Korean War, an American platoon is captured and brainwashed to believe that one of their number heroically saved them during combat. The "hero" has been further brainwashed to serve as a sleeper agent for the Communists.

Alan Drury's 1959 novel, *Advise and Consent,* was designed to show the intricate workings of the U. S. Senate. The narrative posits the nomination to the secretary of state position an individual with liberal politics and a background as a former Communist. The Senate, with a duty to advise the president and consent to his programs, is seen in action, vetting the individual and the implications of his service as secretary of state.

Graham Greene's 1958 novel of politics, *Our Man in Havana,* demonstrates the potential for humor and SATIRE in the political novel. A genial but passive British expatriate working in pre-Castro Havana as a vacuum cleaner salesman becomes a British intelligence agent as a way of making more money to pay for his daughter's convent education. This elaborately constructed satire ridicules the often-unseen consequences of a mismanaged intelligence program. In many if not all his novels, Greene was able to blend his religious and philosophical views with some form of political commentary, yet another demonstration of the flexibility and attractiveness of the medium.

Whenever two or more characters gather, there is some form of politics in play. The writer sees this and takes notes—and incorporates them into his narrative if doing so will enrich the story.

politics

The use of POWER; systematic applications of problem solving; means by which divergent groups or individuals attend ethical, moral, and social issues; POINTS OF VIEW regarding group and individual governance.

All CHARACTERS have politics, whether they know it or not. A basic approach to determine a character's political views comes from investigating that character's family background, both in terms of the character's general political views and also from an assessment of that character's gender, the number of siblings, and when that character arrived in the family. Individuals who are adopted may have yet other political dynamics, including a curiosity to learn the identities of their biological parents. Orphans or characters who have broken relations with family have yet another political as well as psychological dynamic.

For the WRITER, knowing the political petri dish of the character's psyche is vital as it provides information about the character's ATTITUDES, responses, and readiness to form alliances and enmities. Of equal significance, a writer needs to consider his or her own politics or lack of interest in the broader sense of politics, then investigate personal senses of awareness within family, friend groups, workplace associates, and ties with former classmates.

Of all the many influences likely to emerge in the THEMES of a particular writer's work, the writer's personal and broadband politics rank close to the top of the pyramid, influencing choice of characters and the types of CONFLICTS in which those characters engage. As examples of writers whose politics or political interests seem to shine through their pages, Charles Dickens, Jane Austen, John P. Marquand, and Margaret Atwood inspire close study.

PONR (point of no return)

The point in a SHORT STORY or NOVEL where EVENTS have taken the NARRATIVE beyond the place where ACTIONS and their CONSEQUENCES can be cancelled; the place in a narrative where the READER and CHARACTERS realize that the pre-story STASIS can not be revisited.

Point of no return is a close relative of the TIPPING POINT. When the tipping point is reached, any slight DECISION or indecision may send the narrative spilling over into PONR, at which time there is no calling off the QUEST or INTENT that drove the story to this fragile point.

Both PONR and tipping point produce consequences, and these may be unanticipated. When Huck Finn encountered the runaway slave Jim on the river island, then allowed Jim to accompany him, there was no turning back. When young psychiatric resident Richard Diver and his patient Nicole Warren step inside the doorway of a Vienna apartment building to avoid an afternoon shower in F. Scott Fitzgerald's *Tender Is the Night,* then give way to the mounting sexual tension between them by embracing and kissing, Diver "knew from that moment that now, her [Nicole's] problems were his."

portal

A doorway between or entryway from one LANDSCAPE to another; most famously the rabbit hole into which Alice tumbled from the world of reality to Lewis Carroll's world of imagination and SATIRE.

A considerable subset of the FANTASY GENRE is populated with portal stories in which CHARACTERS are able to move variously from one universe to another or one time frame to another. Some famous portals are antique shops, Chinese laundries, apothecaries, and news kiosks, all of which have a habit of offering certain inducements or PRODUCTS to certain characters, then disappearing when the characters, experiencing BUYERS' REMORSE, seek to return.

Yet another famed portal is a park bench in Oxford, England, a site where Lyra Belacqua and her love, Will Parry, characters from the *His Dark Materials* trilogy by Philip Pullman, sit at the same time on the same day of the year, there to hold hands across the boundaries of separate worlds. Less romantic—and less tidy—are the fireplaces and public toilet booths J. K. Rowling employs as portals for Harry Potter and the gang from Hogwarts.

The concept of the portal is not limited to such fantasy-related concepts as ALTERNATE UNIVERSES—and this for the same reason that fantasy fiction is an important construct for all storytellers. In an excruciatingly real way, every NOVEL and short story is set in an alternate universe, one that is somewhat of this present reality and equally somewhat of the author's concept of what this present reality is. Portals allow both writer and reader a glimpse into an alternate universe.

In any convincing story, characters stumble or are drawn into portals they have not recognized as portals; they emerge to discover themselves in a world that may not be hospitable, may in fact be outright menacing, therein to pursue their AGENDAS according to the risks and realities of the universe in which they find themselves. Just as personal traits help define characters, details and conventions of behavior define the world in which characters awaken, then attempt to function in.

Dorothy Gale has been drawn into the Land of Oz through the whirl of a cyclone, while Philip Marlowe is drawn into the shadowy illegalities of the greater Los Angeles Basin through the portal of a scratched and battered office in an undistinguished building on the lower reaches of Hollywood Boulevard. Similarly, through the highly idiosyncratic portal of Yoknapatawpha County, an imaginary venue in the state of Mississippi, we gain access to the alternate universe of the rural United States South, a REGIONAL portal through which is seen a vision of America as variegated and painfully naked as possible, one so specific in its nature that it becomes ironically universal.

How characters come to be in such alternate universes, how they are seen by the denizens of these universes, and how they seek either to remain or find their way out are the essential natures of story.

POV
The abbreviation frequently used for point of view.

power
The capacity a CHARACTER frequently enjoys at the expense of one or more of the others in a STORY is that character's power and it may be anything from political to financial to sexual; it may also be manifest in terms of social standing, high esteem within a family or organization, or even in terms of talent/ability.

Power is often a key element in motivating characters to rebel, escape, seek revenge, or make peremptory moves. They each want their own power; their decision to rebel, escape, seek revenge, or make peremptory moves is an indication of their wish for power of their own, to use as they see fit.

REVERSAL OF POWER is a delicious story element; it often helps dramatize nuances and the not-so-subtle behavior patterns resident in characters who have been affected by turns of fate. One of the many joys available to a READER is to be present at a scene where a bully or tyrant, still acting under the belief of continuing power, discovers the plug has been pulled. And think how noble a character must feel to have caused a switch from being oppressed to being the one who can walk away from a dramatic reversal without having to exact revenge.

It is useful to observe the power dynamic between or among the characters in any given scene; allotting equal power to characters tends to reduce dramatic tension, and since life is notably unfair in the way of power distribution, why start making it so within the confines of a story?

predictable
A NARRATIVE condition that comes to life, then grows critical when the READER correctly guesses the INTENT of a CHARACTER and the outcome of that intent. Any DRAMATIC circumstances in which there is little or no NUANCE, where the reader is neither SURPRISED nor challenged are danger signs, portents for the reader skipping ahead to see if there are good parts or simply abandoning the book for good.

If a reader is truly caught up in a STORY, he will have taken sides, begun to root for the success of some and the failure or worse (humiliation) for others, indulged in the trope of reader as matchmaker and looked for potential romantic entanglements. Additionally, the reader will be able to take cues from the text on a level close to basic reflex. Certain situations in story provoke the speculation that something—a disaster, a REVERSAL, a surprise—is forthcoming. WRITERS who understand the dynamics of story will be aware of these cues and prepare for them in a way that will provoke SURPRISE and keep the reader off guard and guessing to the point of not being able to put the book down.

Never take the reader where the reader wants to go. Leave the reader standing still, and she may easily feel stalled if presented with LAUNDRY LISTS of details, forced to listen to long, philosophical discussions, subjected to weather reports or travel-writing descriptions of scenery. At the extreme least, readers want to feel as though they are eavesdropping on some form of intimacy; better still they wish to feel compellingly caught up with the execution of a particular character's AGENDA.

The writer's task: make the reader feel the intensity of the characters and their involvements with the issues of the story. If the reader is involved in the feelings and agendas of the characters, the reader is joining them in shared vulnerability to the immediate surprise barreling down the narrative highway.

There is no one trick that serves to make a story unpredictable, but studying those who are masters at it can help a writer stretch the imaginative muscles that lift a story out of ordinary. Even if you are not a fan of the suspense-based thriller, it is worth reading at least one novel by Harlan Coben, comparing it with one by Lee Child and Nelson DeMille. Couldn't hurt to read Annie Proulx's *The Shipping News* and Louise Erdrich's *A Plague of Doves* which present yet other variations on the theme of surprise and unpredictability.

Banishing predictability in story provides another set of reasons to learn about acting techniques from the likes of such actor coaches as Stella Adler, Sanford Meisner, and Uta Hagen, wherein actors learn where to find within themselves the emotions, gestures, and visions of surprise. In this sense, surprise is the DISCOVERY the character makes about himself/herself in times of weal and woe—discovery that, before a reader's eyes, can transform the predictable into the truly remarkable.

premise

An as-yet-undeveloped CONCEPT for a NOVEL or STORY; a CHARACTER confronted with a CHOICE or placed in an intriguing or threatening situation; a hypothetical dramatic situation that cannot yet stand on its own.

Premise is like a wobbly three-legged stool or restaurant table; it needs to be stabilized with the shim of ACTION or INTENT or REVERSAL, any or all of which will elevate it toward becoming story. At some point, CHARACTERS, their GOALS, limitations, and strengths need to be articulated, which brings dimension and nuance onto the stage, giving the WRITER and the characters options that will make the development seem to churn up a vacuum, drawing character, READER, and writer along in their wake. The reader will be the litmus test of whether the development is effective.

Two men, each laid off from a promising job, wander into a neighborhood cocktail lounge for solace, where they encounter an up-beat young woman who has just been dumped by her boyfriend.

No hint of story yet, but no lack of possibilities. Premise = the potential for story; it is often the rearranging of dramatic furniture that gets the writer's imagination piqued with the curiosity to see the outcome.

When all else fails, rearrange the furniture.

problem words

Words that seem to enhance ATTRIBUTIONS but actually muddy a given issue; descriptors intended to delineate but which instead blur; words meant to indicate an emphasis or degree of intensity; words that don't enhance the meaning for which they were used.

Problem words are the literary equivalent of hiring relatives; they mean well but ultimately do not understand what is expected of them. To say that John was quite annoying doesn't tell the READER much except that John exhibited qualities that were annoying to some undisclosed person or persons, and that whatever these qualities were, it is impossible to tell to whom or how his behavior caused annoyance; nothing is expressed or implied relative to the accuracy of the statement or its reflection on the reliability of the NARRATOR. It is all right for John to be annoying, but the reader should have some relative sense of how John sets forth on his mission to annoy. Does he chew gum loudly? Does he tell racist or sexist jokes? Then there is the matter of the "quite." Does the "quite" mean "somewhat," "very," "considerably," or perhaps "intensely"? Instead of telling us that John is annoying, show him chewing gum. Show how he chews it—perhaps he makes a long, slurping sound with each bite as he wraps his tongue around the wad to draw it out of his dental work—and then show us how another character reacts to the habit. Once you *show* this exchange to a reader, there is no need at all to *tell* him that John is annoying or to what degree.

Problem words and HABIT WORDS dilute dramatic prose by injecting notes of vagueness and repetition into a narrative, venturing close to the verge of trespass into the terrains of cuteness, patronization, and affectation.

Hint: You are in the literary equivalent of a police line-up, asked to identify miscreant problem words. Before you, in well-lit display, appear "rather," "very," "many," and "somewhat." You blink in recognition of your complicity in using all of them, then point an accusing finger.

process

A sequence of idiosyncratic EVENTS and stimuli leading a WRITER to visualize, orchestrate, and REVISE a STORY; the notional warp and weft of threads the individual writer requires in order to tell a story; the TOOL KIT, techniques, compulsions, and possible superstitions a writer uses in the act of generating material.

Writers come to their craft by accidental discovery, from genetic inheritance, from a desire for REVENGE, or perhaps from a childhood illness that kept them away from school for a prolonged period in which isolated time of physical sickness their imaginative muscles were toned. Writers come from one or more stories that tipped them over into IMITATION, then originality, and from the growing awareness that, for them, no other pursuit is as much fun. There are other processes in which real or imagined pain is an ingredient. Grown men and women confess they would rather do anything but write and then, as a part of their process, trudge to their work area, radiating martyrdom as they settle into the task at hand.

Beginning writers, many of whom are known to have no sense of humor about the career path they have chosen, or who may take writing terribly seriously, begin to wonder if they have the necessary ingredients to tell stories because they do not abuse alcohol or drugs or sex, do not particularly care for driving fast cars, seldom vote in elections, and do not believe they are able to withstand or understand REJECTION. To them, any income under $100,000 a year derived from writing means failure, and reading the works of other writers means time wrenched away from their own creative efforts. But self-doubt, sensitivity to criticism, limited income (if not outright poverty), and learning from most accomplished writers are all strands of the beginning writer's process, which undergoes subtle and individualizing shifts as the process of their own writing continues.

The process of some writers involves first and second drafts written in ink before being transferred to the computer. The process of other writers is to keep a daily journal in which the goal is to evoke at least one EMOTION. Yet other writers believe implicitly in the process of halting a day's work in the middle of a sentence, thus to confront the next day's work with a direct link to work in progress. A considerable number of writers OUTLINE furiously and do not consider beginning text until they have a complete design before them, while an equally considerable number enjoy the high of striking out with no PLOT or plan to hinder their imagination.

All of these processes work for some and, for others, shut the process down completely. The key is to discover for yourself whence cometh the process. Is it anger, politics, a desire to tell cautionary tales, an urge to revise historical outcomes, project futures based on worst-case scenarios? Are you advocating equality for women, same sex marriage, evangelism, creationism, IRONY, ADVENTURE? What is your natural gestalt? Are you an optimist? Is the glass already half empty? Shall we *carpe* the freaking *diem*?

The individual writer's process is a string of stimuli that may have emerged without the knots of culture, family, schooling, or writing books being added. There are those who seem to hear their process speaking to them early on, without having to unlearn things that were painfully acquired in the first place. No sentences that begin with And or But. No one-line paragraphs. A subject for every sentence. A topic sentence in every paragraph.

These are not processes; these are rules. The CONSEQUENCE of disregarding rules should be considered before continuing, but if your process dictates a break, then break away.

A writer's process is much like a pair of shoes one sees in an ad, seemingly a perfect statement of personality, shape, and color. There is a disconnect, however, between the vision of the shoe in the ad and the visit to the shoe store or the arrival of the shoes from Zappos.com. No matter how good the shoe looks in the ad, it is of no value if it pinches at the sides or cramps the toes. You do not take the shoes hoping to "break them in." The writer's process needs to fit, and the best fit is always hand-made.

products

The equipment, merchandise, devises used by CHARACTERS to advance STORY; material goods used by WRITERS to denote living conditions, relative affluence, degrees of decadence, boredom inherent in characters; things people want or conspicuously do not want in stories.

Nowhere in stories are products given a more substantive and metaphoric treatment than the cartoon adventures of Wile E. Coyote. In these iconic dramatic ventures, Coyote lurches forth, a faithful replication of Mark Twain's description of the coyote species from *Roughing It*. Coyote's hunger prods him to consider the Road Runner as prey. The extensive number of Coyote-Road Runner cartoons is an insistent monument to Coyote's abject failure.

The rules surrounding the Wile E. Coyote LANDSCAPE are myriad and inflexible, at once rendering the terrain a crossbreed between Beckett and Krazy Kat. Coyote must not catch Road Runner. Coyote's attempts at catching Road Runner invariably end in his HUMILIATION. Coyote may use devices such as explosive tennis balls, giant mousetraps, do-it-yourself tornado kits, and female Road Runner costumes, but these and all others like them must come directly from the Acme Corporation.

No other organization, neither KAFKAESQUE bureaucracies nor Orwellian imperialists, is so catholic in its offered menu of products as the Acme Corporation; no government or manufacturer has such a smorgasbord of devices which, taken in totality, could be seen to represent the quintessential formula for curing all ills and supplying answers for all needs. Some of the items on the Acme Corporation's list work well enough; they simply do not work for Wile E. Coyote. But rules are rules, meaning Coyote has no recourse; if he is to use products, they must come from Acme.

Probably based on the ubiquity and comprehensiveness of the original Sears, Roebuck mail order catalogues, the Acme Corporation's arsenal of products and their built-in exclusivity for Wile E. Coyote become a metaphor for the writer who is setting forth, beginning with a particular landscape or locale, then basic rules of engagement between the major characters, then the source of materials the characters have at their disposal.

Wile E. Coyote's credit seems to be good so far as Acme Corporation is concerned; there don't seem to be any issues about accounts receivable. There are neither long, elaborate rationales about the Coyote-Road Runner landscape nor the rules governing it. Neither, for that matter, are there distracting questions about the landscape within Beckett plays; Beckett stories hold up while being read, then become iron filings attracted to the magnet of the mind after the reading or witnessing ends. Similarly with Coyote and Road Runner.

The message from Beckett ("Fail again, only next time, fail better") inheres in the Wile E. Coyote cartoons; the after-the-fact paradigm of the cartoons with respect to story also becomes apparent with a personal deconstruction of the entire, precipitous southwestern mesa-butte landscape of the cartoon series.

Tim O'Brien has written a splendid account of American servicemen in Vietnam, *The Things They Carried,* a novel in which products play a major role in defining character and dramatic outcome. In the cartoons, Wile E. Coyote's frequent fate is having his hair singed off, falling to bottoms of steep declivities, being squashed by falling rocks or even the occasional debris from an Acme Corporation product; sometimes Coyote sustains all these fates simultaneously. O'Brien's characters inevitably reveal a distinct, moving relationship to a product, whether the product is a letter from a loved one (or a Dear John letter), a keepsake, a weapon. Coyote and O'Brien's "grunts" are set forth in an atmosphere and landscape that could not have suited Beckett better, thus is there a transcendent plateau reached and recognized when the writer brings characters with purpose and products to a locale, imbues them with constraints, restraints, and possibly even conscience.

protagonist

A front-rank CHARACTER in a NOVEL or SHORT STORY whose AGENDA propels the narrative toward CONCLUSION, an individual whose ACTIONS provoke the actual point of conclusion. A protagonist is often the character with whom the READER most empathizes and for whom the reader roots.

Most dramatic NARRATIVE begins with someone wanting something. (Anne Elliot in Jane Austen's *Persuasion* wants to resume a romance with Captain Wentworth that she broke off a few years back. Ike McCaslin, in William Faulkner's "The Bear," wants to hunt down Old Ben, the eponymous bear.) This desire becomes the catalyst for a series of subsequent EVENTS in which the protagonist strives for the GOAL, achieves it or is frustrated in his attempts, or achieves a negotiated settlement with the Fates and/or other characters.

It has become a conventional standard for critical readers to ask of the protagonist, *What does this person want?* Depending on the length and complexity of the narrative, the goals and outcome of the protagonist's agenda are set forth in some detail. Simply put, Ahab wanted revenge on the whale, Gatsby wanted to fulfill a romantic connection with Daisy, and Huck Finn wanted to be free to live the life he chose. In all three examples, extraordinary interventions complicated the expressed agenda of the front-rank character.

It falls within the realm of dramatic possibility that a protagonist may wish for nothing more passionately than to be left alone, but the vital thing for the storyteller to understand is that passivity in a front-rank character has, in nearly all cases, a fatal effect on story. Thus the protagonist's wish to be left alone requires the connective tissue of being left alone in order to do some thing that has exquisite meaning for him. The protagonist must have an AGENDA that is strong enough to provide forward momentum in spite of and because of opposition from life forces or ANTAGONISTS.

Stories in which protagonists achieve their goals too easily are not good candidates for holding the reader's interest. This is not so much a matter of reader SCHADENFREUDE as it is a matter of the reader wanting to share the moments of insight, determination, and ingenuity that propel the protagonist to have one more try. Given the CHOICE, most readers could accept their protagonist's miserable failure after a noble try rather than have the protagonist achieve the goal by accident.

Answers to the following questions can help the writer bring a credible and pliant protagonist forth from the drawing board:

1. Who is he/she?
2. What does he/she want?
3. What is he/she willing to do to effect the goal?
4. How does he/she handle REVERSAL?
5. How is he/she likely to behave after having achieved the target goal?

The answers to the first question are often simple, "a young person in search of a life's occupation," or "a person looking for a mate," or "a person trying to live down a past mistake."

Useful answers to the second question could be "another chance" or the more direct "revenge," or "to set the record straight;" they could also include "justification," "fame/recognition," or "to discover the truth behind an event or individuals involved in an event."

Answers to the third question are rich in story potential: "give up something important," or "assume a new identity," or "step over some moral boundary," which could easily include "commit some previously unthinkable act."

The fourth answer provides the opportunity to demonstrate the resolve and resiliency of the character, while the fifth answer introduces the possibility of a primary ingredient in fiction, IRONY, which may add layers of meaning and texture to the story. The nature of characters is best revealed when there is an abrupt REVERSAL of fortune. A character who suddenly gains POWER may behave in surprising and revealing ways.

Stories—particularly novels—may have more than one protagonist, but the reader should be able to tell them apart. A splendid example of this is to be found in Henry James's novel *The Ambassadors*. For most practical purposes, Lambert Strether is the main character, but there would be no story had Strether not been sent to Paris by his fiancée, Mrs. Newsome, to persuade her son, Chad, to come home and take over the running of the family business. Mrs. Newsome never appears physically, but her presence is evident on every page. In similar fashion, since it is Strether's "job" to persuade young Newsome to return home, that agreeable young man can be seen as a pivotal presence if not an outright opponent or antagonist. James does an excellent job of bringing us into the orbits of three front-rank players. (See also *Lonesome Dove*, for the seemingly similar Woodrow Call and Gus McRae, who reveal themselves expansively as another instance of differences in protagonists.)

publishers' conventional wisdom

An idiosyncratic sense of "knowing" what the reading public wants; a series of reasons publishers give for taking on some projects and not others; reasons mainstream publishers give for removing mention of oral sex from YA NOVELS; rationale behind enormous advances given on celebrity titles.

Publishers have their individual conventional wisdom, which is their polestar. Similarly, WRITERS have their individual conventional wisdom. This is as it should be. Occasionally the two overlap and a partnership is formed. This, too, is as it should be. Neither should adjust his conventional wisdom to conform to the other; what happens should be of a sincere feeling of chemistry or, better yet, the remarkable symbiosis achieved when particles in a nuclear accelerator crash into one another and produce a reaction. *Hint:* It is one thing for a writer to research a publisher so that the odds of colliding particles is enhanced, but it is yet another for a writer to alter or diminish his own conventional wisdom to suit a conventional wisdom of a particular publisher that is entirely supposition. One of the reasons Kenneth Millar (aka Ross Macdonald) submitted his Lew Archer private eye novels to the publisher Alfred Knopf was because, at the time, Knopf had no mystery list. The best conventional wisdom to follow is this: The more unlike others you are, the more likely you are to find a readership. It may not happen as soon as you wish; it may not happen at all, but you knew that all along and, somehow, the knowledge of it fueled your work.

purple prose

A dangerous condition resident in text when the WRITER mistakes emotion-descriptive words with words that imply or INFER emotion; an excessive romanticizing or sentimentalizing description; an operatic display of METAPHOR, simile, and stylistic flourish executed by the writer in the belief that a love of words and the language is an acceptable excuse; excessive display of descriptive rather than inferential language.

Musicians love notes. Painters love paint. Sculptors love clay. It is a given that writers like words, the proof of which is in the demonstrable chemistry between CHARACTERS, STORY, movement of story, and resolution, a chemistry that produces at least entertainment but in some cases such qualities as solutions to moral problems, revelation of unexamined aspects of human behavior, and a sense of how to get along with other humans on the only known habitable planet. The novels of the late, respected William F. Buckley, Jr. often gave the impression that although he understood story, what he really loved were words and he wrote for the joy of riffing on them. In his fiction, particularly *Memoirs of Hecate County,* the polymath critic Edmund Wilson gave the impression of losing patience with story in favor of the exciting rush of words and connotations. It is arguably fair to render a similar judgment on A. S. Byatt, particularly her novel *Babble Tower,* which seemed to tip its hat to story, then bid it a fond farewell under a welter of words, concepts, and comparisons.

quest

The major goal for any CHARACTER; an intensified apprenticeship undertaken in hopes of achieving virtuoso ability; a SEARCH, study, or other organized pursuit with a GOAL in mind; a systematic and insistent research; an attempt to find a meaning, relic, or understanding.

Sometimes a quest is for a tangible, physical place or thing; other times it is the means by which a POINT OF VIEW or personal commitment is achieved. Everyone in FICTION is on a quest. Often, relationships in fiction are ended because of conflicting quests, thus the importance of knowing what each character in a story wants, how seriously, and to what lengths the character will go to achieve the end results of the quest. Murder? Perhaps. Betrayal of principle? Maybe. Treason? A likely possibility.

A popular add-on to the quest being achieved or realized can be found in IRONY such as is inherent in B.Traven's *The Treasure of the Sierra Madre*. Was Charles Rider's quest in *Brideshead Revisited* any the less ironic? And what about the payoff of *The Maltese Falcon?*

For a writer, knowing what a character wants is a major step toward realizing a memorable STORY; it is no less important for the writer to know how the character might behave having seen the quest through to completion. Would Gatsby have been happy with Daisy? For that matter, would Daisy have remained content to be with Gatsby? And while we're on the subject, Miss Elizabeth Bennett and Mr. Fitzwilliam Darcy each appeared at the conclusion of PRIDE AND PREJUDICE to have arrived at a goal of a companionable, partnership-type marriage, but would they remain so ten years down the line?

Quest is the dramatic boulder of SISYPHUS, poised at the peak of a hill.

quiting

The literary "conversation" in which a WRITER answers or responds to a previously published work; derived from Middle English requite "a return to someone or something." (Thus unrequited love is love that is not reciprocated.)

A noteworthy contemporary example of quiting is Jane Smiley's *Thirteen Ways of Looking at a Novel,* which requites the title and content of Wallace Stevens's poem, "Thirteen Ways of Looking at a Blackbird." In similar fashion, Wallace Stevens requited John Keats's "Ode on a Grecian Urn" with "Anecdote of the Jar." When he composed *Troilus and Cressida,* Shakespeare was requiting Geoffrey Chaucer's Middle English *Troilus and Criseyde,* which Chaucer actually picked up from the *Le Roman de Troie,* written in French in the mid-twelfth century by Benoît de Sainte-Maure. Each of these versions added changes and perspectives, two essential elements to quiting. Similarly, James Joyce requited the poet or poets we now think of as Homer in his famed recounting of *The Odyssey,* known to us as the novel *Ulysses.* Quiting may also be seen as a payback, as Montresor requited or paid back Fortunato in Poe's SHORT STORY, "A Cask of Amontillado." Thus a contemporary writer may indulge in a "conversation" with another writer, even one long dead. American copyright laws that are interpreted to support a writer's use of his property expressly supported J.D. Salinger when another author sought to use characters based on Salinger's own inventions from *The Catcher in the Rye.* In this same construct, no one complained when Valerie Martin retold Robert Louis Stevenson's *The Strange Case of Dr. Jekyll and Mr. Hyde* through the point of view of an Irish maid in her novel *Mary Reilly,* nor of Herman Melville's Captain Ahab in Sena Nasland's novel *Ahab's Wife.* One evident message: if you're going to requite an author, pick one whose work is now safely in public domain. Another message is to make some recognizable contribution to the effect and understanding of the original work.

You could argue that Shakespeare was one of the great quiters, having refurbished or reformulated the works of earlier writers such as Geoffrey of Monmouth (approximately 1100-1155), notably in *Julius Caesar, Cymbeline,* and *King Lear,* not to forget his use of the Danish historian Saxo Grammaticus (1150-1220) for materials inspiring *Hamlet.*

Contemporary quiters have conjoined Jane Austen characters with vampires in what appears to have been a coup for followers of vampire fiction. The late, lamented Ed McBain, creator of the famed, Eighty-seventh Precinct police procedural mysteries, was given to naming junior high schools set in his novels after his friends, a milder but amusing example of requiting.

qy

The common abbreviation for query, usually from editor to author, found on margins of galley proofs or digital documents. Plural, qys. Sometimes rendered au qy.

The qy notation requests a specific answer from the writer. The novelist Barnaby Conrad once referenced the noted gossip columnist Walter Winchell in a manuscript and, when he was sent proofs from his young editor, found an "au qy" tagged to Walter Winchell, "Who he?" The novelist/artist Stephen Longstreet referenced Gustav Flaubert in the text of a novel only to be met with the qy, "Still living?"

~R~

raisins in the matzo

An editorial condition of unnecessary elaboration; a good idea taken too far by an unnecessary element or refinement; the literary equivalent of preparing enough food for twelve guests when only six were invited to dinner.

A matzo is unleavened bread, eaten at the time of Passover to commemorate the flight from Egypt when there was no time to use yeast and leavening. Matzo was and is perfectly good for its purpose. It doesn't need raisins to make it work. First articulated by the WRITER-painter-saloon keeper-teacher, Barnaby Conrad, RITM is a kissing cousin of ANTICLIMAX, thanks to the way it undermines a perfectly good idea by adding embellishments that will distract the READER'S attention for no good reason and a good many bad ones. RITM is a sure sign of the writer's being uncertain of submission to the idea, "If less is more, more is even more."

Watch all DESCRIPTIONS for unnecessary detail, but also watch those perfectly wonderful observations you made and then spoiled by adding another, distracting element. The aforementioned Conrad's observation occurred at the Santa Barbara Writers Conference after a student had piled adjectives onto an already well-described character. "Isn't that putting raisins in the matzoh?" is the twenty-first-century version of the wisdom of William of Occam (1285—1347): "Universes must not be unnecessarily expanded." You could also just say "Keep it simple." You really could.

rate of discovery

The pace at which dramatic information is conveyed to the STORY; appearance to the CHARACTERS and READERS of story issues, DEADLINES, potentials for added disaster, needs for stop-gap or more permanent solutions; introduction of SURPRISE, new menace, and potential disturbance.

The rate of discovery is influenced by the tempo at which seeming STASIS is beset by COMPLICATIONS. A story usually begins on some emotional cusp, where a character may not yet have made up her mind or where an on-going AGENDA has become subsumed by a distraction, possibly one the reader can guess but, as yet, the character cannot. Then comes the discovery of adjunct dramatic information, waiting for an opportunity to catch the characters in moments of VULNERABILITY. Closely following the discovery is some price to be paid, some awareness of down-the-line CONSEQUENCES, which lead the character to recall relevant events from the past.

How much have we really discovered about Romeo and Juliet within the thirty-six-hour time frame of their acquaintance? We have learned the details of the Montague-Capulet feud. We have learned from a Capulet that Romeo is not such a bad kid. And we have learned from watching Romeo and Juliet together that they share a considerable, even consuming attraction. Is it really love? If they'd met under less combustive circumstances, would they have evolved into an enduring partnership? Best not to ask too many questions. Best to take the rate of discovery we've been given and see it for what it is, a romance of the best intentions teenage hormones can afford, running headlong into the dramatic opposition of social COMBUSTION. In a sense, the story is almost larger than the two principals, played out in subsequent forms against backdrops of feuding families, differing ethnicity, and differing religions, opening the doors for the Arthur Laurents, Leonard Bernstein, Stephen Sondheim collaboration of 1957, *West Side Story*, yearning to be recast yet anew, perhaps as a gay version. (See QUITTING.)

If we provide too much BACKGROUND information at once, the risk increases that the reader will begin skimming, thus the warning to slow down the rate of discovery to the point where the reader is not only tolerant and willing to accept but rather impatient, demanding to know. The analogy between cholesterol and discovery, if somewhat a reach, may help:

Cholesterol tends to produce plaque in the arteries; discovery tends to clog up a story, yet each under control is a necessity to its respective system.

As always, the question of how much is the right amount arises, and as always, the answer sounds evasive: It is better to WITHHOLD, to delay information—both action and detail—than it is to pile it on as though it were food portions at a truck stop restaurant. Too much action, too many dramatized moments of complication in too short a time imparts a heavily plot-driven atmosphere to the story. Equally political and evasive at first blush is the rhetorical question, *How much detail?* Would *Moby-Dick* have been more accessible if a first-rate editor had removed forty to fifty percent of the material about whales and whaling? (Probably not.)

Hint: Given the universal story nature of the mystery, select one mystery novel by Frank Morrison "Mickey" Spillane, and one by Kenneth Millar writing as Ross Macdonald. *I, the Jury* and *The Zebra-Striped Hearse* are good choices. Compare the rate at which the two detectives, Mike Hammer and Lew Archer, discover things (including things about themselves), then select your place within that spectrum and discover away. For short fiction, try "Good Country People" by Flannery O'Connor and "The Housebreaker of Shady Hill" by John Cheever.

reaction

A RESPONSE made by one CHARACTER to other characters and/or a stimulus; a dramatic BEAT.

The reaction one character extends—to another character, to groups of characters, and to external stimuli—ratifies the presence of REALITY; it causes the READER to accept FICTION—at least the fiction the characters are in—as PLAUSIBLE. Characters who do not react or, indeed, respond, help to impart a dream-like state to the narrative, making it more like an oratorio, in which the principals are seated together in a pew, than opera, in which the characters interact on a stage, complete with BLOCKING and MISE-EN-SCÈNE.

In successful STORY of any length, one or more characters are working actively to change the status quo. Even if it is the lone, nameless protagonist of Jack London's "To Build a Fire," the reader is made to see the GOAL. The reader already knows the consequences of this character's failure to succeed—literally, a life in the balance. Whatever else the reader may think of this character—how, for instance could he have allowed himself to get into this predicament?—the CONSEQUENCES of failure to achieve the goal are apparent.

Jim Harrison's *Returning to Earth* provides an excellent illustration of how reaction among characters works in a longer, more complex form. The first of a menu of narrators is Donald, mid-forties, a superb athlete when younger and now a man whose profession still keeps him relatively physical.

Early on, Donald is diagnosed with Lou Gehrig's disease, ALS. Donald's reactions alone are worth the investment of time to read the novel. "...it seems I am to leave the earth early but these things happen to people." He begins to dictate his family history to his wife, Cynthia, so that their children will have a record of who he was and whence he came. Subsequent chapters are narrated by Cynthia, by her brother, and by the children of Donald and Cynthia, all of whom are reacting to the feelings set loose by Donald's impending death and his own wishes for how and where his life shall end and where his remains shall be interred.

Characters are neither required to flail about the story ARC in an operatic manner nor be tight-fisted about demonstrating how they are responding to the CIRCUMSTANCES that pester and plague them. Whether the story at hand is a Raymond Carver short story as intended by him or as edited by Gordon Lish, there is no mistaking that his characters are being affected by inner grief and conflicts, possibly even being assisted by such add-ons as severe drink-related problems. In similar fashion, characters in SHORT STORIES and NOVELS by the Irish writer William Trevor present the reader with situations that impinge upon them like tight suits.

A story where one or more of the characters appear to move through the complexities of a torturous PLOT without reacting is suspect, surely not as memorable as stories in which characters demonstrate their feelings by some form of behavior as they pursue their goals, avoid REVERSALS or frustrations, and continue their efforts.

Successful characters have been stoics, cowards, hypochondriacs; they have been afflicted with Tourette's syndrome (Lionel Essrog in *Motherless Brooklyn*) and severe autism (Christopher John Francis Boone in *The Curious Incident of the Dog in the Night-Time*); they have been taciturn and overly emotional, or as self-absorbed and difficult to like as Sherlock Holmes and his contemporary counterpart, Gregory House, M.D. They have in common the fact that they react to the persons, places, and things about them. The reader may not—need not—like them, but the reader knows a character when he sees one.

reader, the

Individual, unknown to the WRITER, who will read and react to the writer's work; person known to the writer who will read the writer's work; individual who knows the writer and is also a writer, who will read the writer's work; critic or individual who considers himself as a critic, who will read the writer's work; person who has some issue with the writer's ethnicity, lifestyle, religion or lack thereof, who will nevertheless read the writer's work; person in search of artistic and emotional insights, who will read the writer's work; individual who will deliberately or innocently misconstrue the writer's work; person who will read the writer's work hoping to evolve her own writing; person who will read the writer's work hoping to find mistakes the writer has made; individual who is convinced he can concoct and render better stories than the writer; individual who is willing to experience transformative moments while reading the writer's work; person who had never considered looking at some person, place, thing, or condition until she saw it portrayed in the writer's work; person who is seeking a miracle, who has come to the writer's words to find it; individual the writer must simultaneously forget entirely and keep entirely in mind.

The writer/reader relationship is complex, somewhat of a piece with exchanging personal secrets with a fellow passenger on a trip, done with the knowledge of the separate and remote lives each party lives, of the unlikely prospect of ever meeting again. And yet. Some writers have a following; some readers anxiously await a new work from a writer.

Readers who admire particular writers often feel as though the writer knows them personally, is writing directly to them. Yet the reader/writer relationship is a partnership of selfishness. Under optimal circumstances, each party profits enormously. The path to achieving that partnership is filled with distraction, frustration, and the underlying SUBTEXT that each contact may be the last, a subtext that tempts the writer to want to say more and the reader to ask more.

One way to approach the relationship begins with the writer, who produces the first draft as though it were a deeply held secret, brought out into the daylight in a moment of recklessness. In subsequent drafts, the writer adds relevant details to the extent that he now feels the secret is out of the darkness and is visible for what it is. At this point the writer becomes increasingly more aware of the reader, simultaneously adding such details as he believes the reader may require, removing such details he believes the reader will already know or will not need to know.

The equation of the Reader/Writer relationship is one of shared secrets: the writer has an idea what the reader wants, then proceeds to offer it.

Hint: Consider the early draft stage of a letter to someone you know or wish you knew. Go so far as to caption the manuscript as you would a letter, "Dear_____." In no sense should the material be thought of as going to an anonymous reader—there is already too much anonymity. If you can't find an ideal person to whom you'd address your "letter," try addressing it to yourself.

reader feeder, the

Relevant dramatic information the WRITER wants the READER to know, inelegantly force fed to the text; it is intrusive authorial introduction of SUBTEXT, BACKSTORY, or information pertaining to relationships among CHARACTERS.

As the name implies, the reader feeder has the effect of turning the reader into the goose who is force-fed to cause enlargement of its liver for a result of *foie gras*. Dramatic information is best communicated by the characters themselves, either through action, dialogue, or a combination of the two—but the action must seem PLAUSIBLE, an extension of the ongoing story; the DIALOGUE could have been said. Conversations that are manufactured or seem too pat and convenient severely undercut the sense that there is a convincing STORY underway. Characters stumbling upon convenient newspaper headlines or just happening to overhear information that will enhance the story become speed bumps, jostling the sense of reality a story conveys.

Exaggerated example: "Say, John, didn't that remarkably attractive redhead over there attend law school with you all the while working a night job and barely eking out a living as a single mom?"

"No, Fred. She wasn't the one who was at the Yale Law School with me. That person did go on to clerk for a circuit judge and later became a U.S. attorney. The one you're looking at now and obviously find yourself attracted to is, however, an attorney, and she did work her way through law school while serving as a night shift checker at a neighborhood grocery."

In a real sense, story is a tactical matter of getting DRAMATIC information on the page through the movement and awareness of the characters, the relevance of the information a pawn in the ongoing chess game of show vs. tell. The more relevant the information is to the nature and outcome of the story, the more onuses on it to be demonstrated.

A workable strategy for the writer: keep out of the NARRATIVE, allow the characters to freight the data wherever possible, and avoid information dumps that seem overly convenient. Even with the given that all the information the writer wants the reader to have is relevant, it is better to under-tell than to over-tell.

A valuable litmus test for the reader feeder: If the passage seems too convenient, it probably is.

reader's first expectation, the

The CHARACTERS, INCIDENTS, and SETTINGS depicted within the story that will cause the READER to SUSPEND DISBELIEF; the primary, receptive state of the reader's mind when approaching a work of fiction.

Readers know in advance that a story is invented. On some basic level of awareness, the reader enters the transaction with the WRITER and the text nursing a conflict of interest: the reader openly wants the text to become a rendition of reality while secretly—even subconsciously—seeking any possible detail that prevents the story from appearing real.

The invention must seem real in every detail; the characters must be plausible, their GOALS and plans to achieve these goals must resonate the sanity of conventional logic. The reader notices anomalies—the left-handed protagonist on page six who suddenly becomes a right-hander on page nineteen, the subway stop in midtown Manhattan where in fact there is no such subway stop, a rifle or pistol of a particular caliber being afforded a range well beyond its real capacity, the winner of the baseball World Series of a particular year being rendered incorrectly—and these lapses in reality jar the reader out of story. The reader does not object, however, to a wrongly placed subway stop in an ALTERNATE UNIVERSE novel, possibly even thinking a subway stop at that particular location would be a good idea. Anomalies must be rendered to have a home in plausibility.

The reader's first expectation is to be given sufficient dramatic, emotional, and physical information necessary to overcome the gap between actuality and projected potential: this story could be happening, this story is in fact happening, these characters are real. The more skilled writers in our midst begin by nurturing a firm belief in their VISION; if they do not have a vision, they add DETAILS in support of one, adding here, removing there until the vision clarifies. They do not try to argue the characters, situations, and locales into being. Least of all do they rely on: "BUT IT REALLY HAPPENED THAT WAY," and "But this character is based on a real person." The reader expects the writer to be right enough to dispel any doubt.

It is instructive to consider our individual lie detector, which usually becomes activated when we see attributes piled on a description of an event or quality, or when materials presented as facts cannot be attributed to reliable sources. Readers have lie detectors, but readers are fighting to believe. Their first expectation is to be able to do so. Give them a reason.

The more convinced the writer is of the characters and circumstances in his story, the less likely he is to pile on attributes and stage directions and in fact the more likely he is to be taken at face value, right from the start.

reader's second expectation, the
A set of conventions found in GENRE/CATEGORY FICTION that are the basic assumptions a READER will make upon choosing and beginning a particular narrative.

In 1942, almost as though he were returning from a mountaintop with freshly etched stone tablet in hand, SCIENCE FICTION writer Isaac Asimov brought forth a short story, "Runabout," with an ethos that subsequently became a tradition—The Laws Governing Robots:

1. A robot may not injure a human being or, through inaction, allow a human being to come to harm.
2. A robot must obey orders given to it by human beings, except where such orders would conflict with the First Law.
3. A robot must protect its own existence as long as such protection does not conflict with the First or Second Law.

In similar fashion, there are EXPECTATIONS if not actual laws covering the relationship between the reader and the genre. Readers of MYSTERIES, for example, have a right to expect intriguing puzzles. They also have a right not to expect Roger Ackroyd-type endings in which, toward the very last paragraph, the narrator casually reveals himself, don't you know, to have been the murderer.

The FANTASY reader has a right to expect some form of magic and, indeed, the ROMANCE reader is entitled to meet an appealing woman protagonist who becomes involved in issues relating to her status as a single person. No less emphatic an expectation is that of the reader of SCIENCE FICTION, who buys into the story hopeful of encountering some significant application and extrapolation of a physical or social science.

Just as readers of genres have expectations, writers of them have obligations:

1. Writers of a genre will have some awareness of the origins and icons of the genre.
2. Writers of a genre will have read at least one hundred of the first generation titles of the genre.
3. Writers of a genre will, even at parties where the punch has been spiked, be able to discuss with some intelligence the expectations inherent in the genre.
4. Writers of a genre will be aware of the works of at least two up-and-coming writers of the genre.
5. Writers of a genre will be able to discuss with some degree of intelligence the direction the genre will take with it into the future. Reading regularly within a favored genre is like having a conversation with the writers working in it, seeing how various writers are pushing the boundaries toward surprise and innovation for the readers and themselves. Reading gives writers new approaches to combining genres or introducing new conventions in ways that will produce surprise. Before Leonard Tourney began his Matthew and Joan Stock mystery series set in Elizabethan England, for example, few mystery writers were mixing mystery with historical. Reading enables the writer to intelligently flout conventions and extends boundaries.

reality
The place and condition WRITERS attempt to replicate in their work; a representative fabric of PLAUSIBLE SETTING, physical, moral, and social conditions of a particular time in a circumstance intended to be conflated with the physical, moral, and social conditions of a specific place or in an imaginary place which is intended to be taken by the READER as a plausible, real place.

Reality is a condition that surrounds EVENTS, living things, institutions, traditions, and conventions. The Salem Witch Trials of 1692 were surrounded by a reality that still affects individuals and institutions of the twenty-first century; the ATTITUDES prevalent at that time have evolved, just as some aspects of civilized society have evolved since then, but various forms of evangelical extremism still exist, informing our contemporary CHOICES and impacting our ability to choose.

Reality affects characters in STORIES in direct proportion to the attitudes of writers writing about their own time or previous or future times. No matter where or when a story is set, it is in effect an ALTERNATE UNIVERSE story because it is filtered through a specific writer's prism of reality, or even that writer's vision of an imaginary reality.

It is the writer's job to visualize and then convey a plausible reality with CONVENTIONS and physical properties most readers *will* accept as valid, perhaps even as rational. It is also the writer's job to present individual characters with ATTITUDES toward the reality in which they live, all the better to convey these characters as being plausible individuals whose behavior is taken as a given, not as a philosophical tenet.

Robert Heinlein is excellent at presenting such alternate realities and plausible characters within those realities *(The Moon Is a Harsh Mistress, Have Space Suit—Will Travel, Stranger in a Strange Land)*. So, too, are Theodore Sturgeon *(More Than Human)*, Ray Bradbury *(Fahrenheit 451, The Martian Chronicles)*, Anthony Trollope *(The Way We Live Now)* and William Faulkner *(As I Lay Dying* and *A Light in August)*.

Story is vital, but it needs the steady plinth of reality on which to perch.

How to convey reality? Believe in the CHARACTERS and their GOALS; believe in the effectiveness of the constraints placed upon these believable characters by their cultures, their FAMILIES, and their own abilities. Believe in the notion that characters need to reach beyond the constraints of their reality, by which action they bring us into sympathy with the reality of the story.

red herring

A false clue introduced in a MYSTERY or SUSPENSE STORY; a plausible-sounding device that convinces the CHARACTERS and READERS of its material relevance to the outcome of the story.

Check the number of times in well-crafted mystery stories when the seeming red-herring falsity of a clue causes the clue to be discredited or rejected out of hand at first blush, only to have it prove to be right on target. (See also MCGUFFIN.)

rejection

An arbitrary condition arising when a PUBLISHER declines an offered WORK;

a situation wherein a WRITER loses enthusiasm for a project and either shelves or discards it; a work that has been denied entry for idiosyncratic, judgmental, or technical reasons; the experiential sense achieved by an author that certain publications, publishing individuals, and random other individuals are not moved by his work; an author, editor, or publisher in a state of denial, for practical or personal reasons.

It is the rare writer who has no experience with having a work refused, either in terms of representation by a LITERARY AGENT or publication from an editorial representative of a publishing venture; rarer yet is the writer who has had no work returned with a memo of notes for REVISION. Rarest of all is the writer who has not, of his or her own accord, set a MANUSCRIPT aside as being unworkable or uninteresting. All these are examples of rejection. Similarly, a note from a publisher's representative expressing great admiration for a work but nevertheless returning it because of its thematic resemblance to a recently published work is still rejection. A note from a publisher accompanying a rejected manuscript that also invites the writer to submit more work is—rejection.

An author, standing in a book store while watching a prospective READER pick up his or her book, thumb through several pages, then set the book back on the shelf, is witnessing rejection of yet another sort.

"There are fifteen types of rejection in connection with writing," Santa Barbara Writers Conference Director Barnaby Conrad said, addressing an auditorium filled with attendees. From the voluminous depths of his blazer pocket, he produced an index card from which he was about to read examples, but before he was able to begin, a voice from the rear boomed, "Sixteen."

Ever the polite fellow, Conrad smiled, nodded. "As I was saying, there are fifteen specific types of rejection." Squinting at the index card for a moment, he continued, "The first instance of rejection is when a writer submits a manuscript electronically or by postal mail and it is subsequently rejected."

Once again the voice from the rear of the auditorium blared forth. "Seventeen!"

Rejection is a living presence in every writer's calculus; even if the writer were to swear off submissions, it could be argued that the writer was rejecting himself. Responses to rejection vary from anger to mild annoyance to conspiracy theory; all of these conditions may or may not be justified, but they may all produce the side effect of listening to and agreeing with the INNER CRITIC, the symptoms of which prevent the writer from writing.

There probably are successful writers who believe their abilities have evolved far enough; they do not worry about becoming better at their craft. The greater number of writers burn off considerable calories with concern about their developmental progress. This is as it should be.

Some letters or notes of rejection address flaws as seen by the rejecter. Unless YOU, the writer, see some way to enhance the effectiveness of the work, or unless a particular editor offers publication of your work if a specific change is effected, a four-letter Latin word, common to publishing, obtains. STET. Let it [the work] stand.

And, of course, move on to another work while this one is making the submission rounds.

relationships

Associations, connections, or the lack thereof among CHARACTERS in a STORY; the attraction or force of OBLIGATION and/or distaste between a character and an institution, organization, or place; an awareness of romantic, social, and ethical potential among characters in a story; the degree of resident empathy between the WRITER and the characters created by the writer.

The writer has created every character in the story, a given that is the baseline of all other relationships in the narrative. Now the writer must establish with each character enough of a relationship to convey by direction and NUANCE the INTENT of the entire ensemble of personalities. Next comes the writer's awareness of each character's GOAL in the story, followed by the writer's awareness of the SUBTEXT among characters in every scene, while each individual is acting on his own AGENDA and intent.

Effectively taking the place of the standard Shakespearean Prologue, the equivalent of three bag ladies off their meds appear. All right, they're witches. They let us know they have some ability to "read" the future. They foresee a meeting "ere the set of sun," on the heath, there to meet with Macbeth. Next scene, establish Macbeth as a loyal captain. Establish also King Duncan, deciding that Macbeth is to be promoted to Thane of Cawdor. We have not seen Macbeth yet, but already we have information about him, including the fact that his promotion comes from his loyal service. Now we're back to the three witches, gloating a bit about their witch-like activities, then, just as they'd foreseen, noting the arrival of Macbeth and his coeval, Banquo—two great chums at day's end. The witches greet Macbeth, first by his old title, then, just as Duncan had decreed, as Thane of Cawdor. The third witch delivers the kicker: "All hail, Macbeth, thou shalt be king hereafter!" Music to Macbeth's ears. He already has inner plans and dreams. Call it a hidden AGENDA. We have barely met him and yet, look at the details of his position and relationships we have gleaned.

Early in *A Streetcar Named Desire*, before she has uttered a word of dialogue, Blanche Dubois is seen taking a quick slug from a hidden bottle, then turning down the lights, giving us a highly intimate view of her relationship with her self-image.

Characters are in the constant flux of defining their relationships to their surroundings, their circumstances, and to those about them. Even in such subjective constructs as sobriety or romantic involvement, a character responds by carefully articulating his movements, thus not to reveal his drunkenness, or to reveal by body language, facial expressions, and words his regard for the object of his devotion. From these definitions of relationships, the reader is able to interpret DRAMATIC intent, then get on with the matter at hand—the story.

reliable narrator

A storyteller who can be trusted to render a fair version of the events within a STORY, possibly extending to judgments about the behavior of other characters and the implications of their ACTIONS as well as his own.

The reliable narrator is one for whom the READER is most likely to be concerned, possibly even sympathetic. The danger for the WRITER who has decided on the most reliable of his narrators is to then kick the unreliable or NAÏVE NARRATORS with adjectives, adverbs, and verbs portraying them in the glare of a biased spotlight. The likely effect on the reader at this point is 1) to lose of interest because the narrative tone is so ON THE NOSE, 2) to be reminded of schoolyard bullies, with their taunts and jibes or 3) to be resentful of the AUTHORIAL INTERVENTION. (See KICKING WHILE DOWN.)

response

An acknowledgment, answer, or reply made by one CHARACTER to one or more other characters; a DRAMATIC answer to a dramatic question; an appropriate or inappropriate answer to an ACTION, ATTITUDE, or question.

The spine of STORY involves confrontation of characters with differing AGENDAS, a confrontation that can be developed within the framework of friendships, family relationships, professional relationships, or any conflation involving the manner in which individuals interact. This can be class- or status-based, a PFC relating to a colonel or general, an employee dealing with an employer; it can also be generational, as in a grandchild dealing with a grandparent. Characters don't go it alone—they react to other characters; this is necessary in STORY and NOVEL—and everything in between.

Some recommended reading for stunning examples of characters who respond to each other:

Elizabeth Bennett and Fitzwilliam Darcy in *Pride and Prejudice.*
Anton Chigurh and the convenience store operator in *No Country for Old Men.*
Bobby Dupea and the truck stop waitress in *Five Easy Pieces.*
Tom Sawyer and his friends, whitewashing the fence in *The Adventures of Tom Sawyer.*
Macbeth and Lady Macbeth after he loses his nerve for killing Duncan in *Macbeth.*

Sherlock Holmes and John Watson, M.D., in any Sherlock Holmes mystery.
Joe Buck and Ratso Rizzo in *Midnight Cowboy.*
Jane Eyre and Rochester in *Jane Eyre.*
Gatsby and Daisy in *The Great Gatsby.*
Frankie Machine and his wife, Zosh, in the climax of *The Man with the Golden Arm.*
Bartleby and his employer in *Bartleby the Scrivener.*
Chief Bromden and Randle Patrick McMurphy in *One Flew over the Cuckoo's Nest.*

In all these examples, the characters have a layered, developing set of responses that grows by accretion as the story ARC develops. To appreciate the interconnectedness of each is an enormous step toward understanding how to bring characters together in ways that enhance the inertia and emotional drive of story.

Hint: There can be no chemistry between characters without response.

retrospect
Looking back at a past moment or era; a POINT OF VIEW containing information or knowledge of the CONSEQUENCES of past action; a NARRATIVE or personal attitude arrived at after the fact, implying some time for reflection on the outcome; Monday-morning quarterbacking.

A significant use of retrospect comes when the details of a NOVEL or STORY are filtered through one or more CHARACTERS, giving historical versions of a STORY, allowing them to consider ATTITUDES or SUBTEXTS of regret, pleasure, or moral superiority over past events. This use of retrospect becomes one of the WRITER'S first major DECISIONS, coming right after who the narrator(s) will be. The issue now becomes at what RATE OF AWARENESS to set the story; is it meant to seem as though it is taking place in the immediate present or at some remove? Was the narrator naïve, reliable, or unreliable when the dramatic activity took place? If the point of view is retrospective, has the narrator remained naïve, reliable, or unreliable?

Huckleberry Finn was told from the narrative eye of a young boy. One of the few anomalies is the likelihood of his being literate enough to have composed any narrative in the first place. His honesty and pragmatism quickly override any tendency to suspend belief. His approach to all matters seems appropriate for a street- and country-wise person of his age, a pragmatism that makes him all the more likable and seemingly truthful. Huck is in touch with his emotions. Would he have been more convincing in his depiction of events if he'd picked up the Conklin fountain pen (the one with which Mr. Twain began the first draft) in his forties or fifties to reflect back on the events? Most likely not—even more likely, the story would not have been so resonant. It needed, in fact, to be told as it was, as though it were happening to a thirteen-year-old boy in the immediate now. As READERS, we "forgive" him his literary abilities as we jump into his explanation of the device by which he came into being in the first place, "You don't know about me without you have read a book by the name of *The Adventures of Tom Sawyer...*"

Twain uses in the opening sentences a stunning device that actually paved the way for Primo Levi and his frequent trespasses into postmodernism. "...but that ain't no matter," Huck assures us, and indeed it isn't, thanks directly to that street-smart honesty. In the second sentence, Huck tells us, "That book was made by Mr. Mark Twain, and he told the truth, mainly. There was things which he stretched, but mainly he told the truth. That is nothing. I never seen anybody but lied one time or another, without it was Aunt Polly—Tom's Aunt Polly, she is—and Mary, and the Widow Douglas is all told about in that book, which is mostly a true book, with some stretchers, as I said before." By the first paragraph, we're in, willing at that early point to trust Huck's retrospective account of *The Adventures of Tom Sawyer.* Shortly after the retrospective account begins, Huck tells of how Aunt Polly's sister, Miss Watson, "took a set at me now with a spelling-book." Between Miss Watson and the soon-to-appear Tom Sawyer, Huck is put on a collision course with literature. Mostly Huck's street smarts win out and mostly we are left with the precious relic of him at the age where he lit out for the territory ahead because Aunt Polly and Miss Watson wanted to civilize him, and he couldn't stand it.

The focus from immediate present to retrospective shifts one-hundred-eighty degrees as the unnamed narrator of Daphne du Maurier's unforgettable *Rebecca* addresses us in as direct a manner as Huck did: "Last night I dreamt I went to Manderley again. It seemed to me I stood by the iron gate leading to the drive, and for a while I could not enter, for the way was barred to me." We now know exactly where we stand in regard to the framework of time, and we have as yet no reason (nor will we have any) to doubt the reliability of the narrator. True enough, she is in at the payoff, telling us, "...it was my lack of poise that made such a bad impression on people like Mrs. Danvers. What must I have seemed like [to Mrs. Danvers] after Rebecca...?" This retrospective assessment makes her all the more believable as a narrator. Unlike Huck, who wants to light out for the territory ahead, this individual is sitting on the veranda with her loved one. "I fix my dark glasses, reach for my bag of knitting. And before us, long as the skein of wool I wind, stretches the vista of our afternoon."

In law and in writing, the perspective of timing and INTENT are everything. Scenario One: Bill goes to the neighborhood pub to collect a bet from Fred, who denies having made the bet in the first place. The two get into a scuffle from which Fred, alas, does not emerge alive. Scenario Two takes us back in time a bit: Bill takes his gun with him as he goes to the neighborhood pub, intending to teach Fred a lesson if Fred decides once again to renege on a bet.

Worst case in Scenario One would be justifiable homicide. In Scenario Two, worst case is premeditated murder.

The differences between retrospective and present time perspectives are that significant.

revelation

A dramatic discovery, experience, or realization, bringing the POWER to change the VECTOR and perhaps even the OUTCOME of a STORY.

In a metaphorical way, a story is like a string of firecrackers, each explosion adding to the collective effect, the individual pop of explosion being a SURPRISE, the final one—the loud, enduring on—being the revelation. Often expressed indirectly, through the medium of a front-rank CHARACTER doing something that becomes a symbolic response, the revelation shows the reader the equivalent of a film or TV close-up reaction shot.

In the novels of nineteenth- and twentieth-century WRITERS, revelations were frequently spelled out in what writer Barnaby Conrad has titled "CAME-TO-REALIZE" moments: "and in that moment, she came to realize that he had been deceiving her all along." From about the 1980s onward, came-to-realize moments were replaced with a more outward display of a character having been struck by the lightning bolt of revelation, imparting less a sense of certainty and resolve, more of a sense of AMBIGUITY tempered with probability; READERS would be certain that Character A knew Character B was wildly attracted to her and had been for some time, at the very least giving her a dramatic power over Character B, but we would not be sure by story's end if Character A were going to do anything about the revelation.

The payoff to Dashiell Hammett's much-anthologized short story "Two Sharp Knives" is an excellent example of how revelation can be used by one character to exploit another and how that exploitation can be used for dramatic effect on the reader.

One of the many revelations to be had from reading the stories of Anton Chekhov is his own understanding and portrayal of how revelation affects characters, and how their movements rather than their INTERIOR MONOLOGUES suggest the OUTCOME.

revenge

A planned, hurtful RESPONSE to a real or imagined injury, a deliberate *quid pro quo* orchestrated by a CHARACTER against another character, group, or institution; an ACT meant to restore a perceived loss of status.

Revenge is aptly thought of as the WRITER'S emotion, honed from an early "I'll show them" (the them being teachers, family, and friends who thought writing was beyond the writer's ability or an undignified profession), extending after the fact of publication to the "them" of critics who may have provided less than exemplary reviews. Revenge stories are often the writer redressing the history of failed romances, failed earlier writings, even failed academic career, allowing writers to refashion past failures, disappointments, and real or imagined slights. A romantic rival may be rendered as a blathering nincompoop; an academic concept may make its way past the stony reception of a tenure committee to a Nobel Prize or, worst-case scenario, a Guggenheim Grant. A former lover may come to regret an intemperate decision to break off a relationship. Revenge, as it plays out in fiction, may even produce a reversal of a known historical event. Woody Allen has used techniques employed by such diverse writers as Italo Calvino (*If on a Winter's Night a Traveler*), Alain Robbe-Grillet (*Last Year at Marienbad*), Michael Cunningham (*The Hours*), and John Fowles (*The French Lieutenant's Woman*) to make the point that a writer writes in part to rewrite a history he does not appreciate. Woody Allen's character in *Annie Hall*, Alvy Singer, is directing a SCENE that is almost word for word a scene that took place in "real life" between Alvy and Annie, except at the ending of the scene, the actress portraying Annie does not leave Alvy the way Annie had in "real life." Quite the contrary. The actress says something to the effect of "Wait, I'll go with you." Alvy turns to the camera (us), with the observation that we always try to make it come out better than it did in real life.

Business has been good for revenge in America. *Moby-Dick* and *The House of Seven Gables* set it in literary stone where it has flourished ever since in such well-known appearances as *The Great Gatsby*, Charles Portis's remarkable *True Grit*, and Donna Tartt's *The Secret History*. From England we have the says-it-all-in-the-title tale of revenge by Jeffrey Archer, *Not a Penny More, Not a Penny Less,* and earlier classics from Dickens, *A Tale of Two Cities* and *Great Expectations.*

Take a character. Insert into that character's BACKSTORY the fact of having been wronged or carrying a grudge for a family member who has been wronged. Add a few measures of revenge fantasy, then start writing.

reversal

Vital points within a STORY in which the plans of the PROTAGONIST take a punishing hit or a disastrous turn; one in a series of accelerating blows to the aspirations of a main CHARACTER.

Story is enhanced by reversal of fortune; the more serious the reversal, the higher the story is borne along. The more PLOT-DRIVEN, formulaic stories use reversal as a vehicle for making it appear to the READER that the lead character's aspirations are done for, that the lead is defeated in some vital enterprise, perhaps even a candidate for a place in the morgue. Without some form of reversal or a direct threat of it, there is no CONFLICT. Without conflict, there is narrative—but no story.

In NOVELS and longer SHORT STORIES, reversals may appear as minor irritations, increasing in intensity to the point where one or more of the characters will wonder aloud, "What more could possibly happen?" And once again the doctrine of the UNTHINKABLE COME TO PASS is evidenced because—if the story is effective—something more always can and does happen.

revision

The systematic review and examination of raw thematic material; a PROCESS of searching for the optimal form and deployment of a STORY (also applies to nonfiction). A final and emphatic editorial vision of a project, reflecting as nearly as possible a unified editorial tone, vibrant CHARACTERS with uneasy choices, and a satisfying, plausible resolution.

WRITERS have been advised from time immemorial by instructors, patrons, LITERARY AGENTS, and editors to revise a recently completed work. Often those same advisors have an inchoate vision of what they mean by the term "revision," adding an entire layer of confusion to a process that can be a joy.

Thus three important revision rules for writers at the outset:

1) Unless a literary agent or editor offers a specific *quid pro quo* offer to represent or publish the work if specified revisions are made, their suggestions are not worth the emails they're written on.

2) Unless the advisor can articulate a specific list of revisions, his suggestions are not as valuable as your own vision of the work.

3) If the revision suggestions do not resonate as appropriate, ignore them unless you have had three or more similar notes from different-but-informed sources.

These are the basic questions that a writer undertaking revision should ask him/herself:

1) Is the work complete? A significant way to determine this is to set the work aside for between one day and a week—or even longer if time permits, then return to read it afresh, hopeful of not discovering any "How could I have forgotten that?" moments. Then, of course, put in the "that."

2) Does it begin in the right place? Always a tricky call, especially if the present opening circumstances were the cause for the work congealing as an idea to pursue. Reread the work for the specific target of finding another place where there is a greater sense of OPENING VELOCITY and character involvement. Stories need not be set in strict CHRONOLOGY; a perfect place for the BEGINNING may be the penultimate or even

final SCENE. Remember, beginnings are not places where much in the way of BACKGROUND is set forth; beginnings are more likely to be eighty percent movement and twenty percent DESCRIPTION. Quirky, interesting people doing quirky interesting things make the most engaging beginnings.

3) Does the READER have someone to root for? Sure, the MANUSCRIPT has a PROTAGONIST, but is the protagonist invested enough in his or her AGENDA to make readers want to become emotionally involved as the characters tread their paths? American readers, for instance, would not seem likely fans of Mr. Stevens, the protagonist of Kazuo Ishiguro's *The Remains of the Day.* After all, what's the big deal about wanting to be a butler? But of course, Mr. Stevens didn't want to be an ordinary butler. And who among us could not root for Fast Eddie Felson, a kid who wanted to be a pool hustler—and not just any pool hustler? Thinking about the dramatic strengths of Carrie Bradshaw and her ultimate goals in Candace Bushnell's *Sex in the City,* we begin to have an emotional stake in her happiness in the modern ambience of that story. Even as we root for Carrie to experience sexual freedoms and fulfillment, we can root for Samuel Richardson's servant girl, the eponymous Pamela, to retain her chastity in her own dramatic venture where the son of the lord of the manor is trying to seduce her for his momentary sexual pleasure.

4) Does it end in the right place? Does it end by explaining itself too strenuously or defensively? Does it bury emotional effect in a welter of logical details to the point of producing ANTICLIMAX? And since we're on a questioning jag, does the ending take the reader well beyond closure? Do the characters and situations have life off the page? Does the current ending foreclose on that delicious sense of AFTERTASTE that appears after the last page has been turned and a final effect appears? Does it usurp reader participation by not allowing the reader to get a word or thought in edgewise, thanks to the control-freak nature of the author?

5) Not forgetting that some types of stories require DESCRIPTIONS of places, clothing, food, local customs and politics, is this story too descriptive, too heavy-handed with theme and atmosphere?

6) Is the story told from the most effective POINT OF VIEW? Could someone have told it better? Think about it. In this case "better" relates to more TENSION, more SUSPENSE, more IRONY, more NAÏVETÉ. Ah, naïveté as in a NAÏVE NARRATOR instead of a worldly or trustworthy one, which takes us back to Mr. Stevens in *The Remains of the Day,* and makes us question the benefits of a trustworthy narrator. Doctors and lawyers frequently complain that they cannot trust their respective patients and clients; should readers be able to trust narrators?

7) Is there a better narrative effect to be had than the present one; is it perhaps too literal? Could the narrative be enhanced with an edgier VOICE?

8) Is the DIALOGUE too conversational and chatty? This sort of question is of particular importance because the answer will have a direct effect on the things characters say to attack STASIS. The intent in dialogue is to have the exchanges sound like plausible exchanges between individuals, remembering as well that dialogue prods, pokes, nudges story forward while simultaneously extending the personality of the speaker, possibly even revealing things the speaker did not intend to reveal.

9) Is the dialogue too literal, falling beyond mere literalness into reader feeder? "As you know, Fred, I have not been feeling myself lately, overcome as I am by the loss of my job, the empty-nest syndrome as my three wonderful children, Manny, Moe, and Jack, have left home to pursue their own lives, and there's my ongoing struggle with my addiction to gambling."

10) Does the dialogue drive the story forward? "You're either with us or you're against us!" "Yo, Macbeth, you gonna whack King Malcolm or what?"

11) Does the dialogue adequately and accurately reflect:
   a) the attitude of the characters
   b) the gap between what characters say and what they feel
   c) the biases or preferences of the characters
   d) the goals of the characters
   e) the familiarity, degree of intimacy between the characters
   f) the social, racial, sexual, and professional coding inherent in the characters
   g) the inner conflicts of the characters

12) How about ATTRIBUTION? Does the reader know who's talking, how the talking is being done (he asked in a sing-songy chirp)?

13) Does the reader have any clue about how what one character says is being received by other characters?

14) Does the dialogue unnecessarily employ adverbial support, he asked nervously? Or, might the dialogue actually profit from adverbial support? (NB: In spite of heavy lobbying from the National Adverb Association for unrestricted use of adverbs, some adverb control is worthwhile, particularly occasionally when they are tacked on to one another.)

15) Does the dialogue feature talking heads, individuals the reader does not know to any degree, having long CONVERSATIONS?

16) Is the NARRATIVE stylistically and psychologically consistent with the point of view? (*Post-it Note*: Unless the narrative structure comes from the author, it should reflect being related by a designated character.)

17) Does the narrative become heavy-handed and obtrusive?

18) Are there places where the narrative becomes redundant?

19) Does the narrative artfully deploy information and make appropriate summary of complex events (best exemplified in MYSTERY FICTION when a detective sums up the alibi/suspect scorecard)?

20) Does the narrative produce the mainstays of drama—suspense or tension?

21) Are all the aspects of your dramatic SCENE necessary? That is to say, are there any in which you are merely showing off, trying to outdo the likes of Noel Coward or Elmore Leonard or Annie Proulx for pithy dialogue?

22) Are there any duplications of scene? Be serious about this. For instance, after a point, most mysteries are simply a series of interviews. Have you taken steps to insure that the interviews have some sense of freshness and divergence from the others?

23) Does each scene develop the reader's understanding of characters and the issues they are facing?

24) Are the characters within each scene interacting and reacting appropriately? When Mary tells John that his dog has died, how does John take the news? As important, how do the other characters who are in the restaurant when Mary gives this news to John react when they see him start to sob copiously?

25) Do the scenes contain suspense, tension, or ominous foreshadowing? Most critical of all, do the scenes leave an emotional impact?

26) Do the scenes end on a note of unresolved conflict or anticipation or do they linger like the last guest at a party?

At some point in the revision process, the writer should make a complete pass in which he becomes a heat-seeking missile trained on spotting and knocking out CLICHÉ of all sorts, whether it is racial, occupational, or narrative. The question often arises in writing groups and beginning classes, *Suppose one of my characters has the trait of speaking or thinking in clichés?* The answer, of course, is that such a character is a fine example of a cliché. If you must have such a character, render that person's linguistic tropes in as fresh a manner as possible in order that the clichés emerge as original as possible, so that the critic will say of you in all sincerity, even this author's clichés are original.

One way to approach this seemingly contradictory task of making clichés fresh is the way Joe Heller did it in *Good as Gold,* using an old saw in a new context or interpretation, in this case by having a protagonist named Gold. Another approach could be changing a letter or word in a cliché to produce a pun, such as the chestnut, "a horse of another color" morphing into this writer's own mystery title, "A Hearse of Another Killer." The cliché character of a paid assassin as a merciless, unfeeling automaton has been moved along by 1) making the assassin a woman, 2) showing the assassin leaving a bowl of milk for his cat, or 3) having the assassin listening to opera or generally engaging in conduct that could be considered "out of character" for an assassin while planning his next attack, such as the remarkable portrayal of the assassin by Robert Duval in *Tango* becoming fascinated at first then seduced by the lure of dancing the tango. A good standard to follow: If you have to ask if a figure of speech or character or situation is a cliché, it probably is.

The last but not least thing to look at is the title, which can and should pose some relevant enigma, pun, double entendre, or even an irony. Clever titles, such as Kate Atkinson's *Left Early, Took the Dog*, often attract favorable attention, but the irony here is that titles obviously intending to be clever can attract negative attention. Nearly all the Lilian Jackson Braun titles in *The Cat Who* series, their sales figures notwithstanding, serve as examples. Sometimes a phrase from the text will suggest a title; sometimes a pun on a well-known situation or condition will fit the writer's purpose. Most famous in this area is John Steinbeck's use of the Robert Burns poem "To a Mouse" for his title, *Of Mice and Men*, but close on its heels is the "lifting" from a John Donne sermon to produce *For Whom the Bell Tolls*. There is good use of irony in Katherine Mansfield's short story "Bliss," but the old standby is the straightforward declarative description as in, say, John Steinbeck's *The Red Pony*.

Another question often asked in writers' groups and beginner classes: *How do I know when I've finished revising?*

Answer: When you make changes no one but you will recognize—when the craft is not apparent to anyone but you.

ridicule

An attack on the status or value of a person, place, institution, or thing, a contemptuous examination; to undermine the status of a person, institution, or social convention by causing that status to appear absurd or in a state of implosion; a tool used by humorists to disrupt the status of superiority resident in an individual or institution.

Ridicule is a lever by which to topple a target from its occupancy of the moral high ground; it is frequently used in connection with EXAGGERATION—though take care with it as it might produce uncomfortable results by causing the target to become DEFENSIVE. Ridicule is at its most effective when the target cannot see itself as the target or when the target actually regards the ridicule as praise and affirmation. Rabelais ridiculed the body politic of his time by creating a landscape of grotesquely overweight individuals with an exaggerated lack of manners in their eating habits—that is, CHARACTERS who would not want to be claimed by the people who are being ridiculed. In modern day, Stephen Colbert is the master of the latter.

In most cases, the major target of ridicule is pomposity, but entitlement and snobbery are not far behind, although there is IRONY in the way some characters ridicule the stupidity of others, indicating in the process their own stupidity. (See Ring Lardner's *You Know Me, Al* stories and Jaroslav Hasek's novel *The Good Soldier Schweik.*)

risk

The potential for and the probability of an unwanted OUTCOME from a venture; the chances a CHARACTER takes when acting or purposefully not acting on a DECISION; the possibility of a character having enhanced VULNERABIL- ITY as a CONSEQUENCE of a prior ACT.

The major defining trait of a character in STORY is AGENDA; close on the heels of agenda comes the risk the character will endure in order to accom- plish the GOAL. Faintness of heart may hang over a character, posing a threat not only of failure but of shutting the story down. A character who acts in spite of the faintness of heart is keeping the story and his hopes alive. READ- ERS want to root for a character who has been pushed by circumstances to risk all in favor of the stated or implied goal. Think Gatsby. Think Ishmael. Think of Dorothy Gale taking on the chores assigned her by the Wizard if she'd known his humbug status in advance.

An integral element of story is the epidemic sense of things going wrong to the point where the characters are often waiting for the next round of things that do go wrong, followed by the existential question, *What next?* Integral to story is the drive and willingness of characters to take risks in such an atmosphere.

If the risks in a given story are not of sufficient weight or CONSEQUENCE, the reader will realize soon enough that the story is a matter of shooting FISH IN A BARREL, the WRITER is inadequate or lazy, and he himself is bored silly.

roman à clef

A NOVEL or SHORT STORY in which the READER assumes the CHARACTERS are representing actual, historical persons.

Somerset Maugham, a well-known employer of *romans à clef*, is univer- sally regarded to have intended his character Charles Strickland, in *The Moon and Six Pence*, to serve as a substitute for the painter Paul Gauguin. Not so well known was Maugham's work *Cakes and Ale*, which is thought to be a *roman à clef* involving the widow of the nineteenth-century novel- ist and poet Thomas Hardy and her subsequent liaison with Horace Walpole, a WRITER who was the Tom Clancy of his day. Not true, said Maugham of the accusations, although there was also a character named Ashenden, a name

Maugham used later in a novel to represent someone with a similar background to his own. Indeed, in that very novel, Ashenden was a former doctor, as was Maugham, and he walked with a limp, as did Maugham...

A *roman à clef* provides a tingle of excitement for those given to seeking and recognizing the real-life counterpart of the characters and situations portrayed. The character of Mark Rampion in Aldous Huxley's novel *Point Counter Point* could easily have been D. H. Lawrence; the character Dill in Harper Lee's *To Kill a Mockingbird* is thought to have been Truman Capote; and Willie Stark in Robert Penn Warren's novel *All the King's Men* is a fanciful-but-plausible substitution for the noted Louisiana political figure, Huey Long. Does anyone really doubt that the married couple in Nora Ephron's *Heartburn* is really Ephron's ex-husband, Carl Bernstein, and Ephron herself?

Romans à clef provide the opportunity to SATIRIZE persons, places, things, and customs—think *Primary Colors* by Anonymous. One of the IRONIES resident in the use of the *roman à clef* is the belief that it is more truthful in its depiction of character and event than a nonfiction rendition; a reader of *Primary Colors* might indeed believe that it is a spot-on record of the 1992 primary season.

The rich history of *roman à clef* in literature serves as a prompt to those writers who are fearful of being called out for basing a character on a family member, friend, mentor, or boss. It is the rare writer who does not at the outset of a new story begin to base characters on individuals from real life.

romance

A genre in which a CHARACTER is forced by circumstances of PLOT to make choices which will affect her lifestyle; the tracking of attraction and desire between two persons as they pursue the potential of a *partnership*; a STORY in which two individuals seek a partnership based on love and affection; a dramatic narrative in which such added themes as adultery, career, homosexuality, death, old age, historical settings, and abusive behavior may be dealt with; a woman's search for romantic connection and the CONSEQUENCES once she achieves it. Romance is the major pillar of genre fiction, outselling all others with ease. As recently as 2008, even in the face of a worldwide financial slump, hardcover and mass-market romance fiction was showing a healthy profit. Of all the literary genres, contemporary and historical romances were the titles statistically most likely to be found in any North American residence.

Romances are primarily about the attraction between a couple and their attempt to build and maintain a loving partnership in the face of obstacles that may result from job pressures, illness, parenting problems, and evolving differences of attitude and opinion.

They have been popular from about the time of the wide success of Jane

Austen's novels and reaching into the present day—and the romance genre has formed a metaphoric marriage with the history category, making historical romances an honorable subgenre.

No matter how popular they are, romance novels are often thought of as the bastard child of literature, snubbed by "real readers" with "taste" and dismissed as being written mostly by frustrated housewives for other frustrated housewives. Beware this attitude. Not just anyone can write an engrossing romance. As with other categories of fiction, the romance requires from the WRITER a respectful approach, a process that includes reading at least one hundred of the classics of the first generation, starting with Samuel Richardson's *Pamela,* then reading another hundred published within the twenty-first century.

Editors and READERS already know this: Romance readers buy more than one romance novel at a time.

romanticism

A narrative attitude in which CHARACTERS act out their positive enthusiasm; a dramatic personal ATTITUDE reflecting a passionate interest in and curiosity about travel, science, history, animals, behavior in general, art, food, drink, literature, all terrains of the imagination; an overwhelming belief in the potential inherent in humanity; an instinctive and vigorous distrust of philosophies or SYSTEMS that diminish or remove altogether the sense of individual choice based on individual responsibility.

Although romanticism and ROMANCE have a brief ARC of overlap, the two concepts, particularly in the literary sense, go their separate ways. The romantic is the Quixote-like character but equally the Tom Jones or Becky Sharp or Asher Lev character, off in the world with a lusty appetite to seek some form of fortune. The romantic is often forced to squint at the accouterments of reality because of the dazzle of reflected light from the GOAL or ideal. A scholarly debate of some vigor argues the likelihood of Geoffrey Chaucer having worked at translation of a medieval French poem, *The Romance of the Rose,* which involved such romantic tropes as dream visions and the true identity of the PROTAGONIST Rose, as in, was she a real person or a METAPHOR for all women? The scholarly debate adds yet another note of romanticism to the persona of Chaucer, who also may or may not have been a spy, may or may not have been involved in a court case where he was charged with rape. Ah, the possibilities.

Romance is more an extended and complex wedding cake display, complete with bride and groom effigies at the top tier. Will a particular couple stop fighting long enough to get married? Will Beatrice and Benedick find true happiness? Will the Wife of Bath finally settle into a good relationship with a man and is her current husband, Jankyn, Mr. Right? As READERS, we already know we feel pretty sure about Jane, so much so that we cannot help wonder if Rochester is going to make her happy. And as we nervously reread the final paragraphs of the ur-romance, *Rebecca,* can we be absolutely sure that the nameless narrator is going to be OK with her Mr. Wonderful?

Both romanticism and romance, however, are considerable forces for a writer to deal with. After rereading *The Crystal Cave* by Mary Renault, we are tempted to observe that romanticism (as well as the English language) is alive and well, thank you. Even though Candace Bushnell exudes a tangy modernity and edge, any of her novels assures us romance—at least in her hands—has not gone vegan on us.

Romanticism, on the other hand, recognizes the nine-to-five job but argues in favor of the intuitive, aggressively emotional state over the more formal, rational, and mechanical. Thus does romanticism become alchemy as it helps transmute the perfervid scientist into Dr. Frankenstein, who may have slightly overreached. Thus does romanticism bring drama into the equation by matching Dr. Jekyll against the neo-Rousseau-ian Mr. Hyde. Indeed, isn't Natty Bumppo the Rousseau-ian noble savage, gone around the bend? What about John Yossarian or, for that matter, Tom Joad? Romanticism gives the WRITER a sterling opportunity to take on established order, one of the most splendid examples of all inherent in the lead character and in the writer of *Huckleberry Finn*—the former taking on social caste and civilization, warts and all; the latter taking on the excesses of Sir Walter Scott (whom he came to loathe), slavery, and race relations in the United States.

sarcasm

Pointed and exaggerated IRONY, intending to derail or deflect a status quo; a blistering overstatement of intentional underplay of a CHARACTER'S self-interest or AGENDA.

Arguably the most difficult EMOTION to convey in writing because of its heavy reliance on CONTEXT, sarcasm found one of its most enduring modern spokespersons in Dorothy Parker. In a review of a book, she said, "This is not a book to be set aside lightly. It should be hurled across the room with great force."

The HUMORIST pokes fun at himself. The ironist pokes fun at the human condition. The SATIRIST is a moralist without the clerical collar. The sarcasm maven wants to elevate his own status at the expense of yours—proceed apace, but be careful with sarcasm, so you don't trip over your own EGO.

A current sarcasm maven worth watching—because of his superb control of the art form—is Stephen Colbert. His targets are well-articulated, his irony extends from verbal acuity to a perfected tone (see DEADPAN delivery) and impeccable sense of timing. So deft is Mr. Colbert, and worth study, that, as mentioned previously, on many occasions even his targets are convinced he is arguing on their side. Few persons are as repelled by his on-stage persona as they are by the persona of, say, of Don Rickles, who turns his sarcasm into scathing personal commentary directed at his audience.

Hint: Even if you find sarcasm attractive, spend some time crafting it before you proceed to using it in the print and digital worlds.

satire

A beloved form of ridicule in which an individual, institution, attitude, or work of academic and/or historical intent is made fun of—and the fun is usually accompanied by some suggestion for solving the occasion of ridicule.

Like its brother and sister aspects of HUMOR, satire is highly moral in its reach. Sparing no feelings in its path to the target, its intended GOALS are a deflation of pomposity and an indicated pathway to better behavior. For WRITERS, satire is an ideal approach to ridiculing prevalent culture, behavior, institutions, and individuals, using EXAGGERATION as a primary tool.

A risk of satire is the potential for offense taken by the target, offense that may easily lead to outrage. Notable historical examples are Jonathan Swift's "A Modest Proposal," which caused a wave of outrage after Swift, a clergyman, suggested a solution for the results of the famine caused by the Irish potato blight.

Beyond the obvious dangers of inciting advocates of the very thing being satirized and their subsequent CONSEQUENCES is the risk of exaggerating too much, causing the entire readership to revolt; thus a good place for satire to stop is somewhere just beyond the boundaries of "This has gone too far." Satire, by its very nature, does go too far in its attempts to call attention to the thing or person being satirized. Joseph Heller went too far in *Catch-22,* but it was a well-controlled too far, which is to say it went slightly beyond probability, but it did not become sarcastic or uncivil, nor did it have to. SARCASM is one of the most difficult emotional registers to capture on paper; sarcasm-driven satire can quickly lose its edge because it tosses control, and thus its effect, out the window.

Although dead for nearly a hundred years, Mark Twain's satire merits study for its tone—neither too sarcastic nor outraged, his intent residing instead in his examples and uses of comparison. His essay "Fenimore

Cooper's Literary Offenses" is a must for writers because it so competently takes its target to task while simultaneously providing valuable literary commentary. Twain is also worth study because his satire is so often delivered deadpan, seemingly without expression. *The Innocents Abroad* and *Roughing It* remain two textbooks for those who would satirize.

Understatement and low-key presentation are two qualities inherent in effective satire, the goal being to convince the reader that the material presented is accurate and PLAUSIBLE. No subject or institution is immune to satire, as *The Onion* (newspaper and website) demonstrates.

scene, the

The basic unit of dramatic storytelling; an integral moment in which one or more CHARACTERS have entered a SETTING with AGENDA and EXPECTATION; the CRUCIBLE to which the heat of ambition, agenda, or desire is applied; a segment of dramatic engagement in a particular setting where personalities and GOALS collide, producing a sense of movement toward a RESOLUTION or trial.

Put enough of these basic units together and they assume a form suggesting a specific path toward some arbitration, trial, discovery, or resolution. As the collection of scenes emerges, the characters in them appear to grow in resolve or stubbornness, producing varying DRAMATIC options to the point where they become memorable enough to eclipse the narrative in which they appear.

In varying degree, scenes have at least the following ingredients: setting, characters, BEATS, PACE, BLOCKING, TENSION, SUBTEXT, DIALOGUE. They may also contain REVERSALS OF FORTUNE for one or more characters, shifts in the POWER exerted by one character or organization over another character or organization, shifts of allegiance within the cast of characters, SURPRISE, DISCOVERY of relevant information, and REVELATION.

The setting is the thematic and physical locale for the scene (see MISE-EN-SCÈNE); the characters are the individuals who come into it, having just been somewhere else. The beats are movements or activities, a pause to consider, a decision to turn a response into a riposte, a reaction to an invitation or an insult. Pace is the tempo with which the beats occur—slow and leisurely or at staccato intensity. Blocking is the sense of movement and placement of characters in the setting—where they will go if they are in motion, where they will remain if sedentary. Tension is the atmospheric pressure of something about to happen, of impending pleasure or gloom or discovery, while subtext is yet another atmospheric pressure, the palpable awareness of the difference between what a character says and what that character is thinking. Dialogue is what the characters say to each other in ways that express who they are, what they mean, what they intend.

Characters come into scenes with expectations, which may be met or frustrated. A character who achieves an expectation, no matter how deserving he may be of the success, may experience buyer's remorse or conversely indulge exuberant celebration. Just as likely, characters may enter scenes with fears, hopes, and prejudices. A character who enters a scene with no expectations needs to be sent home and re-costumed to reflect the basic assumption of story that the characters have within them a sense of being right about something.

A character who is right about something—an interpretation, an entitlement, a sense of being a victim, a sense of having something to protect—has earned admittance to the tent of story and must now pursue the goals that drive him, perhaps tentatively at first, but then with the increasing intensity of ambition.

Some characters require one or more scenes in which to ratify or shore up their sense of being right, which instills within them the glorious dynamic of DEFENSIVENESS, which they are free to interpret as Justice that must be done.

Scenes should be wound about the armature of at least one salient EMOTION. Some characters may not agree with that emotion, may be prevented from recognizing it by the sun-in-the-eyes of their own agenda, but the reader will see through all that and be able to identify the emotion. A significant example of this phenomenon is found in the film *Five Easy Pieces*, in the scene where Bobby Dupea wants nothing more than a conventional breakfast in a small roadside lunchroom. "You want me to hold the chicken?" the waitress asks Bobby, producing not only the CRUCIBLE overflowing but a subsequent persona for the actor Jack Nicholson.

A scene is an ARENA, a place where characters go armed with the baggage of their past, their attitudes, their agendas, fortified with the TOOL KIT of their abilities and hopes.

schadenfreude

Pleasure taken at the evidence of pain or misfortune in another person; delight at the REVERSAL OF FORTUNE experienced by someone else.

One of the many words on loan to English from another language, *schadenfreude* is a shot-gun marriage of two German opposites, damage and joy, thus its meaning: You lose, I smile. This pleasure helps us understand what Aristotle meant when he tied the can of catharsis to the tail of the dog of TRAGEDY.

Schadenfreude allows the reader to feel pleasure when a CHARACTER, say George Amberson Minafer of Booth Tarkington's *The Magnificent Ambersons,* gets a well-earned come-uppance; that such a feeling exists in many humans is often an embarrassment until, on reflection, the larger perspective is revealed: we are able to experience tragedy in literature with EMPATHY for the fall from the heights of the major CHARACTERS, but only after first experiencing relief that we were not the intended targets.

Memorable characters may have *schadenfreude* encoded in their genome, taking a moment or two to gloat when an opponent seems to come out second best in a collision with Fate, but it is best to leave as much *schadenfreude* as possible not to the characters but to the READERS. Equally valid is the notion that the character who has met a tragic downfall or been handed a serious reversal of fortune and goes forth without breast beating or moaning is the character the reader will regard with the most respect. Once again, let the reader do the deconstruction.

Schrödinger's cat

An existential conundrum proposed by the German physicist, Erwin Schrödinger, that demonstrates the dual nature of matter; a useful, literary-related way of looking at the role played by chance or by choice in FICTION.

Schrödinger posited that a cat is locked in a box, along with a radioactive atom that is connected to a vial containing cyanide. If the atom decays—and it surely will over time—it will open the vial. The cat, inhaling the cyanide fumes, will be killed.

When the box containing both the cat and the vial is closed, the observer does not know if the atom has decayed or not. This means that the atom can be in both the decayed state and the non-decayed state at the same time. Therefore, the cat is both dead and alive at the same time—which clearly does not happen in classical physics.

The parallel between the cat and a given STORY is waiting to be drawn, so let's draw it. When asked to list vital constituents of a dramatic incident (story), WRITERS will supply such ingredients as CHARACTER—*How can you have a story without character?*—and such other elements as PLOT, SUSPENSE, and REVERSAL. It is the rare, thoughtful professional who will add one of the key qualities inherent in the fiction of the twenty-first century—AMBIGUITY. (Odds are this metaphorical professional will have read the short fiction of Anton Chekhov, who dispensed with the heavy-handed moral or thematic finality of the short fiction some of his contemporaries—and sundry writers well into the twentieth century—employed.

If we imagine story and Schrödinger's cat to reside on opposing sides of the equal sign, we can "see" and "feel" the power of ambiguity in story. Fiction with the built-in element of duality provides an opening for reader participation, that condition where the reader feels not only close to the characters and EVENTS but becomes immersed in the outcome.

Since about 1902 (picked because James Joyce's *Dubliners* and Henry James's *The Ambassadors* were published then), ENDINGS—CONCLUSIONS, or payoffs—in fiction, particularly in the short form, have tended to move away from the highly visual, seemingly inescapable conclusion, drifting toward uncertainty, opaqueness, and CHOICE, which may be entirely the READER'S to make. Some of this tendency can be related to the uncertainty of the times in which the stories are set; some of this tendency reflects a closer understanding of contemporary human affairs. When we consider the movement away from the fables of Aesop and, more recently, the short stories of O. Henry, we welcome Erwin Schrödinger and his ambiguous cat into the dramatic arena and our storytelling hearts.

science fiction novel, the

A longform NARRATIVE that extrapolates on a hard science or social science theme; a NOVEL in which the major THEMATIC problem and its SOLUTION relate directly to scientific observation; a novel in which laws governing the property of elements, forces, and species are extended to produce a moral problem and its solution.

The common denominator of science fiction is PLAUSIBILITY, demonstrated when the READER, WRITER, and CHARACTERS accept the reality of the CONCEPTS that are inherent to the final result of the STORY. The science fiction READER has no difficulty accepting the speculative reality of Ray Bradbury's *Fahrenheit 451,* which features a repressive society bound up in book burning; nor does it fail to see the issues raised about prolonging the human life span from Aldous Huxley's *After Many a Summer Dies the Swan,* or the issues of morality and prejudice raised in Robert Heinlein's *Stranger in a Strange Land.* These titles represent the broad spectrum of subject matter within the GENRE, which, like other genres, has morphed its way from PLOT-DRIVEN entertainments to CHARACTER-DRIVEN and issue-driven literature. Theodore Sturgeon's science fiction *succès d'estime, More Than Human,* probed the boundaries of the human condition, positing relations among humans that were symbiotic. In one of the few notable cases where a writer's work benefited from honing the art of screenwriting, Leigh Brackett, who began her career writing pulp sci-fi stories, morphed into a hardboiled mystery writer, from which genre she brought an edgier, NOIR type of character into her prolific output of science fiction.

Few if any critics have seen the work of Richard Powers, particularly his 2006 novel, *The Echo Maker,* as science fiction, but thanks to its relentless probing of the meaning of individual identity and the self, it could well be shelved among the more literate and literary works of the genre.

Science fiction bears a close relationship to much mainstream fiction in that each begins with a what-if premise, which is then pushed beyond accepted limitations of known behavior. The writer who is curious about science fiction may discover commentary about it in which it is spoken of as SPECULATIVE FICTION. Philip Roth, for instance, is rarely thought of as a science fiction writer, and yet his *The Plot Against America* speculates an ALTERNATE UNIVERSE theme in which Charles Lindberg became president of the United States.

second-person narrative

A NARRATIVE that addresses the READER directly; it speaks to you as "you," putting you in the position of assuming the role of the PROTAGONIST. A STORY that gives the appearance of intensifying focus on the principal CHARACTER by making events seem as though they are happening in the immediate present.

One of the most prevalent criticisms of the second-person narrative is its seeming inability to maintain plausibility beyond the length of a short story. (Try telling that to Jay McInerney, author of *Bright Lights, Big City*, or William Faulkner in *Absalom, Absalom*, or Richard Powers in *Ploughing the Dark*, to name a few.) Nevertheless, the second-person narrative is more often found in short fiction, where it abounds, notably in Dennis Lehane's "Until Sylvia" and Lorrie Moore's collection *Self-Help*, in which six of the nine short stories are second-person renditions.

One of the reasons second-person narrative is thought not to be as substantial as FIRST-PERSON, THIRD-PERSON or MULTIPLE POINTS OF VIEW has to do with its restricted use: most editors don't like it and MANUSCRIPTS in which it is employed have often, in the past, been accompanied by rejection slips.

As with the other pronouns, "you" is perfectly able to freight a story. While you are doing so with the second-person form, you will discover the small but valuable secret that you can pack in more READER FEEDER information than you could have done with the first- or third-person or multiple points of view. Example: You are not the kind of person to be bound by conventions; it was only natural that you experimented with second person.

secrets

Embarrassing or possibly incriminating information held by CHARACTERS about themselves or other characters; confidences and opinions shared between two or more individuals; closely held details of family or organizational behavior.

So far as dramatic writing is concerned, the more embarrassment or HUMILIATION a revealed secret can inflict, the better. The actual details of the secret, while potentially tantalizing, are not nearly so potent as the imperative felt by the ones for whom the secret must remain closely held.

As all humans do, characters have secrets, data, awareness, lusts, and memories of past behavior, even hidden AGENDAS. It is not necessary for the secret of every character to be revealed, but it is an enormous help to the WRITER to know what secrets lie dormant within the front-rank characters.

The moment Character A confides a secret to Character B, Character A is, in effect, writing Character B a blank check on the bank of power. There are characters who make a point of confessing secrets, sometimes the same secret, to a number of recipients—possibly in an attempt to *give up* power; it is up to the writer to unravel this particular calculus, make something intelligible, dramatic, perhaps even poignant from it.

Characters who inflate the secrets they plan to reveal in confidence may be seen as wanting to achieve some degree of status not readily associated with them. Characters, particularly benign, mild ones who begin by apologizing for the mildness of their secrets, convince us that they are covering some secret too shocking to reveal. The greatest IRONY of all is the character who affects complete transparency.

"I will tell you something I have never told another living person," a character says, and the READER leans forward to listen to it, realizing too late how effective that confession is in eliciting the shifting of body weight to lean forward.

A splendid ratio of effectiveness may be had by the simple expedient of the writer comparing his or her own secrets with the revealed secrets of contemporary dramatic writing, and the triangulation involved in the characters trying to keep, or to reveal, their secrets.

sensory genome, the

A sequence of receptors for touch, sight, hearing, awareness of heat/cold, awareness of taste signals the relative degrees in which CHARACTERS experience sensation; a method of articulating individual characters; an adjunct of the psychological spectrum of a character.

If you were portraying a character in a stage or filmed production, you'd have investigated the individual to the point of at least subliminally assessing the person's tolerance for heat, cold, pressure, and hunger. You'd have an opinion about whether that character was more a "sight" or "hearing" person. Knowing the sensory spectrum of a character helps produce a more plausible and visible representation of that character. Such knowledge helps the writer determine defining specifics for a character: What would his favorite meal be? Was the character a cotton or wool person, dog or cat, wine or beer, vegan or meat lover? When coming into a SCENE for the first time, would the character first be aware of sight, sound, temperature or odor?

The sensory genome merits investigation with all ranks of characters because of the potential spontaneous appearance of thematic or otherwise relevant responses. Example: A pizza deliverer steps into a room and begins sneezing in allergic response to cats, which triggers a furtherance of an argument about whether or not to keep the cat that has been going on between the two front-rank CHARACTERS to whom the pizza is delivered.

Individual character traits should have some relevance, however remote, to the LANDSCAPE, TONE, and OUTCOME of the story, their inclusion determined by their enhancement of plausibility rather than the distraction of mere originality. Thus, in extreme example, a brief discussion of two cowboys during a cattle drive, in which they argue over the relative merits of hemorrhoid analgesic, speaks to the side effects of too much time on a horse, and adds a note of realism. The conversation might otherwise be deleted as having no material effect on the outcome of the story, but its inclusion will insure the characters place in the READER'S memory.

set-up

A strategy for initiating a DRAMATIC event; a means of introducing a CHARACTER with a particular ATTITUDE, skill, or defect into a STORY; establishing a set of circumstances either beneficial or hostile to a character's GOALS and welfare.

Characters rarely go where they should or take up with individuals who are likely associates or lovers; persons in real life may do such things to a significant degree, but not in DRAMA or FICTION. Set-up is the generic name for an elaborate foreshadowing or dramatic description of a physical or emotional LANDSCAPE; set-up is background that will be of interest to the READER because it provides a way for the reader to begin to see the COMPLICATIONS and inherent traps for the characters.

Set-up is dramatic, situational, tense if not suspenseful. A high-energy character wanting to take her boyfriend home to meet parents and relatives is such a set-up, the very mention of it causing the reader to envision older brothers who have no sense of humor and who shake hands as though they mean to hurt fingers of anyone unlucky enough to offer such a greeting. Set-up is nearly CONCEPT, bordering on wanting to be story, certainly an added energy to one or more SCENES. Set-up legitimatizes CONSEQUENCES, a warning that the PROTAGONIST either should have known better or had no choice.

Set-up is analogous to setting a trap for a major character, allowing the reader to see how he or she behaves and how others regard him or her when the trap is sprung. In Graham Greene's chilling morality-play-disguised-as-thriller, *Brighton Rock*, Pinkie, the antihero, sets up Rose via sexual advances, hoping to keep her from testifying against him. At the same time, Ida Arnold, the protagonist, sets up Pinkie by using information she has gained by making advances to one of Pinkie's criminal lieutenants. And look at the marvelous set-up worked on the pompous Malvolio by the rascally Sir Toby Belch in Shakespeare's *Twelfth Night*, in which Malvolio is led to believe the object of his romantic affections has a similar interest in him.

sexual tension

A charged atmosphere when certain CHARACTERS appear together in a

SCENE, causing the READER to wonder if the characters are aware of it, when and how they'll react to it; at-a-distance thoughts and feelings of one character for another; a potential source of HIDDEN AGENDA; a lurking SUBTEXT between characters or between the READER and certain characters.

Sexual tension is THE ELEPHANT IN THE LIVING ROOM, an elephant that is often not recognized much less spoken about. Powerful enough when the involved characters are aware of its presence and actually preparing to act on it, sexual tension is often the force that drives comfortable, secure characters over the edge to a COMBUSTION that produces CONSEQUENCES.

Obvious instances of sexual tension in story must include that between Dolores Haze, aka Lolita, and Humbert Humbert, the gloomy antihero. Humbert even married Lolita's mother as a subterfuge whereby he could have access to Lolita. Lolita was, however youthful, neither innocent of Humbert's intent nor did she wish to blunt it—and Humbert was aware of a ticking clock, knowing Lolita would all too soon outgrow her interest.

Look back into the chemistry sparking between Jane and Rochester in *Jane Eyre.* Did that not create a powerful incentive for the reader to continue, hopeful of more glances and touches of the hand that appeared in the text when Jane and Rochester were in a scene together? And what about Charlotte's kid sister, Emily, so far as *Wuthering Heights* is concerned? Wasn't there profound unresolved sexual tension between Cathy and Heathcliff, made even more agonizing when Cathy agrees to marry Edgar Linton? On a more contemporary level, many of the John Cheever short stories were larded with sexual tension, "The Country Husband" being a notable example of desire's magnetic power to provoke STORY.

Shakespeare knew a few things about sexual tension. This is evident in *Twelfth Night,* where Viola feels it for her "boss" Orsino, and has it felt for her by Olivia. In *Much Ado About Nothing,* the audience is given a pretty strong signal in the tease and banter between Beatrice and Benedick, and the sexual tension between Romeo and Juliet is so powerful from the moment of their first encounter that they are figuratively if not literally screwed, because they are both dead within thirty-six hours.

Observation: When sexual tension is resolved, the story flattens until something comes along—JEALOUSY, GUILT, DISCOVERY—to lift it upward again. Thus observable, smoldering sexual tension becomes a prime mover, a powerful engine for causing characters to take steps either to consummate or to flee from temptation. The crackle of its electricity can cause the reader as matchmaker—or, if you prefer, voyeur—to continue turning pages. Take care to pace this exquisite tension, and not to give it up, as it were, too soon: back in the 1980s there was a television show called *Moonlighting,* an award-winning screwball comedy in which the sexual tension between Cybill Shepherd as Maddie Hayes and Bruce Willis as David Addison was palpable and a main reason that viewers tuned in week after week—until Maddie and David consummated their relationship and the ratings flattened.

shaggy-dog story, the

A long, meandering NARRATIVE, replete with irrelevant or distracting DETAILS, ending with an outrageous, groan-producing play on words—"my homework ate the dog"—or on a totally irrelevant note; a scenario in which the dramatic point resides in the unexpected, leading the READER or hearer—because shaggy-dog stories are often oral—in the lurch, at the mercy of the teller; a STORY in which the joke is on the hearer or reader.

One of the great glosses on the shaggy-dog story comes from Mark Twain. Check out "The Grandfather's Ram" story in his autobiographical tour of Nevada and California, *Roughing It*. In "The Grandfather's Ram," Twain writes of his days as a reporter for the *Territorial-Enterprise*, the freewheeling Virginia City, Nevada newspaper for which he wrote during the early bonanza years of the Comstock Lode. A group of locals had sold Twain on the remarkable tale of a certain old gent who loved to tipple and, thus lubricated, was wont to tell of a ram once owned by his grandfather. Trouble was, the locals assured Twain, the teller of the tale had to have reached just the right, reflective state of tipsiness before he would begin to reminisce. After a number of false starts, the boys assured Twain that the time was now; if he wanted to hear the story, he'd best drop everything and hurry on over to where the teller was holding forth, before a growing audience.

"My grandfather's ram," the old boy recalled with a smile at the memory. "I don't reckon them times will ever come again." And he is off, his brain cells, awash with *spiritus fermenti*, firmly focused. And Twain was hooked.

Trouble was, the old man never referred to the ram again, his story ranging from gossip in his home town to politics, religious preferences, and a remarkable story of a rug weaver who'd fallen into a machine-driven weaving machine and was woven into a six-ply broadloom carpet, making it necessary to bury him rolled up in a long, narrow bundle. The story went on from there until the teller began to nod, then drop off to an early nap. Twain realized this was always the scenario, that the details of the grandfather's ram were largely unknowable, and that he'd been "had" by his friends. This is not to propose that Twain invented the shaggy-dog story, but to show how he expertly demonstrated it in all its living potential.

Life is a shaggy-dog story, a series of often contradictory EVENTS competing for our attention, ending with some awful howler of a conclusion, or worse, ending with no proper conclusive inertia.

When we turn to memoir or biography or fiction, we are looking, in essence, for travel writing—writing that takes us somewhere, a place where the laws of CAUSALITY and determinism have greater effect than they do in real life. This is a place where justice is done, virtue is often rewarded, patience pays off, the good people get laid on occasion, and women are not reduced to having to marry just to get away from home (only to find themselves transported from one dreadful situation to another).

The message here is not that there is more satisfaction in literature than in everyday life but that the two can and should engage in a DIALOGUE, exchange notes, develop a rapport.

One good place to bring this metaphorical pairing of life and story together is in the expectations we bring to our lives and to our reading. All too often when discussing a particular story, we hear the disclaimer: *That could never happen in real life.* Just as often, when discussing the effect of a story and hearing an observation of disbelief about an element, the author will fiercely defend with the observation: *But it really happened that way.* And increasingly, looking at the advertisements for films and TV shows and even the covers of novels, we see the inducement: *Based on a real story.*

One of the Oscars—Wilde or Levant—once observed that in order for history to be effective, it must be rewritten. This observation sets the worm of cynicism into the apple of reality, leaving us with another potent observation: *What is worse than finding a worm in an apple?* Answer: *Finding half a worm in half an apple.*

We must hasten to rewrite the more egregious histories we have allowed to befall us, using our understanding of story and the need to extract some sense of justice and then to transport ourselves to a kinder, more civil place.

Sherlock Holmes

The quintessential essence of the presence needed in a CHARACTER.

Sherlock Holmes is the embodiment of curiosity-as-agenda, happiest when engaged in solving problems, so comfortable with his considerable abilities and deductive process that he walks the sharp cusp between being right and being insufferable. Truth to tell, Holmes, in his deductions, is often right, which has a direct, supportive effect on his insufferable behavior. This volatile combination of traits should and does make it difficult for Holmes to find happiness between mysteries to solve, leaving him vulnerable to boredom, which, in his case, leads to violin playing and cocaine.

Added truth to tell: Sherlock Holmes cannot be trusted with his own POINT OF VIEW; he'd not only put off too many readers, he'd tick them off as well. This sets the stage for John Watson, M.D., a filter for narrating the Holmes adventures, and a perfect foil for allowing Holmes to explain the force of logic behind his reasoning. The presence of Dr. Watson as buffer allows Holmes to talk down to Watson without talking down to the reader while explaining the Holmesian logic. Holmes's creator, Arthur Conan Doyle, was well-aware of this dynamic; in all his writings featuring Holmes, the detective was allowed narration rights only twice, each a brief outing.

The buddy system, as has been noted, has been with us in storytelling as far back as Aristophanes's memorable play, *The Frogs,* in which a slave and his master are setting forth the story through dialogue and action. Sherlock Holmes is MYSTERY FICTION, but buddy teams work—I'll go out on a limb—in every GENRE and medium. A Sherlock Holmes-like character has weathered six seasons of TV in the persona of Gregory House, M.D., emerging as a preternaturally bright diagnostician who is given a team of associates with whom to consult, said consultations often involving House's impatience, irony, bluntness bordering on rudeness, and bluntness bordering on childishness. Instead of Holmes's cocaine use, House is addicted to painkillers; instead of a violin, his musical interests are considerable and extensive. The popularity of the series and its potential for quirky puzzles speaks to the point of major characters who are the literary equivalents of extraordinary individuals wearing ordinary clothing.

Strong characters such as Captain Nemo, Nora Helmer, and Sir John Falstaff do not have to rely on the obvious strength of being diagnosticians, of course; any laser-like focus will do—Pinocchio, for instance, his nose visibly growing longer when he strays from the truth. All support the vision that strength of character resides primarily within an overriding passion for something—and the surplus strength may spill over into morality or even EMPATHY.

Followers of Sherlock Holmes, Gregory House, M.D., and some of the others listed here are well-aware of the numerous puzzles solved by these individuals. Indeed, they are followers precisely to see the solutions. But they are also followers because of the curiosity and simple pleasure of being in the company of these fully formed personalities.

shift of power
The dramatic point where one CHARACTER or group of characters achieves a strategic advantage; a moment in a STORY when a character breaks free of a previously held obligation, belief, loyalty, or romantic attraction; an awareness by a character of a CHANGE in status which results in his being a peer or superior to other characters.

There is an inherent aura of strength in a character pursuing a purposeful GOAL. The READER anticipates and is not surprised to see said character responding well in the face of SETBACK or REVERSAL. When a resolute character suffers a loss of power or loses control, however, there is a tangible shift of emotion among readers and characters. How will those who were formerly subordinate to the character now respond? It all depends, you say. Depends on the kind of person the character was before the loss of power. Will he inspire sympathy, a desire to punish, to humiliate? Perhaps the deposed character will even find himself the focus of a concerted attempt to help him regain lost power.

Look what happened to Edmond Dantes, soon to become Count of

Monte Cristo. His entire story ARC is a shifting of power base to the point where, before events that led him to becoming the Count of Monte Cristo, he was determined to starve himself to death in despair of his miserable circumstances. Look at Mr. Martin, after the shift of power he affected in James Thurber's short story "The Cat-Bird Seat." When the power is shifted, the effect is the same as the "mystery" being solved in a suspense novel: justice is served, and moral order is, for the moment, restored. Of course, the new keeper of the power must not gloat; any victory laps are taken with due modesty.

short story

A dramatic NARRATIVE, conventionally (but not necessarily) advanced in SCENES.

The short story began life as an art form and has held onto that cachet. The short story takes an individual from a point of awareness of a GOAL or PROBLEM through some attempt at striving for the goal or engaging the problem to the point of awareness of the CONSEQUENCES of the success or failure of the venture. It may be rendered in FIRST-, SECOND-, THIRD-PERSON, or OMNISCIENT POINTS OF VIEW.

By its name, the short story intends a word length less than a NOVEL, which is by convention thought to be at least 50,000 words. Conventional short stories run from about 2,500 to about 10,000 words, some of these parameters determined by the availability of space in magazines and journals. Short stories under 1000 words are usually given some designation such as short-short, FLASH FICTION, or sudden fiction, delineating them further from the short story and sometimes, as in the case of under 100 words, making them more a whim or affectation.

Thanks to a review written by Edgar Allen Poe on the occasion of the publication of Nathaniel Hawthorne's *Mosses from an Old Manse*—which Poe quite admired—the short story was accepted as a single-narrator vehicle, its focus on a single issue or situation. The ending was almost invariably a thematic equivalent of the recapitulation of a concerto. Then came Chekhov (1860-1904), who bade farewell to the elbow-in-the-ribs nudge of moral and philosophical resolution, and Joyce, (1882-1941) who used the EPIPHANY or relevant emerging awareness of a character to further the short story along into the twentieth century where such significant voices as John Cheever, John Steinbeck, F. Scott Fitzgerald, Louise Erdrich, Tom Boyle, Alice Munro, Annie Proulx and Deborah Eisenberg rushed the short story into its more elastic and plastic incarnation.

Because of these and other worthies, it is now possible to devise a short story that has more than one featured NARRATOR, that moves about in chronology, refuses to be pinned down in terms of its did-they-or-didn't-they ending, and takes place over a long span of time. Still these standards have to obtain:

the reader must care in some way about the narrator or have a stake in what happens or does not happen to the narrator; someone has to have a goal; even if there is no actual prize, the reader should be able to conceive of an appropriate one; the element of surprise ought to be found somewhere in the calculus—not merely a trick or SURPRISE ending but rather someone doing or not doing something that becomes a surprise or, perhaps, some surprise rendition of format.

show, don't tell

An admonition directed to FICTION WRITERS by everyone from publishers of thick NOVELS to teachers who have written relatively little themselves.

The caution to "show, don't tell" is meant to direct the writer to dramatize important information rather than doing so in NARRATIVE, warning that not doing so is like holding up a sign that informs the audience such details as "it was raining," "the moon is up," "he didn't feel well," "she didn't watch where she as going," rather than showing a CHARACTER getting drenched running through the rain, or having a character move with grace through the night by moonlight, and so on.

"It was raining when Fred got out of his car," if merely an observation, will not offend many READERS, whereas a number might stop reading altogether if Fred takes up too much time and space in performing largely mechanical steps. True enough, fiction is an evocative rather than descriptive art, but seasoned writers have learned the wisdom of telling the smaller, inconsequential details rather than distracting from the emotional bite of the story by overpopulating it with information.

Dramatizing an EVENT gives weight and importance to it. If every step in a STORY appears to be of the same weight, dramatic intensity will suffer. So will the reader's patience. A good ratio to keep in mind is the one between narrative and DIALOGUE: Show what moves the story along, complicates it, and/or reveals information about characters. Tell the rest.

slice of life

A relatively plotless stream of incident from a segment of a CHARACTER'S daily routine; a term used with varying degrees of SARCASM to describe a collection of SCENES that may or may not be a SHORT STORY; a dramatic NARRATIVE of any length.

Earth and ocean scientists frequently take core samplings of terrain under polar caps, oceans and soil strata to examine the processes of sedimentation, weather, pollen/seed density, etc. Similarly, some WRITERS, in the process of building a background on a character, take a sampling of a day or year in the life of that character. A slice of life can be defined as a core sampling of life, being examined.

Instead of a DENOUEMENT or negotiated settlement investigated in much twenty-first-century narrative, slice of life depends on a single, EVOKED feeling, whether that feeling produces laughter, sadness, remorse, or nostalgia. Under close investigation, James Joyce's monumental core sampling, *Ulysses*, is slice of life on steroids, a scrupulously close following of *The Odyssey*, in no way a tie-in to a conventional plot. Another case for argument: Alexander McCall Smith's *The Ladies Number 1 Detective Agency* treads closely along the verges between slice of life and an actual plot. True enough, Mma Precious Ramotswe is given something to solve, but is it really a detective problem or more of a life enigma?

Thus the resident enigma of the slice of life narrative: is it a story—or not?

In slice of life as in the tightly plotted works of Harlan Coben and Lee Child, the inertia is always in the writer's hands. The senses of satisfaction and completion reside within the author; they let the READER rather than the devil take the hindmost.

The writer at some point must arrive at an individual template for what a story is, then compose to the integrity of that template. To encourage the writer to think this point through, answer this question: *Is Tobias Wolff's "A Bullet in the Brain" a SHORT STORY or a slice of life?*

slight

A judgment call and frequent response to MANUSCRIPTS from LITERARY AGENTS and editors; a catch-all criticism implying that the problems and resulting DECISIONS made by the PROTAGONIST of a STORY are inconsequential; an indication that CHARACTERS and their CONFLICTS are too simplistic.

How to avoid such professional responses? One effective way is to recall William Faulkner's definition of FICTION as, among other things, the agony of moral CHOICE. Put characters in situations where they have more to lose than they may realize but which readers recognize as highly probable. Make characters vulnerable to any or all of the seven deadly sins or, instead, invent a BEHAVIOR or indulgence, which, if pursued a tad too far, will emerge as a fresh view of a new sin.

While Frankie Machine nourishes realistic dreams of becoming a professional musician in Nelson Algren's The *Man with the Golden Arm*, his behavior reflects the pulls of guilt and love resulting from the possibility that he may have been the cause of his wife's invalid state. The possibility is equally apparent that Zosh, Frankie's wife, may not be as much an invalid as she appears to be, if she is an invalid at all. Critics and editors have had a number of things to say about *The Man with the Golden Arm,* but none has suggested it is a slight NARRATIVE.

Similarly gritty in its reach and scope, James Leo Herlihy portrays in *Mid-*

night Cowboy the extraordinary friendship between Joe Buck, a young man whose dream of operating his own restaurant causes him to enter a lifestyle as a male prostitute, and Enrico "Ratso" Rizzo, a third-rate con man. However downbeat it is, *Midnight Cowboy* is not slight, particularly not in the CODA portion of its DENOUEMENT.

The temptation to over-respond to slightness may produce an operatic quality to a work in progress, but NB: operatic as a concept has, in recent years, undergone a change that is literally dramatic. Of yore, operatic was associated with broad gestures, which could be seen in the remoteness of the distant balconies, its themes having the equivalency of romance novels. Increasingly so, operatic performers are developing acting techniques as well as their voices; subject matter for operas is being drawn from wrenching social commentary. (For a fine example, see John Adams's 1987 opera, *Nixon in China.*)

A substantive story is rich in layered detail, has more to it than meets the eye. A slight story has less to it than meets the eye.

sorcerer's apprentice, the

The overeager aspirant who sets into motion forces he or she cannot control; a beginning- or medium-stage student who has reached a state of impatience, then acts to outperform the mentor, discovering too late the need for more learning; an ICONIC CHARACTER type who believes things are easier than they appear.

Naïveté, HUBRIS, and impatience seem to be the stars by which the sorcerer's apprentice sets course, a course that in one way or another encourages at first blush the belief that the master's secrets have been digested and taken in as muscle memory. The sorcerer's apprentice, whoever he or she may be, sets a glorious magnet of attraction for the WRITER to use as a CHARACTER who is bound to produce some significant storyline. The inevitable result of the sorcerer's apprentice was well-illustrated in the 1941 Walt Disney film, *Fantasia*—things got out of hand quickly when Mickey Mouse used one of his mentor's charms to enchant a broom to fetch buckets of water that he, Mickey, should have been fetching by hand. Mickey was used to illustrate the Paul Dukas musical suite, which in turn was offered as a musical version of the Goethe poem, "The Sorcerer's Apprentice," which had earlier incarnations from classical antiquity. Thus a dynamic twofer: an example of QUITING and validation of the iconic pedigree of the character type. The sorcerer's apprentice trope is, then, often an innocent, as in Graham Greene's *The Ugly American,* who causes a progression of events other than intended, producing calamitous results. It may be a bit of a stretch, but Greene appears to have done it again in *Don Quixote,* in which a simple parish priest achieves enhanced status through a mild deception perpetrated on a superior. If we focus on the triggering-of-unintended-consequences aspect, Neil Simon's *The Out-of-Towners* presents a role model for things getting out of hand, spiraling down to complete disaster to the point of forcing a theme-related conclusion, then trumping even that with an example of THE UNTHINKABLE, COME TO PASS. The moral of the sorcerer's apprentice tale revolves about the CONSEQUENCES of taking the short cuts of convenience, using them as a substitute for learning.

One of the unintended benefits of the sorcerer's apprentice for the writer is the self-evaluation that may come from undertaking such a STORY and recognizing the personal potential for naïveté, hubris, and impatience. If we posit the work of any admirable storyteller, say a Louise Erdrich or a Jim Harrison, as the literary equivalent of the sorcerer, then we might equate the enthusiasm and inspiration from reading their work with a story of our own—and it is natural and understandable to think we have achieved the spells by which we can duplicate their sorcery. Our failure is not in the attempt but in the inability to recognize how much work these sorcerers have put into learning their craft. In that sense, we are all of us apprentices every time we embark on a new project.

speculative fiction

A NOVEL or STORY that produces an alternate historical reality in which improvised or extrapolated EVENTS occur; a narrative that expands on an if-things-continue-as-they're-going theme; a story framed on the enhanced consequences of political, religious, scientific, or social consequences.

Margaret Atwood's 1985 novel, *The Handmaid's Tale,* takes as its premise the overthrow of the U.S. government as it now exists, replacing it with a totalitarian theocracy under which women are vastly subjugated to the point of being assigned the roles of concubine and producer of babies. This alternate/speculative historical approach allowed Atwood to create a new country, Gilead, complete with different social classes and AGENDAS. Think of *The Handmaid's Tale* and Michael Chabon's 2007 novel, *The Yiddish Policeman's Union,* an adept marriage of alternate history with the mystery/suspense and POLITICAL NOVEL, as bookends for the writer's reference shelf. Some memorable speculative novels that fit between these bookends include at least two by George Orwell, *1984* and *Animal Farm*, and Aldous Huxley's better-known *Brave New World,* that unfairly eclipses his *After Many a Summer Dies the Swan.*

Philip Roth and Saul Bellow have speculated to great effect, but one of the great speculative novels of modern times made its way tentatively as a triad of short stories appearing in *The Magazine of Fantasy and Science Fiction.* Because he participated in the bombing of an Italian monastery during World War II, Walter M. Miller began setting down his own vision of a post-apocalyptic world, starting in a Roman Catholic monastery in the American Southwest, spanning the regrowth of the civilized world. *A Canticle for Liebowitz* has been in continuous print since its 1960 appearance; it is the Universal Bar Code of speculative fiction across the forehead of inventive creativity.

Such is the flexibility of speculative fiction that WRITERS from all genres may resort to it as a means of expressing fables or cautionary tales at the extreme edges of their convictions and imagination. But each of these very different works by very different stylists all began with the same, age-old question: *What if?*

speed bumps

EVENTS, DESCRIPTIONS and reflections that impede the flow of STORY, often imparting a jerky feel to the NARRATIVE; a sense of stylistic devices waving their hands for attention during the otherwise orderly progression of a DRA-MATIC NARRATIVE; the jerky disconnect experienced by READERS when WRITERS are not careful about adding BACKSTORY, description, and the existential wondering of CHARACTERS.

The thing to remember at some point in the telling of a story is that the narrative art is EVOCATIVE, not descriptive; description has its place, usually in small doses, an occasional adjective or adverb, even a clause or entire sentence. The goal is to achieve a smooth mixture of event and explanation within a story, much of a piece with stirring out the lumps in corn bread batter before setting it in to bake.

There are specific times when the make and caliber of a gun, for example, or the year, model, and color of a car bring clarification to the narrative. A character's height or lack thereof, even some descriptive facial tic become not only necessities but tools in the greater process of evoking that individual's presence. Arrogant? Shy? Assured? Lazy? The overarching intent is to suggest. In a delicious IRONY, some writers who should know better fail to see the mischievous potential in verbs, relying instead on the adjective and the adverb.

One last pass in revision to "cure" adverbial abuse is a sure way to remove many speed bumps. As an example, consider the sentence "He felt swelteringly, miserably hot." Compare it with "He mopped perspiration from his forehead before removing his jacket and loosening his tie."

stasis

The state or condition that stops a process or rests it in balance; a situation or series of situations in which dramatic inertia pauses; passages in STORY often referred to as soft spots, where there is no ACTION or REACTION.

The battlefield for WRITERS is populated with two armies: the army of BACKGROUND and explanation, and the opposing army of ACTION. The timid writer worries that the reader will not have enough guidance or information to understand the implications of the STORY, thus slowing it or completely stopping it with BACKSTORY, DESCRIPTION, and EXPLANATION. The more active writer keeps CHARACTERS in constant movement, sometimes to the bewilderment of the READER, who has been given too little understanding of LANDSCAPE and character NUANCE to feel grounded and secure in among all the hubbub of action. By most accounts, the reader is more likely to continue with the latter rather than the former, hopeful of occasional squirts of information.

One truth emerges: if nothing happens for too long, the reader will set the work down with little probability of returning. The culprit is not so much bad writing as stasis: poor management of PACE with necessary development and explanation.

Another truth awaits just below the surface: most readers of fiction enjoy the process of active reading, a process by which they use their imaginations, their ability to deduce, their complete willingness to be led astray. Readers want things to happen; they want COMPLICATIONS to attach themselves to the lives of individuals they have begun to care about.

Stasis is the enemy of fiction. In successful stories, even when nothing appears to be happening, something at some level is advancing the inertia of AGENDA, INTENT, and MOTIVATION.

stet

A term from the Latin *stare* (to be) for "let it be" or "let it stand"; editor or proofreader notation indicating a marked word or passage on a MANUSCRIPT or proof is to stand as now indicated; a WRITER's note to an editorial suggestion or deletion, thus an authorial override on an editorial opinion.

Editors have a complex menu of responses to matter included in a manuscript, ranging from the highly idiosyncratic to the recognition of house conventions. Some responses relate to the use by the author of comma splices or Arabic numerals instead of spelled-out numbers. Other responses are more substantive, involving material the author wants in the final text as opposed to the same material the editor would like to see omitted from the text. When an author answers a query or QY on the manuscript with a stet, the author is having the last word, presumably after taking the editor's query or suggestion into serious consideration.

By the time the decision is made to publish a particular work and the deal has been contracted, notes and queries from the content editor are considered friendly, helpful suggestions, particularly since the editor was probably a party to the arrangement for publication. Editorial notes and suggestions made after the fact of contract are not mandates; the agreement or contract may have had provisional mandates—change the narration from third- to first-person, make the ending a happy ending, don't kill off Uncle

Laird—and the writer will have been aware of these. The stet decisions involve last-minute details. Example: An editor may conclude that a particular exchange of dialogue will by its very use of words and specifics convey that Ms. Kitty is angrily energized and thus mark for deletion the attribution "Ms. Kitty said hotly" as a GOES-WITHOUT-SAYING notation. But the writer, wanting the READER to be sure of Ms. Kitty's frame of emotional mind, may say stet, at which point the editor either says OK or consults with the author to see if a compromise can be reached, depending on how retentive the editor might be, before moving on to the next matter.

COPYEDITORS are more likely to query on usage; their work is mechanical intervention in the service of consistency of use according to a house style. Writers are not likely to get into stet decisions with copyeditors unless the copyeditor is challenging a statement the writer has set as a fact. For an example, in a story in which the writer has claimed that a character who is a professional boxer bears a stylistic resemblance to Muhammad Ali, the copyeditor may circle Muhammad Ali and write in the margin "who he?" The writer may believe Mr. Ali's name needs no attribution and thus lines out the query, then writes stet.

story

A bundle of information bits about CHARACTERS, strategically deployed to produce a series of on-going emotional responses, culminating in a THEMATIC, emotional payoff; the resulting product of one or more characters, individuals who make plans, experience frustration or REVERSAL, then achieve some progress toward their GOAL; a condition reflecting the pursuit of AGENDA against odds; at the very least it is a dramatic expression of VOLITION and INTENT and their CONSEQUENCES.

Longer stories, those over 10,000 words, often referred to as NOVELLAS or NOVELETTES, depending on their length, actually move one or more characters to some kind of change in personality, lifestyle, or understanding. Shorter fictional works running from about fifty words to 10,000 are called SHORT STORIES. Because of their comparative length in relation to the NOVEL, there is less likelihood that shorter works can track a character from the point of awareness of a problem or goal all the way through a complex ending and subsequent change in the character's perspectives.

Short stories may end with a realization or EPIPHANY of stunning emotional impact, as in James Joyce's "The Dead." Stories may also end on a note in which one or more characters, having realized something, resolve to change a course of action, but this resolve stops short of actual CHANGE.

The STRUCTURE of the contemporary short story has changed, moving away from the moral finality or tidy outcome of the ending (see O. Henry), although BEGINNINGS often set a major character in a situation where there is some need for a DECISION. MIDDLES provide occasion for TENSION and SUSPENSE by encouraging the turning up of dramatic heat on the protagonist and/or by adding an atmosphere of texture and complexity to the narrative. ENDINGS propel the lead character to some point where his physical or emotional state produces a direct response from the READER. Most of Alice Munro's, Deborah Eisenberg's, and William Trevor's short stories illustrate the current ELLIP-TICAL state of endings in the short form.

Another characteristic of the contemporary story is the way authors break further away from the traditional narrative restraints and conventional formats. Rick Moody's "Boys" abandons the tradition of a FIRST- or THIRD-PERSON narrator in favor of a pluralistic approach reminiscent of the opening paragraphs of *Madam Bovary*; other short-story WRITERS will render narrative as a series of numbered paragraphs, and yet other writers will either shift from the usual past tense (see VERB TENSES) to a present tense delivery or depart from conventional spelling and usage in favor of Internet chat room or electronic mail abbreviations, acronyms, or symbols.

From time to time, authors will also cast novels in the present tense, use a larger ensemble of characters as active narrators, abandon quotation marks or, as Vikram Seth did in his novel *The Golden Gate,* render his entire text as a series of 690 Onegin stanzas (sonnets inspired by the rhyme scheme of Pushkin's *Eugene Onegin*).

As a dramatic entity, story is nuanced and satisfying enough to allow adjectives to be attached to its name, suggesting types such as MYSTERY story, which by convention has come to mean a story with a focus on the discovery of at least one corpse and the detection of the individual who caused that corpse to come into being. A ROMANCE story is taken by readers to mean a series of events in which an appealing but not necessarily attractive protagonist is faced with the choice of romantic partners. A FANTASY story is set in a more or less conventional venue where the outcome is influenced by a strong element of MAGIC.

There are two basic approaches for the writer to take with the short story, the first being the literary equivalent of the paint-by-numbers approach of arranging a lead character in a beginning-middle-end configuration in which a GOAL or PROBLEM is introduced, followed by a resolve to achieve the goal or solve the problem. Then comes FRUSTRATION and REVERSAL to the point where the goal or solution seems helpless or pointless. Finally, through action and some form of determination, an outcome is forged. Such formulaic approaches can be and often are satisfying, if only momentarily.

The second approach is for the writer to define his own vision of story—including how problems or goals are introduced, and how relatively transparent the characters are—pursuing the avenues of COLLISION and OPPOSITION the characters experience to the point of some fireworks display of emotion that will end the STORY ARC. This is not merely a case of the individual writer moving away from a one-size-fits-all approach to story, rather a case of wanting to establish a defining take on what story should do and what it ought not do; this becomes a matter of the individual writer imposing his individual personality on the story form. Short stories from the contemporary Irish writer, Colm Toibin, are excellent illustrations of this less conventional approach. Because he spends at least half his time teaching in America, Toibin has a close feel for the pulse of American short fiction. Readers wanting a yet closer sense of the "American" take on short fiction will find abundant resources in the work of Deborah Eisenberg, Ann Beattie, and T. C. Boyle. (See SHAGGY-DOG STORY, LIKELY STORY, COCK-AND-BULL STORY, HARD-LUCK STORY.)

structure

The process in dramatic writing where first the WRITER then the READER observe, then respond to the placement of DRAMATIC elements; a systematic arrangement of dramatic events; the order in which key STORY points are set forth with the expectation that they will reveal the writer's INTENT.

The decision Wilkie Collins made to deliver elements of the SUSPENSE THRILLER in *The Moonstone* included his structural strategy for using MULTIPLE-POINT-OF-VIEW narration from key cast members. Thus came an introduction to Franklin Blake as narrator, giving us background about the eponymous jewel and also revealing his love for Rachel Verinder, who is to be given the Moonstone on the eve of her birthday. Rachel, we are pretty sure, also is into Franklin Blake. When the fabled gem goes missing and all are shocked by the crime—Franklin Blake still narrating—Rachel turns on him, saying she never wants to see him again. Stunned, he asks why. Now it is our turn to be stunned. "Because you stole the Moonstone," she tells him. "I saw you with my own eyes." End of chapter.

Collins did not have to end the chapter at that point; he could have chosen other structural approaches, but none would have so effectively created the desired drama Collins wished to present.

F. Scott Fitzgerald experimented fitfully with the narrative of *The Great Gatsby* until, at length, he stumbled on the decision to demonstrate the EVENTS through the eyes of Nick Carraway, a cousin of one of the principals, thus necessitating a change in structure.

Valerie Martin created her own structure with her novel *Mary Reilly* by rearranging the structure of Robert Louis Stevenson's novella *The Strange Case of Dr. Jekyll and Mr. Hyde* and recasting the story through the eyes of an immigrant Irish girl who had signed on as Dr. Jekyll's maid and who ultimately found herself vulnerable when Mr. Hyde developed the polarized feelings of being both romantically attracted to her and paranoid relative to her intentions regarding him.

Hint: A useful way of looking at structure in a SHORT STORY, NOVEL, or play is the positioning of the DISCOVERY. In a MYSTERY, one or more bodies should be discovered early on, with SCENES engineered to suggest to the reader/ viewer the potential for yet additional discoveries. In bedroom farce, the adventurous lover is discovered hiding under the bed or in the closet later in the proceedings.

Structure may take on a life of its own if, as a CONCEPT, the writer questions it during REVISION. The question for the writer to pose at that time is: *Does the inherent energy of this work cry out for a different emphasis?* Depending on the answer to the question, the writer is led by enthusiasm beyond the academic quibble over the difference in meaning between structure and design. The GOAL is to find the most resonant arrangement of CHARACTERS, SCENES, and issues within a particular story.

Hint: For another instructive glimpse of structure, check out Virginia Woolf's 1931 novel, *Waves,* in which she presents monologues of six characters, all of whom are talking about yet another character, Percival, who never appears on stage. In addition, these character-based chapters are interspersed with brief *entr'actes,* each describing a seascape at differing times of the day.

style

The physical fingerprint of the WRITER, demonstrated by such traits as length of sentence, cadence, length of paragraph, use of adjectives and adverbs, punctuation; style may emerge as formal or informal, depending on such idiosyncrasies as the use of "you" instead of "one."

Most writers have a pronounced style, making it possible to identify their work without signposts (Hemingway comes to mind as a prime example), while other writers are said to write *in* a particular style, say journalistic or scholarly or discursive. Some styles, such as material appearing in *The National Geographic,* are so focused on clarity and accuracy that authorial presence tends to retreat into the background except for occasional pronouns.

Style is what remains of a MANUSCRIPT after it has been revised by the writer and subsequently winnowed to achieve for the author a sense of comfort, which is to say that all self-consciousness has been edited out. If the writer is not comfortable or happy with his style, happier results may be found by examining writers with agreeable styles, looking for clues as to what to include or remove from one's own work. Style can be changed by using more active verb tenses, varying the length of sentences, being more observant of the cadence within a paragraph.

The difference between style and VOICE has its origins in the author's INTENT in writing the work; voice comes from an emotional and/or philosophical atmosphere, and is a direct reflection of the author's attitude. Style is more a mechanical function, relating to the way the writer uses tense or where she places commas and other punctuation.

submission

The offering of a NOVEL or SHORT STORY for publication; a presentation of a MANUSCRIPT to a LITERARY AGENT or editor with hopes of impending publication; a practice engaged in by a WRITER in which work is offered to a publishing venue.

The moment comes when a writer knows a particular work is finished, that there is nothing more to be done to it without transforming it into something altogether different from what it is now. If the work is a NOVEL, the writer usually sends it to a literary agent because relatively few publishers will read unsolicited book-length manuscripts unless a writer has been invited to submit the work. If the work is a short story, the writer sends it to the editor of a magazine or journal, hopeful of its being accepted and scheduled for publication. Such is the nature of submission. Writers wishing to have their work published accept the process of submission as a way of life, just as actors accept the reality of audition.

True enough, some writers are invited to submit stories to journals and novels to publishers. These writers are generally veterans of previous publications, which came from previous submissions of previous work.

Writers whose work reflects a difference in THEME and VOICE, while observing an awareness of what makes a story, will have a higher rate of acceptance than writers who strive to make their work less different, possibly even lapsing into derivative or imitative approaches.

Beginning writers see submission as some Sisyphean chore; published writers see submission as a way of writing life.

When Joseph Heller was told he'd have to change the title of his forthcoming novel, *Catch-18*, because it was on the same list as Leon Uris's *Mila 18*, he readily agreed to *Catch-22* because the manuscript had been submitted previously to twenty-one other publishers before being accepted. Although Vladimir Nabokov received numerous letters from publishers proclaiming *Lolita* to have the makings of reaching classic status, he was nevertheless left with no option but to accept the offer of publication from Maurice Girodias at Olympia Press, known for a list that was more erotic than literary.

Hint: Send your work forth and send it forth again and again until it finds a home.

subplot

A secondary or subordinate PLOT line in a larger work of fiction, possibly involving different CHARACTERS than those in the main plot; a thematic counterpoint of ACTION to the major events of STORY; often a related series of EVENTS taking place in an earlier time relative to the SETTING of the main plot; usually a series of events involving characters below front-rank status.

Because of length constraints, SHORT STORIES are unlikely to contain subplots, but in the works of Louise Erdrich, which seem to have been carved from NOVELS or have their origins as platforms for later novels, this construct is an anomaly; ditto Alice Munro. Novels with extensive LAYERS of subplot emerge as being more dramatic and theatrical; this is particularly true of novels with MULTIPLE-POINT-OF-VIEW narration.

If the READER is not able eventually to see a reason for the presence of a subplot, the reader will likely regard it as padding. A good "excuse" for the inclusion of a subplot is parallel development, in which differing groups of individuals are subjected to the same THEMATIC situation within the drama. In ROMANCE novels, for example, the "best friend" is often engaged in a romantic pursuit that serves as a counterpoint to the events faced by the PROTAGONIST. These events may but do not necessarily have to intersect the main plot, but they should provide relevant tangential information to the main story or emphasize thematic threads that have a bearing on the main plot line.

subtext

The vital, often ignored dramatic presence of the space between what a CHARACTER says in a SITUATION and what the character actually feels about the situation; a means of importing IRONY into a situation; a condition of implication by which the READER is able to discern the true feeling of one character at the expense of another.

There are many motivations for subtext, including the stretching of the truth to avoid hurting someone's feelings, transgressing the boundaries of propriety, not wanting to be caught disagreeing with a potential benefactor; there is also seduction, and salesmanship, which is no stranger to seduction. Some of these MOTIVES are noble, others ignoble; thus a character shown being noble in his or her subtextual commentary will convey to the reader added dimension.

An example of the terrain where subtext may blend into THEME is found in Annie Proulx's novel *The Shipping News*. Throughout the novel, each chapter is prefaced with an epigram describing a particular knot, instructions for tying it, and potential uses for it, causing a wrenching pull of nostalgia for the days when securing meant using rope, twine, or string. Although Ms. Proulx used this knot device as chapter epigrams, she did not refer to the knots or their names in the text, nor did her characters make reference to knots or knot tying. Nevertheless, having read these intriguing epigrams, the reader was drawn into the game of looking closely at the text of each chapter to see if the particular knot opening the chapter had any subtext reference to the portrayed events. Proulx's point was that human relationships frequently take on the design complexity of knots, an awareness that encourages the reader to thoughtful reflection about subtext and theme.

surprise

Unanticipated dramatic behavior or circumstances, EVENTS that cause

CHARACTERS to do things they would not normally do. Literary surprises are unplanned turns of events within a drama that nevertheless have feet firmly planted in PLAUSIBILITY. Presented as impulsive behavior erupting within a least-likely-to-rebel character, surprise is a contrived device, intended to catch the READER unaware—but it is also a means by which a WRITER may learn surprising, unintended things about his characters as well as himself. More often than not, surprise comes from CHARACTER-DRIVEN stories, but it is neither unheard of nor unwelcome in PLOT-ORIENTED narratives.

The best foundation for surprise is a deep understanding and knowledge of the front-rank characters, which means the characters will appear to behave in an unanticipated-but-plausible way that may push the story in an entirely original and yet satisfying manner, neither seeming contrived nor accidental. An unanticipated consequence of surprise is the fact of it causing TENSION or SUSPENSE, two of the major elements of story. After one or two surprises, the reader becomes aware of the potential, then begins to wonder where and to whom it will happen next.

suspense

The dramatic quality that makes the READER concerned with what will happen to one or more CHARACTERS; a sense of VULNERABILITY visited on characters by the CONSEQUENCES of their ACTIONS or lack of action; how characters respond to each new stimulus; an overarching sense of danger, disaster, or impending COMPLICATION.

Suspense is one of the major vital signs present in a story; you might call it the life's blood of drama. If the reader feels suspense, the story is alive. Story begins with TENSION or uneasy premonition of impending disaster, which accelerates into suspense— as in how much worse can things get? Suspense is triggered by one or more characters as they act on their goals, attempting to overcome opposition. The rate of suspense increases in direct proportion to the risk and consequences of a character's plan. As suspense builds, so does the SUBTEXT of the UNTHINKABLE, COME TO PASS; how far down can a character's chances descend, and how will that character possibly get free of this latest disaster?

Hint: Consider as an index the correlation between the extent of a character's agenda and the reader's curiosity about what will become of her, now and after the story has ended. Suspense is related to the curiosity a reader feels toward a character, sometimes to a degree WRITERS will find exasperating—at first. But then the writer realizes another fan has signed on for the next story.

synecdoche

A useful figure of speech that is first-cousin to the metaphor; it posits the whole being greater than the sum of its parts or the parts representing the whole, or the parts of one thing relating to the whole or parts of another thing.

A gifted surgeon, for example, may be referred to and represented by her hands. Similarly, there is the synecdoche of long arm of the law, and of plastic being used as a symbol for credit cards, which of course obviate the need for carrying around quantities of paper, or money. Knowing synecdoche may result in a higher SAT score and be good for points in a literary criticism course, but it may also have the unwanted effect of becoming an albatross or weight about the neck (or any other part) of a STORY, so much so that its over abundance will cause editors and READERS to defect.

When the subject of metaphorical writing comes up, regard it in the same way as WEATHER REPORTS and LANDSCAPES are regarded—with extreme caution. For WRITERS such as Raymond Chandler, they—the metaphor and synecdoche—arrived as appropriate devices that shed shorthand light on a situation, an ATTITUDE, a condition, a CHARACTER, not as a blinking neon sign calling attention to the writer's cleverness.

By all means, note and admire these devices when they are found in the work of other writers, but do not try to get them into your own work through some sense of literary homage or obligation. If they are to come in your work, they will come of their own, and even then should be subject to critical scrutiny. Do they make things better, or do they come off as the literary equivalent of an energetic kid showing off in class?

synopsis

A summary or abstract of a SHORT STORY or NOVEL; a compressed outline of the basic PLOT points and MOTIVATION; a guide to the behavior and attitudes of CHARACTERS in a STORY.

The first roadblock a WRITER in search of a LITERARY AGENT and/or publisher experiences is the composition of a synopsis—even if said publisher has already heard about the work in a pitch session and encouraged its submission.

Why, the writer wonders, do they want a synopsis? Why not simply read the manuscript? The answer to these and other publishing-related questions are not entirely rational. For instance, few individuals in publishing (writers included, by the way) have risen through the ranks to at least a journeyman level. Many in publishing have come from business-related areas, their degrees actually MBAs instead of, say, MFAs. But there is another truth at play here, which is that the editor has to produce the prospectus for the work before— in most cases—the work goes to the contract stage. In theory, the editor could write the synopsis. In further theory, it might make sense for the editor to do so because the synopsis would reflect the editor's enthusiasm for the work.

In fact, the author is the better person to write the synopsis because the author's INTENT and enthusiasm emerges, and because the author, however much given to grumbling about the chore of the synopsis, is more likely to produce an emotionally charged work than the editor or literary agent.

Look at it this way: Even though you hate writing synopses and can see no purpose for them, who better than you to synopsize your novel? Onward to the outline: Get some practice. Start by writing fifty- and hundred-word abstracts of short stories. Pick two out of any best-of-the-year collections, settling on one you like and one you don't. You're already halfway to the goal because the stories in the three major best-of collections have appeared in prestigious publications, their validity ratified by a number of critics. Your own sense of liking or not liking particular works allows you to see what the critics may have seen, while offering you the opportunity to disagree with their choices. Start with a character, add a two- or three-word description (a newly divorced mother, a mid-career cop), add an immediate problem (is placed on probation, returns home to attend a funeral, a wedding), then makes a discovery or is suspected of something. READERS of the abstracts are looking for story; story resides in problems, deadlines, discoveries.

After you have the hang of abstracting a shorter work, take a look at the *Books Briefly Noted* section of any issue of *The New Yorker* (which covers fiction and nonfiction). Next, take a longer work that is not your own, then imagine yourself attacking a similar hundred- to hundred-fifty-word critical description. Now you're ready to begin. First step: decide who is the principal teller of the story (POINT OF VIEW). If there is more than one NARRATOR, make a note of all. If there is only one narrator, put the initials POV in parentheses after that individual's name the first time the character is cited. For instance, "Mary (POV) was adopted when she was one year old." If there are other narrators, allow a space break between Mary and the next narrator, say, Fred. Thus, "Fred (POV) is her older brother, adopted prior to Mary's adoption." The next step is to introduce what the novel is about, its primary goal. "Mary wants to learn the identity and locale of her biological parents." Note how this is done in the present tense regardless of the usage in the actual text of the novel. The next step is to introduce some potential for early disagreement or outright opposition. "Fred knows who his biological parents were and where they live. He does not want Mary to learn either fact." Now we have opposition and some conflict, which may be demonstrated with: "Although Mary loves and respects her adoptive parents, Fred, relishing the big brother role, is constantly taunting Mary by questioning her loyalty and devotion to her adoptive parents."

The conventional pattern for the synopsis is to keep it at about three single-spaced pages, but this brings us to a fork in the road regarding the ending. Some synopsis writers "end" the summary with the lead-in to the climactic scene, where the tensions and pressures weigh heavily on the characters and they must face some kind of decisive action. How specific must the ending be? Is it possible to keep the reader(s) of the synopsis in suspense with mere outline and occasional bits of dialogue? On the other hand, if the final confrontation/denouement is left unresolved, won't the literary agent or publisher "have" to read the entire manuscript to see the ending? This is a critical point for all concerned. If the outcome is too detailed, the writer may be stuck with that ending because the editor will have been sold on it ending that way. If the ending is not rendered with enough detail, the editor may become put off, not trusting the author. Thus the trick is to tell just enough to allow the editor to infer what happens, yet continue to hold the editor curious enough to want to read it all the way through to relish the details.

Think of the chore of the synopsis this way: Your book will be taken on by a publisher, printed, bound, sent forth to appropriate reviewers and subsidiary rights agents, along with several thousands of other titles, there to compete in the metaphorical crowded drawing room that is a book store. Someone will provide Wikipedia and possibly even Amazon.com with a description of your book, possibly even spoiling the ending to the point of obviating the reader's need to see how things worked out. Your synopsis can get there first, influencing how your novel will be seen. Repeat slowly: Synopses are not nuisances, they are incentives. Synopses are in fact worked over by the editor and the publishers' marketing department for use in news releases, descriptions for bookstore buyers, and the individuals who write jacket copy. Synopses are indeed not nuisances.

TFS

A useful acronym for FICTION WRITERS and dramatists who are overly given to DESCRIPTIONS and EXPLANATIONS; a reminder of the true task at hand. TFS: Tell the freaking story. READERS are impressed by characters, they luxuriate in stylistic elegance, but they also want the freaking story, and it had better be there.

talking heads

A lamentable condition arising when two or more CHARACTERS in a SCENE/setting, exchange DIALOGUE with only minimal accompanying gestures or inflections; characters seen by the READER as exchanging dramatic information which is little more than NARRATIVE encased in quotation marks; by implication, characters who fail to demonstrate significant dramatic force within a STORY.

Individuals converse in real life. CHARACTERS use dialogue and AGENDA as though each were a volleyball being batted back and forth over a net.

Some writers make use of talking heads in the mistaken belief that they are showing rather than telling, indulging their characters in long exchanges of information framed by quotation marks, but giving no sense whatsoever of what the speaker is seeing, tasting, feeling, or how anyone is reacting to the words being spouted or any other drama-based activity. Such exchanges, because they are notably lacking in SUBTEXT, add a weight of CONSEQUENCE to the narrative that is often fatal, providing the reader with an excellent opportunity to set the story down without intention of return.

Get your characters into a REACTION process with one or more of the other characters in a scene as quickly as possible. Avoid the temptation to have characters utter speeches. Dialogue is spoken, even shouted, perhaps sputtered (although NB: using synonyms for the verb "said" is the equivalent of an invitation to having your work satirized or, worse, unread).

All right, you ask, how do I go about getting important information into the awareness of the reader? Remember, even radio drama has sound effects, noises the characters would plausibly make in their time within a scene—footsteps upon a set of stairs, a door squeaking open, water filling a glass and the speaker pausing to take a gulp. Have one or more characters interrupt or draw the wrong conclusions, or cause an immediate digression. The reader will become FRUSTRATED, which is considerably more positive than if the reader were bored.

Even when you are giving the impression of making things easy for the characters, your best approach is to make it as difficult as possible. In one of Graham Greene's undeservedly neglected thrillers, *The Confidential Agent*, the PROTAGONIST is sent to a foreign city where he is to meet a fellow spy, who is working as an instructor in a language school. They must observe the convention of speaking in an artificial language called Intrenaciono, a take-off on Esperanto. Thus the protagonist must wade through his instructions in this artificial language and not only make sense of it but also translate his own reports. A great deal is at stake during the transaction, but if the two are to avoid detection, they must play by these artificial rules.

The bottom line is that pages filled with talking heads represent missed opportunities at genuine storytelling.

Hint: it will do you no good to complain about the laxity of enforcing such "talky" exchanges in already published work. They have all had the effect of causing LITERARY AGENTS and editors to be more determined than ever that you not be allowed to get away with having your characters emerge as talking heads.

tension

A valuable DRAMATIC entity meaning the anticipation of impending CONFLICT; an upward spiral of the sense of potential MENACE, VULNERABILITY, HUMILIATION, conflict, or REVERSAL hovering over CHARACTERS as they pursue their AGENDAS; a radiant quality of apprehension affecting READERS who have come to have concerns about characters; a dramatic shading valued by some writers to a greater degree than actual conflict.

Tension is the flashing warning light, the buzzing smoke detector that warns of the CONSEQUENCES of conflict.

One instructive way to look at tension is as an atmosphere of dramatic tentativeness, of characters attempting to behave as though nothing is wrong, trying not to recognize the ELEPHANT IN THE LIVING ROOM. Thus by the indirection of SUBTEXT the reader will become apprehensive for the appropriate characters.

theme

The metaphoric or symbolic message of a STORY; an abstract representation of authorial INTENT; a lesson, moral, or observation to be had from considering the CONSEQUENCES of various options.

Theme is similar to authorial STYLE in that it remains resonant after the story has been written, REVISED, and published. Authors are often surprised at the emergent theme of a work after it has been written, an observation that is thematic in itself.

Most themes, when reduced to their basics, tend to sound banal: the brotherhood/sisterhood of humanity; self-interest, nihilism, twilight of the gods, man's inhumanity, etc. Theme, however, is the quality of story that makes the READER think about possible meanings and inferences, as opposed to making the reader wonder why he continued to read for so long—these lingering, larger questions raised within the confines of story are a large part of aftertaste.

third-person narration

A narrative construction that presents STORY as told from the POINT OF VIEW of a CHARACTER rendered variously by the character's name and the pronoun he or she.

Examples: "Mary wanted for today what she'd come to want every day—a day without stress." "Jim Alexander waited patiently for the sun to sink below the horizon before making up his mind. He knew his history of daytime decisions had been remarkably poor."

Third-person point of view shares popularity with the FIRST-PERSON or Icentered narration, its choice being idiosyncratic, often reflecting the WRITER'S unthinking preference. As in all narration modes except the AUTHOR-IAL-INTERVENTION approach, the material being ingested and commented upon must appear to come from the character, reflecting the character's experiences, prejudices, social standing, self-image, and AGENDA. The narrative will also reflect the observing character's vocabulary and any relevant mental or physical deviations from the norm.

Critical and academic arguments abound over which point of view "seems" or "feels" the most intimate but this argument disregards the fact that the goal of any point of view is to cause the READER to forget the presence of the author, to invest instead in the realness of the character.

throughline

A thematic VECTOR linking SCENES and NARRATIVE within a STORY; the driving force or GOAL informing the direction of a NOVEL or SHORT STORY.

time frame

A term that defines the time scheme in which EVENTS in a NOVEL or SHORT STORY take place; a NARRATIVE paradigm that helps READERS see the relative position of events in a story; it includes the use of VERB TENSES as identifiers to help readers orient to the dramatic sequence of events.

Although there is no organized lobby to establish a convention of a strict chronology in a story, there is the tradition of a DRAMATIC UNITY in which a drama shall proceed in real time from start to finish, hence questions about the "legality" of FLASHBACK or other interruptions of time sequence. These arguments are as intransigent and pedantic as the argument addressing the splitting of the infinitive.

It is a rare twenty-first-century story that trudges forward from A to Z without some pause for reflection about past events or an actual shift back to events that took place before the story at hand began. Although his novels are set largely at the time of Elizabeth I, twentieth- and twenty-first-century crime writer Leonard Tourney frequently begins his mysteries with what he calls "a slice of the crime," an out-of-sequence SCENE, where the reader sees a crime being committed, overhears a crime being contemplated, or is present when the results of a crime are being discovered. Other crime WRITERS (Richard Price, George Pelecanos, P.D. James as examples) begin with some provocative event as a preface to the story at hand. Yet other writers (John D. McDonald, for example, in his non-Travis McGee novels) use a combination of a shift-in-time sequence and a shift in POINT OF VIEW to create a CLIFFHANGER effect. Tim Gautreaux's 2009 novel, *The Missing*, begins at the tail end of World War I, moves forward a few years to a major defining moment, then reverts back in time well before the beginning scenes.

One of the most extreme examples of time bending appears in the opening of James Joyce's *Finnegan's Wake,* which begins with a fragment of a sentence,"… riverrun, past Eve and Adam's, from swerve of shore to bend of bay, brings us by a commodius vicus of recirculation back to Howth Castle and Environs." A few hundred pages later, the novel ends with "a way a lone a last a loved a long the…" which, were you to connect it with the opening fragment, would form a complete sentence, setting forth in some degree Joyce's intent of an unending circularity.

A simple recipe for use of time line in the short story or the novel: at least sixty percent of the action takes place in the present. TWO-LINE SPACE BREAKS separate all scenes, but when jumping from time to time and POV to POV, the writer must let the reader know who, when, and where ASAP.

Hint: Time in a short story or novel is the equivalent of setting, the evocation of moments, past, present, and future, each of which have a personality or emotional tint. No two writers would describe the same landscape in the same manner, a fact that sets the hurdle each writer must leap to present an idiosyncratic sense of any particular moment evoked in a story. (See BACKSTORY.)

time sequence

The temporal ARC of a STORY or NOVEL; the chronological order of EVENTS in a NARRATIVE; the arrangement of narrative events to effect the most dramatic result. This differs from TIME FRAME, which is the historical setting of the story and the WRITER'S design for revealing it to the READER. Time sequence is more analogous to the cadence of music, conveying to the reader the sense of passing time.

How long between events? How long has this—whatever *this* is—been going on? How long before *he* gets the idea? How long before *she* asks him if they have a future together? How much time does a Harlan Coben PROTAGONIST have before being discovered rifling the files in an office he has no authority to be in? The PACING or BEATS per minute is another way to measure the way THEME and PLOT establish themselves within the reader's sensibility, helping the reader to remember bits of information as they come forth.

The skilled writer knows ways to manipulate time, showing an event in progress, exhuming an event from the past, switching away from a character who is actually or might metaphorically be hanging from the side of a cliff. Note: it is not necessary to remain with a TIME LINE; you can shuffle various SCENES and confrontations like the dealer in three-card monte.

Romeo and Juliet runs its entire course in about thirty-six hours. James Grady's 1974 novel, *The Six Days of the Condor*, was successful enough to have evolved into a movie in which the time line was cut in half to *The Three Days of the Condor.* William F. Nolan and George Clayton Johnson's novel

Logan's Run had a time line imposed by population explosion:When a character reached the age of thirty, along came a Sandman to put the character to sleep, as in the final sleep. Somewhere along the way between the penultimate draft and the draft submitted to the publisher, Nolan and Johnson decided to cut back on the arc of character life from age thirty as a cut-off point to age twenty-one.

The Iliad begins with the story already having been set in action some seven years previous to Achilles posturing wrath. Tim Gautreaux's 2009 novel, *The Missing,* takes place largely in the late 1920s but begins in the final days of World War I, then flashes back to an earlier time frame before delivering the reader back to the time the protagonist, Sam Simoneaux, returns from his experiences in World War I France to his job in New Orleans, where the main action sets forth.

Words of warning: Forget about extending the sense of time passing with a laundry list of unimportant details or an extended blow-by-blow in a fight or other contest. Readers can tell when a narrative is padded.

tipping point, the

A critical component of DRAMATIC NARRATIVE; the moment where momentum changes to the extent of becoming irreversible; a literary equivalent of irrevocable CONSEQUENCES becoming the guiding force of events; the place in a STORY which, once crossed, makes it impossible for events to return to their previous status.

The tipping point of Linda Sue Park's Newbery medalist, *A Single Shard,* arrives when Tree-Ear, a young orphan boy in twelfth-century Korea, becomes so intrigued while watching a master ceramist create new pots that he sneaks into the potter's workshop to look at more of the potter's work. In the process, he breaks a valuable pot, and must "repay" the potter by working for him for three days.

At almost exactly the midpoint of F. Scott Fitzgerald's novel *Tender Is the Night,* the growing personal attraction between a young patient, Nicole Warren, and her promising young psychiatrist, Richard Diver, has been set in motion, culminated by the two of them taking an afternoon stroll in downtown Vienna, then being surprised by a sudden rain shower which sends them scurrying into a narrow, protective doorway.What do persons who are attracted to one another do when caught in a rainstorm and forced to take shelter in a doorway? They look into each other's eyes. As Fitzgerald put it, "from that moment, Diver knew that whatever Nicole's problems were, they were his problems as well."And were they ever.

Two places where the tipping point or POINT OF NO RETURN can naturally take place in STORY are almost immediately at the beginning or at the midpoint, but the tipping point can fit almost anywhere in a NARRATIVE, just so long as it does appear. It does not have to be as explicit as the examples cited, but it is a present condition in a dramatic narrative. How to develop awareness of it? Read or recall one hundred plays, one hundred NOVELS, one hundred SHORT STORIES. Identify the tipping point in each. Add tipping point to your list of revision chores, insuring you will look specifically for a place where it might have been included, a place you will note and, if necessary, enhance.

tool kit

An assembly of abilities, skills, and talents a CHARACTER carries; an actual collection of tools, implements, and/or weapons a specific character may use in furtherance of his/her AGENDA.

Many characters have few tangible tools or implements, relying instead on such interior qualities as persistence, dignity, honor, which they use as tools to cope with the problems they encounter. For example, such ANTIHERO characters as Sam Spade (*The Maltese Falcon*) use a healthy cynicism or pragmatism to define their activities.

The more or less independent contractor, the samurai warrior, the legendary knights of Arthur's Round Table, an American gunfighter of the legendary Old West all emerge with a different tool kit than what a twenty-first-century soldier of fortune might have. The character's tool kit consists of the specific implements and qualities from which the individual draws to deal with the next-in-line problem.

tradition

A system of customs, rituals, and practices, forming a long-standing literary apparatus for passing myth, history, and cultural beliefs from one generation to the next; a GENRE or platform for presenting STORY or coded cultural lessons and information.

STORY in the aggregate is a record of evolved cultural TRADITION, the PROCESS by which tradition undergoes evolution, both in content and form. Music may be placed in the time of its composition by an assessment of its tonality. In similar fashion, story may be a reflection of cultural growth by close observation of the traditions it extends and perhaps even breaks. SHORT STORIES have evolved more radically than NOVELS, but such novels as Annie Proulx's *The Shipping News* have stretched the traditions of STYLE, place, and internal rhythm; novels such as John Steinbeck's *Of Mice and Men* have stretched the traditions of THEME, place, and the moody sense of life's purpose.

Tim O'Brien broke a number of narrative traditions in *The Things They Carried* (the eponymous "they" being U.S. servicemen in Viet Nam), while Dashiell Hammett and Raymond Chandler broke the traditions of place, MOTIVE, language, and construction in their novels of MYSTERY and SUSPENSE.

Alice Sebold's *The Lovely Bones* broke the tradition and convention in which a principal CHARACTER could not, once dead, be the narrator of a long form story. Susie Salmon, protagonist of *Bones*, is dead by the second paragraph.

While there is no guarantee, a story that somehow pushes the envelope of tradition to the breaking point is more likely to be remembered. That said, story construction is of paramount importance; so are characters, motives, POINT OF VIEW, and VOICE. When they are altered merely for the sake of alteration, nothing is gained or served. When traditions fall in the service of providing a memorable story, then READER, WRITER, and characters are served.

tragedy

A venerable dramatic form based on loss and suffering; it represents pivotal STORY conditions from which there is often no chance of recovery, in which CHARACTERS experience excruciating GRIEF; the actual or metaphorical loss of POWER, position, and happiness; stories in which individual characters appear to be led away from a course of ACTION that would provide them with happiness by personality quirks they cannot control.

In grim metaphor, tragedy has become *The Man Who Came to Dinner* personified, visiting all segments of humanity, seemingly at whim. Tragedy is the Fates on a drunken spree, the forces of Life choosing a victim such as Job seemingly from whim or boredom; it can strike nearly anyone, nearly anywhere; it can find its way into the caves of meditating yogis, the cells of monasteries, the congregations of synagogues, the mosques of the ultra-orthodox. Tragedy can strike at the heart of the most disciplined and severe ascetic, he or she who has renounced all earthly things, by separating that individual from God. Tragedy is the ultimate VULNERABILITY, the ever-present threat that an individual can lose the one thing he most valued, be it life, another person, youth, a special ability, or power.

Over its centuries as a staple in drama, tragedy has become democratized, extending its reach from the noble families of ancient Greece to the middle classes in America, say O'Neill's *A Moon for the Misbegotten,* Miller's *The Death of a Salesman* or *All My Sons,* and thence across the seas to the failed British comic, Archie Rice in John Osborne's *The Entertainer.* We can see tragedy personified in the wrinkled and battered face of actor Tommy Lee Jones, particularly in his portrayals of Ed Tom Bell in *No Country for Old Men* and Hank Deerfield in *The Valley of Elah.* Tragedy inheres in the voice of an Iraqi mother wailing in Arabic over the senseless death of an infant child, an innocent victim of a suicide bomber. Tragedy is everywhere, in actuality, and lurks behind a mere twist of chance.

Tragedy can come at any age. In retrospect, a failed teen romance may seem a trifle in comparison to the loss of a life-long companion. The death of a childhood pet may be trumped by the unthinkable tragedy of a parent outliving a child but, all the same, these early losses may leave life-long scars on the emotions of the individuals involved.

By watching and reading tragedy, the READER/viewer is able to participate in that remarkable human ritual known as catharsis; by sharing in the tragedy of the characters, the viewer/reader is brought closer to the realization of his own personal tragedy.

Much has been made and much more remains to be made of the narrow boundary separating the tragic from the comedic. Laughter, after all, has a cathartic effect of its very own. In that writer-like way of detaching the WRITER self from the self who has experienced tragedy of some measure, we may observe how important timing is. In tragedy, the cadence of events is a heavy presence, plangent, ominous. To achieve comedy, the writer increases the tempo of events. Comedy is tragedy speeded up.

transportation

The PROCESS of being taken to a mental, physical, and/or emotional state by means of STORY; a condition whereby an observer of a staged DRAMA, motion picture NARRATIVE, or televised presentation forges an identity with CHARACTERS and cultures both in and out of his own personal background; a means of accepting and being convinced by the reality of a fanciful or realistic narrative.

The goal of the WRITER is to provide immediate first-class transportation to the READER, with no hassle about lost luggage or chintzy in-flight meals. Transportation recognizes the READER'S passport at the terminal, does not insist on security checks. There are a good many competing conveyances in the world of conventional and electronic publication, so the reader doesn't have to experience any inconveniences. Frequent-flier miles are welcomed.

Any successful story offers this seemingly ineffable quality of transporting the reader from his present, grounded REALITY into another reality in which the rules, conventions, and traditions of story exist to be broken; the ultimate goals are destinations such as disturbance, entertainment, information, and PLAUSIBLE suggestions for dealing with the moral and social conflicts of the reader's immediate present.

Twenty-first-century readers may be transported to the eighteenth century, where they will experience a readily identifiable socio-economic landscape by picking up any of the three novels completed by Jane Austen. Readers wishing an entirely different type of transportation may follow the career path of Valentine Michael Smith in Robert Heinlein's epic SCIENCE FICTION NOVEL—regarded by many as *the* science fiction novel—*Stranger in a Strange Land.* Valentine Michael Smith is the son of two of the eight astronauts of an ill-fated first human expedition to Mars. Smith is raised in the culture of the native inhabitants of the planet, beings whose minds live in another world. By signing on for the trip, we get a picture of differing cultures and their effect on one another.

Each of these two novels, written a tad over a hundred years apart, have provided observations that have influenced generations of readers, the one from a satirical point of view, the other from an imaginative gloss on differing views of human behavior. In order for any work of the imagination to offer transportation, the characters involved must be caught up in some recognizable cultural and social clashes, enhanced by some form of deadline or emotional imperative.

Thus the question: *How does a writer transport readers?* By first transporting himself. Develop the vision of a place, a time, and the individuals who inhabit it, then write with the unfettered energy of enthusiasm for the vision, regardless of whether the vision is dark and gloomy or light and inspirational. Write with the detail and certainty it takes *you* to believe. The more imaginative the LANDSCAPE, which is to say the more it appears to vary from CONVENTION, the more real it needs to seem, so the characters must behave as though the terrain were absolutely, convincingly real. Not easy to do, but not impossible: Your favorite writers do it for you most of the time.

trigger

A sensory recovering device by which sounds, smells, tastes, feelings and visions prompt the recall of previous incidents in the WRITER'S life, which then, by extension, may be transferred into the menu of response for CHARACTERS; a process of recall and substitution allowing the writer to convincingly, *plausibly* portray experiences and emotions the writer may not have actually experienced.

Many writers stumble onto an old actor's technique involving playing music in the background as they work. The music may be used to drown out other ambient sounds—neighbors talking, telephones ringing, babies crying, dogs barking—or to provide an emotional background for the work at hand. The music triggers memories of actual events or memories of previous emotions, which influence the CADENCE, vocabulary, and tone of the work being written.

As the association with triggers increases (or the familiarity with acting techniques becomes more sophisticated), the writer associates memories of the feel of particular places or moods, or the smells, tastes, and sounds associated with past events to create a LANDSCAPE for the work in progress. These sensual implants trigger, in turn, associations within the READER, who is drawn further into the emotions waiting within a NARRATIVE.

Writers familiar with the technique keep lists of music they associate with particular moods or events, then play that music while writing appropriate SCENES. A notable example of a writer who appears to bring his lists into his published text is George Pelecanos (*The Night Gardener, The Turnaround*), whose characters not only appreciate blues, popular, and rock music but also argue about the merits of performers and specific solos. The genres of music and their composers are idiosyncratic and endless, and what a writer plays in the background is vitally dependent on the scene she is writing at the time. My personal short list: Howard Hanson's *Symphony Number 2, "Romantic"* makes me re-experience being in love at seventeen; Theolonious Monk's compositions provide the delights of surprise tonalities even in simple constructions; George Gershwin's melodies, whether popular or classical, evoke the reach and inner resonance of my cultural heritage; Maurice Ravel's textural orchestrations speak to me of the music I would hope to write if I were a musician instead of a writer.

As the process of identifying triggers progresses, the writer will begin to see the value of keeping lists of meals and their varying tastes; beverages and their adjectival and sensual associations; and such potentials as the emotions evoked within the writer by a particular species of flower. This list of emotional associations could be extended to feelings about animals and insects. (Is a particular character a cat or dog person? Perhaps neither—perhaps a bird or a goldfish person. Perhaps allergic. Perhaps fearful or disturbed by spiders or roaches. Or rats. Perhaps he keeps a pet mouse in his vest pocket, as did Count Fosco, Wilkie Collins's great villain in *The Woman in White*.)

Not all persons, much less writers, will have the same emotional response to a particular stimulus. Not all listeners of George Gershwin's *Rhapsody in Blue* will have the cultural background to associate the slightly sour opening swirl of clarinet with klezmer music, nor is that association necessary for them to be drawn into the composition, but such a trigger will immediately have impact on those familiar with klezmer. Keep in mind that one land mine is a potential explosion, but it is not an entire war; one trigger is a potential emotional connection, but it is not the entire STORY.

turn

A shift in the direction and emotional texture of a NARRATIVE, often in the form of a REVERSAL or seemingly complete shutdown of STORY line. Story cannot remain static, and so its participants will devise or be forced into making a turn. You'll hear this movement spoken of at times as "a turn of EVENT"; it is just that, a point where you sense that events in STORY did not evolve the way the CHARACTERS wished, prompting the characters to renewed efforts toward their GOAL or a new set of actions toward another goal.

See how strong the relationship is between turn and event, how each produces one or more CONSEQUENCES. Now compare turn with the individual stroke of action or response known as the BEAT.

Another important and dramatic NUANCE to the turn is its shift in the tone of a SCENE, say from tense to lighthearted, or from carefree to sudden terror, as in the narratives of Steven King.

Don't ignore the potential the concept of turn has in its relationship to POWER; the opening scene of Elmore Leonard's wildly versatile novel *Freaky Deaky* begins with Booker, an obnoxious, power-hungry drug dealer, receiving a telephone call directing him to walk across the room to a particular chair the caller mentions, and then to sit on it. When the caller is convinced the respondent is seated in that very chair, the trap is sprung. That chair has been wired to a bomb, which has now been activated by the sitter's weight. Any attempt to rise without specific instructions and interventions from the caller will trigger a fatal explosion.

Here is turn, a vital tool for a storyteller, demonstrating how event may be used to bring SUSPENSE, TENSION, and COMBUSTION into the narrative calculus to provide dramatic presence.

Hint: The most effective turns will not strike the reader as being manufactured for mere effect. As with all useful tools, the turn will seem a natural and PLAUSIBLE result.

two-line space break

The gap of two double-spaced lines between the SCENES of a NOVEL or SHORT STORY; a visual break in TEXT to signal the reader of a shift in time, place, and/or POV.

Although some WRITERS prefer a row of asterisks (***) or pound key signs (###) to insert a temporal shift in a narrative, hitting the return key twice will have the same effect, allowing the two-line break to take its place with the paragraph indent and the two spaces between sentences as a universal symbol—and, not incidentally, saving your editor, when the MANUSCRIPT is acquired, from having to delete all of those asterisks and pound signs. Do not indent the first line of the paragraph that follows the break in the manuscript and the READER—notably, at the manuscript stage, an editor—will have another visual clue that the break was, indeed, intentional, especially important if your break occurs at a page break.

~U~

unities

The three classical conditions for DRAMA, derived from Aristotle's *Poetics*: 1) a play should have one significant action; 2) it should represent only one place; and 3) it should take place in the time span of a day.

Aristotle, who has made some significant contributions to such diverse things as scientific classification, logic, and the physics of the dramatic experience, has nevertheless been gone since 322 BCE, allowing room for the growth and development of STORY constructs. Even as far back—from our point of view—as Shakespeare's time, the unities were being disregarded, played with fast and loose. One of the delights of story is its ability to include vast shifts of time, some even generational.

Hint: the unities are good things to know about, particularly when reading or considering works from the distant past, but they cannot and should not hinder a WRITER's experiments with TIME, PLACE, THEME, or any other aspect of telling a story.

unreliable narrator, the

A narrative voice that begins to cause the READER an accelerating sense of concern about the presentation of fact and the interpretation of EVENTS.

Presented with a CHARACTER whose dramatic account seems at first reasonable, interesting, even fair-minded, the reader has no reason to feel distrust or dislike, but when that character begins to emerge as biased, flawed, possibly to the point of nursing a grudge or HIDDEN AGENDA, the reader says, "Oh, oh!" Her main questions are: *Whom do we trust? Why?* These practical questions can be answered satisfactorily only if the WRITER has answered some other questions for himself: What purpose does the unreliability serve? Can and should the narrator's unreliability be extended over a greater ARC before the reader is allowed to "get" the concept? Has the author gone too far? In the final analysis, is any narrator completely reliable?

The danger with any too-unreliable narrator rests with the reader's sense of belief. Was Mr. Stevens, for instance, in Kazuo Ishiguro's *The Remains of the Day,* really unable to interpret Miss Kenton's flirting with him? Was he so incurious about Lord Darlington's politics when Lord Darlington asked him if there were any Jews on the household staff? In both instances, the answer is yes, straining our trust in Stevens. And yet, the underlying decency and single-mindedness radiating from Mr. Stevens caused us to hope that he might finally get the awareness we wish for him, simultaneously causing us to admire his creator, Ishiguro, for the deftness of his portrayal.

Another deft ride: Dashiell Hammett's Brigid O'Shaughnessy from *The*

Maltese Falcon. As she became unreliable in her rendition of her agenda and activities, we did not disbelieve her; we became concerned that she'd be able to win Spade over.

An unreliable narrator may not reflect malice so much as pragmatism— such as Becky Sharp in Thackeray's *Vanity Fair.* The unreliable narrator may also be revealed at some point as the ANTAGONIST, to be rooted against in growing fear that the antagonist will best the goals of the PROTAGONIST. Check out the narration in William Faulkner's hilarious romp, *Spotted Horses,* to see how this seesaw of point of view has a direct effect on suspense and reader loyalty.

In real life as well as in FICTION, READERS and audiences will, through their choices of relative reliability in narrators, reveal facets of their own personality and belief.

unthinkable come to pass, the

A condition in STORY similar to the rubber-necking along four-lane highways when there is a pile-up. People want to see the wreckage. The READER wants the worst-case-scenario, is eager to delve the mind of a CHARACTER as the wreck is played out.

Here we are, then, at a crucial point in a story where the WRITER discovers the true site of mischief and energy: the meeting point where the worst fears of the writer and one or more characters meet—and then circumstances up the ante. It is more than a drug deal gone sour (*No Country for Old Men*), or the sudden resignation of one of the team of bank robbers (*Dog Day Afternoon*), or the protagonist of *Vanity Fair* thinking she had married her way into a modicum of respectability. Llewellyn Moss, while out hunting, chances upon the money in *No Country,* and then things become even more unthinkably inevitable when Anton Chigurh enters the story. The two remaining bank robbers in *Dog Day* become enmeshed in a standoff with the police, which was more or less expected—the unthinkable element was the revelation of why the bank was robbed in the first place. Thinking she has achieved some measure of respectability and security in her marriage to the equivalent of a low-echelon civil servant, Becky Sharp is given the following proposal: "Come back and be my wife," Sir Pitt pleads. "Birth be hanged. You're as good a lady as ever I see....I'm an old man but a good'n. I'm good for twenty years. I'll make you happy, zee if I don't. You shall do what you like; spend what you like; and 'av it all your own way. I'll make you a zettlement. I'll do everything reg'lar." At which point "the old man fell down on his knees and leered at her like a satyr."

For an opportunist such as Becky Sharp, how is this moment the unthinkable come to pass? "Rebecca started back, a picture of consternation. In the course of this history, we have never seen her lose her presence of mind; but she did now." Author Thackeray reminds us how the tears now forming in her eyes were some of the most genuine she ever wept. "Oh, Sir Pitt!' she said. "Oh, sir-I-I'm married already."

One would not want to be around at dinnertime, when Becky's husband came home with a sporty kiss and a "Hey, Babycakes, what's for dinner?"

Invention begins in story after the unthinkable has happened. That is when the story kicks into high gear. In its way, the unthinkable may happen to the writer when, in one possible scenario, he is developing the texture and psyche of the ANTAGONIST and begins to realize he has created a much more interesting personality than he'd contrived for the PROTAGONIST.

vector

The direction a STORY takes and the magnitude of intensity with which it moves (see ARC); a line that represents the goal-seeking movement of a DRAMATIC NARRATIVE; the orbital path of the attempt(s) made by one or more CHARACTERS to cope with a dramatic problem.

A vector is a quantity with some degree of magnitude or motion as well as a direction. What better way to look at story: A dramatic force with some inherent inevitability, pointed in some specific direction.

A group of individuals seated at a large dining table is not a story; in fact, it's barely a CONCEPT until someone at the far reaches of the table asks for someone at the other end to pass the mashed potatoes. Now we have an essential ingredient—someone wanting something. All we need now is OPPOSITION, as in someone saying, No, the last time you were passed the potatoes no one else got any. Had the request to pass the mashed potatoes been politely and promptly filled, there would also have been no story because there was neither opposition nor any demonstrable ingenuity on the part of the individual making the request.

Vector is the tracking of initiative against the friction and inertia of opposition. This is another way of saying that the emerging character with some want or need must earn his or her place by taking some steps toward achieving the GOAL, must not be awarded the goal as a result of PASSIVITY or lack of caring about the OUTCOME. It matters less whether the character is successful than if the character tries to implement a strategy. Even though the PROTAGO-

NIST of Jack London's short story "To Build a Fire" is ultimately unsuccessful and dies in his attempts at a relatively simple goal, the story resonates poignancy because the character tried. (See THROUGHLINE.)

venture

A deliberate undertaking or plan; the ACTION taken by CHARACTERS based on a DECISION to proceed with an idea, opinion, or AGENDA; going forth with an agenda as GOAL, against possible risk; an action thought to provide some profitable OUTCOME.

Some characters venture opinions or advice to others, the risk being they may be disagreed with or outright shouted down. Some characters venture forth physically, perhaps tentatively, perhaps even foolishly, hopeful of achieving an inertia or momentum that will carry them further along the path to a goal.

One example of a remarkable and frightening venture is presented to the reader on the first page of Emma Donoghue's novel *Room* when a young woman, herself a captive, attempts to escape from a ten-by-thirteen-foot room with her five-year-old son. Satirist Christopher Moore uses a WRITER'S venture in *Fool,* his wild-ride take-off on *King Lear* where Pocket, Lear's jester, attempts to stave off mischief from Lear's daughters and Edmund, the bastard son of the Earl of Gloucester.

Ventures do not have to be doomed from the start; whether they are ROMANCE, ADVENTURE, or fanciful speculation, they may close on a THEME reflecting the positive joys of making plans, then setting forth to accomplish them.

verb tenses

TOOLS for the dramatic expression of time or the articulation of time filtered through ACTION; a method of measuring when an action takes place; the demarcation between past, present, and future actions.

One notable way to distinguish the accomplished WRITER from the beginner is to notice how much more graceful and conversational the narrative of the accomplished writer emerges. Much of this effect comes from the way the writer deals with verb tenses.

In conventional DRAMATIC NARRATIVE, the writer uses the immediate past tense—the preterit—to convey action taking place now. "John woke up early this morning" is understood by the READER to mean, Here is John, waking up at this very moment. If someone in the scene wants to make sure John is indeed awake, that person will ask, "Are you awake?" or the present participle form, "Are you waking up?"

John may provide a further clue by responding that he is "already up," or that he has been "up for some time." This time frame can be facilitated with the use of already (John was already awake when the alarm sounded) or by the introduction of the auxiliary verb "had" (John had been awake for nearly an hour when the alarm sounded). In every case we have a sense of John's waking progress and the further awareness of his preparedness for what is to come. The only thing we've missed is capturing John at the precise moment of his movement from sleep to wakefulness, which is "John was waking up just as the alarm sounded."

Conditional circumstances are expressed with adverbial help. "Ordinarily John would have slept until six thirty, but this morning was special; he was awake just before five thirty."This construction allows us a peek at John's usual habits, a sense of the specialness of today, as well as the precise time that he awoke on this morning of the story.

Starting about the mid 1960s, narrative writers began employing the present tense to track dramatic action. "John wakes up just as the alarm sounds."To use this verb tense format to indicate that John had been awake for some time, we bring in the auxiliary verb format:"John has been awake for over an hour..."

The conditional approach is rendered in present tense with a slight shift to the tense of the auxiliary verb."John is usually able to sleep until the alarm sounds, but today he is up an hour early."

INTERIOR MONOLOGUE and expressions of subjective volition also have usage shifts that have become conventional. However correct it is for John to wonder in a THIRD- PERSON narrative, "Now what will I do?"—the conventional approach has become a shift in the pronoun and verb tense, "Now what would he do, he wondered." Likewise, while grammatically correct for John to think, "I can't go on like this"—the conventional narrative use has become, "He couldn't go on like this."

Cluing the reader that an action under observation has been completed in the past is done by using the auxiliary verb "had.""John had wanted to go" becomes an indication that John had at one time in the past wanted to go. He may have a different feeling about it now:"At the time, John had wanted to go, but now he was glad he'd remained home" is a straightforward rendition showing us John's past and present feelings and, in the bargain, demonstrating the need to watch one's use of the auxiliary verb *had*, which appears considerably less formal and clunky if used as a contraction as in he'd, she'd, or you'd and I'd.

"I have gone" implies completed past action.

"I went" implies having gone there once, probably witnessed by the reader.

"I used to go" implies having gone there a number of times in the past.

"I might have gone "implies the possibility of not remembering ("Did I or did I not go?") Or it can lead up to a mitigating circumstance that explains why I didn't go.

"I'll do it later" implies future conditional intention.
"I shall do it later" implies future volition.

A good standard for adopting such conventions of verb tense to fit one's individual narrative style is to read writers whose work you admire, noting the places where they so adroitly convey the differences between completed action, recently completed action, ongoing or continuous action, conditional probability, and future probability. The important thing to remember is how helpful verb tenses are in articulating the characters' relationships to the time they are in and the actions they performed, are now performing, or are considering performing.

verisimilitude
The overall sense of believability in the dramatic rendition of a person, place, or thing; a convincing sense of authenticity about a NARRATIVE; an override on the READER's skepticism and sense of disbelief.

In spite of some WRITERS' defensive, "But it happened that way in real life," verisimilitude makes the reader forget about such quibbles and settle into the STORY; it is a quality, almost pointillist in nature, of small, significant details that convey a landscape of authenticity to the reader.

vernacular
The local or native language of a time and place as opposed to the formal, academic, and literary usage of speech and text; a slang or patois of an area or group of individuals; a stylistic rendition of an ethnic, geographic, or social milieu.

To impart a note of ROMANTICISM to vernacular, think of it as the voice of a particular people. To politicize, think of vernacular as the voice of a particular people under contentious circumstances. To dramatize, think of vernacular as the expression of one or more CHARACTERS in a tense, confrontational setting.

Some examples of the exemplary use of vernacular speech:

1. Tom Joad, toward the end of *The Grapes of Wrath:* "I'll be all around in the dark. I'll be wherever you can look. Wherever there's a fight so hungry people can eat, I'll be there. Wherever there's a cop beatin' up a guy, I'll be there. I'll be in the way guys yell when they're mad—I'll be in the way kids laugh when they're hungry an' they know supper's ready. An' when the people are eatin' the stuff they raise, and livin' in the houses they build—I'll be there, too."
2. The entire first chapter of William Faulkner's 1940 novel, *The Hamlet,* is a stand-alone tale, "Spotted Horses," which, in addition to its bursting-at-the-seams humor, brings to vivid life the vernacular of rural Mississippi.

3. Doyle Redmond, narrator of Daniel Woodrell's *Give Us a Kiss,* on the drift from a failed marriage and a floundering life, driving a stolen Volvo:"I had a family errand to run, that's all, but I decided to take a pistol. It was just a little black thirty-two ladystinger and I tucked it into the blue pillowcase that held my traveling clothes. The pillowcase sat on the driver's seat, because you never know when you'll need to slide a hand in there, all of a sudden, somewhere along the road."

The use of vernacular brings to the page an evocation of carpentry so tight and exacting that it requires neither nail nor glue, relying instead on a particular cadence of language as it is thought and spoken and, indeed, a seemingly digitally recorded core sampling of a conversation. Thus do Tim Gautreaux's characters abide with the Cajun drawl of New Orleans, while Luis Alberto Urrea's Mexican characters reach for American words and concepts as though they were the last taco on the plate.

It is not enough to believe vernacular is rendered by removing terminal g's from gerunds or having a character observe how "him and me, we went to the movies." It is more in the order of listening to and engaging in conversation with the people whose language usage you are trying to portray—or, if you are writing a historical piece, of looking at contemporary records for long-since abandoned word usage, checking carefully the dates and notes in the venerable OED, and listening if possible to live sources of individuals speaking the language you are trying to suggest on paper. It is a need to do close research to find out whether the likes of "peachy," as in "That was peachy with me," was favored before "swell," as in "She was sure a swell lady." Or to find out if it was "girl" that was more commonly used in context with swell, as in, "She was sure a swell girl."

There are any number of reasons why a WRITER will try to adhere to Received Standard English (let's thank the newscasters and commentators on NPR for the American standard), including having come forth from an MFA program in Creative Writing. The English writer, Ian McEwan, in comparison with all the writers mentioned above, appears to write in the Received Standard English of the BBC. Other writers to the immediate north of McEwan, which is to say Scotland—writers such as Ian Rankin, Kate Atkinson, or Denise Mina—have evolved a plausible vernacular. These are examples of the writer's need to develop VOICE that serves her and her characters as well as the geographical and chronological situation of her story.

One way of becoming aware of the vernacular voice is to read writers who speak in them, and do it well. "You are not the kind of guy who would be at a place like this at this time of the morning." Thus begins *Bright Lights, Big City*, Jay McInerney's heavily 1980s vernacular novel. "How did you get here? It was your friend Tad Allagash. Your brain is rushing with Brazilian marching powder. You are talking to a girl with a shaved head. You want to meet the kind of girl who isn't going to be here. You want to read the kind of fiction this isn't. You give the girl some powder. She still doesn't want you. Things were fine once. Then you got married.

"Monday arrives on schedule. You are late for work. You buy *The Post* and read the Coma Baby story. Are you the Coma Baby? Of course you are. It's just a fucking metaphor. You reach the lobby of the famous New York magazine for which you work, take the elevator to the Department of Factual Verification and say hi to Megan. You hope your boss Ms Clara Tillinghast aka the Clinger doesn't want the French piece as they'll find out you lied about your fluency in your resume. You want to be a writer, not a fact-checker."

Hint: An actor preparing for a role is much the same as a writer looking for voice in which to cast and then present a story. One way to find out if the voice—especially dialogue and vernacular—works is to read the work aloud until there are no lines to be stumbled over.

victim

A CHARACTER who is the recipient of a real or imagined injustice; an individual affected by adversity; one whose AGENDA, health, plans, and general sense of well-being are diverted or destroyed by an outside force.

Victims have real estate with a view on the literary LANDSCAPE, standing in line to be first to claim the role. A victim, by definition, has experienced (or believes he has experienced) some force of EVENT that has derailed his ASPIRATIONS and his hoped-for rewards, allowing him in some cases to stop all developmental motion, take on the mantle of the martyr, and luxuriate in the misfortune. Other victims of birth or CIRCUMSTANCE or both get up, brush off the dust, then get back to the business at hand.

He or she who proclaims victimhood the loudest is likely suspect of malingering or playing on sympathy. Neither is attractive. A character is a victim as a consequence of having ventured something, taken a RISK, hoped a hope. Such activity is not lost on the READER, who is now prepared to invest hard-earned EMPATHY in such a character.

There is a delicate balance to accepting one's fate; should one go meekly or with a fight? Should one wail loudly after reversal (such as, say, Silas Marner, when his miserly stash was stolen) or be the stoic? It helps to know the character in some detail before inflicting the status of victim on him; his response may well provide the EXIT STRATEGY for the story. Does a SETBACK enhance the character's forward inertia or diminish it?

A character who wishes to avenge victim status is a good candidate for reader sympathy. Even Ahab, setting forth to hunt down the whale, though extreme, nevertheless excites our understanding and sympathy, even our grudging respect. A character who welcomes victim status as an excuse for avoiding future venture is an individual who will not have many rooters among the readership.

Hint: To stir up the potential of mischief for the sake of creating new stories, consider your take on Herman Melville's eponymous Bartleby, "pallidly neat, pitiably respectable, incurably forlorn," then consider his inner core. Consider how you would portray him if you were an actor, and how you would move him forth as a character you had created. Is Bartleby a victim?

vision

The WRITER'S outlook; a philosophical map of a particular segment of humanity; an ATTITUDE toward a system or condition of behavior; an emotional assessment of life and its denizens; the way a writer looks at material.

Along with VOICE, vision is a significant, transformational factor in determining how a writer views CIRCUMSTANCES, turns them into dramatic situations, and populates them with distinctive CHARACTERS. Writers may have a cynical outlook or one that is preternatural in its optimism. There is no right or wrong choice, only the need for honesty. A writer who is notable for technique but no vision will produce work that has the same effect as the floats in the Rose Parade, or piñatas used for holiday or party celebrations, or paper cups intended for single use. The technique will trump the STORY—and while being amazed by the technique, the READER will mourn the loss of DRAMA.

Regardless of the size or nature of the LANDSCAPE, the ripened writer will see it with all its quirks and dents, will know if the undersides of the bureau drawers have been painted or varnished, will be aware if there are any recycled parts within it, and will have taken pains to see that everything is in smooth working order. Whether the setting is a colony on Mars, a girl's school above Mill Valley in northern California, or a patch of backyard garden, the LANDSCAPE will seem important to the reader because of the way it and the characters he has connected to it are regarded by the writer.

Writers variously think the world is going to hell in a hand basket, is a venue for unparalleled chaos, spawns mediocrity, is a splendid opportunity for growth and progress. To the extent they are capable of dramatizing these views, they achieve readerships and, as a consequence of that, exert some influence on what their readers believe. To the extent that writers cannot dramatize these feelings, they push their readers back from direct engagement and end up lecturing their readers rather than entertaining and challenging them.

Pick a handful of writers—say five—who entertain you. Compare these with a group of writers who cannot seem to get beyond the merest semblance of plot and whose characters are as stiff and uncomfortable as though they were first-time visitors at a family gathering of an intended lover. Compare the differences between the two groups of writers. Notice the difference in the physicality of the characters from writers you enjoy, the way their characters react to one another, produce CHEMISTRY, produce a tangible feel of a particular vision. Study, for example, Louise Erdrich's memorable first novel, *Love Medicine*—which will perhaps distract you away from the intent of this exercise thanks to Erdrich's evocations of her characters, but which will give you a full, vivid sense of her overall vision as well as the dramatic energy within her scenes.

Vision and voice—what a writer sees and how the writer relates it.

These questions will help you focus on your vision:

Who are you?

How do you see the world?

Is the world you are creating a safe place? Safer than the world of reality?

If you were writing fantasy, what element would you bring to your fantasy landscape from the world of reality?

What is the prize in your story? How does attaining this prize support or enhance how you see the world? How your character sees the world?

If you had to divide humanity into two opposing approaches, which pair would you choose? Winners and Losers? Givers and Takers? Old and Young? Inner-directed and other- directed?

In your world, are there happy endings or morose ones?

What is the biggest fear held by your protagonist? Your minor characters? Are these your fears as well? How are these fears manifested in your vision of the world?

vital lie

The revealing cultural convention or moral absolute one or more front-rank CHARACTERS in a STORY believes to be true, then COMES TO REALIZE is bogus; an ethical principal or position taken by an ANTAGONIST in opposition to a PRO-TAGONIST; the moral license for politically-motivated behavior.

The vital lie in fiction is the attitudinal and entitled platform of characters who represent a mindset and way of life that appears to withhold acceptance to the PROTAGONIST and his or her associates. The lie may begin with characters from the privileged classes referring to working-class individuals as "good country people," signifying a surface respect that masks a patronizing sneer. It may just as well have its origins in the envy-riddled contempt with which the working classes regard the affluent.

To dramatize the vital lie, the WRITER needs to determine the polestar of a representative character, then construct a plausible path for the character to have followed in order to arrive there.

The vital lie is THE ELEPHANT IN THE LIVING ROOM, the thing that is seen but not acknowledge; it is variously gender prejudice, racial prejudice, and class prejudice. It is story in the making.

Every culture has at least one vital lie it tells itself. Like humor, the vital lie always has a target. The vital lie represents an opportunity for the writer to become political, choosing an accepted explanation offered by a family, an organization, institution, or philosophy, then representing it in a way that conveys to the READER the force of the lie and its consequences. The character of Nora Helmer in Henrik Ibsen's drama *A Doll's House* represents an embodiment of a vital lie, her recognition of it, her decisions to expose it, and the consequences to her, her family, and subsequent generations of women in the real world who were affected by the lie she chose to no longer live.

voice

The resident sound made by a NARRATIVE text when being read; the PITCH and timbre of the author's emotional tone; an intended or revealed-through-betrayal attitude resident in text; the DNA of an author's agenda.

An author seeks and is said to have found voice when a clear tone beyond STYLE and content can be found in all the material that WRITER produces.

Virtuoso musicians are recognized by the manner in which they produce tone, either through an instrument or in vocal rendition. Actors convey voice through their movements, manipulation of time, or projection of attitude. Writers also express voice, which hints at attitude and the degree of emotional involvement with the matter at hand. Voice begins to appear, then deepen in a writer in direct proportion to the writer's honesty in dealing with interests, passions, and philosophy. The writer who has found voice has recognized vital interior forces and concerns.

Voice may be discovered in accidental encounters where the writer dramatizes specific personal concerns that seem, at first, to appear from nowhere. It is the direct result of passions. Voice is the result of caring for someone or something, or recognizing a portion of the writing self as though it were a long lost friend or relative. READERS need not agree with a writer's particular passions or politics to recognize the qualities of that writer's voice.

Often conflated or confused with STYLE, voice is the personality of the writer resident in text. As a young writer develops voice, it can be instructive and rewarding to read aloud from your own work as well as the work of others, to be willing to work harder and think deeper when that voice sounds false or off—and revise and edit toward truth and clarity. It can be instructive to note that the great jazz musician Sidney Bechet was proficient on the clarinet, but his taking up the soprano saxophone secured his distinctive voice and led to his remarkable discoveries as a musician.

Although there is no substitute for story, voice is a major vehicle for expression in all narrative.

Examples of contemporary writers whose work reflects an identifiable—even unmistakable—voice: Ernest Hemingway, Deborah Eisenberg, Annie Proulx, Louise Erdrich, and Daniel Woodrell. Nor would you have difficulty picking out Alice Munro.

volition

A CHARACTER seen in the act of facing a DECISION and making a CHOICE; the ACTS performed or not performed by a character in service of an AGENDA; a necessary quality of determination and purpose resident in a character; the inertial guidance system of a front-rank character.

Integral to any understanding of character and the subsequent empathy for or antagonism to that character, volition is the analog of the purring engine, already converting fuel to energy, ready to move forth with élan. Volition is the engine of personality for a character, the defining set of impressions that determine how the character will behave in a given situation. Will that character elect, as Melville's iconic Bartleby did, to prefer not to? Perhaps the character is more of a mindset with Margaret Mitchell's Scarlett O'Hara, and her memorable "Tomorrow is another day."

Scout, the narrator of Harper Lee's *To Kill a Mockingbird*, who had to make some tough choices about the small Alabama town in which she was raised; what innate force propelled her? What of Hester Prynne in *The Scarlet Letter*? It is highly probable that her early independence and strong-willed nature led her to the rebellious affair that resulted in Pearl, a child born out of wedlock. Although the narrator appears to disapprove of her behavior, his increasing sense of admiration becomes apparent as she, subject to the humiliation and alienation inflicted on her, becomes contemplative as she develops into a more dimensional character than any other in the novel.

For the WRITER, learning who the character *is* becomes the first step in a triad of priority. Given what a particular character wants, at what point will the character's *character* allow her to leap from single dimension into the realm of "yes!" Will the character make that leap? Now comes volition: What is the character willing to do to accomplish the goal? With that awareness radiating within the character and suspected all along by the READER, what explosive results will come forth? With persistence and honesty, the writer is drawn into the equation with the discovery of the depths to which the character will go. Did, for instance, Kate Atkinson, author of *Started Early, Took My Dog,* know the extent of dissatisfaction her retired cop, Tracy Waterhouse, now working as a security guard in a shopping mall clothing store, was experiencing when she made the unplanned (and completely believable) decision to buy? Through Tracy's eyes, we see the young girl being yanked along with great impatience, shouted at with even greater rancor for dawdling. Perhaps the action was as much a SURPRISE to the author as it was to the character. This is more than a hint; it is an imperative: The surprise must also surprise the writer. If it does not, then it is not a surprise—it is a contrivance.

voyage, the

The place a STORY or NOVEL takes a READER; the journey of DISCOVERY made by a WRITER during the course of developing and telling a STORY; a destination neither reader nor writer expected at the outset.

The success of a novel or short story is in direct proportion to the vibrant presence of destination to which the reader and writer are delivered at conclusion.

vulnerability

The risky condition or state CHARACTERS experience in STORIES which leaves them open to be harmed, harassed, or even hurt by external circumstances or by the activities of other characters; a state of unpreparedness or weakness resident in an individual character; a parasitic ATTITUDE or EMOTION such as HUBRIS, pride, prejudice in a character that signals to the READER potentials for dramatic opposition or REVERSAL.

An influential presence in story, vulnerability in a character adds to the impression of PLAUSIBILITY in that individual, enlists the reader in the process of wanting that character to succeed or fail, and paves the way for potential conflicts of interest or changing of AGENDAS.

Questions to ask about a character: What is he/she vulnerable to? Flattery? Enhanced social position? Power? Love? Money? Enhanced professional position? Guilt? Vulnerability, or a combination of vulnerabilities, can help define a character while simultaneously augmenting the dramatic quagmire in which the character struggles. Further question: Is a character who is not vulnerable a plausible human being?

~W~

weather report

Unnecessary description often found at BEGINNINGS of NOVELS and SHORT STORIES, but also in chapter beginnings, where WRITER describes weather conditions with such profundity and éclat as to undercut the presence of CHAR-ACTERS and STORY; an attempt to convince READERS they are in the presence of an author who truly knows how to write; an authorial attempt to infuse thematic content into a narrative.

Weather can and often does have demonstrable effect on story and the characters within it, but—to use a PATHETIC FALLACY—readers appreciate a moderate, unhyperbolic hand in the rendering. Storm clouds may indeed gather in ominous display if they are harbingers of meteorological events; they are not needed to symbolize difficulties in the lives of the characters.

Western novel, the

A longform NARRATIVE, set in the area defined by the western slope of the Rocky Mountains to the east, with Oklahoma, Texas, and New Mexico thrown in, and the Pacific Ocean to the west, from about 1850 until the present day; any pulp, mainstream, or literary narrative dealing with a combination of moral and ethical issues being investigated in an atmosphere suggestive of Western issues and NEEDS; a regional novel evocative of the customs, language, and politics of the American West.

The Western novel was thought by critics and publishers to have had its heyday before the ending of World War II, a belief ratified by the minimal press run of Larry McMurtry's 1985 novel, *Lonesome Dove,* a sprawling, laconic, and limber narrative reminiscent in its evocative way of a clutch of wild horses at playful romp. *Lonesome Dove,* which won the Pulitzer Prize for literature that year, has cowboys, Indians, cattle drives, cattle rustling, saloons, and dance hall girls; it features the dry stoicism of aging lawmen, broken relationships, sudden and violent death, horses, and the relentlessness of the sun scorching everything, including the patience of otherwise taciturn men. Also included are women who resent the dull humdrum of prairie life and the need to have a decent dinner for the men who work the farms and ranches. In short, *Lonesome Dove* has humanity, just as surely as McMurtry's earlier works, *Horseman, Pass by,* and *The Last Picture Show* captured core samplings of the artifacts and ZEITGEIST of particular times in the American West.

Early Western classics were unabashed celebrations of the openness and scope of the country, the individuals who were drawn to it and, in particular, those who brought independence of spirit and vision to it. For a time, the hot Western topic was the sense of being on the cusp of change—from openness to enclaves of civilization, as in Glendon Swarthout's 1975 contribution, *The Shootist.* Elmore Leonard's 1961 title, *Hombre,* dealt with the issue of race in the form of a protagonist who was half-white, half Apache, demonstrating with acuity the risks of living in both worlds. Since about 1980, the emerging themes for the Western have been nostalgia—fond recollections of what was—and the inevitability of change. The West was touted as America's manifest destiny; the Western, ever evolving, is an apt vessel for its literary future.

The Western novel began with Owen Wister's 1902 epic, *The Virginian,* which helped articulate and define codes of behavior that through CLICHÉ and repetition became stereotypes of what to expect of the genre. That seemingly iconic 1912 work from dentist-turned-author Zane Grey, *Riders of the Purple Sage,* gave us Lassiter, a prototype Western hero who can also be seen in Jack Schaefer's *Shane,* published in 1949 and, although more NUANCED and believable, in Schaefer's 1981 portrait of the life of a cowboy, *Monte Walsh.*

Walter Van Tilburg Clark's 1940 Western, *The Ox-Bow Incident,* is set in the Nevada of 1885, taking on the theme of frontier justice and its applications to strangers appearing in the midst of a small town where everyone knows everyone else. A.B. Guthrie's 1947 novel, *The Big Sky,* uses three fictional mountain men to dramatize the early Caucasian denizens of the West—foragers and hunters-and-gathers, to use the anthropological terms—setting the stage for the farmers and ranchers to follow. *The Big Sky* is undershot with a sense of Paradise about to devolve, of a persistent sense of impending foreclosure as humanity *en masse* moved to encounter it. The Western novel is a HISTORICAL NOVEL, just as likely to have its pulp and mainstream visions as any other genre, but equally apt to have works of substantial worth that accurately define and dramatize the human condition, as it was and as it still is. Even with the enormous success of *Lonesome Dove,* however, the historical WRITER is likely to find a sense of publishers' CONVENTIONAL wisdom that the Western has seen its heyday, but it would be a shame for the writer who has a genuine feel for the land, people, history, and potential of the American West to be barbed-wired off by such conventional wisdom.

whale, the great white (aka Moby-Dick)

A dramatic partner to the PROTAGONIST in STORY landscape; a presence eventually discernible as having an AGENDA opposing the protagonist. (See WORTHY OPPONENT.)

what is the story about?

An inventory of dramatic essentials for the WRITER to keep in mind during REVISION; a template defining the behavior and GOALS of CHARACTERS and generating the outcome or PAYOFF.

Many writers embark on a STORY to see what it is really about only to discover it is about ways to achieve the stated goal of the PROTAGONIST, as well as possibly to better understand how to cope with some existential situation—love, death, birth, career, perhaps even ethical conflict. It's equally true that basic answers to the question sound banal, insubstantial: *The Wizard of Oz* is about Dorothy getting home; *Hamlet* is about a son avenging his father's murder, *Great Expectations* is about Pip being unspoiled by his rise in social class.

Not sure what your story is about? Try asking what the main character wants. If that produces an unsatisfactory answer, try factoring in what the ANTAGONIST wants. The dramatic premise of even such a dense work as *Les Miserables* can be articulated so simply: John Valjean wants, more or less, to have his debt to society deemed paid but Inspector Javert's insatiable demand for justice stands in his way. The story is about the convergence of two powerful forces—as is, at its core, almost every story ever written.

where would they rather be?

A provocative, useful question to ask of CHARACTERS before introducing them into any SCENE. It is quite possible for them to want to be in the current scene, AGENDAS and AMBITIONS burning brightly or fearful of potential consequences. Also it is possible they would prefer to be elsewhere, doing things other than what is required of them in the instant moment.

The answer to the question informs what the character thinks, says, does; it keeps the character on track moment to moment; it keeps the WRITER focused on the needs of the STORY, and it keeps the READER guessing (which is the place the reader wants to be—readers who stop guessing tend to go on to other books). The ACTION or overwhelming NEEDS of a scene, combined with the character's desire to be in it will influence the choice of words used in rendering the character and the PACE with which the character performs.

It is important to realize that the character's preference does not operate on a right-wrong basis but rather on an opportunity-providing basis. The waiter working the dinner shift may want instead to be attending an acting class or, better still, be a character in a performance in a theater, providing the temptation for that waiter to behave at the present task of serving meals in ways that produce a chemistry to the scene and perhaps even a CONSEQUENCE.

Wile E. Coyote

A scruffy, scheming, cartoon CHARACTER who, on appearances and behavior, would go unnoticed among the individuals in a Dostoevsky NOVEL. Coyote lives in the butte- and mesa-littered American Southwest. On closer consideration, the Coyote and the desert are as right for one another as Dostoevsky's characters are right for the press and scurry of the urban landscape they inhabit.

The Coyote has one essential goal: to capture and devour Roadrunner, a bird of the cuckoo family who haunts the hardscrabble terrain of the Southwest. He, of course, will never succeed in his quest. Not only is Roadrunner a fast, shrewd cookie and WORTHY OPPONENT, but because of the simple dramatic principle that were Coyote to realize his goal, there would no longer be a story. Doomed to a series of near misses and frustrations in his attempts to outsmart Roadrunner, Coyote's constant companion is humiliation. We watch him with fascination and admiration at the way he shrugs off his last humbling defeat, then sets forth again.

A literary descendant of Joel Chandler Harris' iconic B'rer Fox, the Coyote is a candidate for beatification and ultimate sainthood as the patron saint of characters. He has a singular, ongoing goal that occupies him every moment he is on stage. His devices and stratagems have the complexity born of mounting desperation. He is so intent on bringing The Roadrunner to ground that he frequently finds himself in mid-air, his paws cycling in wild attempts to gain some footing—but it is too late; he has only the downward fall to disaster. He is, as Mark Twain wrote of the generic coyote, "a living, breathing allegory of want. He is always hungry." The Coyote frequently obtains materials and devices from The Acme Company, a mail-order distributor. These items, in their ludicrous way, add to the Coyote's plight; they are technology gone mad. They are particularly out of place here on the mesas and buttes. After a time, we no longer question the Coyote's use of such absurd contraptions, recognizing them as growing signs of his desperation. These extreme remedies plus the Coyote's own hunger-driven ingenuity comprise his TOOL KIT.

The dramatic center of The Coyote is in his single-minded pursuit of his agenda, making him worth concentrating on while creating any front-rank character. As you create characters or encounter them in your reading, consider comparison points between The Coyote and CAPTAIN AHAB or, for that matter, the other notable Herman Melville creation, Bartleby the Scrivener. Jay Gatz, better known to us as *The Great Gatsby*, is Wile E. Coyote incarnate. You don't think so? Look what Gatsby did in pursuit of Daisy. So is that other morose character from Fitzgerald's *Tender Is the Night*, Dick Diver.

Look closely and you will see traces of the Coyote in such historical forerunners as Jane Eyre and Becky Sharp. Now that you think of it, doesn't Inspector Javert of *Les Miserables* bear resemblance? Shakespeare, too, had his own pre-coyote characters in the likes of Sir John Falstaff and Coriolanus. Not to forget Don Quixote.

Wile E. Coyote is the antithesis of Joseph Campbell's Hero's Journey, instead the Natty Bumpo/Deerslayer of NOIR FICTION, leading us away from the happy and manufactured endings of the early days of the novel and into the still unexplored dark sides of reality and humanity Huck Finn set after when he lit out for the territory ahead.

willing suspension of disbelief, the
   Believability.
   Coined by critic-poet Samuel Taylor Coleridge in 1817 in his *Biographia Literaria*, the concept accounts for the inertia of skeptical disbelief a WRITER must overcome in a READER in order to have his narrative accepted as real. Got that? The writer has to sell them on her STORY. That's *sell*, as in convince the customer to buy. With so many books being published and so many sources apparent for short stories, readers are daring writers to be more convincing at pain of not pursuing a story to its conclusion. Sophisticated readers have come a long way from the early days of the NOVEL and SHORT STORY; they certainly know the CHARACTERS are inventions of the author. But they also know that a skillful writer can make them forget this fact, empathize with fictional beings, root for their favorites, and experience severe distress when their favorite CHARACTERS experience reversals.
   One way a writer can do this is to quickly present characters in the midst of their attempts to solve a problem or a REVERSAL of fortune—to plunge the reader into the thick of the action. Another way to accomplish this goal is to show characters setting off on a QUEST, a perilous journey, or a new venture that will accelerate their risk. Yet another approach is to endow the character with some physical or emotional flaw that they must struggle to overcome. Johnny Tremaine, the young, eponymous apprentice to Paul Revere, experiences an accident early on; molten silver is spilled on his hand, permanently fusing his thumb to his palm. In Tracy Chevalier's novel *Girl with a Pearl Earring*, a young peasant girl is forced to take a job as a maid when her artisan father is blinded by an exploding kiln.
   Every SHORT STORY and NOVEL, regardless of how fantastic or quotidian, has to cope with this problem: Does the reader believe implicitly in the characters and situations?
   Step One in this remarkable alchemy, from the dross of initial concept to the gold of finished work, begins with the *writer* believing in the characters. By indirection, the key to overcoming disbelief is VULNERABILITY; no matter what the characters are vulnerable to—greed, love, fear, confusion, ambition—that vulnerability becomes a wedge that lifts the fence of plausibility. The flaw of vulnerability lends the fictional character humanity; we might like Indiana Jones for taking us along with him on his grand adventures, but we love him because he's afraid of snakes. (See PLAUSIBILITY.)

wisdom
   A system, vision, or range of *a priori* experience that will lead an individual, a culture, or group to presume functional understanding of the behavioral qualities on which the universe functions; a sense of presumption of knowledge by CHARACTERS in a STORY; an attempt by characters to understand how and why things, systems, and people behave.

Wisdom is a quality young characters in COMING-OF-AGE stories are reminded they lack by older characters, making immediately for generational CONFLICT, a primary cause in the story. Wisdom is a quality of understanding that younger characters believe they can do without, coming, on occasion, to regret that earlier belief and, incidentally, making incrementally for a secondary cause of conflict in longer stories.

A character who is sadder but wiser is a character who regrets not having appropriate wisdom at the right time. The shrewd writer will see that wisdom is as change-ridden and ephemeral as the human condition, making it and its acquisition as vital a dramatic force as the rival forces of accruing financial fortune and inspiring love.

withholding dramatic information

A strategy for creating narrative TENSION and/or SUSPENSE; keeping information from the READER or one or more CHARACTERS; using the curiosity or lack thereof in a character to influence AGENDA; creating awareness in the reader and/or in characters of SECRETS relating to the theme or actual OUTCOME of a STORY.

Story, however ambiguous in nature or ELLIPTICAL in ORBIT, is an outgrowth of a natural inclination to assign NARRATIVE to EVENTS whether they are as complex and intertwined as generational family history or as random as boy-meets-girl—or boy-meets-boy or girl-meets-girl.

Story is implicitly and sometimes explicitly a tale told to provide evidence that life has meaning, that certain events were ordained if not preordained, that human behavior and destiny is not a mere series of random events, atomic particles spinning about in a reactor or collider that can be turned off for the night. The DOMINO THEORY, CAUSALITY, and DETERMINISM—these are not merely items in a WRITER'S TOOL KIT, they are the stuff of life. And as we are living our lives, we don't always—we may, indeed, rarely—have all the facts at hand that would impact our decisions in the moments in which they must or should be made.

The reader likes to see parallels between the stuff of story (causality and consequence) and the seeming inevitability of events in real life because this dramatic parallelism produces a sense of reality in the story, while at the same time producing tension.

The skilled writer has learned to withhold vital information, making the reader curious about it, avid for more. CURIOSITY ranks just below TENSION and SUSPENSE as an important mortar, holding the isolated bricks of dramatic detail together. Until the reader has become interested to the point of empathy, details about a particular character often bore more than they illustrate. Some of the background material, for instance, about Eilis Lacey, Colm Toibin's protagonist in his 2009 novel, *Brooklyn*, is inconsequential until the reader has seen Eilis performing in social situations, at which point the events become poignant to the point of being heart-wrenching: this information has been artfully manipulated so that it appears to emerge from the character rather than Post-It notes from the author.

Never tell the reader more than the reader wants to know at any given time is an underlying mantra of *The Fiction Writer's Handbook*. Observing it becomes an effective restraint for the writer to keep in mind. Withhold, then pay out in slow, incident-related doses. The downside of too much withholding can be seen in the novels of Ian McEwan (see *Saturday; The Innocent;* and *The Child in Time*), where the secrets to be discovered and the DEFINING MOMENTS present, on closer consideration and however bravura his technique, the image of a highly skilled dealer at a casino rather than a storyteller such as Michael Chabon (see *The Wonder Boys; Secrets of Pittsburgh;* and *The Yiddish Policeman's Union*).

What is the right balance between withholding and being manipulative? First of all, forget any stigma attached to the word "manipulative"—all storytellers manipulate, having chosen the beginning point of the story and the ending payoff, at the very least. Secondly, write from your own point of curiosity, playing to your own RATE OF DISCOVERY. Third, try not to attach too complex a meaning to things deliberately held in secret, traumas from past events that were completely or semi-occluded, or repressed memories suddenly unloosed on the consciousness. Secrets seem complex because of the downstream consequences readers and writers attach to them, which is, after all, part of their job, but while the "secrets" are being constructed, try to think of them in brief descriptions such as betrayal, pay-back, skeleton-in-the-closet, and the rewriting of family history. The devil of these secrets is in the details. Hinting at them and paying them out slowly gives them their full dramatic effect.

Wizard of Oz, the

The ideal NARRATIVE to examine for its thoughtful inclusion of basic elements supportive of STORY integrity. Just follow the yellow-brick PLOT line.

There is never any doubt of the answer to the question, *Whose story is it?* (Dorothy Gale's.)

There is no doubt about the GOAL or prize of the story. (For Dorothy to return home.)

The OBSTACLES are laid out carefully before Dorothy, and the DISCOVERY she makes is a learning experience (the Wizard is, although good natured about it, a humbug), as is the awareness, "There's no place like home."

Give this classic a close reading. Dissect it with detailed care; it is the READER's equivalent of a GPS, guiding you through the directional workings of a novel. By starting with *The Wizard of Oz,* and noting its construction, you'll be able to take on something as remote in style and as nuanced in content as Henry James's *The Ambassadors.* That story's hero, Lambert Strether, is not as remote from Dorothy Gale as, on first blush, it might appear. He, too, is yanked out of a familiar LANDSCAPE, and plunked into Paris, France—every bit as foreign to him as Oz is to Dorothy. Go ahead, take it from there, and keep your copy of *The Wizard of Oz* close by for reference when taking apart a work that puzzles you or when constructing your own new work.

worthy opponent

A CHARACTER whose personal and/or organizational interests run antithetical to the PROTAGONIST of a NOVEL or SHORT STORY; an individual of significant enough stature to insure a sense of fear in the reader that the protagonist will either lose outright or have to relinquish some of the PRIZE.

The concept of shooting FISH IN A BARREL comes to mind when considering the dynamics of the worthy opponent. It would take a poor shot indeed to miss hitting at least one fish thus constrained. By extension, an ANTAGONIST who is made to seem evil for its own sake or merely contrary for the sake of being contrary proves no real threat to the protagonist or the READER, leaving additional metaphors such as 'paper tiger' or 'tempest in a teapot' to hover over the story.

An ideal opponent for a protagonist in a story is a person who is in his or her own way every bit bigger-than-life than the protagonist, a person of steely desire and purpose, equipped with such tools as a brilliant sense of humor, an obvious intelligence, adaptability, charm, and that great catch-all, people skills. Try matching the rascally Harry Lime of *The Third Man* with the protagonist, Western adventure writer, Holly Martins.

The goal is to provide the worthy opponent with enough clout that the OUTCOME of the story is in doubt to the very end. A plausible opponent is one who might, in a MYSTERY, outwit the detective; win the heart of the protagonist in a ROMANCE; supply superior magic in a FANTASY; have a grittier social/existential problem than the protagonist in a YA NOVEL; have loftier motives than the protagonist in a SCIENCE FICTION NOVEL. There is no GENRE in which an unworthy opponent should feel at home.

We may begin historically with Achilles and Hector in *The Iliad*, where it is still possible to root for Hector against the anointed hero, Achilles; then we can move to a platform where a personified Nature presents a worthy opponent, first as the whale in *Moby-Dick*, then as the marlin in *The Old Man and the Sea*.

In the original *Star Trek* TV series, the Romulan commander tells Captain Kirk, "I regret that we meet in this way. You and I are of a kind. In a different reality, I could have called you friend." In the TV drama *The Wire*, OMAR LITTLE was heard to observe, "A man got to have a code." Little had such a code, lived by it, and, reminiscent of Greek tragedy, died by it. Another splendid example of worthiness in opponents also appeared in *The Wire*, where the characters of Avon Barksdale and Russell "Stringer" Bell were school chums, then loving partners in a flourishing Baltimore drug trade before a clash of philosophy led each to ACTION that betrayed the other. The common denominator here among worthy opponents is that the WO plausibly stands between the protagonist and the protagonist's GOALS.

One of the dividing lines between the worthy opponent and the mere opponent is fairness. The WO plays fair, in large measure because he is confident of his abilities and his cause. The mere opponent uses any means at his disposal to win. A helpful recipe for creating the WO: give him or her ten percent more in some relevant, thematic ability than you give the protagonist. Heat to boiling, then serve.

writer. the
> You.

At this point in your writing career, you've developed a measure of narrative and dramatic skills, even produced a modest body of NOVELS or SHORT STORIES. In all probability, you've experienced extraordinary, idiosyncratic pleasures, and known severe disappointments. You understand loss. Somewhere along the path of your decision to become a writer, you read one or more books or stories by other writers and were so taken by them that your decision to become a writer was formed.

How unfortunate for you that these same writers and their work made writing seem so simple that you believed writing was easy.

Only one way out now: Master your craft, then keep reaching.

writer's block
A strategic NARRATIVE impasse often analogous to a hangover, the culprit in this case not alcohol but over-thinking during writing time; the unwelcome presence of a cultural super-ego; a side-effect of the beginning WRITER's belief in the notion of a narrative arriving all at once in near perfect condition.

One of the more effective approaches to coping with this affliction is to move on to the next SCENE, leaving a Post-It note at the 'blocked' place— "confrontation between Bill and Jim goes here," or "sex scene goes here."

Another effective approach is to stop thinking about THEME- and PLOT-related matters in terms of questions. "What would Bill do now and is it plausible that Jim would want to stop him?" Move instead to the id-related mode by asking, What does Bill want now? Then listen for Bill's answer. If it turns out that Bill doesn't want anything right now, move on to the moment where he does want something.

During early draft stages, thought is not a helpful ally; rather it is the equivalent of the dog or cat that jumps up on the bed at night, wanting the precise place on the mattress occupied by the writer. The true, helpful ally is what the writer wants—repeat *wants*—to write, not what the writer thinks should be written. The Inner Editor is going to be trying to distract with you with complaints about your vocabulary, your punctuation skills, your grammar, and that dreadful D-word, that the work might be *Derivative*. "You are derivative," the Inner Editor will claim. "Worse yet, you are not even derivative of writers you admire." This is the one editor you do not want to heed; there are enough skilled and devoted ones out there for when the time comes. At the moment, you need to get words down on paper. Imagine yourself hanging a "Do not disturb" sign on the door of your brain, then begin to write, if only nouns and verbs at first. *Bill wanders into the room. Sees Mary reading, becomes curious, moves closer to see what she's reading.* Even this kind of writing brings you toward some kind of confrontation. No matter what the Inner Editor throws at you, throw something back. "Here," Mary said, "hold my glasses." *You call that writing?* the Inner Editor demands. Answer: Yes; you've got something coming. "What for?" Bill says. "So they won't get scratched when I take off my blouse," Mary answers. By which point, regardless of your age, gender, or sexual orientation, you will have become interested in the possibilities here and Inner Editor will scarcely matter.

writers conferences

Places where, under the guise of wanting to learn more about their craft, writers congregate in order to defend the rightness of what they have written. If they are able to secure agency representation to the point where they will have regular contact with editors, their entire sense of being right about what they have written will change.

writers workshops

A gathering of writers who meet to read and discuss their works in progress. Writers workshops are craft-oriented rather than occasions to show knowledge of critical terms. First-draft material is not only acceptable, it is encouraged.

Writers workshops should be moderated by an individual who has editorial and/or significant publishing experience. English teachers and professors are welcomed as group members but not as workshop leaders because English teachers and professors have the potential to think too much, which leads to compound verb tenses, diagrammed sentences, and the use of passive voice so common in academic writing.

If your workshop mates do not respond at all to something you have written, their non-response becomes the declarative sentence telling you to go back to the drawing board and take a close look at your dialogue for traces of conversation, at your narrative for soft spots, and at your interior monologue/free independent discourse for unnecessary attributions and explanation. Should your workshop mates tell you they want more details and BACKGROUND for your CHARACTERS, it means they are hooked. Never take the READER where the reader wants to go.

YA novel

A novel intended for the young adult readership (roughly between ages twelve and twenty); a novel with a protagonist in that age range; a novel with significant themes, problems, and issues relative to individuals of the twelve-to-twenty age group.

Remember: Young READERS read up—they like protagonists of at least their own age but enjoy identifying with characters from one to five years their senior.

YA fiction has increasingly moved toward cutting edge themes, language, and characterization, as for example Steve Berman's 2007 *Vintage:A Ghost Story*, in which a gay protagonist deals with issues of gayness, loneliness, and suicide; Judy Blume's *Forever*, which moves quickly past first sexual encounter into teen parenthood; Alice Hoffman's *Green Angels*, which dramatizes self-mutilation; and David Belbin's *Love Lessons*, which dramatizes teacher-student sex.

This is an exciting and demanding GENRE, one that has traditionally been the conscience of U.S. reading matter by staying on top of issues that appear at first blush to offer a helping hand to young readers who are overwhelmed by the apparent demands of the adult world, but which at the same time forces self-reflection in the adult world. Many adult readers were propelled into their reading habits by YA titles, some of which they discovered long after leaving their YA years behind them. J.D. Salinger's *The Catcher in the Rye*, Judy Bloom's *Hello, God, It's Me, Margaret*, and Robert Heinlein's *Have Space Suit—Will Travel*, all still in print, come to mind.

you

The unique persona of the WRITER; the experiences, opinions, tastes, and prejudices of the WRITER; the ATTITUDES, curiosities, and fears of the writer emerging through portrayal of CHARACTER, THEME, and RESOLUTION of STORIES. The totality of the resident writer within as it emerges in the writer's stories.

Each writer brings to story a particular set of sensitivities, sensory awareness, and attitude in the same way each actor puts his own stamp on a role. Could we imagine James Dean playing Hamlet? Could we imagine Norman Mailer capturing the angst and wrench of "Brokeback Mountain"? Similarly, could we imagine Mel Brooks doing Lear or Dustin Hoffman doing Rocky Balboa?

The question for the writer on any given story is *Why you?* This question is not by any means in the sense of *How dare you?* but rather *What do you bring to the story that gives it the ridges and whorls of your own writer fingerprint?* Would you bring Mel Brooks's antic humor to Lear or would you bring his incredible sadness over the loss of his wife, Anne Bancroft? Possibly a hint of both? What could make Dustin Hoffman want to do Rocky Balboa? What could possibly have possessed Philip Seymour Hoffman, a large man, to take on the portrayal of Truman Capote, an elfin presence?

There are no *right* answers as long as there are, indeed, answers, specific answers reflecting the reasons you were drawn into writing and find resonance in it—revenge, envy, proprietary power, exuberance at being alive, wanting to share a vision, wanting to take down a vision.

Look at it this way: In the beginning, your focus is primarily internal, finding the VOICE from which you write, getting words down on paper and learning to craft them into an intriguing whole. Later, that focus extends outward, to finding agency representation, then publication. After a few publications you will, if fortunate, be compared to other writers, living and dead. But then the focus will change once more, unless you take steps to prevent it, to where you are labeled with the dreaded d-word, *derivative*. When you are seen as deriving all your energy, voice and THEME from other writers—or, possibly, even your own early work—you will have either lost the YOU that drew you into writing or settled into a certain comfortable niche as writer, becoming lazy about the work that will allow *you* to mature. You will have become not a voice but a shrewd compiler of collage, bits and snippets pulled from elsewhere, arranged in some generic formula, a quick read while being stranded in an airport, but afterward a candidate for remainder dump bins, thrift store bargain shelves, and the 'free reading' pile at coffee shops. You'll have learned what some of the tools are, even how to use some of them, but you will not have listened to the genie in the bottle that is you, waiting to be let forth.

zeitgeist

The spirit or ghost of the time, from the German *zeit* = time, *geist* = spirit/ghost; a physical, emotional, and historical sense of a time and place.

A WRITER's job—among others—is to convey through dramatization the feel of a particular place at a particular time, among a particular group of people. CHARACTERS, whether directly or not, reflect the zeitgeist of their setting, whether at a family reunion, a school reunion, an application for a job, or the angst of delivering parents to a senior living facility. Some zeitgeists are gay, ebullient, filled with optimism; others reflect uncertainty or a the-sky-is-falling terror of things unseen and the uncertainty of the future. Every STORY has a zeitgeist, but it does not have to be expressed directly, rather being allowed to refract through the behavior of the characters.

Hint: at some point during the construction of a story, pinpoint the spirit of the time in which the story was set, then use that awareness as a polestar to guide the spoken and unspoken behavior of major characters. F. Scott Fitzgerald's characters, through their use of language and behavior, reflect the zeitgeist of the 1920s, the Jazz Age; Tim O'Brien's *The Things They Carried* reflects the zeitgeist of the Vietnam War; Jane Austen's *Pride and Prejudice* reflects the zeitgeist of nineteenth-century England.

BIBLIOGRAPHY

The following titles are not mere recommendations; they are essentials for the professional writer and the avid reader. The sooner and closer they are read, the better.

REFERENCE

Bloom, Harold. How to Read and Why, Scribner, 2001.
An insightful introduction to the kinds of close reading a thoughtfulreader and writer employs for optimal understanding of the text.

Booth, Wayne C. *The Rhetoric of Fiction*, University of Chicago Press, 1961.
For the reader and writer of serious ambition, this sure-footed analysis of narrative technique provides the tools, examples, and vocabulary for a working knowledge of dramatic fiction. It is the literary equivalent of the Journals of Lewis and Clark—true discoveries in every chapter.

Browne, Renni and Dave King. *Self-editing for Fiction Writers, Second Edition*, Harper Paperbacks, 2004.
As basic a tool for writers as a jack is for car owners. It covers areas where even accomplished writers show weaknesses; an invaluable help in revision.

Burroway, Janet. *Writing Fiction: A Guide to Narrative Craft, Eighth Edition*, Addison Wesley Longman, 2010.
The teacherly tone is mitigated by Burroway's own splendid fiction and its resident techniques.

Busch, Frederick. *A Dangerous Profession: A Book about the Writing Life*, St. Martin's Press, 1998.
So you want to know what the writing life is? Busch is the man: an excellent teacher and a superb crafter of short story and novel.

Cassil, R. V. *Writing Fiction, Second Edition*, Simon & Schuster, 1975.
Out-of-print but filled with contemporary relevance; Cassil was a writer-teacher and his take on narrative is worth absorbing.

Chabon, Michael. *Maps and Legends*, McSweeney's, 2008.
Electrifying, satisfying, and useful essays on genre fiction.

Conrad, Barnaby. *The Complete Guide to Writing Fiction*, Writer's Digest Books, 1990.
An anthology of craft-related articles by the workshop leaders of the Santa Barbara Writers Conference, not the least of which is Chapter Four, "How to Make Your Characters Work for You," by Shelly Lowenkopf.

——*101 Best Beginnings Ever Written*, Quill Driver Books, 2008.
Great focus on the need for opening velocity.

Delany, Samuel R. *About Writing*, Wesleyan University Press, 2006

Dillard, Annie. *The Writing Life*, HarperCollins, 1989.
Makes you realize where to expend the energy necessary to become and
remain a writer.

Fagan, Brian. *Cro-Magnon*, Bloomsbury Press, 2010.
Watch carefully how Fagan makes people who lived over 30,000 years ago
seem as though they're in the living room with you.

Fiedler, Leslie. *Love and Death in the American Novel*, World Publishing, 1962.
For the politically- and thematically-inclined reader and writer, Fiedler's spir-
ited analysis of novels from *Huckleberry Finn* through those published in the
first half of the twentieth century will provoke and inspire the understanding
of the momentous force resident within story.

Fish, Stanley. *How to Write a Sentence: And How to Read One*, HarperCollins,
2011.
Takes you back to the basic arrangement of words, energizing you with the
potential for getting your own thoughts expressed with clarity and concision.

Forster, E.M. *Aspects of the Novel*, Perseus Press, 1956.
A collection of a series of lectures Forster gave nearly a hundred years ago,
this book belongs next to Aristotle's *Poetics* in the writer's and reader's reference shelf. It focuses on the seven elements Forster thought necessary for a
successful novel, using specific examples. This guide is essential.

Frey, James N. *How to Write a Damn Good Novel*, St. Martin's Press, 1987.
If you are a reader or a writer, you probably collect books on writing; all these
Frey titles will make your understanding of the reading and writing process
more complete.

——*How to Write a Damn Good Novel, II*, St. Martin's Press, 1994.

——*How to Write a Damn Good Thriller*, St. Martin's Press, 2010.

Gardner, John. *The Art of Fiction: Notes on Craft for Young Writers*, Alfred A.
Knopf, 1984.
Over the years since its publication, this has become a writer's must-have.
Gardner's vision will also inspire readers, who will wonder why, with the
exception of his masterful novel, Grendel, he did not follow his own advice.

LaMott, Anne. *Bird by Bird: Notes on Writing and Life*, Anchor, 1995.
Her chapter on first drafts has become a legend among writers.

Lawrence, D. H. *Studies in Classic American Literature*, Penguin Classics, 1990.
A valuable critical review of American literature from an iconoclastic English
novelist, superb short story writer and poet. Helps you search for your own
identity as a writer.

Lowenkopf, Shelly. *Secrets of Successful Fiction Writing: A Guide to Techniques
and Approaches the Professionals Take for Granted*, Santa Barbara Writers
Conference Shop Talk Series, Charters West Publications, 1991. Good stuff.

Macauley, Robie, and George Lanning. *Technique in Fiction*, Harper & Row, 1964.
Invaluable advice, complete with useful examples from two respected editors.

McCormack, Thomas. *The Fiction Editor, The Novel, and the Novelist*, Paul Dry Books, 2006.
This helpful book goes a long way to defining and suggesting ways to enhance editorial sensibilities.

Newlove, Donald. *First Paragraphs: Inspired Openings for Writers and Readers*, Henry Holt & Company, 1993.
More valuable insights into the selection of the right moment for a story to begin.

Prose, Francine. *Reading Like a Writer*, HarperCollins, 2006.
The most helpful and inspiring book of its sort, closing the gap between reader and writer with intelligence and grace.

Seger, Linda. *Creating Unforgettable Characters*, Holt Paperbacks, 1990.
A helpful adjunct to its title, and a big boost toward understanding the needs and dynamic of dialogue.

Smiley, Jane. *Thirteen Ways of Looking at a Novel*, Knopf, 2005.
As is all of Smiley's fiction, this helpful work is a joy for reader and writer. Of particular worth are her editorial notes on one hundred novels.

Stein, Sol. *Stein on Writing*, St. Martin's Griffin, 1995.
Stein, a publisher and editor as well as a writer, has become the go-to source for fiction writers. This book explains why. His other books on writing leave too many questions.

Tierno, Michael. *Aristotle's Poetics for Screenwriters: Storytelling Secrets from the Greatest Mind in Western Civilization*, Hyperion, 2002.
What a great idea.

Twain, Mark. *Life on the Mississippi*, Vintage Books/Library of America, 1991.
This stunning work is a textbook example of how to blend dialogue, narrative, raucous humor, and story, enlivened by Jonathan Raban's introduction.

Williams, Joseph M. Style: Toward Clarity and Grace, University of Chicago Press, 1990.
A stylish look at the uses and implications of style in fiction. A valuable tool for reader and writer.

FICTION

Atkinson, Kate. *Started Early, Took My Dog*, Little, Brown and Company, 2011.
The exquisite use of character and dialogue in this novel shove it out the door of a genre detective novel and into the living room of great originality.

Boyle, T. C., *T. C. Boyle Stories*, Viking, 1998.
Wildly famous for his novels, Boyle has an impeccable feel for the short form. This doorstopper volume includes twenty-five years' worth of his work and merits close reading.

Chaucer, Geoffrey. *The Canterbury Tales*, Norton Critical Editions, 1989.
Six hundred years and still going; difficult to beat the enormous layering of techniques in these pitch-perfect visions of the human condition.

Dickens, Charles. *Great Expectations*, Penguin Classics, 1996.
A convenient package of text, good notes, and chronology for one of the two grand first-person narratives in the English language.

Donoghue, Emma. *Room*, Little, Brown and Company, 2010.
A bravura use of evocation and point-of-view.

Eisenberg, Deborah. *Collected Stories*, Picador, 2010.
One of America's finest short story writers demonstrates her stage-like visions of pestered individuals in action, trying to get a handle on life.

Erdrich, Louise. *Love Medicine*, Harper Perennial, 1993.
A major step by which a collection of short stories may become a novel.

——*The Plague of Doves*, HarperCollins, 2008.
The narrative form, imaginative use of point-of-view, awl-sharp dialogue and deft attention to landscape make this a textbook on novel writing.

Faulkner, William. *As I Lay Dying*, Random House, 1930.
Fifty-nine chapters, fifteen points of view, and Faulknerian dark humor; what more do you need to know?

Fitzgerald, F. Scott. *The Stories of F. Scott Fitzgerald*, Scribner, 1989.
Fitzgerald's stories, even the commercial ones, hold up well into the twenty-first century, in large measure because they are poems in dramatic disguise.

Hughes, Dorothy B. *In a Lonely Place*, The Feminist Press. 2010.
Hughes's work opened the door for the reappearance of noir for women in modern crime fiction. Hughes has always been among the most intelligent and piercing crime writers; her novels are role models of craft and point-of-view.

Lahiri, Jhumpa. *Interpreter of Maladies*, Houghton Mifflin, 1999.
Lahiri's work is of inestimable value to the reader and writer for the order in which she places events in her stories, her sharp-eyed vision when it comes to "getting" characters, and her pitch-perfect ear for dialogue.

Lehane, Dennis. *The Moonlight Mile*, William Morrow, 2010.
With every new venture, Lehane keeps improving his already considerable chops. Study his dialogue, his seemingly easy way with conflicting characters.

Leonard, Elmore. *Freaky Deaky*, Arbor House, 1988.
The opening is a textbook for narrative hook devices.

——*The Hot Kid*, William Morrow, 2005.
How to break through genre barriers the Leonard way: not with mirrors but with characters.

Mansfield, Katherine. *Selected Stories*, Oxford University Press, 2002.
Thirty-three piercing short stories from a gifted and highly observant writer, along with explanatory notes. Mansfield, dead at thirty-four, was the only writer her contemporary, Virginia Woolf, was jealous of.

Moore, Christopher. *Fool*, William Morrow, 2009.
How to sustain satire, book length. How to be funny without trying.

Price, Richard. *Lush Life*, Farrar, Straus & Giroux, 2008.
As always, spot-on renditions of characters, best dialogue in any genre, textbook authority in demonstrating ways to make compelling stories from small chunks of event.

Prose, Francine. *Hunters and Gatherers*, Farrar, Straus & Giroux, 1995.
How to make the absurd seem real; how to make the real seem funny; how not to beat up on quirky characters.

Proulx, Annie. *The Shipping News*, Scribner, 1993.
Read closely several times for character articulation, cadence of dialogue, cadence of narrative, and seamless blending of setting to story.

Steinbeck, John. *Of Mice and Men*, Viking, 1937.
For structure, pacing, dialogue and concision, this haunting short novel is nothing less than a beacon to writers and an introduction for readers to the consideration of thematic materials.

Trevor, William. *The Collected Stories*, Viking, 1992.
The short fiction of a major presence, covering twenty-five years of his work, all of which is remarkable for its insightful use of character, its deft uses of humor, irony and inference as well as its steadfast reliance on omniscient point of view.

Twain, Mark. *Huckleberry Finn*, Norton Critical Editions, 1998.
Every time you reread this work, you will learn something you hadn't realized you needed in your work. Read carefully up to the point toward the end, where Tom Sawyer is reintroduced—and learn from that as well. Ranks with *Great Expectations* as the essential guide to first-person narrative.

TELEVISION

Simon, David, producer/director. *The Wire*, 2008.
This five-volume set of compact discs represents a dramatic storytelling triumph, bringing together sixty episodes of a complex, gritty, absorbing novel for television. At least three of the writers, Dennis Lehane, George Pelecanos, and Richard Price, are respected noir novelists. The remarkable ensemble cast brings together social issues, nuance within personal agenda, psychology, and the edgy presence of dramatic truth.

ABOUT THE AUTHOR

Shelly Lowenkopf taught in the University of Southern California's Master of Professional Writing Program for 34 years, has taught at the annual Santa Barbara Writer's Conference since 1980, and has been guest lecturer in many schools and conferences. He is currently Visiting Professor at the College of Creative Studies, University of California, Santa Barbara, with classes in noir fiction, the modern short story, genre fiction, and developing a literary voice. Lowenkopf has served as editorial director for literary, general trade, mass market, and scholarly book publishers, seeing over 500 books through the editorial and production process. His own short fiction has appeared widely in the literary press.

WELCOME TO
WHITE WHISKER BOOKS

Thank you for buying *The Fiction Writer's Handbook*. White Whisker Books, named for our mascot cat, Maggie, who has one white whisker, specializes in fiction. Go to **www.WhiteWhisker Books.com**, to see what we currently offer. At this writing, we have three authors in addition to Shelly Lowenkopf:

Christopher Meeks is a fiction writer who has two collections of short stories, *The Middle-Aged Man and the Sea* and *Months and Seasons*. His novel *The Brightest Moon of the Century* is a bildungsroman (look up the word in this book) that follows a young Minnesotan named Edward from 14 to 44 through college in Colorado, love in a trailer park in Alabama, and a film career in Los Angeles. *Love At Absolute Zero,* a Book of the Year Finalist at *ForeWord* magazine, has a star physicist look for love using the scientific method. Also available is Mr. Meeks' produced play, *Who Lives?*

E. Van Lowe specializes in young adult novels, and his current series, the Falling Angels Saga features *Boyfriend From Hell*, *Earth Angel*, and *Heaven Sent*. All revolve around 15-year-old Megan Barnett from Glendale, Arizona, who at first fights to keep the devil from dating her mother. All hell breaks loose. Then things get worse.

David Scott Milton writes noir mysteries. His latest is *Iron City*, about a disgraced police detective who returns to his hometown of Pittsburgh to find out who murdered one of his childhood buddies and why.

White Whisker Books believes that in fiction you can find truth. With the book in your hands, Shelly Lowenkopf, unlike the Wizard of Oz, lets you look behind the curtain to show you how our writers—and you as a writer—can use the elements of fiction to get to the truth.

Printed in Great Britain
by Amazon.co.uk, Ltd.,
Marston Gate.